WARRIORS FOR THE WEST

"Outdoorsmen must read *Warriors for the West* to see how enviro-wackos are trying to turn Americans into disconnected city punks. If they had their way, Bobby Unser would have gone to prison, John Shuler, who killed a grizzly bear in self-defense, would have lost his ranch, and my friend Kathy Stupak-Thrall couldn't put a boat out on her lake."

—**Ted Nugent**
Guitarist, outdoorsman, and bestselling author of *God, Guns, & Rock 'n' Roll*

"Defenders of religious liberty will be stunned to learn, as *Warriors for the West* reveals, that, while the federal courts use the Establishment Clause to ban almost any hint of Judeo-Christian religion in the 'public square,' they have upheld the right of American Indian religious practitioners to demand and federal agencies to order the closure of public and private land that is 'sacred' to pantheists. This is indeed a call to action."

—**Hugh Hewitt**
Author of *Painting the Map Red*

"Those of us who are deeply opposed to race-based public policies celebrated when the Supreme Court's ruling in *Adarand v. Peña* came down on June 12, 1995. We read the decision as a heartening—and presumably lasting—blow to the pernicious sorting of Americans on the basis of the color of their skin. But politics often emasculates the high Court's decisions, and in the last decade, through two administrations, our hopes for a new day have been dashed. That sobering story is just one of many that William Perry Pendley tells in *Warriors for the West*."

—**Abigail Thernstrom**
Co-author of *America in Black and White: One Nation, Indivisible*

To R. I. Hlousek —
one of the true

WARRIORS
FOR THE WEST !

Best regards,

Perry

February '07

Supreme Court of the United States

October 31, 2001

No. 00-0730, Todd Crespi, Supreme Court artist, *Adarand Constructors, Inc. v. Mineta*

WARRIORS
FOR THE WEST

FIGHTING BUREAUCRATS, RADICAL GROUPS, AND LIBERAL JUDGES ON AMERICA'S FRONTIER

WILLIAM PERRY PENDLEY

Since 1947
REGNERY
PUBLISHING, INC.
An Eagle Publishing Company • Washington, DC

Library of Congress Cataloging-in-Publication Data
    Pendley, William Perry
    Warriors for the West: fighting bureaucrats, radical groups, and liberal judges on America's frontier / by William Perry Pendley.
    p. cm.
    ISBN 1-59698-006-0
    1. Trials—West (U.S.) 2. Environmental law—United States—Popular works. 3. Environmental policy—West (U.S.)—Popular works. I. Title.
    KF220.P46 2006
    344.7804'6—dc22

                                                            2005036595

Published in the United States by
Regnery Publishing, Inc.
One Massachusetts Avenue, NW
Washington, DC 20001
www.regnery.com

Distributed to the trade by
National Book Network
Lanham, MD 20706

Manufactured in the United States of America

10 9 8 7 6 5 4 3 2 1

Books are available in quantity for promotional or premium use. Write to Director of Special Sales, Regnery Publishing, Inc., One Massachusetts Avenue NW, Washington, DC 20001, for information on discounts and terms or call (202) 216-0600.

DEDICATION

This book and the efforts it represents are dedicated to H. A. "Dave" True, Jr., the "Wyoming Wildcatter." In his professional career in the energy and agricultural industries, Dave embodied the philosophy that man can develop and use our land's resources while conserving our land's beauty and gifts. In his personal life, his passion to see our laws applied justly and with accountability was second only to his passion for good fly fishing and his family. Without Dave, none of the successes of Mountain States Legal Foundation chronicled here would have been possible.

CONTENTS

ACKNOWLEDGMENTS

I am grateful first to the men and women of these pages who coura-geously stepped forward to fight for a cause because they believed it was right. That did not make their decisions any easier, and the realization that they were in for the long haul, not to settle or com-promise but to win, made those decisions even more difficult and, in the end, remarkable. Without them, there would be no stories to tell, no victories and legal precedents to celebrate, and no lessons to learn, however painfully, from the long battles on their behalf.

Thanks as well to the tens of thousands of Americans who, with absolutely no direct financial or legal interest in the battles that are being undertaken, still have a "dog in the fight," their commitment to constitutional liberties and the rule of law. Their contributions make it possible for the courtroom battles set forth in these pages to be fought as well and as long as they are fought. I value most the single dollar bill tucked into an envelope with a scribbled note, "This is all I can afford. Keep up the good work!"

Furthermore, the men and women who serve and have served as Directors and members of the Board of Litigation of Mountain States Legal Foundation (MSLF) are indispensable to this great undertaking. They help manage the organization, raise the financial support, approve the cases, applaud the victories, and offer encouragement after the defeats.

MSLF's legal staff over the years has been a remarkable blessing. Those lawyers and staff members came because they believed in the cause; they stayed because they came to believe in the clients. In particular, I am grateful to Steven J. Lechner, Esq., Managing Attorney, whose indefatigable spirit and attention to detail are more than any client could wish. Although never as optimistic as I am, he shares the same passionate commitment to victory. I am thankful as well for J. Scott Detamore, Esq., Senior Attorney, whose thoroughness and mastery of the record ensures, if not success, at least a belief that all that could be done was done. As well, I extend my thanks to attorneys Joseph F. Becker, Jayme Ritchie, Ronald W. Opsahl, Joel M. Spector, and Elizabeth Y. Spencer, as well as Steve and Scott, not only for their past and current efforts on behalf of our clients but also for reviewing these materials for accuracy; my thanks also to our legal secretary, Jane Baer. I am particularly appreciative of paralegal Judith Stoeser, not only for her day-to-day work but also for her painstaking attention to detail in ensuring the proper formatting and accuracy of this manuscript. The rest of MSLF's team deserves great credit: Janice Alvarado, Diane Patrick, Cindy Berrios, Maryann O'Brien, and Janice Chase.

I am most appreciative of the support of my friend Marji Ross, president and publisher of Regnery, and her editor in my cause, Anne Sorock. Both are a pleasure with whom to work.

Finally, I thank my wonderful spouse, friend, and law partner, Elisabeth Y. Pendley, Esq., for her support while I abandoned every other responsibly and wrote this manuscript; in fact, at my request she read it more than once and offered her always-excellent advice. I enjoy as well the wonderful support of our children: 1st Lieutenant William P. Pendley, USMC, his wife Blair Pendley, D.V.M., and our son Luke Taylor Pendley, actor, screenwriter, and student.

I take full responsibility for any errors in these pages; any credit that may be accorded for what I have written here must go to the clients who lived these stories.

INTRODUCTION

I n *War on the West: Government Tyranny on America's Great Frontier*, I set out the details of the attack embarked upon by the Clinton administration and its allies in various radical environmental groups on the ability of westerners to live, work, and play in the American West. On reading my manuscript, my good friend Al Regnery proclaimed, "You ain't seen nothing yet." He was right, of course. Clinton's efforts were not the first; early in his run for the presidency, Jimmy Carter had made an alliance with radical environmental groups and was eager to do their bidding after he was elected.

Although Jimmy Carter was busy scheduling the White House tennis courts and running the economy into the ground, the attack on the West by his appointees was sufficiently strong to engender what was called the Sagebrush Rebellion. When the man who proudly proclaimed, "I am a Sagebrush Rebel," Ronald Reagan, was elected president, many thought the War on the West was over forever. It had only taken a brief hiatus.

William Jefferson Clinton, his scandals notwithstanding, unleashed his minions, many of whom were on leave from the radical groups that had allied themselves with the Carter administration. Over the eight years that Clinton was in office, he and his appointees were relentless in their efforts. No western issue was too insignificant to draw their attention and an attack. There was one positive aspect of the Clinton administration, however; a grassroots response began, a response that took its leaders and members to Washington, D.C., to confront federal agencies and Congress and, with the aid of nonprofit, public interest law firms, to federal district and appellate courts and, ultimately, the U.S. Supreme Court.

My colleague and ally, Mark R. Levin, in his remarkable work, *Men in Black: How the Supreme Court Is Destroying America*, provides ample evidence that, all too often, when cases make it to the Supreme Court, the Court gets it wrong, on a host of issues of vital importance to the American people. As much of a problem as that is, and Mark Levin is absolutely right that it is a huge problem, almost a crisis, the greater problem is that for 99 percent of the cases serious enough to merit an appeal to that Court, the nine justices are not the final arbiters. Instead, the court of last resort is a three-judge panel in San Francisco, Denver, or Washington, D.C. In other words, it is not just that the Supreme Court, all too often, makes bad law, but also that scores of appellate court panels, without fear of review and reversal, are doing the very same thing.

Of course, first one must not only get into court, one must stay there. The order of battle for the U.S. Department of Justice increasingly mandates an attack upon the ability of westerners to challenge a government agency's decision in the first place. Thus, federal lawyers do not file an answer to a complaint; instead, they assert that: the case is not ripe; the court lacks jurisdiction; it's the wrong court; the plaintiff has failed to exhaust his administrative remedies; or the plaintiff lacks standing—that is, he has not been injured, at least by the agency, and, even if he has been injured, the court is not able to remediate that injury. If a westerner survives those challenges and obtains a ruling on the merits in federal district court, a new team of Justice Department lawyers becomes involved at the appellate level and once again challenges ripeness, jurisdiction, standing, and all the rest. All too often, district court and court of appeals judges are eager to dispense with a case for procedural reasons, which has two positive features from the judges' point of view: it is quickly done and unlikely to be reversed.

If a litigant survives these procedural challenges and gets to the merits of his case, he is battling: the world's largest law firm in the U.S. Department of Justice, a powerful adversary in federal agencies to whom time and money is irrelevant and to whose "expertise" the federal courts defer, friend of the court support from the nation's richly endowed radical environmental and other such groups, and a federal judiciary that became increasingly liberal with eight years of Clinton appointments. Furthermore, the litigant must run a legal gauntlet in which he is disadvantaged by the tendency of appellate judges: not to rock the boat, not to file dissenting opinions, and not to question the decisions of their colleagues by granting further review. Finally, the brass ring of Supreme Court review is an unreachable dream for most litigants. For the lucky few, however, it offers a chance to change their world.

Goodness knows there is an abundance of targets of opportunity. The Clinton administration did not truly end when Bill and Hillary drove off with the White House furniture in January 2001. Over the eight years of their administration, hundreds of their loyalists imbedded themselves in the federal bureaucracy. In addition, the changed culture that took place over those years in agencies like the U.S. Forest Service caused the departure or early retirement of careerists of a different era and orientation. Federal employment always has held more attraction for those left of center; the Clinton era only heightened that reality. Notwithstanding the arrival of George W. Bush and Dick Cheney and their appointees, the change that they brought is only skin deep; scratch the surface in many federal agencies and the careerist who is implementing the Bush agenda likely was put there during the Clinton administration.

Furthermore, the laws that those officials are implementing were written by a Congress that tends to the Left and if not the Left then at least to a political correctness in its legislative enactments that permits a creative bureaucrat or an activist judge to give the laws a left of center spin. Too often Congress, not wishing to offend anyone and wishing to please everyone, leaves its terms and meanings undefined creating an empty vessel into which bureaucrats and judges pour their own views. Then there are the incredibly well-funded, highly motivated, and media-savvy radical groups: they lobby when the legislation is drafted; they exert pressure when the regulations are written; and they sue when the laws and rules are interpreted.

This then is the battlefield onto which Warriors for the West who wish to fight back must enter. The battle is not for the faint of heart, those lacking in commitment to principle, or those in a hurry. Occasionally, it has its rewards. Too often it results in heartbreak. But, for those who love liberty and find truth and inspiration in the vision of the Founding Fathers, it is the only way. Thus, over the last decade or so, the men and women of these pages have been Warriors for the West, fighting against incredible odds.

They fight environmental laws; bureaucrats who break the law and lawyers who cover for them; racial preferences undertaken in the name of trust responsibilities to American Indians; Clinton's monument decrees; attacks on logging, mining, and energy development; seizure of private land for public recreation; closure of public and private land as worship sites for American Indian religious practitioners; government's refusal to abide by the contracts it enters into; government when it becomes a bullying bad neighbor; criminalization of almost all activity in the name of protecting the environment; racial quotas and preferences; racial gerrymandering of voting districts; taking of private property for ostensible public use without just compensation; denial of access to private land contrary to guarantees by lawmakers more than one hundred years ago; and, the newest battles of the day, illegal immigration and restrictions on the ability of Americans to speak out and be heard.

As it is not the destination, but the journey, so these tales are not about victories and defeats but about men and women who, knowing that defeat was likely, undertook the fight anyway because if victory came it would have been worth it, not just for them but for all the others like them. They may not be heroes to everyone, but they are heroes to me.

CHAPTER 1

FIGHTING THE "PIT BULL
OF ENVIRONMENTAL LAWS"

The right to defend one's property has long been recognized at common law [yet] the Government...make[s] it unlawful for [a man] to "harass, harm, [or] pursue" [grizzly bears] when they come to take his [sheep]. [I]f the Government decided (in lieu of the food stamp program) to enact a law barring grocery store owners from "harassing, harming, or pursuing" people who wish to take food off grocery shelves without paying for it, such a law might well be suspect under the Fifth Amendment. For similar reasons, the Endangered Species Act may be suspect....

U.S. SUPREME COURT JUSTICE BYRON WHITE[1]

It was a dark and stormy night in Dupuyer, Montana, one of the oldest towns along the Rocky Mountain Front Range, just south of the Blackfeet Indian Reservation and Glacier National Park and due east of the Flathead National Forest, the snowcapped peaks of the Flathead Range, and the Great Bear Wilderness.[2] On the outskirts of town, John Shuler, who raises sheep for a living, heard a disturbance outside his house. He knew the sound well—it was grizzly bears; they had come to kill and eat his sheep.

Quickly, John Shuler jumped up, grabbed his rifle by the door, and ran out into the darkness. He hurried to the sheep pen where he came upon three grizzlies. He fired at the bears and they fled, disappearing into the night. Thinking the danger was over, he settled his sheep, which were frightened and cowering under the sheep creep, and turned to go back into his house.

Suddenly, a ferocious grizzly appeared in his path. It rose onto its hind legs, spread its mighty paws, and let out a vicious roar. At that moment, John Shuler was sure of only one thing: if he did not act fast, he was dead. His powerful .375 caliber rifle was quickly at his shoulder; he fired and the bear fell. Just as quickly, however, the grizzly sprang up and vanished into the night. As snow began to fall, John Shuler heard the rattle of his gate. The grizzly had gone over the fence toward the Flathead.

Fearful that the grizzlies would return and that he would lose more sheep to their voracious appetites, John Shuler spent the night awake, his rifle across his lap, and his dog Boone by his side. As the snow deepened outside, he wondered whether he had killed the grizzly. Had it gone off somewhere to die or was it headed toward a neighbor's property? A wounded grizzly was a danger to everyone. John Shuler knew that, at first light, he had to find the grizzly.

Early the next morning, John Shuler and Boone climbed into his pickup truck and set off in hopes of finding the grizzly bear's carcass. As they neared where John Shuler thought the carcass might be found, John Shuler let Boone out of the truck and followed behind until Boone disappeared from sight. After waiting a couple of minutes, he began to get anxious and drove to where he had last seen his dog. John Shuler stopped the pickup and called for Boone, but he got no response. He got out of his pickup to stretch his legs and it was then that he spotted Boone on point. Thinking that Boone must be pointing at the carcass of the grizzly bear, John Shuler grabbed his rifle from the pickup and walked toward where Boone was pointing.

Observing nothing in that direction, John Shuler turned toward his pickup and glanced to the northwest. It was then that he spotted the grizzly bear, only 150 feet away. They locked gazes for an instant and then the grizzly bear charged. Fearing for his life, John Shuler raised his rifle and fired, but missed. As he quickly reloaded and fired again, the bear was only 100 feet away. The bear fell to the ground, then was back on its feet, charging once more. As it came within 50 feet of John Shuler, he fired again. The third shot knocked the grizzly bear to the ground; it skidded and clawed its way into a clump of willows. John Shuler cautiously approached the grizzly bear and, realizing that it was dying, ended its suffering.

When John Shuler got home, he received a call from a wildlife official wondering if he were "having any problems" with grizzly bears. "Yeah," John Shuler replied, "we got hit last night. I killed a bear." A few days later, U.S. Fish and Wildlife Service employees arrived at Shuler's ranch and officially pronounced the bear dead. As John Shuler poured the men hot coffee, he told them his story. While it was not the first time grizzlies had come calling—they had killed eleven sheep and even eaten his wife Carmen's peaches off their picnic table—it was the first time John Shuler had killed one. He had acted out of necessity, and it never crossed his mind that the federal employees who packed up the grizzly carcass would think any differently. He felt relieved that he had kept the injured bear from causing any further harm and breathed a sigh of relief as he bid the officials goodbye.

It wasn't goodbye—in fact, he was about to say hello to real problems. The Fish and Wildlife Service charged John Shuler with violating the Endangered Species Act, legislation that protects grizzly bears as "threatened," and sought a $7,000 fine.[3] Although there is a self-defense exception in the Endangered Species Act, under which John Shuler's actions were exempt, the Fish and Wildlife Service asserted that John Shuler did not act in self-defense.[4] John Shuler now needed legal counsel.

Before the matter could go to federal court, it was necessary to obtain what federal law refers to as final agency action, for, although the Fish and Wildlife Service thought that John Shuler should be fined, the secretary of the U.S. Department of the Interior, to whom the Fish and Wildlife Service reported, had not made a final decision. Yet, even before the secretary made that decision—or it was made in his name—it was necessary to ascertain exactly what happened on John Shuler's ranch that dark September night. The initial finder of fact and determiner of law would be, as it always is in cases involving the Fish and Wildlife Service and other similar Interior Department agencies, an administrative law judge (ALJ).

The ALJ conducted a two-day hearing in Great Falls; John Shuler testified, as did a number of other witnesses called by John Shuler's lawyers and the United States, but there was one surprise witness. After John Shuler had killed the grizzly, a state wildlife official met with him to discuss sharing the cost of an electric fence to prevent grizzly predation of his sheep and to eliminate any need for John Shuler, in self-defense, to kill another grizzly. Eventually John Shuler agreed to his $1,500 share of the cost and installed the fence, as federal and state wildlife agencies had requested. It came as a surprise, therefore, that the man was called as a witness.

This surprise witness testified that John Shuler was "glad he killed the grizzly,"[5] but his testimony had no impact on the ALJ's ruling, which was issued some months later.[6] In his factual findings, the ALJ ruled favorably that, on the night of the killing, John Shuler was in reasonable fear of death or serious bodily injury—the test for validating a self-defense claim.[7] So far, so good, John Shuler's lawyers thought, as they read the ALJ's opinion; John Shuler will win. It was quite unexpected then, that the ALJ ruled, as a "matter of law," that John Shuler had no legal right to go outside because, by doing so, he was placing himself in the "zone of imminent danger."[8] John Shuler was ordered to pay a fine of $4,000.[9] It was a stunning ruling that disregarded a freedom westerners had enjoyed ever since homesteaders first came west: the right to arm themselves and go freely about their private property.[10] John Shuler appealed.

John Shuler's appeal was to the Ad Hoc Board of Appeals with the U.S. Department of the Interior in Washington, D.C., whose decisions constitute the final agency action necessary for an injured party to proceed to federal court. Briefs were filed by attorneys for John Shuler and the Fish and Wildlife Service. The two-member panel took its time; three years after briefing was completed, the panel ruled.[11]

John Shuler was correct, concluded the panel. He had the right both to arm himself and to go outside into his yard. The ALJ's decision in that regard was in error. Nonetheless, ruled the panel, John Shuler could not claim self-defense because he was legally at fault in another respect. The panel concluded that, because John Shuler had taken his dog Boone with him, and, because Boone had gone on point when Boone saw the grizzly, Boone had provoked the grizzly. Since the law is quite clear that anyone who provokes a situation that gives rise to a self-defense claim or escalates that confrontation may not claim self-defense, the panel held that John Shuler was liable under the Endangered Species Act and was required to pay a fine of $5,000![12] At least, John Shuler's lawyers reassured him, there is a final decision from the United States that could be taken to federal court.

John Shuler filed a lawsuit in Montana federal district court challenging the fine levied against him and the constitutionality of assessing a $5,000 fine without providing him a right to a trial by jury.[13] Based on the factual record established before the ALJ and the Ad Hoc Board, briefs were filed and arguments held. Finally, the district court ruled that John Shuler had acted in self-defense and had not violated the Endangered Species Act. At last John and Carmen Shuler were out from under the fine that the Fish and Wildlife Service had sought to impose; they could go about their lives.

That certainly was good news; however, the bad news was that it had taken John Shuler and his attorneys eight years to win. Moreover, the value of the free legal services that John Shuler had received exceeded $225,000. Because federal law authorizes a court to order a federal agency to pay a person's attorneys' fees when he prevails and the federal government's position is "not substantially justified," John Shuler's attorneys asked to be paid. Amazingly, the district court ruled that the Fish and Wildlife Service had been "substantially justified" in the legal actions it had taken against John Shuler.[14] That ruling was appealed to the U.S. Court of Appeals for the Ninth Circuit. In his appeal, John Shuler asked, rhetorically, which of the positions taken by the Fish and Wildlife Service over the eight years of its persecution of him had been "substantially justified":

- Shuler had not acted in self-defense when he shot the grizzly the night it attacked him;
- Shuler had not acted in self-defense when he shot the grizzly the next morning when it attacked him;
- Shuler could not claim self-defense because he was at fault for going outside, the "zone of imminent danger";
- Shuler could not claim self-defense because he was at fault for allowing his dog Boone to provoke the bear by going on point;
- Grizzlies are entitled to a higher standard of self-defense than are humans because grizzlies are not capable of sapient thought.

John Shuler believed that only the Fish and Wildlife Service's attempt to determine the facts before the ALJ was "substantially justified"; every other legal stratagem pursued by the Fish and Wildlife Service had no legal basis whatsoever. Nonetheless, the Ninth Circuit ruled that John Shuler's lawyers were owed nothing.[15]

Oddly, John Shuler's victory was not a defeat for the Fish and Wildlife Service. The Fish and Wildlife Service had demonstrated to everyone in grizzly-bear country that it would aggressively prosecute anyone who killed a grizzly bear in self-defense. It also sent a message that such persecution would be incredibly time consuming—requiring at least eight years! Finally, it put all on notice that the cost of defending against Fish and Wildlife Service prosecution would be costly—$225,000 or more—and that anyone who killed a grizzly bear in self-defense would be better off just paying the fine. The message does not simply affect the decisions people make *after* they act to save their lives during a grizzly-bear attack; it affects what they do in life-and-death situations, which is what the Fish and Wildlife Service intended.

In October 1998, Pat vanVleet from Evanston, Wyoming, went hunting near Dubois, Wyoming.[16] Suddenly, he heard the sound that everyone in grizzly-bear country fears: the sound of a grizzly charging. He looked up, saw the grizzly, and, armed with a powerful hunting rifle, did an amazing thing. He laid his rifle down, took a can of pepper spray off his belt, and stood at the ready. When the grizzly got to him, Pat vanVleet let the bear have it with the pepper spray. The grizzly stopped, took a big whiff, and then charged through the mist.

The grizzly clamped his jaws tight on Pat vanVleet's stomach, catching his belt and large belt buckle, and started flinging him around. Suddenly, a shot rang out and the grizzly fell dead. Pat vanVleet's hunting partner had come running and fired a lucky and life-saving shot, but his friend was badly hurt. From his hospital bed, Pat told reporters in Jackson, Wyoming, "I wanted to do the right thing... I didn't want to lose my hunting license so I put my rifle down."

Months later, after he had recovered, he was asked if he had really said what the newspaper quoted him as saying. He verified his remarks. When asked why he had done such a brave and perhaps foolhardy thing, he responded, "I had heard about John Shuler and I did not want to happen to me what had happened to him."[17] What an amazing admission; a man facing a charge from the most dangerous animal in North America fears his government more than he fears the attacking grizzly. The Fish and Wildlife Service must be very proud. No wonder that John Shuler soon became and remains the poster boy for Endangered Species Act reform.

THE PIT BULL OF ENVIRONMENTAL LAWS[18]

The Endangered Species Act has many flaws, all of them well documented. To begin with, many of the species are not truly endangered, the critical habitat set aside for them is unnecessary, and, furthermore, the Endangered Species Act is not saving anything.[19] Perhaps its greatest defect, however, is that, notwithstanding the perception of the vast majority of the American people, the decisions made by federal employees who implement the act are not made on the basis of science—let alone good science.[20] No wonder efforts have been underway for many years to reform the statute to rectify these and many other deficiencies. Sadly, those efforts have gone nowhere because most members of Congress represent urban districts unaffected by the draconian impact of the Endangered Species Act. For those representatives, voting against reform, the stance that radical environmental groups demand, is a cheap and easy environmental vote. While their constituents enjoy the benefit of believing they are saving species, westerners bear the burden imposed by the Endangered Species Act, so they fight on!

It is often a very frustrating fight, due in part to the failure of federal agencies to play by the rules, the difficulty of challenging illegal agency actions, and the preferential treatment accorded federal employees.[21] The case of Lin Drake of Cedar City, Utah, provides an example.

In 1995, the U.S. Supreme Court issued a ruling on the Endangered Species Act in *Babbitt v. Sweet Home Chapter of Communities for a Great Oregon*.[22] In large part the ruling favored the Fish and Wildlife Service; however, one aspect of the decision was helpful to landowners. The Court ruled that property owners could not be fined for disturbing habitat unless the Fish and Wildlife Service could demonstrate that, by disturbing habitat, the person charged with a violation actually harms or kills a protected species.[23] As a result, a person who plows the proverbial north 40 and does not actually harm or kill a species may not be charged under the Endangered Species Act simply because the agency says that the land he plowed is habitat.

Lin Drake owns land in Cedar City, just off Interstate 15 some sixty miles north of St. George and the Utah-Arizona state line, which he uses for agricultural purposes as well as for housing developments. Aware that there exist in the Cedar City area prairie dogs protected under the Endangered Species Act, Lin Drake consulted with Fish and Wildlife Service employees regarding whether any of those prairie dogs were upon his property. In fact, Lin Drake went farther; he hired an expert to advise him as to whether he could develop his property. On more than one occasion, Lin Drake walked his land with various Fish and Wildlife Service employees; during those visits no one discovered any evidence that the protected prairie dogs were there. Moreover, Lin Drake was told the same thing by his expert. As a result, Lin Drake plowed his property for planting. Almost immediately, the Fish and Wildlife Service charged him with disturbing habitat and fined him $15,000.

Before an ALJ, Lin Drake argued that there were no prairie dogs on his property and that, without evidence that prairie dogs were actually harmed or killed, the Fish and Wildlife Service could not fine him for disturbing habitat. The ALJ ruled that there was no need for Fish and Wildlife Service employees to produce evidence of harmed or killed prairie dogs—they asserted that they were reluctant to recover the dead prairie dogs that they believed existed because doing so would disturb the living prairie dogs—because those employees had testified that the prairie dogs had been on Drake's property and they were no longer there.[24] Furthermore, ruled the ALJ, federal employees were to be believed in cases such as this because, after all, they are merely doing their jobs and have no reason to lie.[25] Federal officials, lawyers, and bureaucrats at the U.S. Department of the Interior were so excited about the ALJ's panegyric that they took the very unusual step of publishing the opinion in *Interior Decisions*.[26] Not surprisingly, the Interior Board of Land Appeals (IBLA) upheld the ALJ's ruling.[27]

Thus, notwithstanding the Supreme Court's ruling, the Fish and Wildlife Service, at least as to Lin Drake in southern Utah, believes it has no obligation to demonstrate that a person who disturbs habitat has harmed or killed a protected species. Unless and until a court of appeals, or maybe even the U.S. Supreme Court, rules that the Fish and Wildlife Service must obey the rules, it will do as it pleases.

The Fish and Wildlife Service similarly plays fast and loose with the requirements for listing a species for protection under the Endangered Species Act. In May 1998, the agency, in response to the demands of environmental groups, listed the Preble's Meadow Jumping Mouse (PMJM) for Endangered Species Act protection, declaring that it was found only along the Rocky Mountain Front Range from Colorado Springs, Colorado, to Casper, Wyoming.[28] Skeptics quickly noted how very convenient the listing was given complaints by radical environmental groups about "uncontrolled growth" on Colorado's Front Range. Some went so far as to assert that, just as those groups had discovered the Northern Spotted Owl in the Pacific Northwest, which they then used as a weapon to kill logging in the region, so the groups had discovered the PMJM, which would be used to put the brakes on growth in two of the ten fastest growing counties in the country, Colorado's Douglas and Elbert Counties.[29]

Soon Fish and Wildlife Service employees and environmental groups were out in force demanding that every land use be halted until provisions could be made to ensure the survival of the PMJM. Small farmers in Wyoming's Wheatland Irrigation District were told they could not burn their ditches, which they must do in the early spring to prepare for planting; rural counties in Wyoming and Colorado were told that they had to come up with expensive plans for protecting the PMJM's habitat; elderly ranchers were told they could not subdivide their property; state highway projects, including a bridge at a dangerous intersection near Fort Collins, Colorado, were put on hold until the safety of the PMJM could be guaranteed; and millions of dollars worth of property, in the midst of planned communities, was set aside for the PMJM.

One of the people harmed was Robert B. Hoff of El Paso County, Colorado. A real estate developer, Mr. Hoff smelled a rat, not a mouse, in the sweetheart deal between the Fish and Wildlife Service and the environmental groups. In July 1999, Mr. Hoff filed a petition to delist the PMJM asserting that the evidence used by the Fish and Wildlife Service to list the PMJM was no evidence at all and presenting substantial scientific and commercial information and analysis himself.

The Endangered Species Act requires that the Fish and Wildlife Service make a preliminary determination about any such petition within ninety days and an additional determination within twelve months. Nonetheless, over the next four years, the Fish and Wildlife Service took no action on Mr. Hoff's petition. In fact, in response to Mr. Hoff's frequent written requests that the agency obey the law and act on his petition, he was advised that the agency could not take action "any time in the near future" because it was developing a recovery plan for the PMJM.[30] Mr. Hoff responded that, if the Fish and Wildlife Service would delist the PMJM as he requested, there would be no need for a recovery plan. Finally, in June 2003, Mr. Hoff sued the agency. Six months later, the Fish and Wildlife Service confessed error and paid Mr. Hoff for his attorneys' fees.[31]

Shortly before Mr. Hoff settled his case, Mountain States Legal Foundation filed a lawsuit against Secretary of the Interior Gale A. Norton asserting that the listing of the PMJM was not based, as the law requires, on the "best scientific and commercial data available" given that one of the Fish and Wildlife Service's own contractors had advised the agency, in 1992, that there were no baseline data for the species. Another expert pointed out that the agency had been unable to locate the species or to identify its habitat. Yet another expert noted that the agency was using, not primary sources, as required by law, but secondary sources. Plus, none of the agency's data had been subjected to peer review. Furthermore, the agency had failed to review the listing of the PMJM, which is required every five years, despite acquisition of new data by people using Fish and Wildlife Service permits. Finally, the lawsuit charged, the agency's designation of 57,446 acres of critical habitat along 657 miles of rivers and streams was illegal because the data used for the designation were inadequate and unreliable and the area was defined so vaguely that the burden of determining habitat was imposed illegally upon landowners.[32]

Within a matter of weeks of the filing of the lawsuit, the Fish and Wildlife Service asked the federal district court to suspend the case while it considered removing the PMJM from the list.[33] In January 2005, after its PMJM expert recanted, the Fish and Wildlife Service announced plans to delist the PMJM.[34]

HE WHO OWNS THE GOLD MAKES THE RULES

The apparent victory over the illegal and unsupportable listing of the PMJM is a rare victory that demonstrates why those who oppose the abuse of the Endangered Species Act by avaricious bureaucrats and radical groups keep up their battles. How difficult those battles can be, not substantively, but procedurally, is evident from a legal battle over the Endangered Species Act in northern Montana.

Phillips County, in north-central Montana along the Canadian border, contains miles of sparse scrub grass, low native plants, gravel, and rocks. Hostile and forbidding, bitterly cold in the winter and aridly hot in the summer, it contains mountain lions, coyotes, rattlesnakes, antelope, deer, and black-tailed prairie dogs. The people, about one person per square mile, are outnumbered by the prairie dogs.[35]

Gary Marbut and Dr. Philip Barney, with fellow Montanans, formed a club to promote firearms safety and to engage in an activity as old as mankind's first encounter with the land of Phillips County: hunting. That land is primarily federal land, managed by the Bureau of Land Management of the U.S. Department of the Interior. Since its creation, the Interior Department has kept those lands open to the shooting of unregulated wildlife, such as prairie dogs, one of the few recreational activities in this desolate region.

The Federal Land Policy and Management Act (FLPMA) requires federal agencies to develop plans setting forth the manner in which federal land are to be managed, which must involve active, public participation. In 1994, the Bureau of Land Management developed such a plan, the Judith Valley Phillips Resource Management Plan or JVP RMP, for the 2.8 million acres under its control in Phillips, Fergus, Petroleum, Judith Basin, Valley, and southern Chouteau Counties. A portion of the 2.8 million acres covered by the JVP RMP lies within Phillips County and includes 20,000 acres of land referred to as the 40 Complex. Under the JVP RMP, approved by the Bureau of Land Management in 1994 after extensive public participation, Messrs. Marbut and Barney and their fellow Montanans could use the public land of the 40 Complex for hiking, camping, hunting, and the recreational shooting of unregulated wildlife.

Meanwhile, the Fish and Wildlife Service decided to introduce a minimum of twenty surplus black-footed ferrets in 1994, and annually thereafter for two to four years, into north-central Montana, including the 40 Complex. The agency also announced that the ferrets would continue to be protected under the Endangered Species Act. A short time later, without notice or opportunity for public comment, the Bureau of Land Management closed the public land in the 40 Complex to the "discharge or use of firearms" to "protect habitat for the reintroduction of the black-footed ferrets." Violations of the closure order would result in "a fine not to exceed $1,000 and/or imprisonment not-to-exceed 12 months." Since issuance of the closure order, Messrs. Marbut and Barney and their fellow Montanans have been denied the ability to engage in an activity allowed by the JVP RMP: the recreational shooting of unregulated wildlife.

The federal government is not seeking to protect the prairie dogs because they are listed under the Endangered Species Act; prairie dogs in Montana are not listed. Nor is the federal government seeking to prevent the shooting of ferrets, which are protected by the Act; there is no danger of that. What the government is seeking to save are the prairie dogs so that the ferrets may invade their homes and eat them. "The prairie dog colony provides prey base and habitat for the survival of the ferrets"[36] and "[b]lack-footed ferrets depend almost exclusively on prairie dogs and prairie dog towns for food and shelter."[37]

The natural extension of this interpretation of the Endangered Species Act is mind-boggling: any plant or animal could be placed off limits under the Act because it is used, as food or shelter, by a plant or animal protected by the Act! However, that big picture issue is not what concerns Messrs. Marbut and Barney and their fellow Montanans; they simply want the government to obey the law so that they may go hunting again. As a result, in September 2001, they filed a lawsuit contending that the federal agencies had violated federal law.

In the meantime, the Fish and Wildlife Service convinced the Montana state legislature to remove the area from the unregulated hunting of wildlife. As a result, the Bureau of Land Management lifted its closure order and moved to dismiss, as moot, the lawsuit filed by the Montana hunting enthusiasts. The hunters' lawyers argued that the case was not moot because the federal government asserted that it could issue a similar closure order at any time. Moreover, the Supreme Court has held that the voluntary cessation of illegal activity does not cause a case to be moot; instead, the court hearing the matter must complete its consideration of the case and issue a final order.[38] Nonetheless, nearly two years later, the District of Columbia federal district court dismissed the case as moot.[39]

The hunters appealed to the U.S. Court of Appeals for the District of Columbia, arguing that, because federal lawyers adamantly maintained that federal agencies had the right to engage in the illegal land closure challenged by the hunters and could engage in that illegal conduct at any time in the future regarding the Montana land or land anywhere in the West, the case was not moot and a ruling on the legality of the closure order must be issued. The three-judge panel rejected that appeal ruling, incredibly, that while the standard for mootness cited by the hunters does apply against private individuals and entities, it does not apply against the federal government![40]

If Supreme Court rulings regarding important issues like preventing a court from denying an injured party his day in court do not apply against the federal government, from what else is the federal government exempt?[41] Apparently, Congress is exempt from the U.S. Constitution and, in particular, its Commerce Clause.

As every high school student used to know, the federal government is one of enumerated powers, all other powers being reserved to the states.[42] One of those enumerated powers is the Commerce Clause, the primary source of Congress's authority to enact national legislation.[43] For years, the Commerce Clause was interpreted to impose strict limits on the types of laws that Congress could write;[44] however, from 1937 on, the Commerce Clause imposed absolutely no limits on Congress's power to write laws.[45] Then, in 1995, the Supreme Court rediscovered the Commerce Clause when it invalidated the federal Gun-Free School Zones Act of 1990.[46] Suddenly, advocates of federalism, the rights of states to address their issues creatively, and property rights were given new hope. If Congress could not use the Commerce Clause to prohibit guns in school yards, how could Congress use the Commerce Clause to regulate, for example, a species that exists only within a state or a part of a state? Maybe the answer was in Texas.

In 1983, Dr. Fred Purcell and his brother purchased an interest in 216 acres in Travis County near Austin, Texas, which lie within 1,200 acres and sit at the intersection of two major highways in a rapidly growing commercial and residential area. The Purcells' property, on which they installed water and wastewater gravity lines, force mains, lift stations, and other utilities, contains a number of caves. In 1988 and 1993, the U.S. Fish and Wildlife Services declared six invertebrate species of cave bugs (arachnids and insects, some with eyes, some eyeless), which range in length from 1.4 mm to 8 mm, "endangered" under the Endangered Species Act. These cave bugs are found only in parts of Travis and Williamson Counties; there is no commercial market for them, nor do people travel to Texas to see them.

In 1989, the Fish and Wildlife Service told the Purcells that development of their property would violate the Endangered Species Act because it would constitute a take of cave bugs. In 1990, in an effort to alleviate the agency's concerns, the Purcells deeded six acres, containing caves and sinkholes in which the cave bugs were known to live, to a nonprofit environmental organization. But then, in 1993, after Dr. Purcell cleared brush from his property, the Fish and Wildlife Service told him that he was under criminal investigation for taking endangered species. In 1998, after years of stonewalling, which drew a rebuke from a federal judge, the agency barred the Purcells from using their property.

In 1999, the Purcells and their partners sued, contending that application of the Endangered Species Act to the Texas cave bugs violated the Commerce Clause in the same way that the federal school yards gun law violated the Commerce Clause. In 2001, a Texas federal district court ruled for the Fish and Wildlife Service, holding that application of the Endangered Species Act to Texas cave bugs was related substantially to interstate commerce.[47] In 2003, a three-judge panel of the U.S. Court of Appeals for the Fifth Circuit upheld the lower court's decision, ruling that, because takes of cave bugs threaten the "interdependent web" of all species, the cave bug's habitat may be regulated, under the Commerce Clause, by the Endangered Species Act. In the panel's view, although the taking of cave bugs does not itself affect interstate commerce, the taking of all listed species, viewed in the aggregate, affects interstate commerce.[48]

The Purcells and their partners asked the entire Fifth Circuit to rehear the case. In February 2004, the Fifth Circuit refused to rehear the case *en banc* over the dissent of six judges—only one shy of the number necessary for a rehearing.[49] The dissenting judges condemned the panel's opinion as giving new meaning to the term "*reductio ad absurdum*" and said that the panel's circle of life analysis was based on unsubstantiated reasoning that embraces "a remote, speculative, attenuated, indeed more than improbable connection to interstate commerce."[50] Moreover, the panel's opinion was in direct conflict with the Supreme Court's ruling in *Lopez*, which had come out of the Fifth Circuit. Thus, the very federal appellate court that had been reversed in *Lopez* had not received the message the Supreme Court was sending in *Lopez*.[51]

In May 2004, the Purcells and their partners asked the Supreme Court to hear their case and to announce whether, in interpreting the Commerce Clause consistent with the vision of the Founding Fathers in the Court's 1995 *Lopez* ruling, the Court really meant it. Sadly, in June 2005, notwithstanding the clear conflict of the Fifth Circuit's ruling with the Supreme Court's ruling in *Lopez*, the irritation and limitless reach of the Fifth Circuit's Commerce Clause analysis, and the powerful dissent filed by so many Fifth Circuit judges, the Supreme Court declined to hear the case.[52]

Perhaps the Supreme Court concluded that it was wrong in *Lopez*.[53] Perhaps the Court believes that Congress may not make a federal crime out of carrying a gun on a school yard in San Antonio, Texas, but may make a federal crime out of violating Elton John's *Circle of Life* regarding tiny cave bugs seventy-eight miles up the road in Austin. Perhaps the Court is tired of Commerce Clause cases. One thing is sure, property owners grow weary of fighting the Fish and Wildlife Service and its application of the pit bull of environmental laws, the Endangered Species Act.

Westerners have it tough enough with the laws that Congress writes, the regulations that federal agencies promulgate, and the decisions that ALJs and judges issue; too often these laws, regulations, and rulings impinge on westerners' constitutional rights. But when bureaucrats lie and cheat, well, "Katy, bar the door!"

CHAPTER 2

FIGHTING LYIN' CHEATIN' BUREAUCRATS

Don't Steal. The Government Hates Competition.

BUMPER STICKER

I Love My Country but Fear My Government.

WESTERN BUMPER STICKER

If there is a place out West where the correct answer to the question "Where is it?" is "You can't get there from here!" it would be Jarbidge, Nevada. Tucked into the extreme northeastern corner of Nevada in Elko County, nestled deep in the Independence Mountains in the Humboldt-Toiyabe National Forest beneath the 10,839-foot Matterhorn and along the Jarbidge River, is the old mining town of Jarbidge. Its name, purportedly, comes from a Shoshone word meaning "a bad or evil spirit."[1]

Although ranchers had settled the area years before, gold was discovered in Jarbidge Canyon in 1909. Soon prospectors were flooding into the town searching for their fortune and the town boomed to five hundred souls. By 1919, the Long Hike mine led the state in gold production and continued to do so in 1920 and 1921; the mine also produced an appreciable amount of silver. By the late 1930s, however, the area was played out; most folks left and, in 1942, the school closed.[2] Today, Jarbidge is relatively popular for summer recreation—the Jarbidge Wilderness Area is nearby—and autumn hunting. Only a few hardy souls remain in Jarbidge year round. One of them is John Bernt.

John Bernt, like the men who came to Jarbidge in the early part of the last century, is a miner. He searches out and identifies likely mineral deposits on federal land that is available for the purpose and, in accordance with the General Mining Law of 1872, locates or stakes claims to those deposits.[3] Once he does, his claims are good against all the world—except the United States, which may challenge whether or not he has made a "valuable discovery" that would cause a "prudent man" to expend his time and energy developing the claim.[4] John Bernt searches for mineral deposits on the U.S. Forest Service land of Elko County.

On January 3 and 10, 1996, John Bernt located five mining claims on land managed by the Forest Service. On January 19, 1996, the Bureau of Land Management (BLM) entered a notation upon its official records for the land on which John Bernt had located his mining claims, indicating that the land was no longer available for the staking of mining claims.[5] Because John Bernt had located his mining claims prior to the BLM's "withdrawal" of the land, he had valid, pre-existing rights.

On January 12, 1996, John Bernt checked the Forest Service office in Elko to see if there had been any recent withdrawals of land in the area where he had located his claims; one of the Forest Service men told him, "No." Then, on January 22, 1996, John Bernt got a telephone call from the same Forest Service man who said, indeed, there had been a withdrawal, for a future land exchange, on January 19, 1996. John Bernt knew that, because his claims were prior in time to the Forest Service withdrawal, his claims were protected; however, he wanted to make sure. On February 2, 1996, John Bernt told the same Forest Service employee of his valid, pre-existing claims on the now withdrawn land.

In late February 1996, John Bernt received a copy of a Forest Service "Notice of Exchange Proposal" to conduct a land exchange of the very land on which John Bernt's valid, pre-existing claims were located. John Bernt took a careful look at the notice, which was dated February 13, 1996; sure enough, it stated that the land had been withdrawn "beginning January 19, 1996," that is, after he had located his claims. Once again, John Bernt knew his claims were protected!

Nonetheless, and just to make sure, on March 6, 1996, John Bernt again notified the Forest Service of his valid, pre-existing claims on the very land the Forest Service was proposing to exchange. When he did not hear from the Forest Service, John Bernt, on April 12, 1996, called and asked why his claims and correspondence regarding those claims had not been acknowledged. One of the Forest Service employees told him that the man he had spoken to earlier now believed that the land where John Bernt had staked his mining claims had been withdrawn in November 1995. In other words, she said, he thought the land had been withdrawn before John Bernt staked his claims!

On April 15, 1996, however, after researching BLM public land records, she told John Bernt that those records proved, in fact, that the land had been withdrawn from mining in January 1996, not November 1995; that is, after John Bernt had located his claims. Out of an excess of caution, on April 17, 1996, Bernt reviewed and copied the official records at the BLM office in Elko, which showed a single withdrawal date of January 19, 1996. John Bernt wondered where the Forest Service man had come up with the November 1995 date; there was no record of any withdrawal activity during that time.

That same day, over at the Elko Forest Service office, the man and woman from the Forest Service showed John Bernt "new" official records that they had received from the BLM Nevada State Office in Reno just the day before. Those "new" official records showed that the land on which John Bernt's claims were located had been withdrawn both on November 27, 1995, and on January 19, 1996. It made no sense to John Bernt.

On May 3, 1996, John Bernt again reviewed the BLM official records at the BLM office in Elko. This time, however, those records were the same as the "new" records he had been shown in April. John Bernt later attempted, unsuccessfully, to obtain clarifying information from the Forest Service and the BLM regarding the withdrawal, only to be told that all documents relating to the January 19, 1996, withdrawal had been voided or destroyed.

On April 24, 1996, John Bernt spoke to the BLM man who had handled the withdrawal. Incredibly, he admitted that he had entered the January 1996 withdrawal on the official records prior to entering the November 1995 withdrawal. Moreover, he disclosed that he had altered and backdated the records to make it appear as if the November 1995 withdrawal had been entered on the official records before the January 1996 withdrawal.

On June 27, 1996, John Bernt visited the BLM office in Elko where he discovered that the BLM official records had been altered once again, this time to make it appear that the land had been withdrawn first in November 1995; that is, the notations had been reversed and the November 1995 withdrawal now preceded the January 1996 withdrawal. John Bernt copied the newer official records; however, when he asked the BLM man for the original official record, the one showing only the January 1996 withdrawal, he was told that it had been destroyed. Other records showed that the January 1996 date had been entered "in error."

Meanwhile, on May 24, 1996, the BLM had invalidated John Bernt's mining claims asserting that they were not valid on the day he located them because the public records showed that the land on which he had located his claims had been withdrawn in November 1995, prior to the date on which he had located the claims.

John Bernt hired a lawyer and, in October 1996, appealed the BLM's decision to the Interior Board of Land Appeals (IBLA) by filing a "Statement of Reasons for Appeal" and his sworn affidavit, which set out the facts of what had happened to his claims. Under IBLA rules, the BLM was required to respond officially to John Bernt's Statement of Reasons and John Bernt was to have the opportunity to reply to what the BLM argued in its filing. Amazingly enough, the BLM never responded! That is, neither John Bernt nor his attorney were served with or made aware of any BLM filing before the IBLA. Much later, however, John Bernt discovered that, in September 1998, the IBLA had received documents from the BLM. In fact, John Bernt discovered that there had been a great deal of correspondence between the BLM and the IBLA. This kind of communication is referred to as *ex parte* communication, which means in the absence of one of the parties to a case.

Not surprisingly, given the chicanery between the IBLA, a quasi-judicial tribunal, and the BLM, one of the parties in the case, in March 1999, the IBLA affirmed the BLM's decision to declare John Bernt's mining claims void on the day that they were staked.[6] The IBLA based its decision entirely upon its *ex parte* communications with the BLM.[7] Even worse, as far as John Bernt was concerned, the official documents given to the IBLA by the BLM clearly indicated erasures and alterations, yet the IBLA did not demand an explanation from the BLM.

On December 29, 1999, John Bernt was examining public files in the BLM Nevada State Office in Reno when he made an amazing discovery: a handwritten letter from a BLM employee to one of the man's supervisors just before the man retired from the BLM. This was the same BLM employee who had prepared the official records of the withdrawal and to whom John Bernt had spoken three years before. He wrote:

> As far as the Mister Burnt [sic] thing goes and for the last time, somehow the [official records] got noted as to the [January 1996 date] before the [November 1995 date]....I changed the [official records] to show what I thought happened....I remember telling you and [the Forest Service] about it and I also explained all of this to the solicitor. He said no problem and not to worry about it and that's the way I left it. What a mess this case was!

That was not all. John Bernt also found a copy of the official records showing both of the withdrawals: the January 1996 withdrawal and the November 1995 withdrawal. He had never seen this record—it had not been made available as part of the official public land records nor had it been provided by the BLM to the IBLA. John Bernt made a copy of this revealing and incriminating document.

The following month, January 2000, John Bernt's attorneys filed a Freedom of Information Act ("FOIA") request with the BLM. In response, Bernt received copies of documents dated March and April of 1996 referencing the withdrawal of January 1996 even though John Bernt had been told numerous times by BLM and Forest Service employees that all those documents had been destroyed. Moreover, those documents had not been provided to the IBLA. Thus prepared, John Bernt sued the United States.

In February 2000, John Bernt filed suit in Nevada federal district court seeking judicial review under the Administrative Procedure Act of the IBLA's decision and a court order striking the IBLA's decision and reinstating his claims as of January 1996.[8] He also charged employees of the BLM and the Forest Service with fraud. Generally, a fraud claim against the United States must be brought under the Federal Tort Claims Act (FTCA), in which the United States is liable to the same degree that a private party would be liable for a tort (civil wrong) under state law.[9] However, fraud that is due to misrepresentation or deceit is excluded from the FTCA.[10]

Because John Bernt had charged federal employees with fraud, federal lawyers were required to conduct a fact finding to determine if the employees had been acting within the scope of their employment and thus were immunized from a lawsuit and permitted to have the United States substituted for them in the case. Not only was the federal lawyers' "certification" to this effect to be "substantiated," if John Bernt then provided evidence refuting the certification, the federal lawyers would be required to provide evidence and analysis to support their conclusion that the fraudulent conduct had occurred within the scope of employment. Even after that evidence was provided, John Bernt would be permitted to conduct discovery or even to demand that an evidentiary hearing be held to resolve disputed issues of fact.

Nonetheless, federal lawyers declined to conduct the required review. Instead, they summarily certified that the BLM and Forest Service employees had been acting within the scope of their employment and, in July 2000, they moved to substitute the United States for the individually named employees and to dismiss all of John Bernt's claims.[11] In March 2001, the Nevada federal district court held a "hearing" by telephone and shortly into the hearing ruled from the bench and dismissed all of John Bernt's claims. Specifically, the district court ruled that the BLM and Forest Service employees had not committed fraud even if their conduct were "overly zealous," "mistake[n]," or "on the fraudulent side." Essentially, the district court held that backdating government documents was "within the scope of employment" because federal agencies should expect that their employees would engage in that activity.

In so ruling, the Nevada federal district court ignored not only applicable Nevada law on "scope of employment," but also federal law on what is to be expected of federal employees. For example, the United States may not assume its employees will engage in fraudulent actions to fulfill their duties as federal employees; in fact, the United States is obligated to deal honestly and fairly with those who come before it.[12] There is an expectation that individuals charged with administration of an elaborate statutory scheme will act fairly and honestly, which expectation "is not based on blind hope or naiveté, but on a shared expectation of how the Government will conduct itself."[13] Moreover, it is presumed that public employees will perform their duties "correctly, fairly, in good faith, and in accordance with law and governing regulations."[14]

In May 2001, John Bernt appealed to the U.S. Court of Appeals for the Ninth Circuit; however, officials in Washington, D.C., soon learned of the Nevada district court's holding that backdating documents is within a federal employee's scope of employment. Fearing the impact such a decision, if upheld by the unpredictable Ninth Circuit, could have on personnel actions taken in the nine states comprising that appellate court, they settled John Bernt's case. John Bernt's travails with the federal government were over; however, how had it all come to pass?

It started simply. On November 20, 1995, the BLM received a letter, dated November 15, 1995, from the Forest Service requesting that certain public land be withdrawn from the mining law. For whatever reason, the withdrawal requested by the Forest Service in November 1995 did not occur until January 19, 1996. A short time later, someone discovered that, because of the delay, the land that was to be exchanged was now encumbered with five mining claims. One person had made a mistake. That was bad enough, but not as bad as it was going to get.

Someone decided to fix the mistake, then others got involved. Fraud piled upon fraud, deceit upon deceit, lie upon lie; so far, just in Nevada. Then, agency lawyers were told and did nothing. Lawyers and bureaucrats responsible for dealing with the IBLA provided that tribunal with selective documents in an *ex parte* manner. Judges at the IBLA did not object to those *ex parte* communications, failed to demand answers of the BLM to questions made obvious by an official document containing erasures and alterations, and failed to conduct a factual inquiry. Federal lawyers refused to conduct a factual inquiry into the alleged fraudulent enterprise, declined to interview the defendants, and stonewalled efforts by John Bernt to learn the truth so that it might be presented to the federal district court.[15] And the federal district court? It viewed the case as unimportant, conducted a cursory telephone hearing, and issued a problematic ruling.

That is not all. John Bernt's case was brought to the attention of senators and representatives; after all, fraud had been committed and was being covered up. John Bernt was rebuffed. Because the matter was "in litigation," these elected officials could not become involved, not even as part of their oversight responsibility to ensure that the laws passed by Congress are executed faithfully and the money appropriated is spent properly.

At any point in the five years of John Bernt's case, especially in the first days, weeks, or months, someone could have yelled, "Stop! This is serious; this is fraud." No one did. As one of those involved wrote, "What a mess. . . ."

BITTER TASTE IN SWEET GRASS HILLS

In the mid-1980s Ernest Lehmann and his company, Mount Royal Joint Venture (MRJV), located several mining claims and bought surface and mineral leases in Toole and Liberty Counties in north-central Montana, in an area known as the Sweet Grass Hills area. The Sweet Grass Hills area consists of private, state, and federal surface and mineral interests spread over a vast area of plains and buttes, which has been prospected for gold, iron, and fluorspar since 1885. MRJV's gold deposit, the Tootsie Creek Deposit, compares most favorably with other existing or planned gold mining operations in the Western United States.

In February 1992, MRJV filed a plan of operations with the BLM so that it could develop the Tootsie Creek Deposit. After conducting a lengthy environmental review, the BLM concluded in September 1993 that it would approve the plan; however, in a June 1993 memorandum to the director of the BLM in Washington, D.C., a BLM employee wrote, "[w]ith careful handling, the approval [of MRJV's plan of operations] could be delayed many months or even years." The director initialed the document and wrote back, "Proceed immediately. Do Press. See Me."

As a result, instead of approving the plan, the BLM withdrew, from operation of the General Mining Law, all federal mineral land in the Sweet Grass Hills area, some 19,700 acres, for a period of two years. The withdrawal took effect in August 1993 and, at the same time, the BLM notified MRJV that it was "hereby suspending processing" of MRJV's plan of operations.

In July 1995, as the BLM's withdrawal period was about to expire, then U.S. Representative Pat Williams of Montana introduced a bill, "Sweetgrass [sic] Hills Protection Act of 1995,"[16] which proposed to withdraw all federal land in the Sweet Grass Hills area from mineral entry and location. This bill was neither considered by any committee nor otherwise acted upon by Congress. Nonetheless, a short time later, the BLM issued a withdrawal, "in aid of legislation," of the 19,700 acres withdrawn in 1993 and set forth in Mr. Williams's legislation, which took effect in July 1995.

Then, in March 1997, as the BLM's second withdrawal order was nearing its expiration, the BLM obtained yet another withdrawal order from operation of the General Mining Law of the same 19,700 acres, this time for 20 years.

Because none of these withdrawal orders was legal, that is, each violated the strict procedures set forth in the Federal Land Policy and Management Act (FLPMA) as to how withdrawals may be executed, because the BLM had no evidence to support the reasons claimed for the withdrawals, and because the withdrawals were made to prevent development of the Tootsie Creek Deposit, in October 1999 MRJV filed a lawsuit in federal district court in Washington, D.C.[17]

It would not have been unreasonable, and would have been rather predictable, for Clinton administration attorneys to have defended vigorously the challenged actions by high-level officials. Along about May 2001, however, when federal lawyers were filing their motion for summary judgment, one would have thought the case deserved a hard look from the new team in Washington, D.C., for several reasons. First of all, the Clinton administration, whose war on the West was one reason why Governor Bush and Secretary Cheney ran successfully in flyover country, had played fast and loose with federal land law and there was much to undo.[18] Had the Clinton administration violated the law regarding the Sweet Grass Hills of Montana? Second, any time a public official writes that he is taking a particular action to put the screws to a citizen, the government attorney ought to ask if that action merits any defense, let alone a spirited one. Third, any attorney reasonably familiar with federal land law knows there is, for example, no such thing as a withdrawal "in aid of legislation." Thus, on the face of it, that part of the case should have been conceded.

Nevertheless, the United States continued to defend most zealously the actions undertaken by the Clinton administration to prevent Ernest Lehmann and MRJV from using their mining claims. That defense was not merely ill-advised, unjustified, and imprudent—at least in one respect, it was unethical.

In 1915, in *U.S. v. Midwest Oil Co.*, the U.S. Supreme Court ruled that Congress had acquiesced in the Executive's usurpation of Congress's power over federal land.[19] But, in 1976, Congress ended its acquiescence and repealed "the implied authority of the president to make withdrawals. . . ." Nonetheless, the Bush administration, in its brief in support of the BLM's authority to withdraw lands in the Sweet Grass Hills in "aid of legislation" cited to *Midwest Oil* for its holding that the president's man at the BLM has "implied authority. . . to make withdrawals."[20]

Lawyers are supposed to be zealous in representing their clients; however, federal lawyers are held to a much higher standard.[21] Is it too much to expect that attorneys from the U.S. Department of Justice will, of all things, seek justice? Yet, that does not seem to be their prime directive, which is instead, to win on any basis whatsoever—on standing, on ripeness, on jurisdiction, on the merits with questionable facts and law—and at all costs.

Ernest Lehmann's lawsuit against the United States for illegally withdrawing the federal land on which his claims were staked and thereby killing his plan of operations to develop his gold deposit, first filed in October 1999, was briefed fully and ready for oral argument, and subsequently a decision, in July 2001. No decision was forthcoming; in fact, the District of Columbia federal district court denied Ernest Lehmann's motion for oral arguments. Finally, the case was assigned to a Florida federal district court, which declined to hear oral argument and then ruled in favor of the United States.[22]

RELIEVING A NON-EXISTENT DEBT

Americans love to hate the IRS, often with good reason. The IRS, for example, is notoriously bad at giving advice. According to the Treasury Department's inspector general, over one four-day period, 47 percent of the answers given by IRS officials was wrong![23] Furthermore, the IRS has taken the old saw, "What's mine is mine and what's yours is negotiable," to new heights with its demand that all is "gross income" and hence "taxable," unless the taxpayer can prove Congress meant for it to be exempt. It is that approach by the IRS that has caused an uproar among many Americans forced to depend on pro bono legal services to vindicate their constitutional rights and the non-profit lawyers who provide those services.

Decades ago, Congress adopted a number of federal statutes as a result of its concern that, unless folks had some assistance in paying for their lawyers, they would not be able to sue the federal government for what was rightfully theirs, either relief from illegal decisions or payment of debts owed.[24] In addition, Congress sought to ensure that, if government bureaucrats did wrong, their employer would be punished, in some small way, by having to pay the citizen's legal fees. Plus, thought Congress, perhaps such payments would cause federal agencies to exercise more caution in any future actions. These law are referred to generically as "federal fee-shifting statutes."[25]

In the past few years, it has come to the attention of several public interest law firms (PILFs) that the IRS believes that, when pro bono attorneys receive attorneys' fees under federal fee-shifting statutes, the fee is gross income to the clients. The IRS has taken no formal position on this subject and has not issued any revenue ruling; in fact, the revenue rulings it has issued seem to say just the opposite. Nonetheless, these rumors are disturbing and, perhaps most troubling of all, they are consistent with something the IRS has been doing in another area, that of contingent fees received by for-profit lawyers.

The IRS has maintained consistently that the portion of a court award or settlement decree that the client is required, pursuant to his contingency-fee agreement with his attorney, to pay to his attorney is gross income to the client. The IRS asserts that this is either the "anticipatory assignment of income" or the "relief of a debt." Most of the federal appellate courts had agreed with the IRS; however, a handful had ruled to the contrary.[26] Thus, the IRS recently urged upon the U.S. Supreme Court cases from two of those divergent circuits to resolve this split. The Court agreed to hear the cases and, in January 2005, ruled 8–0 in favor of the IRS, concluding that attorneys' fees paid under those conditions are gross income to the client because the payment involves the anticipatory assignment of income.[27]

Although the issue of federal fee-shifting statutes generally and, in particular, as they affect non-profit, public interest law firms was not before the Court, several PILFs filed friend of the court (*amici curiae*) briefs to ensure that the Court would not issue an overly broad ruling that might permit the IRS to contend that the rule enunciated by the Court as to for-profit, contingent-fee agreement attorneys applied as well to non-profit, representation agreement bound, public interest law firms. The Court brushed aside that request believing, mistakenly, that the issue involving payment of attorneys pursuant to federal fee-shifting statutes had been resolved.[28]

Because the Court declined to address the issue, it remains possible for the IRS to contend that attorneys' fees paid to public interest law firms pursuant to federal fee-shifting statutes are gross income to clients; however, the IRS would be wrong.

First, as the Supreme Court noted in January 2005, the "first principle of income taxation [is] that income must be taxed to him who earns it."[29] As between a PILF and its client, it is the PILF that earns any attorneys' fees awarded under a federal fee-shifting statute because non-lawyers who represent themselves are not entitled to attorneys' fees under federal fee-shifting statutes.[30] Thus, because the PILF earned the attorneys' fees paid under the fee-shifting statutes, those fees are not taxable to its client.

Second, a PILF does not enter into the contingent-fee agreements that the Supreme Court addressed in January 2005 because it may not consider the "likelihood or probability of a fee" when selecting cases and, generally, may not accept cases in which the client has a financial interest at stake.[31] Thus, the agreement between a PILF and its client provides pro bono representation; it does not contain contingency fee provisions. Although it may contain a provision that the PILF will seek attorneys' fees under federal fee-shifting statutes, those fees are sought and paid, not in accordance with the representation agreement but pursuant to the applicable federal statute.

Third, the Court's January 2005 opinion provides that "when a litigant's recovery constitutes income, the litigant's income includes the portion of the recovery paid to the attorney as a contingent fee."[32] When a PILF receives attorneys' fees, those fees are not paid out of a "portion of the recovery," and the litigant's "recovery," whether or not it constitutes "income," is not reduced by the payment of the PILF's attorneys' fees. Instead, a PILF's attorneys' fees are paid by the United States in accordance with federal law.

Finally, the IRS has issued a ruling, with regard to a union that provided free legal services to its members, that the legal fees received by the attorney, as part of a settlement, did not constitute gross income to the union members.[33] In this case, the IRS applied the "first principle of income taxation: that income must be taxed to him who earns it."[34]

All of these are excellent tax code, revenue ruling, and legal holding types of reasons why the IRS has no basis to declare that the money received by a pro bono attorney for winning for his client who could not afford to hire an attorney is taxable to the client. But there are additional reasons:

First, the client never gets the money; his pro bono lawyer gets it!

Second, if the client had to pay taxes on that money, those taxes would reduce the money awarded by the court to reimburse him because, for example, his property was unconstitutionally taken from him. Thus, the client would not have received the just compensation that the Constitution requires.

Third, sometimes when a person beats the federal government in court and his pro bono attorney is awarded legal fees, he did not seek or get a cash award; all he wanted and all he got was a court ruling that he did not owe penalties that bureaucrats illegally assessed against him.

It almost appears as if the IRS has declared war on conservative legal foundations and their clients to silence those who fight conservative causes! Consider this:

- The ACLU, which gets millions of dollars in legal fees for lawsuits for people who object to the Ten Commandments or prayer, has not been told that its fees are taxable to its clients!
- The Sierra Club, which gets millions of dollars in legal fees for lawsuits for people who want to save endangered species, has not been told that its millions are taxable to its clients!
- Scores of civil rights groups, which have gotten millions of dollars in legal fees for various well-publicized lawsuits, have not been told that their millions are taxable to their politically correct clients.

In the last category, contemplate the famous case of Shannon Faulkner, who sought admission to The Citadel, the Military College of South Carolina.[35] After she prevailed, her powerful legal team was awarded $4.5 million in attorneys' fees.[36] Yet the IRS never insisted, never even suggested, that this mammoth award was gross income to a young woman barely out of high school. If the IRS did not try to collect on that award, one wonders why the IRS is casting a covetous eye at the paltry sums collected by attorneys for folks throughout the West who must fight to vindicate their rights.

Lawyers are often urged to first argue the facts—unless the facts are against them. Then, they are urged to argue the law—unless the law too is against them. At that point, they are advised to argue the Constitution and for all they are worth. Such it is with federal bureaucrats when they seek to accord special privileges that neither the facts nor the law support. In fact, neither does the Constitution!

CHAPTER 3

FIGHTING RACIAL PREFERENCES DISGUISED AS TRUST RESPONSIBILITIES

> Within two or three generations, the [United States] will possess hundreds of semi-independent "tribes" whose native heritage consists mainly of autonomous governments and special privileges that are denied to other Americans.
>
> FERGUS M. BORDEWICH, *KILLING THE WHITE MAN'S INDIAN*[1]

Sandra Shook went deer hunting on her neighbor's private property in Sanders County in northwestern Montana. She had a deer hunting license and tag as required by Montana Big Game Hunting Regulations and, perhaps just as importantly, her neighbor's permission.[2] Nevertheless, after she had killed and tagged a white-tailed deer, Sandra Shook was cited by the Montana Fish [and Game], Wildlife & Parks Commission for hunting in violation of Montana law.[3] The reason: her neighbor's property is a "closed area" because it is within the exterior boundaries of the Flathead Indian Reservation and Montana limits hunting within the boundaries of Montana Indian reservations to tribal members, even if the property is owned in full, that is, in fee simple absolute, by a non-Indian.[4]

Sandra Shook believed that the Montana law violated her constitutional rights. After all, it was her neighbor's private property and he could give her permission to hunt there. So Sandra Shook contested the citation.[5] Eventually, her case made it to the Montana Supreme Court. There, in response to Sandra Shook's claim that the Montana law violated the Equal Protection Clause of the Fourteenth Amendment to the U.S. Constitution, the Montana Supreme Court relied on a 1974 U.S. Supreme Court decision in which the Court upheld the constitutionality of an American Indian-only hiring preference adopted by the Bureau of Indian Affairs (BIA); the U.S. Supreme Court held that the classification was "political," not "racial." Thus, Montana Fish, Wildlife & Parks' policy was similarly protected from constitutional challenge, the Montana Supreme Court ruled.[6]

Specifically, the Montana Supreme Court held that "laws that afford Indians special treatment are constitutional as long as those laws can be tied rationally to the fulfillment of the unique federal obligation toward Indians."[7] Moreover, reasoned the Montana Supreme Court, because the obligations imposed on Montana when it entered the Union require it to adhere to all federal obligations, "federal Indian law regarding the rights of Indians is binding on the state."[8] Thus, "the state equal protection guarantee … must allow for state classifications based on tribal membership if those classifications can be rationally tied to the fulfillment of the unique federal and consequent state, obligation toward Indians."[9] "Therefore, we need only address whether the state regulation that prohibits non-tribal members from hunting big game is rationally tied to the fulfillment of the unique obligation toward Indians. We hold that it is."[10]

Sandra Shook knew there was something wrong with the Montana Supreme Court's ruling, and her lawyers told her that she was right. First of all, the U.S. Supreme Court's 1974 decision related to the authority of Congress and, as a result of the delegation by Congress, the authority the BIA had vis-à-vis American Indians; no similar authority had been given to Montana and its Fish, Wildlife & Parks Commission. Second, there was some substantial doubt as to whether the Supreme Court's 1974 decision had survived the Court's 1995 ruling on the ability of the federal government to distinguish between and among Americans on the basis of race.[11] In fact, dissenting from the 1995 landmark decision, Justice Stevens asserted that the 1995 ruling would eviscerate the Court's 1974 decision.[12] Third, while Congress certainly had a special relationship, given the Constitution's Indian Commerce Clause and the treaties into which the United States had entered with the various American Indian tribes, Montana had no such special relationship.[13] Given all these problems with the Montana Supreme Court's decision, Sandra Shook decided to ask the U.S. Supreme Court to hear her case.

In her petition for *certiorari*, Sandra Shook challenged the holding of the Montana Supreme Court noting that the U.S. Supreme Court had held: "It is settled that 'the unique legal status of Indian tribes under federal law' permits the Federal Government to enact legislation singling out tribal Indians, legislation that might otherwise be constitutionally offensive. States do not enjoy this same unique relationship with Indians. . . ."[14] Moreover, argued Sandra Shook, Montana does not have a special "trust relationship" with American Indians as a result either of the Montana Constitution[15] or the treaties entered into by the United States with American Indians.[16]

Sandra Shook also argued that Montana's law is a racial classification that is unconstitutional under the Supreme Court's 1989 decision regarding the use of racial classifications by Richmond, Virginia.[17]

That is, because membership for each one of the eleven Indian tribes that resides on a reservation in Montana requires a certain blood quantum, it is impossible for a non-Indian, that is, a person without the requisite degree of American Indian blood, to simply apply for and be granted membership with a tribe in order to hunt within the reservation.[18] The Montana Supreme Court's decision was also in conflict with a more recent U.S. Supreme Court decision.[19] Finally, Sandra Shook contended that the Montana Supreme Court decision was in conflict, not only with several U.S. Supreme Court opinions, but also with a persuasive decision of the U.S. Court of Appeals for the Ninth Circuit.[20]

Nonetheless, in October 2003, the Supreme Court declined to hear her case.

ABUSING THE TRUST RESPONSIBILITY

The Montana Supreme Court's claim, in ruling in Sandra Shook's case, that Montana is obligated by federal law to accord American Indians special treatment is unique and perhaps unprecedented. What is much more typical, even common, is the assertion by federal agencies that they may do what is otherwise impermissible under the Constitution (certainly following the Supreme Court's 1995 ruling on racial preferences) with regard to their treatment of American Indians. An example of this claim is the approach of two federal agencies to a particular commercial and recreational activity at Grand Canyon National Park.

In the northwest corner of Arizona, running along the Colorado River and the majestic canyon that it cut deep into the sandstone over the course of millions of years, Grand Canyon National Park is 277 miles long and encompasses 1.2 million acres—an area the size of Delaware.[21] For more than 70 years, small businesses have offered air tours of Grand Canyon National Park. In fact, of the more than 5 million people who visit the Grand Canyon annually, approximately 750,000 tour by air. Of these visitors, many are elderly, disabled, or otherwise mobility-impaired individuals.

In August 1987, Congress enacted the Overflights Act,[22] which required the Federal Aviation Administration (FAA) and the National Park Service (NPS) to achieve "substantial restoration of the natural quiet" at the Grand Canyon. As a result, over the years, the FAA adopted various rules restricting air tours to certain areas of the park culminating, in December 1996, in a rule that eliminated recreational air tours over 90 percent of the Grand Canyon and restricted the number of aircraft each recreational air tour provider could utilize. Then, in April 2000, the FAA published an even more restrictive limit on the number of air tours that the recreational air tour providers could fly at the Grand Canyon.

In accordance with federal law,[23] the FAA prepared a study that concluded that between 2000 and 2009 recreational air tour providers would lose a total of $155.4 million in net operating revenue; annual losses for some recreational air tour providers would be as high as $6.3 million dollars.[24] Finally, the FAA concluded that the annual per capita impact on recreational air tour providers and their roughly 1,500 employees would be $10,333.[25] Despite its predictions of the economically ruinous impact the new rules would have on the recreational air tour providers, the FAA adopted the rules.[26]

The economic impact of the new rules on another group of recreational air tour providers, however, did cause qualms for the FAA. The FAA disclosed that the annual per capita impact of the rules on the 2,500 members of the Hualapai tribe would be roughly $700.[27] In addition, the FAA concluded that "youth activities and other social programs on the Reservation" would be affected adversely.[28] That impact, concluded the FAA, was unacceptable; it would violate the agency's "general trust responsibility to Native American tribes or

Nations, [which requires the agencies to] act[ ] in the interest of the Tribe…particular[ly] concern[ing] the economic development and self-sufficiency of the Native American Tribe or Nation."[29] Thus, after concluding that its "economic analysis…indicates that th[e] rulemaking would significantly adversely impact the Hualapai tribe's economic development and self-sufficiency," the FAA exempted all flights to the Hualapai reservation from the new rules.[30]

In May 2000, some non-Indian recreational air tour providers challenged, among other things, the decision by the FAA to exclude American Indians from application of what was in essence an environmental statute, asserting that the exemption violated the Constitution's equal protection guarantee. In their arguments before the U.S. Court of Appeals for the District of Columbia, they relied on the Supreme Court's 1995 decision regarding racial preferences in government contracting.[31]

In August 2002, the D.C. Circuit rejected the argument that the new rule "violates the equal protection component of the Fifth Amendment because it exempts flights to and from the Hualapai Indian Reservation." In so doing, the D.C. Circuit relied, not on the Supreme Court's 1995 ruling, but instead on its 1974 ruling in *Mancari*.[32] The D.C. Circuit concluded that the Supreme Court, in that 1974 decision, had "upheld an employment preference for Indians in the face of an argument similar to that of [the recreational air tour providers], declaring that, '[a]s long as the special treatment can be tied rationally to the fulfillment of Congress's unique obligation toward the Indians,' such treatment must be upheld.'"[33] Therefore, the D.C. Circuit, declaring that the Hualapai exemption is "at least rationally related to 'the government's interest in fulfilling its trust obligation' to the Tribe," rejected the recreational air tour providers' equal protection argument.[34] As to the recreational air tour providers' contention that the Supreme Court's 1995 decision had overruled the

1974 decision, the D.C. Circuit declared, "the Supreme Court has made clear that the lower courts do not have the power to make that determination."[35]

In December 2002, a single recreational air tour provider, AirStar Helicopters, whose president, Ron W. Williams, had flown combat helicopters in Vietnam for the U.S. Army and who, given his service there, found the racial distinction particularly offensive, sought U.S. Supreme Court review.[36] In his petition he asked the Court to resolve the conflict between its 1974 and 1995 holdings.[37] Unfortunately, in April 2003, days after oral arguments in two highly controversial racial preference cases, the Supreme Court declined to hear Ron Williams's appeal.[38] Perhaps the Court was exhausted by its consideration of the issue or thought the applicability of the equal protection guarantee to American Indians should wait for another day. Whatever the reason, one day it must make that decision because, for millions of Americans, the issue will not go away.

THE MODERN-DAY TREATMENT OF AMERICAN INDIANS

In the nation's early days, the United States sought to balance its "Manifest Destiny"—to settle, colonize, and utilize the resources of the land—with the desires of the independent and diverse indigenous peoples who inhabited that land and used its resources and who wanted to keep both. Thus, it was not racial hostility that drove the western expansion; it was the desire of a predominantly rural population for free land and the promise of wealth that went with it. In fact, the official government policy was more the result of a Jeffersonian ideal that American Indians would one day, along with the nation's non-Indian population, "become one people."[39]

Although historically, indigenous or aboriginal peoples either had been annihilated or absorbed by the larger, militarily more competent newcomers, that did not take place in the United States. Instead, from 1850 to 1887, Congress created a reservation system to prevent the extinction of the tribes and their members by reserving parcels for those tribes out of their original land holdings. These reservations were viewed as temporary—ultimately, American Indians would become full members of society.[40]

To accomplish this Jeffersonian ideal of assimilation, from 1887 to 1934, Congress adopted the allotment system, which provided agricultural land to American Indians in the hopes that American Indians would become self-supporting and self-sufficient members of American society.[41] As it turned out, the primary effect of the allotment system was a precipitous decline in the total amount of land held by American Indians as a result of its sale or lease to non-Indians.

After the failure of the allotment system, Congress adopted the Indian Reorganization Act of 1934, also known as the Wheeler-Howard Act, which ended the allotment system and extended indefinitely the period for holding existing allotments in trust.[42] The Wheeler-Howard Act encouraged tribal self-determination, allowing tribes to organize and to adopt constitutions and bylaws, subject to the approval of the Secretary of the Interior, and to organize as federally chartered corporations.

In 1953, during the Eisenhower administration, Congress formally adopted a policy of "termination" under which American Indians would be "subject to the same laws and entitled to the same privileges and responsibilities as... applicable to other citizens of the United States, [and] to end their status as wards of the United States...."[43] Under this policy, the special government-to-government relationship between the United States and tribal governments would end and American Indians would be subject to state law. States, however, raised concerns about the policy, noting that their responsibilities under the

Act involved substantial expenses. Moreover, because states were unable to tax tribal property to pay these expenses, they insisted on substantial funds from the federal government to support their new obligations. In addition, American Indian tribes adamantly opposed the termination policy.

By the late 1960s, the termination policy was regarded as a failure as plans for assimilation began to fade. In 1970, President Nixon issued a statement on Indian affairs that still represents the federal government's policy toward American Indian tribes.[44] He declared termination a failure and called upon Congress to repudiate it. Although President Nixon stressed the continuing importance of the trust relationship between the federal government and American Indian tribes, he urged Congress to adopt legislation to permit all tribes to manage their own affairs with a maximum degree of autonomy.[45]

In 1975, Congress established the American Indian Policy Review Commission, which undertook a review of federal Indian policy and, in 1977, recommended rejection of assimilation, reaffirmation of the status of tribes as permanent self-governing institutions, and reauthorization of increased financial aid for tribes. In 1982, Congress adopted the Indian Tribal Government Tax Status Act, which accorded tribes many of the federal tax advantages enjoyed by states, including the ability to issue tax-exempt bonds to finance tribal projects.[46] In 1988, Congress declared the nation's commitment to "the development of strong and stable tribal governments."[47] In 1994, President Clinton instructed all federal agencies to operate "within a government to government relationship with federally recognized tribal governments."[48]

Thus, contrary to the histrionics of the Ward Churchill-types who would characterize the treatment of American Indians as a vicious campaign of genocide based on racial hatred, the history of the federal government's treatment of American Indians has not involved overt, intentional racial hatred, but instead an attempt to achieve a Jeffersonian ideal of a United States of America in which all adopted the English language, Christian religion, and Anglo/American culture and lived side by side. Furthermore, the history of the federal government's treatment of American Indians has been that of dealing with indigenous peoples through treaty, paternalism, occasionally war, and, eventually, the provision of the assistance thought necessary for self-determination, preservation of culture, separate tribal government, and freedom from dependence on the United States.

Today the federal government's policy toward American Indians, or more properly toward American Indian tribes and tribal governments, is represented most clearly in the Supreme Court's 1974 *Mancari* decision. This decision authorizes the federal government to treat American Indians differently than it treats non-Indians insofar as that policy affects non-Indians and the constitutional rights guaranteed them. The wisdom, not to mention the constitutionality, of that decision is now in serious dispute as a result of three interrelated phenomena: the incredible wealth generated by tribal casinos, the exclusion from taxation of all tribal activity, including those casinos, and the demographic changes taking place in the American Indian community.

THE CHANGING LANDSCAPE

As a result of an act of Congress, American Indian tribes are now authorized, after entering into compacts with states, to undertake gaming on their reservations.[49] To say that these enterprises have been a phenomenal success would be an understatement. In 2004, the 405 American Indian casinos generated $19 billion dollars in revenue, an increase of 12 percent over 2003.[50] Tribal casinos in California grossed $5.3 billion in 2004, which was twice that of Connecticut where the two largest casinos in the world generated $2.2 billion.[51] The financial future looks even brighter as old casinos are expanded and new ones are opened either by newly recognized American Indian tribes[52] or by existing tribes on newly acquired tribal trust land, following required certification by the U.S. Department of the Interior.[53] The recent proposal by two American Indian tribes—the Cheyenne and Arapaho of Oklahoma—to trade their claims to 27 million acres of land, some 40 percent of which is in Colorado, for the right to build a casino near Denver International Airport is one of many currently pending.[54]

Although these casinos have been unqualified financial successes, their economic and social impacts are less positive. For example, a 2002 study documented increases in auto thefts, larceny, violent crime, and bankruptcy in surrounding counties four years after the opening of a casino and increases in bankruptcies within 50 miles of a new casino.[55] Plus, because the profits from casinos are tax exempt, casinos' "presence in many states possibly diverts funds from a taxable activity (e.g. dining at restaurants, going to movies) and negatively impacts state and local public finance."[56] More definitive information as to the adverse social and economic impacts of American Indian casinos is as yet unavailable[57] for a variety of reasons,[58] but the casinos' tax-exempt status has drawn fire already.

Arnold Schwarzenegger's declaration during his campaign for governor of California that, "[American Indian] casinos make billions, yet they pay no taxes and virtually nothing to the state," was the turning point for his candidacy; he surged in the polls.[59] The Terminator's tough stance struck a chord among voters disgusted that his predecessor had received $1 million from tribes for his 2002 reelection campaign and had endorsed legislation to give American Indian tribes authority to halt development by designating "sacred tribal land" and that Arnold Schwarzenegger's opponent received $8.2 million in direct and indirect contributions from California tribes.[60] After his election,

Governor Schwarzenegger asserted that he thought that payment of 25 percent of American Indian gaming revenues to the State of California, or $1 billion a year, would be gaming tribes' fair share.[61]

It is not just about the vast sums of tax-exempt money being generated by tribal gaming; it is about what is being done with that money and why it is tax exempt in the first place. As was the case most famously in California with Governor Gray Davis and Lieutenant Governor Cruz Bustamante, those revenues have resulted in awe-inspiring political contributions. Remarkably, given the hue and cry over the purported need for campaign finance reform, American Indian tribes are exempt from the McCain-Feingold Campaign Finance Reform Act.[62] The exemption looks more like a "loop-chasm" than a loophole.[63]

The controversy surrounding American Indian gaming is also about what is not being done with the money, which is collecting from and paying state sales taxes for non-Indian customers. The Supreme Court ruled in 1991 that, while American Indians are required to collect those taxes, no effective mechanism exists for states to enforce that obligation; because of "tribal sovereignty" states may not sue tribes to collect those taxes.[64] In fact, on two separate occasions, attempts by the State of Oklahoma to compel tribes to pay those taxes were rebuffed by the Court.[65] American Indian tribes have been extremely aggressive in challenging any state tax that they believe interferes with their sovereignty or right to self-determination. One such case was decided recently by the U.S. Supreme Court.

In 1997, the State of Kansas adopted a tax on the first receipt of motor fuels by all wholesale distributors who, in selling that motor fuel, are not prevented from increasing the price of that fuel by some or all of the amount of the tax. Some of these distributors sell to the Prairie Band of the Potawatomi Nation, a federally recognized tribe that sells the motor fuel from a convenience store and gasoline station near its casino in Jackson County. In May 1999, the tribe filed suit in Kansas federal district court to bar Kansas from imposing the tax on distributors who sell to the tribe.

In January 2003, the district court held for Kansas, ruling that the tax was not preempted by federal law and did not interfere with the tribe's sovereign right to self-government. In August 2004, the U.S. Court of Appeals for the Tenth Circuit reversed on both issues, concluding that the motor fuel sold by the tribe is an "integral and essential" part of the casino and its value is attributable solely to the reservation, not in any way to the efforts that occurred off reservation to get that motor fuel discovered, developed, refined, and transported to the distributor. In February 2005, the Supreme Court agreed to hear the case.

The National Association of Convenience Stores, the Petroleum Marketers Association of America, and the Society of Independent Gasoline Marketers of America, which together represent 80 percent of the nation's convenience stores, 8,000 independent petroleum marketers, and 250 independent motor fuel operators, urged the Supreme Court to reverse the Tenth Circuit. They argued that, because the tax is on non-Indian, off-reservation economic activity, federal law does not preempt it and that any federal preemption must be unequivocal. Plus, because the value of the motor fuel is due to off-reservation activity, Kansas's interest is paramount. They also predicted that, if not reversed, the Tenth Circuit's ruling would destroy competition in the sale of motor fuel,[66] disrupt state tax administration, prevent states from raising revenue, increase federal litigation, and create commercial chaos. Remarkably, but perhaps not surprisingly, the United States filed a friend of the court brief in support of the tribe.[67] Nonetheless, in December 2005, the Supreme Court ruled, by 7–2, in favor of Kansas.[68]

There is yet another controversy brewing regarding what American Indian tribes do with their casino earnings: spend it on new tribal— and hence tax exempt—enterprises. Tribes near urban centers that have benefited from casino operations use the funds thus generated to acquire additional land; they put that land into trust with the United States, and then they engage in further commercial activities on that land. Because these tribal enterprises are tax-exempt as well, they have a tremendous competitive advantage over their taxpaying competitors. The result is the shrinking of local tax bases for states and their political subdivisions and unfair, often ruinous, competition.

In New York State, for example, a recent study concluded that 25 percent of smokers surveyed traveled to Indian reservations to buy their cigarettes, which is not surprising given that the $1.50 tax on all packs of cigarettes results in a price per carton of $50; on reservations, cigarettes sell, per carton, for between $10 for generic brands and $30 for premium brands. No wonder that western New York State convenience stores lost 25 to 50 percent of their cigarette sales after the 2000 tax increase.[69]

QUESTIONING SOVEREIGN IMMUNITY

In 1991, Justice John Paul Stevens declared that "the doctrine of sovereign immunity is founded upon an anachronistic fiction."[70] How much more true are those words fifteen years later given the incredible, maybe even unimaginable wealth generated at American Indian tribal casinos? For now, politicians like Governor Schwarzenegger are talking only about the money; however, the day may soon come when Congress and the Supreme Court will be asked to take a serious and very hard look at whether there remains a need for the federal government's policy of paternalistic protection and its dependent and immune sovereignty treatment of American Indian tribes. The day may come sooner than many expect given that, with ever declining blood quantum per tribal member, recognized tribes may soon be little more than associations of financial convenience.[71]

The request for that serious and hard look will no doubt come as well from portions of the American Indian community given the immunity of tribes from lawsuits,[72] the inapplicability to tribes of many federal civil rights laws,[73] the ability of tribes to banish members, without due process, and thus exclude them from the valuable benefits, including casino payouts, derived from tribal membership,[74] and the absence of the fundamental civil rights that all Americans, except American Indians, take for granted.[75] American Indians are discovering that sovereign immunity is not only a shield to resist all challenges to tribal actions and decision making, but also a sword to be wielded by the tribe against American Indians. A case seeking review at the U.S. Supreme Court is an example of just such a use.

In June 1999, Thomas Lee Morris, a member of the Chippewa tribe from the Leech Lake Reservation in Minnesota, was cited for speeding near Ronan, Montana, on the Flathead Indian Reservation. Although Morris and his family have lived on the Flathead Reservation, which is the home of the Confederated Salish and Kootenai tribes, for nearly fifteen years, neither Morris nor any member of his family belongs to either tribe. Mr. Morris filed a motion to dismiss for lack of jurisdiction, which was denied. Mr. Morris then filed suit in Montana federal district court.[76] The United States intervened.[77]

Mr. Morris challenged the constitutionality of the 1990 Amendments to the Indian Civil Rights Act,[78] which affirm tribal court jurisdiction over all Indians, not just those Indians who are members of the prosecuting tribe. After the federal district court dismissed Mr. Morris's lawsuit without considering his constitutional arguments, the Ninth Circuit reversed and directed the district court to do so.[79]

On remand, the Montana federal district court ruled against Mr. Morris, holding that "Federal regulation of Indian tribes ... is governance of once-sovereign political communities; it is not to be viewed as legislation of a 'racial group' consisting of Indians."[80] Therefore, ruled that district court, Mr. Morris could not claim the benefit of the Supreme Court's jurisprudence regarding disparate racial treatment. Moreover, noted the district court, because Indian status for federal criminal jurisdiction requires voluntary membership or affiliation with a federally recognized tribe, in addition to an ancestral or racial element, an individual subjected to a foreign tribe's criminal prosecution could always give up his tribal enrollment to escape that tribe's jurisdiction! Finally, the district court brushed aside the Supreme Court's most recent pronouncements on the use of race by federal and state legislative bodies as "beside the point."[81] Yet even if those Supreme Court decisions controlled, declared the district court, the 1990 Amendments met the Court's test:

> The United States and the tribal governments have compelling interests in the self-governance of the tribes, the public health, safety, and welfare of the reservations, and effective and thorough law enforcement on the reservations. The [1990] [A]mendments are necessary and narrowly tailored to meet those needs.[82]

In other words, Congress amended the Indian Civil Rights Act not to meet the needs of American Indians but to serve the interest of the federal and tribal governments. Later, Mr. Morris's second appeal to the Ninth Circuit was unsuccessful.[83]

All of these are much larger questions that will concern Congress and the Supreme Court for the next several decades. In the meantime, tribal sovereignty and federal and state deference to it have more on-the-ground consequences.

Randy Roberts, a non-Indian, is entitled to hunt on approximately 1,500 acres of deeded land within the exterior boundaries of the Crow Indian Reservation in Montana. Although Randy Roberts currently operates a commercial bird shooting preserve on the property, he has been prohibited by Montana State law from hunting or allowing others to hunt big game on that property for the last thirty-five years. After learning about what happened to Sandra Shook, he decided that was long enough. He filed a lawsuit in Montana federal district court.[84]

In recent years, westerners have become accustomed to the manner in which the federal government has abused it trust responsibilities regarding American Indians. Nothing, however, could have prepared westerners for the arrogant and audacious abuse of the Constitution, federal law, and the facts in which Bill Clinton engaged as he approached the presidential election of 1996.

CHAPTER 4

FIGHTING CLINTON'S ABUSES OF THE ANTIQUITIES ACT

The political purpose of the Utah event is to show distinctly your willingness to use the office of the President to protect the environment...Designation of the new [Grand Staircase-Escalante National M]onument would create a compelling reason for persons who are now disaffected to come around and enthusiastically support the Administration.

MEMORANDUM TO PRESIDENT CLINTON, AUGUST 1996

One way for [President Clinton] to get past the Monica [Lewinsky] legacy is to create the public land legacy by locking up public property.

U.S. SENATOR BEN NIGHTHORSE CAMPBELL (R-CO), JUNE 2000

On September 18, 1996, President William Jefferson Clinton dropped a huge bombshell on the State of Utah. Standing on the edge of the Grand Canyon in Arizona, more than seventy miles from the Beehive State, Clinton announced creation of a 1.7 million acre Grand Staircase-Escalante National Monument.[1] The national media were there to record the event, as were Clinton's friends and supporters from national environmental groups and other prominent Americans, including Robert Redford, who had been alerted in time to make the trip. Missing from the assembly, however, was any elected official from the State of Utah. Not a single member of its congressional delegation or its governor was there.[2]

In fact, Utah's senators and representatives had been told, consistently and repeatedly, that Clinton had made no decision regarding a monument in Utah and that if any decision were reached, the delegation would be told. Governor Leavitt was afforded slightly more deference; at 2:00 a.m. on September 18, the White House advised him that Clinton would make the announcement later that day. As Clinton and his friends celebrated in Arizona, the president was being hanged in effigy in Kanab, Utah, in Kane County, which along with its neighbor Garfield County, were two of Utah's poorest counties. It was in the midst of these two counties that Clinton had decided to make his first use of the Antiquities Act of 1906.[3]

The Antiquities Act, as is clear from its very specific language and its legislative history, was intended by Congress to apply to items of antiquity, which means, in common parlance, "relics or monuments of ancient times."[4] The final version of the statute, the result of six and one half years of lobbying by archeological organizations,[5] was written by the archeologist Edgar Lee Hewett, who at last agreed to write the more expansive language favored by the U.S. Department of the Interior—though he did not go as far as Interior suggested. Although Hewett's concerns were with prehistoric antiquities, he added the phrase "other objects of historic or scientific interest." The acreage limitation of "320 to 640" was abandoned as well and, in its place, "the smallest area compatible" language was inserted. Despite the changes, the will of Congress, both as to the items to be designated and the size of the designations, remained clear:

> There are scattered throughout the Southwest quite a number of very interesting ruins. Many of these ruins are upon the public lands, and the most of them are upon lands of but lit-

tle present value. The bill proposes to create small reservations reserving only so much land as may be absolutely necessary for the preservation of these interesting relics of prehistoric times.[6]

As if to demonstrate what did not meet the requirements of the Antiquities Act, shortly after its enactment, Congress created Mesa Verde National Park to protect cliff dwellings in Colorado spread over an area of 216,960 acres.[7] It appears that Congress made the site a park because it was too large for designation as a monument.[8] The narrowness of the legislative authority provided the Executive by Congress was clear, even to advocates within the Department of the Interior, which had called for more expansive power, including the right to designate scenic areas:

> I have at times been somewhat embarrassed by requests of patriotic and public-spirited citizens who have strongly supported applications to create national monuments out of scenery alone...The terms of the [Antiquities Act] do not specify scenery, nor remotely refer to scenery as a possible *raison d'etre* for a public reservation.[9]

The very first national monument, Devils Tower, declared on September 24, 1906, by President Theodore Roosevelt shortly after the Antiquities Act was passed, was well within the statutory limits intended by Congress. It covered a mere 1,153 acres—one one-thousandth the size of the Utah Monument—and was of unquestionable scientific interest given the intense debate as to how it was formed.[10]

Clinton acted, a congressional report would later reveal, not to save manmade works of earlier cultures, which the Antiquities Act was adopted to protect, but to resolve a debate over wilderness. Utah has more than 3.2 million acres of federal land set aside by Congress pursuant to the Wilderness Act of 1964, land where "man is a visitor" and no motorized vehicles or commercial use is permitted. Although environmental groups and activists outside the West favor more designations under the National Wilderness Preservation System, most westerners and their leaders oppose closing more federal land to recreational and economic use.

The reason is simple. In most rural western counties, federal land predominates, which means local economies require use of that land. Since 1872, national parks have been off limits to all but the narrowest of uses; then, in 1964, Congress, at the behest of a nascent environmental movement, developed a new federal land designation, wilderness, where use would be restricted even more. After a flurry of state wilderness bills, supported by each congressional delegation and state and local leaders, westerners sought to end the possibility that more land would be locked up as wilderness. In 1976, Congress adopted the Federal Land Policy and Management Act (FLPMA) or the Bureau of Land Management (BLM) Organic Act,[11] and, among a lengthy list of other matters, put a deadline on the study of BLM land for future wilderness designation by Congress.

In 1991, the Utah BLM ended its review of the 20 million acres of Utah's BLM land: 5.4 million acres were examined; 3.2 million acres were placed in "wilderness study areas"; and 1.9 million acres were recommended for wilderness designation by Congress, a recommendation that was sent to the secretary of the Interior and the president. That recommendation was still in Washington, D.C., in 1993 when President Clinton was sworn in as the nation's 42nd chief executive.

Not surprisingly, environmental groups, by 1993 a powerful monolith and often an important component of Democratic Party politics, were not satisfied with the BLM's recommendation; they wanted 9 million acres of Utah's BLM land recommended and designated as federal

wilderness. While Utah's leaders, its governor and congressional delegation, favored additional wilderness designation, in their view, the
land to be set aside was much more limited, targeted, and discreet.
There the impasse stood when, in July 1996, Clinton's Secretary of the
Interior Bruce Babbitt ordered a re-inventory of Utah's BLM land to
find more land "suitable" for wilderness designation.

Meanwhile, federal employees were completing a study required
by the National Environmental Policy Act (NEPA)[12] regarding an
underground mine in Kane County, the Andalex Smoky Hollow
Mine, which would affect 60 acres of surface area on the Kaiparowits
Plateau, which covers 1,650 square miles.[13] The extraction of the
thick-seamed (easily mined), low-sulfur coal would provide high-paying jobs for nearly 1,000 local citizens and generate $20 million a year
in local revenue.[14] As the NEPA study—an Environmental Impact
Statement (EIS)—neared completion, after the expenditure of $8 mil-
lion and seven years of comprehensive study and analysis,[15] it became
clear that the Smoky Hollow project posed no "threat[]" to the environment or proposed wilderness areas in the region and that its
impacts would be "minor" or "negligible."[16] So, while Utah's leaders
were enthusiastic about economic activity in this depressed region,
environmental groups were enraged. The latter took their concerns to
the White House.

The Clinton administration got the message. In March 1996,
Clinton officials sought a means of circumventing Congress's
wilderness authority given the refusal of the Utah delegation to support the wilderness legislation demanded by environmental groups.
Could the Antiquities Act of 1906 be used, the Clinton White House
asked?[17] Later: "[i]s there another Utah hook?" besides the stalemate
on wilderness legislation.[18] The "hook" was the "threat" of an underground coal mine, which the White House chose to "rope in" to
achieve "the president's overall purpose,"[19] even though the Council

on Environmental Quality (CEQ) admitted, "these lands are not really endangered,"[20] and the Office of Environmental Policy and Compliance (OEPC) declared: "it strains credulity to base a 'go' or 'no go' decision on an analysis of two alternatives which appear to indicate no significant difference in environmental impacts for the area of either permitting or not permitting the proposed Smoky Hollow Project."[21] Tellingly, in all of the White House communiqués, no mention is made of environmental concerns, antiquities, or impending threats to those values, nor is there mention of real scientific or historical concerns by any of the government agencies involved.[22]

The decision made, on August 14, 1996, the CEQ advised Clinton of the reason for the Utah monument. "The political purpose of the Utah event is to show distinctly your willingness to use the office of the President to protect the environment . . . Designation of the new monument would create a compelling reason for persons who are now disaffected to come around and enthusiastically support the Administration."[23] A month and four days later, in Arizona, Clinton expressed his "concern[] about a large coal mine proposed for the area" as well as his belief that "we shouldn't have mines that threaten our national treasures."[24]

Perhaps it was about the coal after all. Two reporters suggested, at the time, that Clinton's decision was motivated, not by the environment, or even by a desire to garner votes, but by a *quid pro quo* for campaign contributions. Wrote one, "With a stroke of his pen [President Clinton] wiped out the only significant competition to Indonesian coal interests in the world market."[25] That was important, wrote another reporter some weeks later, to "the Jakarta-based Lippo corporation [which] has business interests related to coal."[26] The link was simple: "Lippo's founder, billionaire Mochtar Riady, his family members and associates have contributed heavily to Clinton and the

Democrats."[27] Nationally syndicated columnist Paul Craig Roberts wrote on the topic and *The Washington Times* editorialized about it.[28]

One strictly circumstantial connection is the following set of events: *U.S. News and World Report* reported that "the monument was on the fast track from late July to its creation on September 18."[29] Coincidentally, *USA Today* reported that on July 30 President Clinton had a private, fundraising dinner at the Jefferson Hotel, "one of the capital's most exclusive hotels," an intimate dinner that included Lippo Group official, James Riady, and no other member of the administration except for Clinton. Don Fowler, Democratic National Committee co-chairman, who was present, said of the dinner, "The president would speak for five or ten minutes, and then people could say what they wanted."[30]

Whatever his reasons for decreeing the Utah monument, Clinton must have been pleased with the results; over the next three plus years, he designated or expanded twenty-two national monuments. Of particular significance were these: January 2000: Agua Fria National Monument in Arizona (71,100 acres) and Grand Canyon-Parashant National Monument in Arizona (807,881 acres); June 2000: Ironwood Forest National Monument in Arizona (129,022 acres), Canyons of the Ancients National Monument in Colorado (163,892 acres), Cascade-Siskiyou National Monument in Oregon (52,947 acres), and Hanford Reach National Monument in Washington (195,000 acres); November 2000: Vermilion Cliffs National Monument in Arizona (280,324 acres) and Craters of the Moon National Monument in Idaho (271,847 acres); and January 2001, on his way out of the Oval Office: Carrizo Plain National Monument in California (204,107 acres), Upper Missouri River Breaks National Monument in Montana (374,976 acres), and Sonoran Desert National Monument in Arizona (486,603 acres).[31]

Clinton may have been pleased, but folks in Utah were not. In October 1996, Mountain States Legal Foundation (MSLF), on behalf of its members in Kane and Garfield Counties, filed suit in Utah federal district court.[32] Subsequently, Governor Mike Leavitt and the Utah Association of Counties (UAC) joined in the litigation, although the former later withdrew. MSLF and the UAC averred that Clinton had violated several federal statutes including the Antiquities Act and its requirement that designations be only of "historic landmarks, historic and prehistoric structures, and other objects of historic or scientific interest" and "be confined to the smallest area compatible with the proper care and management of the objects to be protected."[33] They also complained that Clinton had violated the Wilderness Act, which limits wilderness-style designations to Congress, and had acted *ultra vires*, that is, without legal authority. Environmental groups called the litigation "frivolous" and stayed on the sidelines.

Clinton's Utah monument was not the first opposed by states and local citizens. That distinction belongs to a monument designated in Wyoming by President Franklin D. Roosevelt. Wyoming sued and, for the first time, a federal judge considered the authority of a president to act under the Antiquities Act.[34] In fact, Wyoming raised many of the same issues that would be raised more than fifty years later by people in Utah:

> [First, the new monument] is outside the scope and purpose of the Antiquities Act [since it] contains no objects of an historic or scientific interest... [second, it] is not confined to the smallest area compatible with the proper care and management of a National Monument; [third, it is] an attempt [] to substitute, through the Antiquities Act, a National Monument for a National Park, the creation of which is within the sole province of the Congress....[35]

Although the federal government challenged Wyoming's right to file its lawsuit, the court held that it possessed the requisite jurisdiction:

to investigate and determine whether or not the Proclamation is an arbitrary and capricious exercise of power under the Antiquities Act so as to be outside of the scope and purpose of that Act by which the President in the exercise of its provisions has exceeded or violated a discretion thereby conferred.[36]

The case even proceeded to trial, during which evidence was presented; however, after a brief recitation of that evidence, the court demurred, noting:

> [I]n an ordinary suit the Court would be confronted with the task of determining where the preponderance of evidence rests and render a decision based thereon. This in substance, amounts to no more in the end than the Court's opinion of what evidence in the case purports to show and itself implies an exercise of the Court's discretion.[37]

Instead, ruled the court, it would defer to the president and his proclamation, "[i]f there be evidence in the case of a substantial character upon which the President may have acted...."[38] Nonetheless, the court did recognize that there were outer limits to the president's authority:

> For example, if a monument were to be created on a bare stretch of sage-brush prairie in regard to which there was no substantial evidence that it contained objects of historic or scientific interest, the action in attempting to establish it by proclamation as a monument, would undoubtedly be arbitrary and capricious and clearly outside the scope and purpose of the Monument Act.[39]

Although two cases involving national monuments reached the U.S. Supreme Court, neither concerned the issues raised by Wyoming in 1945 or Utah in 1996.[40] Furthermore, in the decades since the Wyoming case, federal land law has changed significantly. Prior to 1976, Congress, which possesses the sole constitutional power over federal land under the Property Clause,[41] acquiesced in the withdrawal, by various presidents, of millions of acres of land from 1910 to 1976.[42] However, with the adoption of the Federal Land Policy and Management Act (FLPMA) in 1976, Congress acquiesced no longer.[43] Thus, the Antiquities Act may not be interpreted in isolation, but must be interpreted in light of FLPMA, which, notwithstanding the strict limits it imposed on the authority of the Executive to withdraw federal land from public use, left the Antiquities Act in place. This then was the setting when the legal challenge to Clinton's Utah monument decree went to court.

In July 1998, federal lawyers moved to dismiss or for summary judgment in the challenge to the Utah monument. Over the next four years, the parties battled over attempts by MSLF and UAC to engage in discovery, a dispute that was later amicably resolved. Meanwhile, in November 1998, federal lawyers filed a motion to dismiss the case asserting that, by action or inaction, Congress had ratified President Clinton's decree. In a forty-one-page opinion, the Utah federal district court denied the motion.[44] In July 2000, the U.S. Court of Appeals for the Tenth Circuit declined to hear an appeal by federal lawyers on the matter.[45]

By now, various environmental groups had decided that the lawsuit was no longer frivolous. Therefore, in March 2000, they moved to intervene to defend Clinton's decree. In June 2000, the Utah federal district court denied their motion; however, in July 2001, the Tenth Circuit reversed that decision and, in September 2001, the environmental groups were granted intervention.

Meanwhile, Clinton's monument decrees had drawn the attention of other users of the public land of the West, including the Blue Ribbon Coalition (BRC), a family-oriented group that uses multiple use federal land for off-highway motorized recreation. In January 2001, MSLF and BRC challenged Clinton's designation of six national monuments in four states averring that Clinton's actions were *ultra vires* in violation of the Constitution's Property Clause. Specifically, MSLF and BRC challenged the Hanford Reach in Washington, the Cascade-Siskiyou in Oregon, the Canyons of the Ancients in Colorado, and three monuments in Arizona: the Grand Canyon-Parashant, Ironwood Forest, and Sonoran Desert. In March 2001, federal lawyers and various environmental groups, which had intervened, filed separate motions to dismiss arguing that President Clinton had complied with the Antiquities Act of 1906.

By now, of course, Governor George W. Bush had been sworn in as the United States's forty-third president. The Bush administration's position on the Clinton monuments was uncertain. After all, both Governor Bush and Secretary Dick Cheney campaigned throughout the West by opposing Clinton's monuments.[46] Bush, for example, was quoted in a June 2000 story in the *Seattle Post-Intelligencer* as saying he did not know if he could "unscramble the egg" regarding Clinton's monuments, but that Clinton's actions had "virtually shut down the ability of a lot of people to use lands." Moreover, on a related issue, Bush promised to reverse Clinton's closure of sixty-million acres of "roadless" forest land.[47] Secretary Cheney was even more forthright. In an August 2000 speech in Oregon attacking Clinton's "willy-nilly" designation of monuments throughout the West, Cheney promised a review and possible reversal of the monument decrees.[48]

It was not to be. Although Attorney General John Ashcroft and Secretary of the Interior Gale Norton were confirmed and in place within days of Bush's inauguration, they were, as the media joked, "home alone," since their deputies were not confirmed for months. In fact, Assistant Attorney General Thomas L. Sansonetti, of the Environment and Natural Resources Division, was not in place to manage the litigation involving Clinton's monuments until November 30, 2001. By then, more with a whimper than a bang, word leaked out that the Bush administration would not withdraw any Clinton monuments but might, in the right case, make boundary adjustments. But, by that time, the litigation strategy of the Bush administration had been decided for months; it was to be the same strategy as existed during the Clinton administration: defend Clinton.

In November 2001, the federal district court for the District of Columbia heard oral arguments regarding the legality of the six monuments. Immediately after those arguments, the court ruled that it lacked jurisdiction to review the president's actions beyond the face of the challenged proclamations; that is, because President Clinton had declared in his proclamations that the designated monuments contained items "historic and scientific" and were "confined to the smallest area compatible with the proper care and management of the objects to be protected," the court could inquire no further.[49] Thus, Clinton's use of such "magic words" barred judicial inquiry.[50] The court reached the same decision in a challenge by Tulare County to Clinton's designation of the Giant Sequoia National Monument in south-central California in April 2000.[51] All plaintiffs appealed.

In October 2002, the U.S. Court of Appeals for the District of Columbia reversed the district court's holding, in both cases, that it lacked authority to conduct the inquiry sought.[52] The District of Columbia Circuit declared that "review is available to ensure that [monument] Proclamations are consistent with constitutional principles and that the President has not exceeded his statutory authority."[53] Moreover, ruled the appellate court, "[c]ourts remain obligated to determine whether statutory restrictions have been violated" given that "the Supreme Court has indicated generally that review is available" to ensure presidential compliance with statutory obligations.[54]

The D.C. Circuit affirmed the dismissal of both complaints, however, by holding that neither complaint "presented factual allegations that would occasion ... *ultra vires* review of the Proclamation."[55] The holding was curious given the differing approaches of the two complaints. Whereas MSLF and BRC had utilized bare-boned notice pleading, setting forth the details of the monuments being challenged and alleging, in a single count, that President Clinton had acted *ultra vires* in their designation,[56] Tulare County had crafted a detailed 215-paragraph complaint. Tulare County alleged, for example, that "Sequoia groves comprise only six percent of the [Giant Sequoia National] Monument." Oddly, neither complaint, one very short and to the point, the other quite long and detailed, in the D.C. Circuit's view, met notice pleading requirements. Frankly, the appellate court's holding in this regard was ridiculous. In January 2003, the Court of Appeals denied MSLF's and BRC's petition for *en banc* review.[57] Likewise, and perhaps not surprisingly given the procedural issues presented, the U.S. Supreme Court denied the two petitions regarding these seven monuments.[58]

While the D.C. Circuit was willing to reverse the district court in order to state correctly the law of the D.C. Circuit as to its authority to review presidential actions, it was unwilling to mandate that the district court review President Clinton's designation of the seven monuments. Therefore, it merely dismissed both complaints as defective thereby assuring that the Supreme Court would not review the matter.

By this time, the challenge to the Grand Staircase-Escalante National Monument was ready for briefing and arguments. Bush administration lawyers stood on the motions filed by Clinton administration lawyers in July 1998. The environmental groups, after some delay, filed their brief in March 2003, to which MSLF and UAC responded; thus, the matter was joined. Oral arguments were held in January 2004.

The Utah federal district court's decision was awaited eagerly. After all, none of Clinton's monuments had generated the controversy and outrage that had taken place in Utah following Clinton's 1996 announcement. Furthermore, in subsequent years, court orders regarding the protection required by the Endangered Species Act for the Mexican spotted owl had closed down the timber industry in southern Utah and northern Arizona. In addition, the district court had gone out of its way, government attorneys thought, to slap down the Clinton administration's congressional ratification gambit. Finally, during oral arguments, the court had brushed aside assertions by a lawyer for the various environmental groups that the economies of Kane and Garfield Counties had benefited from, not been burdened by, the Utah monument.

Nonetheless, in April 2004, the Utah federal district court granted the federal government's motion to dismiss and for summary judgment, concluding simply that the court had no authority to determine whether Clinton's actions were in accordance with the requirements set forth in the Antiquities Act.[59] In doing so, the court relied on the very case relied upon, unsuccessfully as it turned out on appeal, by the D.C. district court.[60] Moreover, that case is a slender reed upon which to rely given that: the decision turned on a specific provision in the Tariff Act, which expressly limited judicial review; the statutory delegation at issue committed the decision entirely to the discretion of the president; and the issue involved foreign affairs, which, under the Constitution, is the primary responsibility of the president.

Furthermore, the U.S. Supreme Court has recognized repeatedly the availability of non-statutory review of executive action, that is, review not predicated on a specific or general statutory review provision.[61] Such review flows from the general presumption of judicial reviewability of executive action, a remedy that is particularly necessary when one is injured by an act of a government official allegedly in excess of his express or implied powers.[62] Thus, courts will "ordinarily presume that Congress intends the executive to obey its statutory commands and, accordingly, that it expects the courts to grant relief when an executive [] violates such a command."[63] That is the conclusion reached by the D.C. Circuit in ruling for MSLF and BRC, at least with regard to the duty of courts to review national monument decrees. "[T]he [president's] power must be exercised consistently with the structure and purposes of the statute that delegates that power."[64]

Because of its initial ruling as to its limited jurisdiction, the Utah federal district court declined to apply the "intelligible principles" of the Antiquities Act to the Clinton decree.[65] Had it done so, MSLF argues, it would have been compelled to strike the Utah monument. First, the legislative history of the Antiquities Act demonstrates its extremely limited scope. The House Committee wrote of the need to protect "interesting relics of prehistoric times" and the Senate Committee referred to "historic and prehistoric ruins and monuments." Moreover, Congress specifically declined to include authority to set aside areas of "scenic beauty" and "natural wonders."[66]

Second, Congress provided the specific statutory mechanisms for protecting many of the values purportedly protected by Clinton's Utah decree. In 1964, Congress adopted the Wilderness Act as the sole means by which to withdraw land from public use so as to protect "scenic beauty," "natural wonders," and "wilderness values."[67] In 1973, Congress adopted the Endangered Species Act as the sole means by which to protect threatened or endangered wildlife.[68] In 1976, Congress adopted FLPMA, setting forth the only mechanisms by which federal land was to be withdrawn from use by the public and limiting strictly that withdrawal authority. Also, in FLPMA, Congress provided the sole mechanisms by which certain environmental values were to be protected; for example, Congress described how to protect "areas of critical environmental concern."[69]

Third, even a facial comparison of the Utah proclamation with the Antiquities Act reveals a conflict with the will of Congress. The monument purports, for example, to protect "bold plateaus and multi-hued cliffs," "sedimentary rock layers," "a wide variety of formations," canyons, "many arches and natural bridges," and "1,600 square miles of sedimentary rock,"[70] as well as various "vegetative communities," "unusual and diverse soils," grasslands, trees, wildlife (over 200 species of birds), "fragile cryptobiotic crusts," and "numerous types of endemic plants and their pollinators."[71] Although the proclamation generally describes the "cultural resources" to be protected, including "[h]undreds of recorded sites," such as "rock art panels, occupation sites, campsites, and granaries," as well as "many more undocumented sites," the proclamation fails to identify any particular ancient ruin or artifact to be protected by the monument reservation.[72] Finally, the proclamation laughably asserts that 1.7 million acres "is the smallest area compatible with the proper care and management of the objects to be protected."[73]

Why then did the Utah federal district court wash its hands of this challenge to Clinton's Utah monument? After all, this was the same district court that took the Clinton administration to the woodshed over its assertion that Congress had ratified the Utah decree. Perhaps, it was one thing for the district court to question Clinton's actions when it appeared that there might be another point of view, at the presidential level, on the legality of the Utah designation; however, it was quite a different matter when Bush administration lawyers argued vigorously in support of Clinton's action.

Nonetheless, the matters that the Utah federal district court refused to address are now before the U.S. Court of Appeals for the Tenth Circuit.[74] Today, more than nine years after Clinton traveled to Arizona to designate a national monument in Utah, the controversy continues. With another year likely before a ruling by the Tenth Circuit and potentially a year before U.S. Supreme Court review, a final legal resolution of the issue will have taken more than a decade. Yet, even with all of that time, the questions that the people in Kane and Garfield County are asking remain worthy of answers from the Supreme Court:

- Is the Antiquities Act a limited grant of power to the president?
- If the Antiquities Act grants unlimited power to the president, has Congress violated the Delegation Doctrine?
- Do federal courts have the authority to determine, not only whether Congress has exceeded its constitutional power, but also whether a president has exceeded the power delegated him by Congress?
- Has the president, by his broad application of the Antiquities Act, usurped unconstitutionally Congress's Property Clause authority over federal land?

Those westerners who are suffering as a result of Clinton's decrees are most frustrated by the failure of those in a position to do something about it to act. For example, Congress enacts laws that are limited in scope, then looks the other way when those limits are exceeded. Judges, appointed and confirmed to enforce the Constitution, check out the political landscape, then demur or defer. Presidents, and there is nothing new about this but it is vexing nonetheless, promise action but fail to take that action or fail to ensure that their promises are kept by political appointees and career bureaucrats alike. No wonder westerners believe they must go to court.

With his designation of vast portions of the American West as national monuments and hence "wilderness" areas off limits to economic and recreational activity, Clinton gave environmental groups a victory they could not have achieved in Congress. It is not enough for them, however; they want an end to the very economic activities that permit people to live, work, and recreate in the West.

CHAPTER 5

FIGHTING FOR LOCAL COMMUNITIES

In the wake of Hurricane Betsy forty years ago, Congress approved a massive hurricane barrier to protect New Orleans from storm surges.... The project was stopped in its tracks when an environmental lawsuit won a federal injunction on the grounds that the Army's environmental impact statement was flawed.... [T]he corps' former chief counsel [] said the project was estimated to cost $85 million in 1965, or just over $500 million, adjusted for inflation. Estimates of the costs of Katrina's damage and reconstruction exceed $100 billion...

"A BARRIER THAT COULD HAVE BEEN," *L.A. TIMES*, SEPTEMBER 9, 2005

Bruce Vincent is a third-generation logger who lives with his extended family in Libby in Lincoln County, Montana, in extreme northwestern Montana. Hard up against the Canadian border and just east of the Idaho Panhandle, 78 percent of Lincoln County is owned by the federal government—land that is managed primarily by the U.S. Forest Service as the Kootenai National Forest. The Cabinet Mountains lie to the south, the Purcell Mountains run up the spine of Lincoln County, and to the east, the Kootenai River flows south out of British Columbia to meet Libby Dam and to form

Lake Koocanusa, which Bruce Vincent and his neighbors refer to jokingly as Lake Whocanuseit. People like Bruce Vincent who are users of the national forest for economic and recreational activities make such jokes because much of the federal land of their county is off limits for almost any use.

Today, Bruce Vincent is a nationally known advocate for the right of local communities like Libby and the nearby towns of Troy and Eureka to survive by ensuring the availability of long-lasting, high-paying jobs—jobs like logging and mining.[1] Because the geological forces that created the Cabinet and Purcell Mountains also deposited vast mineral wealth beneath the lodgepole pine forest that covers the deep valleys and steep slopes of the Kootenai National Forest, there are riches there that may be developed to provide jobs and local revenues, all while protecting the environment. Bruce Vincent and his neighbors care about the environment; that is why they live where they do: to hunt, and fish, and hike, or simply to marvel at the beauty of it all. But to do those things they need jobs. There is another reason why people in Lincoln County favor logging: they know that if the trees are not harvested in a timely manner they will burn. Folks in Libby, Montana, are particularly sensitive about wildfires because of what happened in their community in 1910. "For two terrifying days and nights—August 20 and 21, 1910—the fire raged across three million acres of virgin timberland in northern Idaho and western Montana. Many thought the world would end, and for 86, it did."[2] That fire remains the largest, in terms of acres burned, and the fastest moving fire in U.S. history.

No wonder the people of Lincoln County were concerned when, in 1972, the U.S. Forest Service discovered that a mountain pine beetle infestation was killing a number of lodgepole pine stands in the Upper Yaak River drainage of the Kootenai National Forest. It was not just that the infestation would destroy the value of those trees for later commercial use; the trees were now ripe for a catastrophic fire, a fire that, perhaps, during times of periodic drought, would be as bad as the 1910 blaze. After all, the life span of a lodgepole pine is about eighty to ninety years. Unfortunately for the folks of Lincoln County, the plans by the Forest Service to harvest that timber were stopped dead in their tracks by a ruling of the U.S. Court of Appeals for the Ninth Circuit in response to a lawsuit filed by environmental groups.[3] The reason: the Forest Service had failed to comply with the National Environmental Policy Act of 1969 (NEPA).[4]

Although NEPA is referred to as an environmental statute—its name includes the word "environment[]" and its purposes section is replete with save the planet fluff—NEPA is not entirely an environmental statute. NEPA is a planning statute that requires federal agencies, before the "irretrievable commitments of resources" for "major federal action" that "significantly affects the quality of the human environment,"[5] to take a "hard look"[6] at all available information. The home workshop counterpart to NEPA would be "measure twice, saw once." Moreover, like almost all acts of Congress, NEPA includes in its purposes section extremely broad, all-things-to-all-people language, such as the need to "achieve a balance between population and resource use which will permit high standards of living and a wide sharing of life's amenities."[7] In fact, NEPA might even be described, not as an environmental statute, but as a good government statute in which federal agencies "foster and promote the general welfare" in order to "fulfill the social, economic, and other requirements of present and future generations of Americans."[8]

Yet, as Bruce Vincent and his neighbors from Libby discovered in 1988 when environmental groups put a stop to timber harvesting plans, federal courts interpret NEPA primarily as an environmental statute. Thus, federal courts use NEPA to prevent the most remote and speculative of harm to the "environment" even if, in the process, the "social" and "economic" needs of the folks of Lincoln County suffer and they are denied "high standards of living and a wide sharing of life's amenities." Bruce Vincent and his neighbors discovered something else: even though they live, work, recreate in, care deeply about, and want to protect the environment that surrounds them,[9] they are not the kinds of people who, according to federal courts, are within the "zone of interest" that Congress intended to protect when it passed NEPA. Therefore, only so-called environmentalists and environmental groups have what is called "prudential standing" to sue for violations of NEPA. This interpretation is particularly ironic given that NEPA proclaims, "each person has a responsibility to contribute to the preservation and enhancement of the environment."[10] Bruce Vincent did not understand how he and his neighbors have "a responsibility" under NEPA but may not sue to enforce it.

In 1990, the Forest Service finished the environmental impact statement (EIS) mandated by the Ninth Circuit. That was the good news. The bad news was that, in one particular sale area, the Forest Service had cut allowable timber harvest by 43 percent to achieve a 1 percent increase in grizzly-bear habitat. With environmental groups using NEPA to challenge more and more timber sales and with cutback after cutback by the Forest Service, locals feared for the survival of their mills. They also feared the results of a catastrophic fire in the pine beetle killed lodgepole pine forest surrounding their homes. They decided to fight back. As Bruce Vincent put it, "We used to think that it was a radical notion to sue our government. We now know that what is radical is for us to sit back while the other side destroys us."[11]

In 1992, Bruce Vincent's grassroots group, Communities for a Great Northwest, several local units of governments, and others sued in Washington, D.C., federal district court.[12] In 1995, the District of Columbia federal district court dismissed Bruce Vincent's case holding that none of the plaintiffs had the legal right, or standing, to sue contending that the Forest Service had violated NEPA or the other federal statutes at issue.[13] Even though all those who had filed the lawsuit lived, worked, and recreated in the Kootenai National Forest and were affected adversely by the decisions made by the Forest Service when it acceded to the demands of environmental groups, they had, according to the district court, no right to be heard, not even with regard to the increased likelihood that their forest would burn down and them with it, which the district court brushed aside as "mere speculation."[14] The folks from Lincoln County appealed.

In 1996, the U.S. Court of Appeals for the District of Columbia reversed the federal district court, ruling that "persons physically close to the potential fire [may] question the [Forest Service's] decisions."[15] Moreover, "individuals who hike, camp and fish in the forest are thus intended beneficiaries [of the various federal statutes involved] and [the groups] to which they belong are suitable champions"![16] Finally, held the appellate court, these individuals' "economic interests do not blight [their] environmental interests in the quality of public lands where [they] hike[], camp[], fish[], etc."[17] Sadly, the District of Columbia Court of Appeals ruled that the increased risk of a catastrophic fire that resulted from the Forest Service's decision was not sufficiently high to be called "arbitrary and capricious" and hence illegal.[18] Plus, the Court of Appeals deferred to Congress's adoption of the Endangered Species Act holding, "There is nothing arbitrary or capricious about an officer's incurring some incremental wildfire risk if the [Endangered Species Act] requires him to do so."[19]

Bruce Vincent and his neighbors had won! They had proved, with a victory before the second most important court in the country,[20] that they had the right to sue to enforce federal planning and environmental statutes to protect local jobs as well as the environment where they lived, worked, and played. However, the case had taken four years and even if the court had ruled against the Forest Service and held that it should harvest more timber, implementation of that decision would have required more Forest Service planning and decision documents on which environmental groups could sue. For Bruce Vincent and the people of Lincoln County, they needed decisions, rulings, and action. Delay meant death: death to the lodgepole pine forest and death to local jobs.

And that is what happened to Lincoln County's once vibrant timber industry. In the years of the Clinton administration, Forest Service officials decreased allowable timber harvest, environmental groups sued asserting that the plans, even for those vastly reduced sales, violated numerous federal statutes, but always NEPA, and activist federal judges ruled in favor of the environmental groups and sent the Forest Service back again and again to the drawing board. Although local mills retooled and retrofitted to deal with less and less lumber and smaller and smaller logs, the Kootenai National Forest was effectively closed to business.

Even after the end of the Clinton administration, the slow-starting efforts of the Bush administration to effect change in the management of the forests of the West were not enough to counter the double-barrel efforts and effects of radical environmental groups and leftist activist judges.[21] For example, in August 2004, the U.S. Court of Appeals for the Ninth Circuit reversed an Idaho federal district court's ruling and held that the Forest Service needed to perform more studies regarding a plan proposed in 1996.[22] Nearly every proposed timber sale was subjected to the same treatment. In May 2005, Lincoln County's last mill, Owens & Hurst Lumber Company, shut its doors for good.[23] Libby, Troy, and Eureka were not the only Montana towns affected; since 1990, Montana has lost twenty-three mills and 2,240 high-paying jobs despite an annual growth rate of 1.4 billion board feet of federal timber.[24]

NEPA-style lawsuits are not only killing logging jobs. Although one mine near Troy, which closed in 1993 due to low metal prices, reopened in December 2004 and has hired one hundred workers,[25] two extremely valuable mining projects that held out great hope for Bruce Vincent and his neighbors are dying the death of a thousand paper cuts, NEPA style. Revett Mineral's Rock Creek silver and copper project, which would provide 330 high-paying jobs over a thirty-year mine life, is an underground mine that accesses the ore body from Sanders County to the south but would provide jobs to folks from Lincoln County as well.[26] A plan of operations for the mine was submitted to the Forest Service in 1987; NEPA review began in 1989 and was the subject of a Final EIS in September 2001, twelve years later. There followed more study, this time by the U.S. Fish and Wildlife Service, which issued a decision in June 2003. In March 2005, a Montana federal district court judge told the Fish and Wildlife Service to redo its study.[27]

The second potential mine, this one located physically in western Lincoln County, is in the distant future, if anywhere. The Montanore project, a silver and copper deposit, could employ 250–300 workers with an average annual payroll of more than $10 million and purchases of $200 million worth of supplies.[28] Although approved back in 1998, after ten years in the permitting process and an investment of $100 million, it was abandoned due to unrelenting NEPA-type pressure from environmental groups. In January 2005, a new company submitted a thirteen-volume application for re-permitting. Bruce Vincent thinks that maybe, just maybe, his grandchildren might have a chance at one of the mine's very high paying jobs if they wish to remain near their grandparents in Libby, Montana.

Meanwhile, after years of Bruce Vincent telling jokes about the fiction that is rural tourism jobs,[29] Lincoln County, in desperation, began to plan a ski hill on some Forest Service land near town. After Lincoln County scraped together several hundred thousand dollars, the ski hill died a sudden death when local Forest Service officials learned that

President Clinton had issued instructions to lock up sixty million acres of purportedly roadless Forest Service land. Once again, Bruce Vincent's Communities for a Great Northwest returned to the District of Columbia federal district court.[30] That lawsuit was dismissed, after years of inaction by the federal district court, when the Bush administration adopted new regulations that voided the Clinton plan.[31] There is some hope in Libby that there might be new life in the ski hill plan; however, timber and mining jobs are years away, thanks to NEPA and lawsuits by environmentalists.

NEWSPAPERS AND AN AGENCY'S EXPERTISE

Bruce Vincent and his mining and logging neighbors may take some small solace in one thing: they are not alone. Folks in Montana and Wyoming who are trying to ease the nation's energy crisis and accompanying record-setting prices for gasoline and home heating oil are having the same problems with NEPA. Take, for example, Wyoming's Powder River Basin.

The Powder River Basin in northeastern Wyoming covers the entirety of Campbell County as well as portions of the surrounding seven Wyoming counties. Years ago, the Powder River Basin and Gillette, Wyoming, became famous when large-scale strip mining of the thick, low-sulfur coal deposits began in earnest; many ranchers became rich and Campbell became the state's most prosperous county.[32] The strip mines are still producing, the coal trains still head east, and the royalties still roll in, but today the hottest activity is development of coal-bed methane, which the Wyoming State Geological Survey describes thusly: "Coalbed methane (CBM) is natural gas found in coal beds and used for a variety of purposes that range from domestic, commercial, industrial to electrical power generation."[33]

Because much of the mineral estate in the Powder River Basin is owned by the United States and managed by either the Bureau of Land Management (BLM) or the Forest Service, extraction of CBM requires compliance with NEPA. In February 2000, the BLM, after preparing several NEPA documents, conducted a competitive oil and gas lease sale for what is known as the Buffalo Resource Area of the Powder River Basin. Pennaco Energy, Inc., a subsidiary of Marathon Oil Corporation, bought three of the parcels, located in Campbell and Sheridan Counties, with the intention of developing CBM. The Wyoming Outdoor Council and the Powder River Basin Resource Council, two environmental groups famous for opposing all natural resources activity in Wyoming, immediately filed a protest of the lease sale with the BLM arguing that, in issuing the leases, the BLM had violated NEPA. One of the assertions made by the environmental groups in their protest was that the NEPA studies prepared by the BLM had addressed only traditional oil and gas activity and not specifically CBM activity, which, the groups asserted, had "unique" impacts.

In April 2000, the Wyoming office of the BLM dismissed the protest after concluding that the NEPA documents had studied all oil and gas activity, including CBM, that CBM development did not have unique impacts in so far as traditional oil and gas development sometimes produced abundant water, and that the BLM had taken the hard look at the environmental consequences of its planned leasing program. The two environmental groups immediately appealed the dismissal to the Interior Board of Land Appeals (IBLA) at the U.S. Department of the Interior in Washington, D.C.

In April 2002, the IBLA ruled in favor of the two environmental groups: the BLM had indeed violated NEPA, it concluded.[34] The environmental groups were right, opined the IBLA, there were "unique problems" and "critical air quality issues" caused by CBM development; however, the IBLA did not identify those "problems" or "issues" or its bases in evidence for such findings. Instead, the IBLA referenced "newspaper articles, budget request materials, a memorandum segment, and its own prior opinions."[35]

In June 2002, Pennaco filed a lawsuit in Wyoming federal district court. In May 2003, the Wyoming district court reversed the IBLA, ruling:

> The fact that the IBLA cited only to dubious evidence such as newspaper articles and budget request materials does not inspire confidence that its opinion was grounded in more reliable data from the record. The evidence cited by the IBLA simply does not constitute substantial evidence.[36]

Moreover, concluded the Wyoming district court, "when the two [BLM] documents are considered together, they provide the BLM with all the information it needs to take the requisite hard look before making its leasing decisions."[37] It is important to remember, the district court pointed out, that the NEPA requirements at the pre-leasing stage, during which no on-the-ground activity may yet take place, are more general. Later, when the leaseholder proposes to engage in on-the-ground activity, such as submitting an application for permit to drill (APD), much greater specificity is not only possible, it is mandated by NEPA. In conclusion, the district court wrote, the IBLA's opinion "arbitrarily and capriciously elevates form over substance" and in the process "impose[d] undue procedural burdens upon the BLM."[38]

In July 2003, the two environmental groups appealed to the U.S. Court of Appeals for the Tenth Circuit. In August 2004, the Tenth Circuit reversed the decision of the Wyoming federal district court, holding that it owed no deference to the Wyoming court; instead, it owed deference to the IBLA.[39] Furthermore, held the Tenth Circuit, it did not have to uphold the IBLA's opinion based on what the IBLA wrote was the basis for its opinion; it could look elsewhere, even if there were evidence elsewhere that contradicted what the Tenth Circuit found to support the IBLA's ruling.[40] How ironic. Evidence that would not be admitted into federal court as unreliable could be relied on by the appellate court to defer to a federal agency's decision. Moreover, the Tenth Circuit defers to the agency by rejecting the bases for its decision and using instead some other bases.

Traditionally, courts do defer to agency expertise, recognizing that there are matters in which an agency, as a result of years of experience in a particular area, has accumulated expertise that the court lacks. In this case, however, the IBLA's opinion did not evince any expertise to which the appellate court should have deferred. Moreover, if there were an agency with expertise, after three decades developing, preparing, and relying on NEPA documents pursuant to issuing oil and gas, coal, and geothermal leases, it would be the BLM. Nonetheless, the Tenth Circuit made clear that it owed its deference, not to the BLM, but to the IBLA.[41] The Tenth Circuit instructed the Wyoming federal district court to reinstate the IBLA's decision. As a result, the lease sale was invalidated and, with it, Pennaco's leases.

Meanwhile, the BLM pressed ahead with the NEPA documents regarding CBM development in Montana and Wyoming, which it had initiated some months before in anticipation of an adverse ruling.[42] Soon after those new NEPA documents were released, environmental groups sued alleging NEPA violations.[43]

There was one bright spot in this rather depressing and time-consuming effort. In April 2002, the BLM held a competitive oil and gas lease sale for land in Wyoming's Powder River Basin, similar to the one on which Pennaco had bid successfully in February 2000. At the 2002 sale, Nance Petroleum Corporation of Billings, Montana, bought ten parcels, primarily for the production of CBM. The same two environmental groups immediately protested the sale of these oil and gas leases, just as they had protested the leases issued to Pennaco. As a result, the BLM withheld its decision regarding those ten leases. When Pennaco filed its lawsuit, Nance Petroleum intervened believing that the Wyoming federal district court's decision, if favorable, would bind the BLM and the IBLA with regard to the leases issued to Nance Petroleum.

After the Wyoming district court issued its decision, Nance Petroleum demanded that the Wyoming State BLM issue it the ten leases. Soon thereafter, the BLM dismissed the protest filed by the environmental groups and issued the leases. In December 2003, the groups appealed to the IBLA arguing, once again, that the documents relied on by the BLM violated NEPA; they also asked for a stay of the BLM's decision to issue Nance Petroleum its leases. Nance Petroleum, in turn, asserting that the legal sufficiency of the environmental documents had been determined by the Wyoming district court and that the IBLA had no authority to rule otherwise, filed a motion to dismiss the appeal because the environmental groups lacked standing to challenge the leases. In January 2004, the IBLA denied the environmental groups' motion for a stay and ordered them to show cause why their appeal should not be dismissed for want of standing. Subsequently, the groups moved to dismiss their appeal, which occurred in February 2004.[44]

Nance Petroleum's success in having a NEPA-style challenge dismissed because the environmental challengers lack standing is the rare exception. One of the vexing aspects of NEPA is the ability of almost anyone to assert an interest in the area where the federal action is proposed and hence an ability to challenge alleged deficiencies in the documents themselves. Bruce Vincent tells of a young man from Brooklyn, New York, who, though it is doubtful he has ever crossed the Hudson, let alone the Flathead, appeals every timber sale in the

Kootenai National Forest.[45] And ranchers in Montana's Powder River Basin complain that a fellow from Vermont challenges CBM sales due to his fear that harm will befall the Mountain Plover, which he favors.

The reason that people like these bother to file their challenges is that they are consistently, notoriously, and ubiquitously successful. It is like folks say about driving on the highway: if a person is pulled over by a police officer, he is going to get a ticket; a cop can always find something that he did wrong. So it is with NEPA documents: if a judge has an inclination to put a stop to a copper mine, a oil well, or a timber sale and a hankering to find fault with the NEPA document that, if approved, would allow that project to go forward, he will find that fault. Moreover, it is not just his mindset; odds are, there is something wrong.

First of all, judge the source. There are many capable people working in the federal government; however, if they were truly skilled at their jobs, they would probably be in the private sector. Nonetheless, even with their skill levels, federal employees should be perfectly capable of preparing a NEPA document; after all, it is not rocket science. Or is it? Fact of the matter, it is akin to rocket science, what with thousands of highly educated, anally retentive, tree-hugging radicals fly-specking every page of the hundreds of pages of fine print that make up such NEPA documents as "Environmental Assessments" (EAs), "Findings of No Significant Impact" (FONSIs), and "Environmental Impact Statements" (EISs).

Second, although at one time environmental documents were supposed to include just off-the-shelf science, beginning in 1986 agencies were required to disclose "incomplete or unavailable information" and, if the cost of filling that gap were "not exorbitant," the agency was required to get that information.[46] Thus, a judge inclined to find fault with a NEPA document could conclude that the agency's knowledge was incomplete or the agency failed to disclose that its knowledge was incomplete and, because the cost of filling the gap was not exorbitant, the agency failed to comply with NEPA.

Third, environmental groups attack the purpose and need for the project, such as, for example, why does the nation need another gold mine that will be used to make expensive jewelry?[47] Or, why does the nation need this gas field developed when, if it were America's only source of gas, it would only supply the nation's needs for "x" days? Then the attack turns to whether a sufficient number of reasonable alternatives were considered by the agency during the NEPA process; if a judge is willing to second-guess an agency, he can always come up with more reasonable alternatives that the agency could have considered. As one expert points out, these attacks on reasonable alternatives are attempts to "sandbag the process" well after the money has been spent and the study completed.[48]

Just how much money is involved in preparing NEPA studies? No one really knows. One estimate, considered low, maintains that an environmental impact statement costs between $250,000 and $2 million; however, a 1997 EIS for the Glen Canyon Dam Operating Criteria cost in excess of $100 million.[49] Certainly, NEPA's original sponsors never intended studies of this size, scale, and expense, yet that is the modern-day NEPA, a law for which, like the Endangered Species Act, cost is no object; America is to spare no expense. Moreover, because, as regards NEPA, no one in Washington, D.C., is able to give a definitive "yes," those who have an interest in NEPA as a mechanism for stopping projects are able to find some way or someone to say "no." Over the last three decades, NEPA has morphed beyond recognition because it is a creature of case law, case law written, at the urging of forum-shopping radical groups, by activist public policy-making judges, especially at the trial court, but also at the appellate level. And there is no one to rein them in: not the Executive, not the Congress— save for the recent example of the Healthy Forest Restoration Act—

and rarely the U.S. Supreme Court; after all, when did the Court last issue a major NEPA ruling?[50] The result is that, once an agency, or the project proponent, has paid millions for a NEPA document, all that it has bought is a ticket to a federal courthouse.

No project is too small to draw a NEPA challenge. Macum Energy, Inc., is a tiny oil and gas exploration and development company located in Billings, Montana; its president and sole stockholder is Ralph S. Gailey and its only full-time employee is his wife, Nancy. Macum owns interests in several federal, state, and private oil and gas leases in and around the Leroy Field, which is located in north-central Montana in and around the Missouri River Breaks National Monument, designated by President Clinton in January 2001.

In the fall of 1999, Macum applied for a right-of-way across federal land to install a natural gas pipeline to transport and sell natural gas from wells on leases that were well outside of the area that became the monument. In November 1999, the BLM granted the right-of-way to Macum after, as far as Macum knew, the BLM had complied with the requirements of NEPA. In the winter of 1999–2000, Macum installed a 4-inch pipeline in the right-of-way, in accordance with all applicable federal and state laws, at a cost of $120,000. A short time later, Macum began using the pipeline to transport its natural gas to a gas transportation company, which purchased the gas from Macum.

In March 2000, an environmental group sued the BLM and Macum contending, among other things, that the environmental assessment (EA) prepared by the BLM for the right-of-way for Macum's gas pipeline was defective because an American Indian represented by the group had not been consulted about a tipi ring on private property near the right-of-way. The group asked a Montana federal district court to invalidate the EA, to order the shutting in of the gas wells, and to direct the BLM to tear up the pipeline.[51]

No project is too circumscribed to draw a NEPA challenge. In January 2005, the BLM approved an oil and gas leasing plan, which had been months in preparation, for New Mexico's Otero and Sierra Counties. The final plan provides for leasing of federal minerals on more than 1.9 million acres of public land; however, 40,500 acres bar any surface use, 484,100 acres allow only limited surface use, and 1,406,600 acres contain standard lease terms and restrictions. Furthermore, the plan strictly regulates and carefully monitors activity and allows a maximum surface disturbance of only 1,589 acres in Otero and Sierra Counties from well pads, roads, and pipelines—less than one-tenth of one percent of the total surface area. At most, 141 exploratory wells can be drilled, resulting in no more than 84 producing wells. Experts assert that the plan is the most restrictive oil and gas leasing plan ever issued by the BLM.[52]

Nonetheless, New Mexico Governor Bill Richardson demanded that more than 1.5 million acres in the area be placed off-limits to oil and gas leasing. After the BLM concluded that the governor's demands did not provide a reasonable balance between federal and state interests, the governor, in April 2005, filed a lawsuit in New Mexico federal district court arguing that the BLM plan violated NEPA.[53] Environmental groups quickly filed a related lawsuit. No wonder local communities feel compelled to fight back.

When Bill Reilly, decades-long advocate of federal land-use planning,[54] headed the Environmental Protection Agency for President George Herman Walker Bush, he declared, "Private property rights are a quaint anachronism which society cannot afford."[55] Whether the nation can no longer afford private property rights, or the nation wants environmental purity on the cheap, or Americans have become the most covetous, "I want it; give it to me," people in the history of the planet, the fact is that it is not just federal officials and bureaucrats who want, without paying, what westerners own.

CHAPTER 6

FIGHTING "YOUR LAND IS OUR LAND" STATE BUREAUCRATS

> This land is your land, this land is my land
> From California, to the New York Island
> From the redwood forest, to the gulf stream waters
> This land was made for you and me.
>
> As I went walking I saw a sign there
> And on the sign it said "No Tresspassing."
> But on the other side it didn't say nothing!
> That side was made for you and me!
>
> In the shadow of the steeple I saw my people,
> By the relief office I seen my people;
> As they stood there hungry, I stood there asking
> Is this land made for you and me?
>
> "THIS LAND IS YOUR LAND," WOODIE GUTHRIE © 1956[1]

In November 2004, as Marines were engaged in a bloody fight to liberate Fallujah, Iraq, nationwide headlines broke news of another battle—this one a little closer to home. In the quiet north woods of rural northwestern Wisconsin, amidst rolling woodlands of maple, hemlock, and yellow birch, six people lay dead or dying. Amongst the victims were a teenager, young woman, and four others. Those who hadn't perished were struggling to survive after a hunter had opened fire on them with a SKS rifle.[2]

Within hours, the details emerged. At noon on November 21, the second day of deer season for guns, a group of unarmed hunters spotted a stranger hunting from their deer stand, a small platform in trees typically fifteen to thirty feet high. They advised him that he was on their private property and in their tree stand and asked him to leave. He agreed; however, after walking forty yards, he turned and began shooting. When the unarmed hunters ran, the stranger gave chase, leaving the dead scattered over a hundred yards.[3] The killer remained hidden in the woods until night fell, when he emerged, weapon empty, and was arrested. He was charged with several counts of murder and attempted murder.[4]

The tragic news from Wisconsin had particular significance for Robert and Judith Benson and Jeff and Tricia Messmer of South Dakota. They were awaiting a ruling from a state court in a case in which the attorney general for South Dakota had argued that, because South Dakota would no longer enforce the families' private property rights against hunters, they had to engage in the very action that had got the folks in Wisconsin killed: confront armed hunters and order them to leave. The prospect of ordering armed strangers off their property terrified them and made the wait for a ruling in their case even more nerve racking. How in the world had they found themselves in this situation?

Robert and Judith Benson live in Winner, South Dakota, in Tripp County where, since 1965, they have operated a 5,890-acre ranch, primarily for agricultural purposes, including the raising of livestock and a variety of crops. They own approximately three thousand acres of the ranch property on which they maintain a home, as well as an employee's home, a hunting lodge, barn, hay sheds, cattle sheds, machine shops, grain bins, and extensive corrals and feedlots.

Jeff and Tricia Messmer live in Wessington Springs, South Dakota, in Jerault County where, since 1989, they have operated a

three thousand acre farm, which includes a cattle and grain operation, crops, and pasture, as well as a private hunting lodge and private hunting grounds. They own approximately 320 acres of the
farm property and on that property they maintain a home and other
farm buildings.

For decades, South Dakota law allowed hunting along section lines
or other roads if such rights-of-way are used for vehicular traffic;[5]
however, hunters were not allowed to fire over or onto privately
owned land without the landowners' permission.[6] In fact, since 1973,
South Dakota had barred hunting on private property without the
owners' permission, including firing over and onto that private property, and had recognized the right of owners to deny entry to all others.[7] That South Dakota law protected landowners' property rights
became abundantly clear in 2002 when the South Dakota Supreme
Court upheld the conviction of a hunter who shot game over private
property from a public right-of-way road ditch.[8]

Members of the South Dakota legislature were livid and moved
quickly to change the law. In March 2003, the legislature amended
South Dakota's hunting law to provide that "hunting on highways or
other public rights-of-way" includes shooting at small game that is in
flight over private land if the small game has taken flight from or is in
the process of flying over the right-of-way.[9] This new law allowed
hunters, for the first time in South Dakota history, to shoot onto and
over private property from any public right-of-way.

Not surprisingly, the Bensons and Messmers were deeply concerned. Their properties are bordered by several miles of county and
township roads that are used for road hunting. Plus, because the hunting season for some small game is year-round and the season for other
game extends from early fall through early winter, the ability of the
Bensons and Messmers to use their private property exclusively and
safely was impaired perpetually.[10] Their worst fears were soon realized.

With the new backing of the state legislature, road hunters became bolder and more aggressive.

The Bensons routinely heard shot hitting both their home and a nearby tin shed; the Messmers observed hunters shooting around their home, buildings, and cattle. Road hunters were attracted particularly to the Bensons' property because part of it was cultivated as pheasant habitat for the Bensons' private hunting business. Knowing that the U.S. and South Dakota constitutions both bar the taking of private property for a public use without just compensation and aware that the South Dakota legislature had included a provision in the new hunting law that would invalidate the law if the South Dakota Supreme Court ruled that it caused a "taking" without just compensation, the Bensons and Messmers sued.[11]

The U.S. Supreme Court has long held that "'a permanent physical occupation' of the property, by the government itself or by others," is a taking.[12] Moreover, "a physical invasion is a government intrusion of an unusually serious character"[13] because "the right to exclude others is one of the most essential sticks in the bundle of rights that are commonly characterized as property."[14] Furthermore, a "permanent physical invasion" occurs when "individuals are given a permanent and continuous right to pass to and fro, so that the real property may continuously be traversed, even though no particular individual is permitted to station himself permanently upon the premises."[15] In fact, "even if the government physically invades only an easement in property, it must nonetheless pay compensation,"[16] for, "no matter how minute the intrusion, and no matter how weighty the public purpose behind it,"[17] an invasion is still a taking.

As to what constitutes a landowner's property, the Supreme Court ruled, in 1946, that "[t]he landowner owns at least as much of the space above the ground as he can occupy or use in connection with the land."[18] Furthermore, ruled the Court, government action would result in a taking "if the [government], with the admitted intent to fire across the claimants' land at will[,] should fire a single shot."[19]

With such strong support from the U.S. Supreme Court, the Bensons and Messmers went to state court relatively confident of their ability to prevail; after all, what could the South Dakota attorney general argue in response, certainly he could not argue the Constitution. Then came the stunner: in addition to other procedural arguments, such as that South Dakota had not consented to be sued and could not be sued by the Bensons and the Messmers, the attorney general asserted that the state legislature had merely decriminalized hunting on private land. Using a separation of powers argument, the attorney general asserted that South Dakota courts had no authority to review the South Dakota legislature's decisions as to what acts to criminalize; thus, the Bensons and the Messmers could not sue to compel the courts to conduct that review. Furthermore, said the attorney general, the Bensons and Messmers still had other remedies available to them: explicitly, civil lawsuits against trespassing hunters, and, implicitly, self-help. That is, they could tell hunters they were trespassing—the very thing that got the landowners in Wisconsin killed!

The attorney general's argument was ridiculous.

First, the state legislature had adopted the new law for one purpose: to allow hunters to hunt where South Dakota law had barred them from hunting in the past, as recognized by a recent South Dakota Supreme Court decision. The attorney general's asserted basis for the new law was nothing more than a lawyer's *post hoc* rationalization, which courts have rejected consistently.[20] Laws must be stricken or sustained on the bases asserted by legislatures, not on the bases dreamed up by lawyers on their way to the courthouse.

Second, the legislature was notifying, not law enforcement as to who could be arrested for trespass, but hunters as to where they could lawfully hunt. In fact, South Dakota ensured that the right group—hunters—got that message when it rewrote the South Dakota hunting handbook to provide that shooting onto private land is now lawful.[21] By defining what is lawful, the hunting handbook places hunters on notice that hunting pursuant to the new law is not a trespass and those who hunt in this manner may not be prevented from doing so by landowners and are free from self-help or civil or criminal court action by landowners.

Third, the legislature sent a message to landowners like the Bensons and the Messmers; it was not only hunters who were put on notice of the change in the law and where they could now lawfully hunt. The legislature intended for landowners to get the word, and they did. After all, the legislature had changed the law following the conviction of a hunter for trespassing on private property. Moreover, South Dakota law continued to provide for criminal sanctions for any landowner who interfered with those hunting in accordance with South Dakota law.[22]

Nonetheless, as ridiculous as was the attorney general's argument, it could still carry the day given the deference courts too often give to government attorneys and the diffidence judges often display when asked to resolve constitutional violations; courts seem to look for any reason to dismiss rather than to decide a case! Fortunately for the Bensons and the Messmers, a South Dakota Circuit Court brushed aside the attorney general's argument. "Either the state legislature has chosen to allow hunters to invade private property under color of law and thus free of interference by landowners or the state legislature has told hunters that they may invade private property while hunting but at their own peril. The latter makes no sense." "[T]he former is the law now in South Dakota."[23] Then the court proceeded to the merits of the case.

Had South Dakota denied landowners "exclusive use and peaceful enjoyment of their property?" the court asked, noting that the right to exclude others is "one of the most essential sticks in the bundle of rights that are commonly characterized as property," that the right to exclude extends to any physical invasion, "no matter how minute," and that the firing of bullets over and onto private property is such an invasion. The court said, "Yes."[24]

Although the state legislature had authority to regulate road hunting in South Dakota, the court declared, "it must do so within the framework of the Constitution."[25] In this case, the court held, "the legislature went too far when it granted hunters the right to shoot onto private land. This is the very kind of thing that the Takings Clause, which " 'stands as a shield against the arbitrary use of governmental power' was meant to prevent."[26] South Dakota immediately appealed to the South Dakota Supreme Court.

In the meantime, however, as the Bensons and the Messmers await a Supreme Court ruling, the circuit court, in striking South Dakota's new hunting law, may have done more than prevent an unconstitutional taking; it may have prevented bloodshed.

COME ON IN: THE WATER'S YOURS AND MINE

In the summer of 2000, horrific wildfires engulfed Montana. Nearly 2,500 fires covering almost one million acres of land blazed during one of worst fires seasons in state history.[27] On August 16, 2000, the governor declared the entire state a disaster area.[28] Then, on August 22, 2000, all national forests, all federal Bureau of Land Management land, and all Montana state land was closed to the public to prevent more deadly fires.

While most Montanans worried over the fires, some urban dwellers were worried about something else: where would they go fishing? Fortunately, Montana newspapers had the answer. Although federal and state land was closed, the public could go onto private land and fish from any non-navigable streams there.[29] The reason, a Montana law enacted some years before barred property owners from excluding anyone who wanted to engage in "recreation" along the non-navigable streams on their private property.[30]

Indeed, that is exactly what the Montana Stream Access Law provides. It all started with the Montana Supreme Court, which, in 1984 ruled that, under the "public trust" doctrine, the public had a right to recreate in the non-navigable streams on private property.[31] By way of background, all waters in Montana belong to the state, which its citizens may "appropriate" or use, according to state law, by applying that water to a "beneficial use."[32] The land beneath "navigable waters," as that term is defined by state law, belongs to Montana, all the way up to the high water mark; however, the land beneath non-navigable waters belongs to the landowners. For example, in Wyoming, while someone may fish from a boat on a non-navigable stream, he may not step out of the boat onto the streambed; that would be trespassing.[33] Thus, while Wyoming landowners with non-navigable streams on their property may bar trespassers, because of Montana Supreme Court's 1984 decision, similarly situated Montana landowners may no longer exclude all others.

Not surprisingly, the decision by the Montana Supreme Court was extremely controversial. After all, one of the most ubiquitous signs in the West, one sees it on nearly every pickup truck, reads, "Ask Before Hunting or Fishing on Private Land." Landowners were furious that they had been robbed of one of the essential sticks in the bundle of sticks that is private property rights: the right to exclude others. People who wanted to engage in recreational pursuits without asking permission or to charge people for taking them to the best fishing spots welcomed the change. In the end, the Montana state legislature passed legislation codifying the Supreme Court's decision.[34] It did so, it asserted, to end the conflict over the issue. Landowners thought it odd that the public's demand to have what it did not own could be resolved by the legislature by giving it to them anyway. The landowners also thought it was unconstitutional. They sued in the Montana Supreme Court and lost, then lost heart and gave up.[35]

Over the years, matters got worse and worse. The Montana Stream Access Law allowed people to enter upon private land for "recreation" (the term was not defined) on the non-navigable stream up to the "ordinary high water mark" (another term that was not defined) and to "portage" further onto private land around any "obstruction" (still more undefined terms) that they might encounter. Landowners were powerless to stop anyone who wanted to come onto their property. Robbed of any incentive to take care of the property that strangers were using for free, landowners stopped doing so, although they were required still to pay taxes on land that they owned but that the public had the right to use. Entrepreneurs took photographs of beautiful stretches of streams on private property and included those photographs in their brochures to show potential customers where they would be taken, for a price. Not surprisingly, people defined recreate quite broadly and fished, cooked, camped, urinated, defecated, and left their trash on these privately owned lands. After all, it was not their land!

The most poignant tale came from an elderly woman in Bozeman, Montana. Some thirty-five years before, she had moved to Montana and bought fifty acres on which an ankle-deep creek flowed. She paid her taxes and was, in her words, a good steward: eschewing chemical sprays, protecting the wildlife, and preventing erosion. Whenever anyone asked to fish on her property, she gave her permission. After the state legislature changed the law, no one asked permission anymore, they did not have to ask. So now:

Many of us came to Montana seeking peace and quiet . . . investing our life savings in a home and small plot of land, hoping to find a safe place to raise our children. [Now] the public is allowed to wade down [our] and similar small streams into people's back yards at any time, bringing their dogs and stereos...hav[ing] beer parties, eat[ing] picnic lunches, sleep[ing] or even camp[ing] [on our land] without permission. ...[Because] homeowners are required to open up their very back yards for public access...it's almost as if a public highway had been opened up through people's backyards....

I'd like to know...who is going to pay for cleaning up the beer cans and picnic leavings and other trash on our half-mile of stream and who will build up the banks to prevent erosion and flooding if it is public property? I am a senior citizen and I like to walk in the bottomland of our property but now I'm almost afraid to go alone for fear of encountering drifters lounging (doing drugs or drinking) in the dense trees and shrubbery along the stream. I'm also afraid to allow my own young grandchildren to play freely down there....

By May 2000, a number of landowners, people whose forefathers had been original homesteaders in the 1800s, decided they had had enough and they sued.[36] They did not seek just compensation for the taking of their property—the time for that had long since expired—but sought instead invalidation of the law as contrary to the Due Process Clause. They argued that the "due process of law," without which they could not "be deprived of life, liberty, or property," required that Montana demonstrate a rational basis or even, given that property is a fundamental right, a compelling governmental interest for denying them the most basic right of every landowner: the right to exclude others. No reason cited by Montana or environmental groups as the basis for adopting the Montana Stream Access Law met either test.

In January 2001, the Montana federal district court granted motions filed by Montana officials and a host of environmental groups, which had lobbied for the right of people to access whatever stream they desired, and dismissed the landowners' case.[37] Relying on a ruling by the U.S. Court of Appeals for the Ninth Circuit, the district court held that the landowners' only constitutional remedy was to seek just compensation for a taking of their property for public use. The landowners appealed to the Ninth Circuit.

In December 2002, the Ninth Circuit, relying on one of its earlier rulings, upheld the district court's decision. The Ninth Circuit held that, because the Fifth Amendment grants property owners the specific right to just compensation if their property is taken by governments, the more general protections afforded "life, liberty, [and] property" by the Due Process Clause are null and void.[38] In other words, property owners could not challenge the authority of governments to regulate or seize property as a violation of the Due Process Clause; owners may seek only just compensation. With its ruling, the Ninth Circuit had read the words "property" and "public use" out of the Due Process Clause.

Because the Ninth Circuit ruling, not surprisingly, conflicted with rulings of the U.S. Supreme Court and other federal appellate courts, the Montana landowners asked for Supreme Court review.[39] Nonetheless, in May 2003, the Supreme Court declined to hear the case.[40]

Although the fight by Montana landowners against the "your land is our land" crowd is over, much work remains. The Ninth Circuit's continued insistence on reading "property" and "public use" out of the Due Process Clause awaits future challenges, especially given the unfortunate fact that the Supreme Court's rulings on the subject are not the picture of clarity. Furthermore, although seven circuits have recognized, generally, that a property owner is protected by both the Takings Clause and the Due Process Clause, only two circuits have reached that express holding.[41] Finally, there is just something that urban dwellers and their elected representatives simply do not understand about the constitutional protection afforded private property. Take the folks in Coeur d'Alene, Idaho.

In April 1994, Jack and Virginia Simpson bought property on Lake Coeur d'Alene in Coeur d'Alene, Idaho. Lakefront Drive separates their property into an upland parcel and a waterward parcel; the latter has 230 feet of lake frontage.

The Simpsons installed a wrought iron fence around the upland parcel. Then, in December 1997, when people began to trespass on the waterward parcel, they installed two sections of fence along the western and eastern boundaries of the waterward parcel. The City of Coeur d'Alene issued a stop-work notice and informed the Simpsons that their fence was a "non-conforming structure" that violated city ordinances. After issuing more threats, the city brought legal action against the Simpsons and instructed its police officers not to cite trespassers on the Simpsons' land! The Simpsons claimed that their constitutional rights had been violated.

In October 2002, an Idaho district court ruled in favor of the city and ordered the Simpsons' fences on their waterward parcel removed.[42] The Simpsons appealed to the Idaho Supreme Court, which in February 2005 found no constitutional violation and ruled for the city.[43] Subsequently, the Idaho Supreme Court agreed to rehear the case.[44] Property rights advocates have their fingers crossed that this time the Idaho Supreme Court will get it right! After the U.S. Supreme Court's terrible ruling in *Kelo v. City of New London, Connecticut*,[45] in which the Court ruled five to four that "public use" was whatever a governmental unit said it was, it is vitally important that Idaho

Supreme Court and other courts follow the lead of, for example, the Michigan Supreme Court.[46]

LAND USE REGULATION IN THE PEOPLE'S REPUBLIC

In August 1954, McKay and Velma Allred bought a lot on which they built their home in newly platted Longs View subdivision in Boulder County, Colorado. In 1958, the Allreds bought two additional lots, contiguous to their original lot, with the intention of building homes for resale on those lots. However, in July 2005, Boulder County issued a written determination that the Allreds' lots constitute a single legal building site. That is, the only home that Boulder County allows on the three lots is the Allreds' original home.

What happened to the Allreds is the result of a 1993 amendment to the Boulder County land-use code that permits Boulder County, under a host of circumstances, unilaterally to merge separate adjacent empty lots into "a single building lot." The Allreds are not alone.

In 1992, Joe Kellogg, another Boulder County resident, bought a two-plus acre parcel that was adjacent to property that his mother and aunt had owned since 1965. He was delighted to have property in his own name for the first time in his life. Then, in May 1993, his mother and aunt presented him with a wedding gift, title to their nine acres. As he reports, "my joy and happiness of receiving the nine-acre gift lasted approximately one week." Later that same month, Boulder County Commissioners unilaterally ruled that contiguous parcels like the ones that he owned would be limited to one building site. If he had known what Boulder County was about to do, he said, "I would have graciously declined my mother and aunt's well-intentioned and generous gift. I had hoped to sell one parcel so I could use the money to build a house on the other, but the commissioners stripped me of [that right]."[47]

Frances MacAnally owns adjacent lots in Boulder County that she and her late husband bought in 1970 and 1972. They built their home on one of the lots; the other lot they kept vacant for their retirement. Today, she would like to have the money that the sale of the vacant lot would generate, but Boulder County's merger rule has robbed her of that opportunity. Moreover, she was not informed of the county's 1993 decision and continued to pay separate taxes on her two properties; when she sought to recover the excess taxes that she had paid over the years, the assessor's office advised her that she would receive a tax refund for only two of the seven years that she had overpaid.

When Frances MacAnally consulted an attorney regarding challenging the involuntary merger of her property, he "informed me that it would cost approximately $30,000 to try to have my lots separated again. There would be no guarantee that I could win or that the County wouldn't change their mind the following year!"[48]

So controversial was Boulder County's unilateral action that the Colorado state legislature enacted a law requiring that counties give notice to the landowner and obtain landowner consent before merging adjacent properties.[49] That legislation, which took effect in October 2003, affects only future mergers; property owners in Boulder County like the Allreds, whose adjacent lots were merged into a single unit before the new law took effect, are unaffected. For the Allreds to get their right to use their own property returned to them they will have to take Boulder County to court, after they seek and are denied a variance from Boulder County. Already Boulder County has erected a barrier to that undertaking by demanding that they sign a virtual blank check to the county for the cost of processing their request. Boulder County refuses to disclose how much that will cost.

Even after the Allreds are denied their variance they will be required, by a longstanding ruling of the U.S. Supreme Court, to take their challenge to the constitutionality of Boulder County's merger policy first to the Colorado Supreme Court.[50] Only after the Colorado

Supreme Court has ruled against them may the Allreds initiate a lawsuit in Colorado federal district court maintaining that their right to own and use their property was taken in violation of the rights guaranteed them under the U.S. Constitution's Fifth Amendment. The difficulty with proceeding in this fashion is that, not only will it delay by several years the Allreds' vindication of their constitutional rights, it may even cause them to lose those rights.

In 2005, the U.S. Supreme Court upheld a ruling by the U.S. Court of Appeals for the Ninth Circuit that a decision by the California Supreme Court that a landowner's constitutional rights had not been violated precluded any future lawsuits on the same issue in federal district court.[51] The Supreme Court upheld the Ninth Circuit's ruling that the landowner's rights under the California Constitution were equivalent to its rights under the U.S. Constitution, even though the landowner expressly reserved assertion of its federal constitutional rights.[52] With this ruling, the Supreme Court has denied to itself jurisdiction over a cause of actions specifically granted to it and the federal courts by the Constitution.[53] Thus, the Supreme Court requirement for exhaustion of Takings Clause claims has become, as one writer labeled it, an elaborate bait and switch.[54] There is one small glimmer of hope in the Supreme Court's most recent ruling: four of the justices urged that the Court reconsider its earlier decision requiring exhaustion.[55]

The Allreds believe that, after they have overcome the procedural hurdles facing them, they will be able to demonstrate that the rights guaranteed them by the U.S. Constitution have been violated by the actions of Boulder County. First, the Due Process Clauses of the Fifth and Fourteenth Amendments guarantee not only that proper and just procedures will be used whenever a government deprives a person of his "life, liberty, or property," but also that a person's "life, liberty, or property" may not be deprived him without appropriate governmental justification, regardless of how proper are the procedures utilized to deny life, liberty, or property.[56] Unfortunately, economic liberties such as the Allreds' right to use their property have minimal substantive due process protection; a government entity need only demonstrate a "rational basis" for its decision to deprive a person of his property. Nonetheless, the Allreds believe that Boulder County lacks even a rational basis for merging their properties; after all, had another person owned the land, he could have built upon the site.

Second, the equal protection guarantees of the Fifth and Fourteenth Amendment are violated when a government treats similarly situated classes of persons differently, even classes composed of but one person.[57] If that disparate treatment involves a fundamental liberty interest, then the government must pass "strict scrutiny"; that is, it must demonstrate that it is seeking to achieve a "compelling governmental interest" in a manner that is "narrowly tailored" to achieve that interest.[58] On occasion, the right to own and use property has been held to be fundamental.[59] If the Allreds are unsuccessful in their arguments that their right to use their property is fundamental, then Boulder County may prevail if there is a rational basis for its merger policy. Although this is a much less demanding test and much easier for governments to pass, the Allreds believe that Boulder County will fail because its policy is irrational, arbitrary, and capricious.

Finally, the Constitution forbids the taking of private property for public use without just compensation. The U.S. Supreme Court has held that, when a government denies a person all economic use of his property, a *per se* taking has occurred. The Allreds believe that they have been denied all economic use of their adjacent lots.[60]

Unfortunately, it will be years before the Allreds fully vindicate their right to own and use their properties. Sadly, Boulder County officials realize this, which is why they appear so willing to ignore the Constitution.

Just as property owners must continue to litigate to protect their rights as intended by the "just compensation" and "public use" provisions of the Takings Clause, so too must they continue to litigate to ensure their right to challenge any seizure of their property by governments that violates the Due Process Clause. Fortunately, scores of property owners have demonstrated the courage to do just that.

Of all the fears that westerners have regarding what their governments might do, they have no fear, after decades of litigation by anti-religious zealots and goofy, hair-splitting decisions from the Supreme Court and federal courts of appeals, that their governments will have anything to do with religion. That is taboo; that is, unless governments endorse, not Judeo-Christian religion, but, for example, pantheism.

CHAPTER 7

FIGHTING THE CLOSURE OF "SACRED" PUBLIC AND PRIVATE LANDS

[W]hen reviewing [] Establishment Clause challenges to federal action protecting Native American interests, courts [must] apply...the Indian trust doctrine....Under that test, [federal agency] actions are constitutional...[b]ecause preservation of Native American culture, including traditional religious practices, is a legitimate government objective [and not] an establishment of religion in contravention of the First Amendment.

NATIVE AMERICAN RIGHTS FUND[1]

Native American tribes, are not solely religious in character or purpose. Rather, they are ethnic and cultural in character as well....[T]he Establishment Clause does not bar the government from protecting an historically and culturally important site simply because the site's importance derives at least in part from its sacredness to [Native American] groups.

U.S. COURT OF APPEALS FOR THE NINTH CIRCUIT[2]

Wyoming Sawmills, Inc., is the largest non-governmental employer in Sheridan County, which lies in north-central Wyoming next to the Montana border. The lumber mill itself is in downtown Sheridan, northeast of the historic Sheridan Inn[3] and between the Burlington Northern and Santa Fe Railroad yards and Interstate 90, which runs north and south along the Big Horn Mountains to the west. In business since 1964, Wyoming

Sawmills's philosophy is "to use every bit of every log we process and find outlets for all of our byproducts. Wood shavings, dry sawdust, bark, chips: all are sold to become useful products."[4]

The prime source for its raw materials is the vast Bighorn National Forest and its abundant lodgepole pines. Created in 1897, the Bighorn National Forest is eighty miles long, thirty miles wide, and covers 1.1 million acres, including portions of four Wyoming counties (Sheridan, Big Horn, Washakie, and Johnson). It is nearly as large as the State of Delaware.[5] Under federal law, the Bighorn is managed in accordance with multiple use principles—that is, the land is to be available for use by a variety of users, including ranchers, miners, energy developers, recreationalists, and loggers, like Wyoming Sawmills.[6] In fact, the National Forest System was created by Congress in 1897 to serve two primary purposes: to generate water and timber.[7]

For decades, the U.S. Forest Service recognized and fulfilled its statutory obligations regarding its management of the Bighorn. Those portions of the forest that were capable of being managed as a source of timber were made available for sale to timber companies like Wyoming Sawmills. In the process, not only were fees paid to the Forest Service, 25 percent of which were returned to the county where the timber was harvested, but also jobs and wealth were created and taxes paid all while ensuring the health and viability of the forest itself.[8] In 1996, however, the Forest Service decided to manage nearly fifty thousand acres, about seventy-eight square miles, of the Bighorn in accordance with the demands of American Indian religious practitioners.

Various American Indian groups maintain that, notwithstanding its prehistoric origins, the Medicine Wheel, a designated National Historic Landmark on the western peak of Medicine Mountain in the northern part of the Bighorn just off Alternate Highway 14, is sacred to them.[9] In recognition of this belief system, the Forest Service granted free and open access to the Medicine Wheel to permit Amer-

ican Indian religious practitioners to engage in the free exercise of religion, even though that exercise would occur on federal or public land.
In fact, the Forest Service granted the practitioners unlimited ceremonial use of Medicine Wheel, agreed to close the feature during ceremonial usage to ensure privacy, and authorized the presence of
American Indian "interpreters" during tourist season to proselytize
about their faith.[10] Even these extraordinary allowances were not
enough for the practitioners. They maintained that any activity to
which they objected that was audible or visible from the Medicine
Wheel would interfere with their religious practices. Specifically, they
objected to timber harvesting and demanded the closure of huge portions of the Bighorn to that activity.[11]

The process had begun in June 1993, when the Forest Service
entered into an agreement with a variety of governmental and non-
governmental groups, which did not include any members of the private sector, such as Wyoming Sawmills, that established the Forest
Service's management priority for Medicine Mountain and Medicine
Wheel as "continued traditional cultural use" of nearly twenty thousand acres as a "sacred place and important ceremonial site."[12] In addition, the agreement formed the groups into a permanent body called
the "Consulting Parties" to determine how the sacred areas of the
Bighorn would be managed. In April 1996, the Forest Service,
responding to a "resurgence of Native American spiritualism and new
information that all of Medicine Mountain [is] of religious importance to American Indians, not simply the Medicine Wheel," published a draft management plan that affirmed "the importance of the
Medicine Wheel as a American Indian Shrine."[13] In September 1996,
the Forest Service published its final plan in which it announced that
its "management priority" was to bar any activity that might "detract
from the spiritual and traditional values" associated with "Medicine
Mountain and the surrounding area."[14] Then, in October 1996, as part

of its statutorily mandated planning process, the Forest Service adopted an amendment to its forest plan under which all of Medicine Mountain, nearly twenty thousand acres, would be managed as a "sacred site."[15]

Previously, 15,840 acres of the sacred site area had been designed by the Forest Service as available for timber management and more than six thousand acres had been designated as available for timber harvesting.[16] In fact, the Forest Service regarded the timber there as especially valuable because the trees were mainly "large and very large."[17] Additionally, as a result of a pest infestation that has plagued the area since 1990, 1,135 acres had "a large amount of dead standing trees" and was selected for thinning in order to achieve "the desired state of forest health" and to reduce "potential wildfire risk."[18] As a result of the Forest Service's agreement with American Indian religious practitioners, this federal land was now off-limits to timber harvesting.[19]

Ten months later, the Forest Service completed its environmental review of a timber sale plan that had been issued first in 1988 and determined that the sale could proceed.[20] Almost immediately the Consulting Parties objected.[21] Although the sale area was several miles north and outside of the twenty thousand acre sacred site area, the sale would require timber hauling on a Forest Service road, a small portion of which was within the far eastern boundary of the sacred site area. In deference to the demands of the religious practitioners, the sale was cancelled.[22] By putting that road off-limits to timber hauling, the Forest Service added an additional thirty thousand acres to the land being managed as "sacred."

Wyoming Sawmills, which planned to bid on the sale and needed the timber for its mill, filed a lawsuit against the Forest Service contending, among other things, that managing fifty thousand acres of federal land as a sacred site violates the Constitution's Establishment Clause and its mandate of government neutrality regarding religion.

THE ESTABLISHMENT CLAUSE

The First Amendment to the Constitution reads, in part, "Congress shall make no law respecting an establishment of religion, or prohibiting the free exercise thereof . . ."[23] The first phrase is referred to as the Establishment Clause and the latter, the Free Exercise Clause. Since 1971, and its decision in *Lemon v. Kurtzman*,[24] the U.S. Supreme Court has defined expansively what governmental activities violate the Establishment Clause; the short answer, for the Supreme Court and the various federal appellate courts, is that nearly any government involvement with religion is unconstitutional.

Under *Lemon*, so as not to violate the Establishment Clause, governmental action "respecting" religion: (1) "must have a secular... purpose," (2) "must... neither advance[] nor inhibit[] religion" in "its principal or primary effect," and (3) "must not foster 'an excessive government entanglement with religion.'"[25] The *Lemon* test is supplemented with the "endorsement test," which asks, "whether, irrespective of government's actual purpose, the practice under review in fact conveys a message of endorsement or disapproval."[26] What the Establishment Clause requires, says the Supreme Court, is that government:

> [N]ot coerce anyone to support or participate in a religion, or its exercise, or otherwise act in a way which "establishes a [state] religion or religious faith, or tends to do so."... [For] [w]hat to most believers may seem nothing more than a reasonable request that the nonbeliever respect their religious practices... may appear to the nonbeliever or dissenter to be

an attempt to employ the machinery of the State to enforce a religious orthodoxy.[27]

Furthermore, a government may not send an "ancillary message to members of the audience who are nonadherents 'that they are outsiders, not full members of the political community, and an accompanying message to adherents that they are insiders, favored members of the political community.'"[28]

Applying these tests to the Forest Service's action in the Bighorn National Forest seems to compel that a court issue a ruling that the Forest Service had abandoned its constitutionally required neutrality. In fact, in two earlier instances that is exactly how the U.S. Court of Appeals for the Tenth Circuit and, eight years later, the U.S. Supreme Court ruled. In both cases, unlike the Forest Service in the Bighorn, the federal agencies involved refused to accede to the demands of American Indian religious practitioners.

In 1980, the Tenth Circuit ruled regarding the demands by several American Indian leaders and organizations that the National Park Service (NPS) restrict tourist activity at Rainbow Bridge National Monument in south-central Utah due to the needs of American Indian religious practitioners. The Tenth Circuit held that restricting public access to the Monument's land would violate the Establishment Clause:

> "The First Amendment...gives no one the right to insist that in the pursuit of their own interests others must conform their conduct to his own religious necessities..." [] Were it otherwise, the Monument would become a government-managed religious shrine.[29]

In 1988, when members of three American Indian tribes in northwestern California sought to prevent timber harvesting and road construction in a portion of the national forest traditionally used for religious purposes, the Supreme Court declared:

> Nothing in the principle for which [American Indians] contend, however, would distinguish this case from another lawsuit in which they (or similarly situated religious objectors) might seek to exclude all human activity but their own from sacred areas of the public lands.... Whatever rights the Indians may have to the use of the area, however, those rights do not divest the Government of its right to use what is, after all, *its* land.[30]

JUSTICE DELAYED IS JUSTICE DENIED

By October 1999, Wyoming Sawmills's lawsuit, filed the previous February, had been briefed fully and argued before the U.S. District Court for the District of Wyoming. Nonetheless, the district court did not issue its decision until December 2001, ruling, incredibly—because it could have issued its ruling within days of oral arguments—that Wyoming Sawmills did not have the legal right ("standing") to file its lawsuit.[31] Although the district court agreed that Wyoming Sawmills had suffered an injury, which was its lost opportunity to bid on the timber sale, the district court held that it could not redress that injury because it "could not eliminate the Medicine Wheel as it is a protected National Monument."[32] Either the court was being obtuse—because addressing the constitutionality of the Forest Service's closure of fifty thousand acres to timber harvesting would not affect the designation of the Medicine Wheel's 110 acres—or obstinate—because it did not want to apply the earlier holdings of the Tenth Circuit and the Supreme Court.[33] Perhaps it was a little of both; Wyoming Sawmills appealed.

At last, in May 2003, Wyoming Sawmills appeared for oral arguments before the Tenth Circuit, the matter having been briefed by Wyoming Sawmills, the U.S. Forest Service, which under the Bush administration continued to support the constitutionality of the closure,[34] and a group of American Indian religious practitioners.[35] The good news for Wyoming Sawmills was that the Tenth Circuit agreed that the district court's redressability holding was in error. The bad news was that the Tenth Circuit held that Wyoming Sawmills had suffered no injury whatsoever, neither the loss of its opportunity to bid on a timber sale nor its having been "directly affected" by an Establishment Clause violation. Even worse, the Tenth Circuit went so far as to accept the argument of the Forest Service that a corporation is not capable of suffering an injury under the Establishment Clause.[36]

The Tenth Circuit's ruling was particularly curious given that, for more than thirty years, any one "offended" by government action that allegedly "respect[s] an establishment of religion," has been found to have been "directly affected" by that purported violation and given standing to sue. Famously, for example, the Tenth Circuit held that a local citizen offended by seeing an image of the Mormon temple on the seal of the City of St. George, Utah, had standing to challenge the seal's constitutionality.[37] In fact, according to the Tenth Circuit, all but one of the other federal appellate courts, and the Supreme Court, anyone who comes into direct contact with governmental action regarding religion has standing to file an Establishment Clause lawsuit.[38] Nonetheless, for unspecified reasons, the Tenth Circuit did not apply that test to Wyoming Sawmills. When the Tenth Circuit denied Wyoming Sawmills's petition to have the Tenth Circuit panel's decision heard by all Tenth Circuit judges, that is *en banc*, Wyoming Sawmills asked for Supreme Court review. In October 2005, the Supreme Court denied Wyoming Sawmills's petition.[39]

The refusal of the Supreme Court to hear Wyoming Sawmills's challenge, which was not surprising given that the Court grants only one percent of the petitions filed, reveals an often overlooked aspect of federal litigation. For all intents and purposes, the three-judge panel of a federal appellate court, whether the Tenth, the Ninth, or the District of Columbia, is the court of last resort, the supreme court, for almost all federal litigation. That is almost assuredly the result, regardless of the importance of the issues raised—such as whether federal land may be managed to suit the demands of American Indian religious practitioners—if the appellate court resolves the case on procedural or technical grounds, such as "the plaintiff lacks standing." Almost as unlikely is that a federal appellate court will hear the matter *en banc*, that is, before all the judges of the circuit. If two members of a three-judge panel agree on a decision, the third judge is encouraged to sign on as well, out of a spirit of comity. In the rare instance of a 2–1 ruling, the dissenting judge, often as not, declines to file an opinion. Finally, a circuit judge is disinclined to vote for *en banc* review of the decisions of his colleagues just as he would prefer that his colleagues withhold that vote on his rulings. Not surprisingly, when the Supreme Court considers a petition for *writ* of *certiorari*, a unanimous three-judge panel ruling, the absence of a written dissent in a 2–1 ruling, or the denial of a petition for rehearing *en banc* without dissent almost always dooms that petition.

If the law is so clear, one may ask in light of the Supreme Court's 1988 ruling regarding demands by American Indian religious practitioners for exclusive use of public land, how may an appellate court refuse to follow it in addressing the issue of purportedly sacred federal land? The answer is that the appellate court will recognize the Supreme Court's holding but will conclude that it lacks the jurisdiction to apply that holding in the case before it. The Supreme Court is highly unlikely to review such a holding. Even if the appellate court rules on the merits and refuses to apply, for example, that Supreme Court ruling or applies the ruling incorrectly, again the odds are that the Supreme Court will decline to review the matter given that "misapplication" of the law is not a basis for Supreme Court review.[40]

For more than a decade, that has been the fate of challenges to decisions by Clinton administration federal land managers restricting public use of purportedly sacred federal land either pursuant to Clinton's 1993 Executive Order[41] on the subject or, with that order as cover, to prevent activity that environmental groups or local land managers or both oppose. Thus:

- When commercial and recreational climbers challenged the National Park Service's decision to restrict June climbing of Devils Tower in northern Wyoming in deference to the demands of American Indian religious practitioners,[42] the Tenth Circuit ruled that none of them had standing to challenge the policy.[43]
- When local members of a national trade association challenged the U.S. Forest Service's decision to close nearly 1 million acres of federal land in north-central Montana to oil and gas exploration and development,[44] the Ninth Circuit ruled that they lacked standing and that the Forest Service's action met the *Lemon* test.[45]
- When visitors to Rainbow Bridge National Monument, who were told they could not approach Rainbow Bridge because it is god incarnate to some American Indian religious practitioners, sued,[46] the Tenth Circuit overruled the Utah district court and held that none of the visitors had standing to challenge the NPS's policy.[47]

DALE MCKINNON AND WOODRUFF BUTTE

Designating federal or public land as sacred to a particular religious group and thus off-limits to what the Supreme Court calls "nonadherents" is one thing; after all, as the Supreme Court declared in the opposite context, it is "*its* land."[48] For the government to declare private land sacred to American Indian religious practitioners and off-limits to the owner's use is quite something else entirely! Or is it?

Woodruff Butte is private property located about ten miles southeast of Holbrook, Arizona, which is ninety-three miles due east of Flagstaff. Mr. Dale McKinnon and his family own Cholla Ready Mix, Inc., which first leased and then purchased Woodruff Butte to mine the unique and valuable aggregate found there for use in highway construction projects. In 1990, the Hopi, Zuni, and Navajo Indian tribes passed resolutions against the mining of Woodruff Butte because they consider it a place of religious significance or sacred. On that basis, in or around 1990, the Arizona State Historic Preservation Officer declared Woodruff Butte eligible for listing on the National Registry of Historic Places (NRHP) over the objections of Mr. McKinnon. Woodruff Butte has yet to be listed on the NRHP.

In June 1991, the Arizona Department of Transportation (ADOT) granted Cholla a commercial source number allowing aggregate mined from Woodruff Butte to be used on ADOT projects. Nonetheless, beginning in 1992, ADOT took steps to bar the use of Woodruff Butte, which culminated in new ADOT rules adopted in 1999. Under those new rules, Cholla was required to apply for a new commercial source number, which application was denied solely as a result of the religious significance of Woodruff Butte to the three tribes.

In June 2002, Dale McKinnon's Cholla Ready Mix sued ADOT in Arizona federal district court claiming that ADOT's actions violated the Establishment Clause. In January 2003, the district court dismissed Cholla's complaint holding that ADOT's regulation—Historical and Cultural Resources Regulation—"[o]n its face . . . is aimed at protecting sites of historical and cultural significance. That a protected site also has religious significance does not make the regulation unconstitutional."[49] After the district court denied Cholla's motion for reconsideration, Cholla appealed to the U.S. Court of Appeals for the Ninth Circuit.

In September 2004, the Ninth Circuit affirmed dismissal of Cholla's complaint holding that "[n]o evidence could bolster Cholla's Establishment Clause claim because it is premised on flawed analysis of the governing law."[50] Although the Ninth Circuit upheld the Arizona federal district court's dismissal of Cholla's complaint, it issued a published ruling on the merits in which it declared: "[T]he Establishment Clause does not bar the government from protecting an historically and culturally important site simply because the site's importance derives at least in part from its sacredness to certain groups."[51]

After oral arguments in the case, but before the panel ruled, another Ninth Circuit panel ruled on the constitutionality of a Latin cross erected on federal land in the California desert to commemorate those who died in World War I. In that case, *Buono v. Norton*, the panel ruled that, despite the historical and cultural significance of the Latin cross, it remained a symbol of the Christian faith and therefore had to be removed.[52] In September 2004, in light of the clear conflict between two panels of the Ninth Circuit, Cholla petitioned for a rehearing *en banc*. In October 2004, the petition was denied, as was Cholla's Supreme Court petition for *writ* of *certiorari* a few months later.[53]

Nonetheless, the Ninth Circuit may yet have the opportunity to decide which one of its opinions, *Buono* or *Cholla*, controls when considering American Indian religion, the use of public land, and the Establishment Clause. In January 2005, the Nevada federal district court upheld the constitutionality of a decision by the Forest Service to close Cave Rock near Lake Tahoe to climbing in response to the demands of American Indian religious practitioners.[54] Relying on the Ninth Circuit's ruling in *Cholla*, the district court declared, "The Establishment Clause does not require government to ignore the historical value of religious sites[;] protecting culturally important Native American sites has historic value for the nations [sic] as a whole because of the unique status of Native American Societies in North American history."[55]

The Forest Service, in barring climbers from Cave Rock, engaged in a more blatant endorsement of American Indian religion than did the National Park Service, ten years earlier, when it closed Devils Tower to June climbing. Perhaps the federal government's string of procedural victories had made agencies much bolder; if no one could challenge sacred land closures to determine whether they violated the Constitution's Establishment Clause, then the agencies had *carte blanche* to accede to the demands of American Indian religious practitioners regarding public land. Whatever the reason, the Forest Service documents that accompanied its Cave Rock decision are breathtaking in their advocacy on behalf of American Indian religious practitioners.

The Forest Service characterized the religious "power" of Cave Rock as a "renewable" resource and concluded that the Forest Service had to take action to ensure that "the short-term uses at Cave Rock ... will not compromise the area's long-term [religious] productivity."[56] That was not all. Wrote the Forest Service:

> In the Washoe Tribe's view, effects of rock climbing, including physical alterations of the rock associated with sport climbing, the placement of climbing equipment, and the presence of visible and audible persons on the rock, are considered to be insensitive, distracting, and incompatible with the traditional spiritual activities.... According to Washoe traditional belief, the intimate contact between climbers and Cave Rock leads to an exchange of power between the rock and climbers.... Washoe believe the presence of people at the rock can have ill effects on both the visitor and the Washoe people.[57]

One alternative considered by the Forest Service to preserve the religious power of Cave Rock would have "voluntarily or mandatory prohibit[ed] all activities under Forest Service jurisdiction, other than Washoe spiritual uses, during specific time periods."[58] The Forest Service rejected that alternative because American Indian religious "practitioners cannot follow a predictable schedule in knowing when the power that Cave Rock provides will be needed...this alternative would not meet the needs of the traditional tribal users....[T]o implement it would unnecessarily restrict public access without benefiting the group for which the regulation was being established."[59] Thus, the Forest Service rejected this alternative, not because such a closure is patently and facially unconstitutional,[60] but because it would not limit public access for as much of the year as American Indian religious practitioners demanded.

Preserving the power of Cave Rock was not the Forest Service's only concern. The Forest Service determined that recreational activities by climbers and non-climbers would "disturb traditional users of the property, [and] would affect the property's pre-European encroachment feel and association."[61] Furthermore, conversations by those recreating on Cave Rock "contribute to the generation of noise," which, although the Forest Service recognized was "not the dominant noise source in the area, current noise levels affect use by Washoe spiritualists, as rituals are intended to occur during serene and tranquil periods; this would affect the feel and association of the property."[62] Finally, the Forest Service noted the need to protect American Indian religion. "If current adverse impacts to [Cave Rock] continue, it is possible the Washoe Tribe would abandon its [religious] practices at Cave Rock."[63]

In the end, the Forest Service barred use of Cave Rock by climbers and those on educational field trips, limiting access to American Indian religious practitioners, hikers, and picnickers.[64] Because hikers "only occasionally visit the cave, and more commonly walk up the backside of Cave Rock up to its summit," American Indian religious practitioners will be the primary users of the face of Cave Rock and the cave itself.[65] Effectively closing Cave Rock to all but American Indian religious practitioners was not enough; the Forest Service also included in its management plan a "signage component and a brochure designed to inform people of the cultural [that is, religious] significance of Cave Rock."[66]

It is remarkable, given Establishment Clause jurisprudence by the U.S. Supreme Court and the U.S. Court of Appeals for the Ninth Circuit, that the Nevada federal district court upheld the constitutionality of the Forest Service's actions at Cave Rock. After all, in *Buono*, the Ninth Circuit had ruled that the mere presence of a Latin cross on federal land in California constituted an Establishment Clause violation.[67] As to Cave Rock, not only did the Forest Service agree that Cave Rock is sacred, it labeled the religious power of Cave Rock a "resource" to be protected by the Forest Service and barred non-believing climbers from recreating on Cave Rock.[68]

Furthermore, the Nevada court's holding with regard to the unique status of American Indian religion and its blending of history, culture, and religion ignores that other Americans celebrate faiths that have rich histories and are part of their culture and the culture of this country.[69] Judeo-Christian religion, for example, imbued every aspect of the early American culture and history.[70] Moreover, even if American Indian religion were unique, that uniqueness does not exempt it from application of an Establishment Clause that has been applied to every other religious faith. It would appear that the Ninth Circuit must reverse the Nevada district court's decision and rule that the Forest Service's actions at Cave Rock are unconstitutional. Whether the Ninth Circuit will do so remains in doubt.

THE TEN COMMANDMENTS AND AMERICAN INDIAN RELIGION

When the Ninth Circuit decides the Cave Rock case, its ruling will be informed by two recent U.S. Supreme Court rulings regarding public display of the Ten Commandments.

In June 2005, the Court ruled that display of the Ten Commandments in the McCreary County and Pulaski County courthouses was unconstitutional. In a 5–4 ruling authored by Justice Souter and joined by Justices Stevens, O'Connor, Ginsburg, and Breyer, the Court held that, given the actions of the counties, "[t]he reasonable observer could only think that the counties meant to emphasize and celebrate the Commandments' religious message."[71] In determining the counties' purpose, the Court looked to "readily discoverable fact[s] set forth in a[n] ... official act."[72] The Court demanded that the counties' purported secular purpose "be genuine, not a sham, and not merely secondary to a religious objective;" that is, the secular purpose must be "'preeminent' or 'primary.'"[73] Finally, the Court had to "be familiar with the history of the government's actions and competent to learn what [that] history has to show."[74]

The same day, the Court ruled that a six by three-and-one-half-foot granite monolith containing the Ten Commandments set upon the Texas State Capitol grounds was constitutional. Chief Justice Rehnquist delivered an opinion in which Justices Scalia, Kennedy, and Thomas joined. Justice Breyer, who expressly declined to join the Chief Justice's opinion ("I cannot agree with today's plurality analysis."[75]), concurred in the judgment. Justices Stevens, O'Connor, Souter, and Ginsburg dissented.

Justice Breyer called the case "borderline," given that "the Commandments' text undeniably has a religious message."[76] Eschewing any particular Establishment Clause test and embracing instead the Establishment Clause's purposes, Justice Breyer concluded, after an "exercise of legal judgment," that the physical setting of the display "suggests little or nothing of the sacred."[77] Most compelling to Justice Breyer, however, was that "[t]his display has stood apparently uncontested for nearly two generations[which] helps us understand that as a practical matter of *degree* this display is unlike to prove divisive."[78]

Therefore, the Supreme Court's two Ten Commandments cases provide no support for the Ninth Circuit's ruling in *Cholla*. If the Ninth Circuit rules, in the Cave Rock case, that federal land may be closed to public access because it is regarded by American Indian religious practitioners as sacred, then the tests adopted by the majority in *McCreary County* and espoused by the dissent in the Texas case compel reversal. Moreover, Justice Breyer's test in the Texas case does not apply in the Cave Rock case given that the Forest Service's access decision was challenged immediately. However, this does not mean that the Ninth Circuit will adhere to the Supreme Court's commands regarding the Establishment Clause and invalidate the Forest Service's closure of Cave Rock to climbing. Nor does it mean that, if the Ninth Circuit, as is its wont, ignores the Supreme Court's jurisprudence, the Supreme Court will hear the case. Finally, it does not mean that, even if the Supreme Court hears the Cave Rock case, it will apply to American Indian religion the same principles that it has applied to Judeo-Christian religion.

Until the Supreme Court does just that, the law of the land regarding government activity "respecting an establishment of religion" is Judeo-Christian, "no," and pantheism, "yes." As long as that is the law, millions of acres of federal land and goodness knows how much private land could be declared sacred and off-limits to the public and the people who own it. The people who use those public land, for recreation and for economic purposes, will continue to challenge these unconstitutional closures until the Supreme Court issues a ruling on the issue.

The federal government is not always the federal landowner and manager or the federal overseer and regulator; sometimes, the federal government steps down from its throne of sovereignty to stand shoulder to shoulder with its citizens in a business relationship, albeit only briefly. Then, when things go wrong, it once again cloaks itself in immunity, denies any and all responsibility, and asserts that it is not a partner but, once again, in charge.

with the federal Geothermal Steam Act of 1970, for land near Las Cruces in southern New Mexico, just north of El Paso, Texas. The lease provided, as did all geothermal leases, that it would be in effect for "a primary term of ten (10) years" and last so long as "geothermal steam is produced or utilized in commercial quantities" but not more than forty years. The lease could not be cancelled, the lease assured, "with[out] notice and an opportunity for a hearing."

The lease was held by a small Denver, Colorado, geothermal company, Chaffee Geothermal, Ltd., that Stanley Mann headed up. Chaffee spent $850,000 exploring and developing the lease between 1981 and 1983; in fact, it successfully drilled and completed two geothermal wells, which were each capable of producing geothermal resources in commercial quantities. In 1985, Chaffee assigned the lease to Stanley Mann.

Stanley Mann teamed up with a friend, Larry Hall, formed a company, Crowne Geothermal, Ltd., and initiated discussions with, among others, the town of Las Cruces, New Mexico, with respect to providing a clean, environmentally safe, energy supply for a proposed industrial park. In fact, by 1988, Larry Hall had designed a unique, state-of-the-art greenhouse facility to use the abundant geothermal resources of the lease.

In September 1989, Stanley Mann began teaching at Pepperdine University and rented a tiny apartment in Malibu, California. In March 1990, a February 16, 1990, letter from the BLM was forwarded to Stanley Mann; the letter inquired about the bond on the lease held by Stanley Mann. The letter had been addressed to Crowne Geothermal, Ltd., in Brighton, Colorado. Within days, Stanley Mann wrote a letter, on Pepperdine University stationery, advising the BLM that his bond was still in place. At the top of the letter, Stanley Mann stamped his Malibu, California, address.

CHAPTER 8

FIGHTING THE FEDERAL GOVERNMENT WHEN IT WEARS TWO HATS

Government is not reason, it is not eloquence—it is force! Like fire, it is a dangerous servant and a fearful master.

GEORGE WASHINGTON[1]

Government's view of the economy could be summed up in a few short phrases: If it moves, tax it. If it keeps moving, regulate it. And if it stops moving, subsidize it.

RONALD REAGAN[2]

S tanley K. Mann had an idea, an idea of producing abundant, clean, and efficient energy in southern New Mexico. He believed he could make a pretty penny and the country would be better off for what he had accomplished. The energy source was geothermal, which for decades had been one of the "soft" energy paths that environmentalists had demanded the nation take. Stanley Mann wanted to take a tiny part of New Mexico down that path.

Stanley Mann's company had a geothermal lease issued by the Bureau of Land Management (BLM) in October 1981, in accordance

In April 1990, Stanley Mann received a letter from the Minerals Management Service (MMS), a sister agency to the BLM in the U.S. Department of the Interior that collects royalties on producing oil and gas and geothermal wells. That letter too had been sent to Crowne Geothermal, Ltd., in Brighton, Colorado. The letter, as well as an earlier one from the MMS that Stanley Mann had not received, sought clarification on the nature of the geothermal lease. In a telephone conversation with an MMS official, Stanley Mann informed the MMS that the geothermal lease had commercial quantities of steam, was shut in for economic reasons, but that its future development was being actively pursued and that the lease was now a long-term, that is, forty-year lease. The MMS thus changed the status of Stanley Mann's lease.

In May 1990, Stanley Mann confirmed the telephone conversation with a letter to the MMS official. Then, in a request that would prove ironic and prophetic, Stanley Mann wrote, "Would you also be kind enough to make sure the records of our current address get properly changed. Although we gave the correct address to the [BLM] office in New Mexico, we continue to have mail forwarded from our old address, and I am not sure I gave you the current address during our telephone conversation." He then provided his Malibu, California, address, which was also stamped at the top of the letter.

In September 1990, the BLM issued a "notice" regarding Stanley Mann's lease, which it sent to him in Malibu, California, advising him that the MMS was now Stanley Mann's point of contact with the U.S. Department of the Interior and that "all reports and monies must be sent to that office." As a result, Stanley Mann had numerous telephone and written communications with the MMS official with whom he had spoken earlier. In addition, in October 1991, Stanley Mann made his "minimum (because his lease was shut in) royalties" payment of

$2,560; later, he would make his "minimum royalties" payments for the years 1992 through 1996.

Meanwhile, in April 1991, the BLM called Stanley Mann in Malibu, California, regarding his lease bond. Stanley Mann responded immediately, on Crowne Geothermal, Ltd., letterhead, with a letter to the company that had posted his lease bond. He advised the bonding company of the new address for Crowne Geothermal, Ltd., in Costa Mesa, California, where Stanley Mann's partner, Larry Hall lived. To make sure that the BLM knew that Stanley Mann had ensured that the bond was still in place, Stanley Mann sent an unsigned, courtesy copy of the letter to the BLM.

When the BLM got that letter, someone (no one will say who) decided to change Stanley Mann's personal address in the BLM's records from Malibu to Costa Mesa, California. It was later discovered that one reason the BLM made this mistake was that earlier the BLM had made an even bigger mistake: it had listed Crowne Geothermal, Ltd., and not Stanley Mann, as the owner of the lease.[3] Ultimately, in January 1992, the BLM changed its records to reflect that Stanley Mann owned the lease, but that would be too late for Stanley Mann. However, regardless of who owned the lease, the address should never have been changed absent, in accordance with official BLM written policy, a letter specifically requesting a change of address!

In November 1993, the BLM issued a "lease determination," which provided that "geothermal lease NMNM 34793 [sic] shall expire thirty days after receipt of this decision unless satisfactory evidence is provided . . . that diligent efforts to utilize the geothermal resources are in fact being made."[4] Thus, the lease determination was an "interlocutory decision;" that is, only if Mr. Mann did not provide the requested evidence of "diligent efforts" within thirty days would the BLM terminate his lease.

Incredibly, the BLM sent the notice to Costa Mesa, California. In one bit of irony, the BLM also sent the notice to the MMS. Although the two agencies are both part of the Department of the Interior and both are involved with energy leases, the BLM never bothered to inquire of the MMS about Stanley Mann's geothermal lease, and the MMS, once it had received the BLM's notice of pending cancellation, never advised the BLM that the lease term had been extended and that Stanley Mann was paying royalties.

In August 1995, Stanley Mann and his fiancée visited the BLM office in Las Cruces, New Mexico, to discuss options for using the geothermal resources on his lease. Stanley Mann was astonished to learn that, according to the BLM, his lease had been terminated over a year earlier.[5] The BLM advised him, however, that he could reinstate his lease if he would pay the unpaid royalties and show that he had made a good-faith effort to use the geothermal resources. Stanley Mann responded that his lease had been extended, that he had been paying the necessary minimum royalties for the last four years, and that he had continued to make good-faith efforts to utilize the geo-thermal resources.

What a mess, thought Stanley Mann. Certainly the BLM would make things right. Fact is, these things happen; people in business make mistakes all the time. Then, they do the right thing; they fix it! After all, the lease was not cancelled; commercial quantities of geo-thermal resources had been discovered and their production was being actively pursued; and, Stanley Mann had paid all the royalties due on his lease! But Stanley Mann's optimism was unwarranted.

In September 1995, uncertain as to whether the BLM would make good on the assurances of the Las Cruces BLM office, Stanley Mann's attorney filed an appeal and a petition to stay the BLM's decision to cancel Stanley Mann's geothermal lease with the Interior Board of Land Appeals (IBLA). The BLM responded by acknowledging that the notice it had tried to send to Stanley Mann was procedurally defective and that the BLM had failed to provide Stanley Mann the due process rights to which he was entitled after the BLM received the notice marked by the U.S. Postal Service as "unclaimed." In fact, the BLM admitted that it had done nothing regarding the notice it had tried to send to Stanley Mann—that is, until he and his fiancée walked into the Las Cruces BLM office. Nonetheless, the BLM had made the decision to cancel retroactively Stanley Mann's lease effective sixty days from the day it had received the unclaimed letter, that is, as of February 1994. Therefore, asserted the BLM, the Las Cruces BLM office was wrong when it told Stanley Mann that his lease could be reinstated; it was too late for that!

In November 1995, the IBLA said the same thing and it dismissed Stanley Mann's appeal as "untimely." The IBLA ruled that the BLM had sent its letter to Stanley Mann's last "address of record" when it sent it to Costa Mesa and that Stanley Mann had "constructively received" the notice. Therefore, Stanley Mann had until January 7, 1994, to file an appeal with the IBLA; because he had not filed an appeal until September 1995, he was too late.[6] When Stanley Mann filed a motion for reconsideration with the IBLA, arguing that he had never lived in Costa Mesa, the IBLA made a "finding" that Stanley Mann had "intended" to change his address.[7]

Stanley Mann could not believe it. The federal government's position was constructed on a series of legal fictions: the BLM had sent the notice to his "last address of record"; Stanley Mann had "intended" to change his address; the BLM had given him "constructive" notice; and, in September 1995, the BLM had cancelled his lease as of February 1994. The federal government refused to admit that it had made a mistake, and it certainly did not offer to make things right. Instead, it decided to circle the wagons and to fight! Stanley Mann was determined to fight back.

In May 1998, Stanley Mann filed a lawsuit in the U.S. Court of Federal Claims, the sole court in which to obtain the damages against the United States of the amount that Stanley Mann thought he was owed. He claimed that the BLM had breached its contract with him. In September 2002, the Court of Federal Claims ruled against Stanley Mann, holding that he had "constructive notice" of the BLM's letter regarding his lease and that his claim to the BLM and his appeal to the IBLA had been untimely.[8] Stanley Mann immediately appealed the decision.

On June 3, 2003, oral arguments took place before the U.S. Court of Appeals for the Federal Circuit. A mere twenty-four days later (a record for a federal appellate court), the Court of Appeals reversed the lower court and ruled in favor of Stanley Mann! It ruled that "a lessee's 'last address of record' is the place where the party to receive documents has declared he will receive such delivery," that by sending a courtesy copy to the BLM, Stanley Mann did "not expressly indicate an intention to change his mailing address," and that "the BLM did not mail the [notice] to Mr. Mann's last address of record."[9] The Federal Circuit remanded the case to the Court of Federal Claims for "a determination of an appropriate remedy," which Stanley Mann interprets is the millions of dollars he is owed because the BLM took his extremely valuable property.[10] That fight, due to years of foot dragging by the federal government and its lawyers, is still underway.

More than twelve years after the BLM sent a letter to the wrong address—a problem that could have been rectified with a couple of telephone calls—the matter continues in litigation. Federal lawyers are fighting Stanley Mann every step of the way while their supposed clients, federal bureaucrats at the BLM and elsewhere, could not care less about doing the right thing—adhering to the terms of the contract the BLM made with him, saving the United States time and money, and producing geothermal energy and jobs for the people of southern New Mexico. In time, Stanley Mann will receive some recompense for what has happened to him, but at seventy-two years of age it will come a little late in the day. With oil prices at all-time highs, Stanley Mann wishes he had had that lease all these years. He knows he could have made winners of all concerned: himself, the federal government to which he would have paid royalties, the local economy for which he would have provided jobs and tax revenues, and the environment, which would have benefited because geothermal energy is clean, efficient, and endlessly renewable.

Why did no one in the federal government seem to care back in 1994 when this all started? Why does no one in the federal government seem to care even today?

First, people in government do not like to make decisions unless they are forced to do so. Career bureaucrats want to keep their jobs until they can collect their retirement; making controversial decisions might disrupt their plans. Political appointees avoid making controversial decisions because doing so might interfere with their promotion to an even better job in the federal government, or election to higher office, or being hired by a big law firm or major corporation.

Second, the attorney-client relationship in the federal government is unlike that in the private sector, where the client is always in charge. Moreover, both attorneys and clients in the federal government use that unique relationship to each one's individual advantage. Federal bureaucrats defend their failure to act by saying, "the lawyers are calling the shots"; government lawyers shrug, "this is what the client wants."

Third, higher level political appointees—those nominated by the White House and confirmed by the Senate, those ultimately responsible for their agency—refuse consistently to become involved. Their excuse: they do not wish to usurp their subordinates' decision-making authority, so they defer to them.

Fourth, elected officials have adopted a hands-off policy regarding litigation. If a matter is in litigation, then U.S. Senators and Representatives assert that they may not become involved. Even when the federal government's initial illegal or wrongful action, or the federal agency's subsequent failure to do the right thing, or the federal lawyers' adoption of a scorched earth litigation strategy results in an unfair or even ethically questionable decision, Congress rarely wants to know what happened. When it does inquire, either the decision makers have long since departed or no one can recall who made the various bad decisions along the way.

Finally, federal agencies, unlike everyone else facing litigation, never really incur the cost or pay the price of litigation. That a case that could have been settled for a million dollars results in a court award of five million dollars paid out of the federal government's "judgment fund" is irrelevant to the agency, its officials, and its lawyers.[11] That a case that could have been settled for minor legal fees, which must, under federal law, be paid to certain deserving plaintiffs, results in a final award of hundreds of thousands of dollars in legal fees is irrelevant to the agency and its officials, even though that award must come out of the agency's budget. After all, no one will be fired; no programs will be cut; no one's heat or air conditioning will be shut off. And, even though the federal government's take-no-prisoners litigation strategy of using every jurisdictional, procedural, and tactical trick in the book did not work in this multimillion dollar case, maybe it will work in the next case and the citizen will be sent home with nothing! That's what happened with the Cannon family in Utah.

WE ONLY MAKE OTHER PEOPLE CLEAN UP THEIR MESSES

In 1945, as U.S. Marines continued their assault on the islands of the Pacific and the units of the Japanese Imperial Army massed there, the federal government approached Jesse Fox Cannon of Toole County, Utah, for permission to use 1,425 acres encompassing 89.5 patented mining claims he owned near the Army Dugway Proving Grounds in west-central Utah. Jesse Fox Cannon quickly agreed and entered into a contract with the U.S. Army that allowed it to survey and to perform exploratory and construction work in a section of Mr. Cannon's property on and near his Yellow Jacket mining claims.

The army's "Project Sphinx" was to be conducted on mineshafts to simulate Japanese cave fortifications like those the Marines had encountered on Saipan and Iwo Jima. Contrary to terms of the contract, however, the army not only bombed all of Jesse Fox Cannon's claims, it also used non-explosive munitions. In total, the army utilized more than three thousand rounds of ammunition containing either chemical or incendiary weapons. It used twenty-three tons of chemical weapons, including "the choking agent phosgene, the blood agent hydrogen cyanide, and the blistering agent mustard,"[12] and incendiary weapons including "butane, gasoline, and napalm."[13] To make matters worse, the army continued using Jesse Fox Cannon's property, without permission, until the 1960s.

Although the contract between the federal government and Jesse Fox Cannon provided that, within sixty days from the end of its testing, the army would "leave the property of the owner in as good condition as it is on the date of the government's entry," the army did no reclamation.[14] In September and October 1945, the federal government paid Jesse Fox Cannon $2,819.48 for some of the damage to the timbering in his mine shafts, but when he submitted another similar claim in 1950 for $3,000 the federal government denied it. In 1954, Dr. J. Floyd Cannon acquired the property from his father; he made repeated requests that the federal government clean up the property, which were ignored. In 1980, Dr. Cannon died, leaving the property to his four children.

Meanwhile, in 1979, the federal government released a report regarding testing in the "Yellow Jacket Area" that, not surprisingly, noted the need for more information on the extent of contamination in the area. In 1988, the federal government updated its 1979 report finding that the "Yellow Jacket Area" was "potentially contaminated with hazardous materials" and was being subjected to an "environmental assessment."[15] In July 1994, the federal government notified the Cannons that it was performing a "geophysical survey of property known as the Yellow Jacket Mines" to discover "[if] these lands have been impacted by unexploded ordinance."[16] In August 1994, the federal government held a press conference to announce that it was undertaking an "Engineering Evaluation/Cost Analysis (EE/CA)" study to "determine risks associated with former defense sites including the Yellow Jacket Area."[17] Finally, in August 1996, the federal government released a draft of its EE/CA study in which it concluded that the Cannon property was "highly contaminated."[18] Because full-scale removal of munitions and related debris would cost $12.4 million, the EE/CA study recommended the Cannon property be purchased by the United States and then sealed off and closed to the public.[19]

In April 1998, Margaret Louise and Allan Robert Cannon presented the federal government with a damage claim that the federal government summarily rejected; in December 1998, the Cannons filed a lawsuit for $8 million in damages. The federal government argued that the Cannons had waited too long; they should have sued, asserted government lawyers, before the federal government issued its August 1996 report! The Utah federal district court rejected the federal government's argument, ruled that the army's weapons testing was a continuing trespass and nuisance, and awarded Margaret and Allan Cannon $166,000. The federal government appealed, contending that it could not be sued.

In August 2003, the U.S. Court of Appeals for the Tenth Circuit lamented that, fifty-eight years after the federal government had reached its agreement with Jesse Fox Cannon, "[it] has yet to fulfill its contractual obligations to the Cannon family [or] to recognize and appreciate Jesse F. Cannon's contribution to National Security during World War II."[20] Moreover, the Tenth Circuit acknowledged that, notwithstanding the federal government's 1996 report, "the only action the Government has taken associated with [its] conclusions and recommendations is to defend this lawsuit."[21] Nevertheless, the Tenth Circuit agreed with the federal government that the Cannons, instead of "waiting until the Government informed them of the extent of their injury," should have sued immediately.[22] Concluding that the Cannons' "remedy at this stage is political, however, not legal," the Tenth Circuit dismissed their case.[23]

So, instead of trusting that, in the end, the federal government would do the right thing, the Cannon family should have hired a lawyer and sued. Indeed, should any one ever trust what the federal government says, even in print. The Kidmans of Page, Arizona, would probably say, "No!"

THE FRYING PAN OR THE FIRE

For nearly twenty-five years, Richard and Shauna Kidman have owned and operated RD's Drive-In in Page, Arizona. Page, which abuts the Glen Canyon Dam and Lake Powell just south of the Utah border, is seventy-five miles east of Kanab, Utah, and 125 miles north of Flagstaff, Arizona. The vast Navajo Nation is to the east, the Glen Canyon National Recreation Area to the west. Tourism is an economic mainstay—that, and the nearby Navajo Generating Station.[24]

The Kidmans and their seven children have worked hard to make RD's (the initials are those of Richard and Dean, a former partner) a success. Over the years, they have hired and trained almost 1,100 employees; many were school students and almost 90 percent were

Navajos. Today, the Kidmans' six daughters have moved on and only son Steve, their oldest child, remains to help run RD's.

Early in 2000, the Kidmans learned of a problem feared by all businesses, large and small. The Kidmans began to receive complaints from employees and customers that some of their Navajo-speaking employees were speaking rudely, crudely, and inappropriately. In addition, the language was sometimes sexually offensive, derogatory, and insulting, thus creating a hostile and harassing work environment for which the Kidmans could be held liable under federal law. Worst of all, the Kidmans did not know it was happening; the offenders were using the Navajo language, which none of the Kidmans spoke. Later, the Kidmans discovered it was not just other employees who were offended and quit; Navajo customers were repulsed by the vulgar language and stopped dining at RD's.

Fearful that more employees would quit or, worse yet, file a legal action against them for permitting a sexually hostile and harassing work environment and concerned about what the loss of older customers was doing to their business, in May 2000, the Kidmans asked Steve to research if they might restrict workplace communications to English. His research, done using the Equal Employment Opportunity Commission (EEOC) website and other resources, led the Kidmans to conclude that an English-language workplace policy is permissible so long as: (1) the policy is necessary for conducting business, (2) the employees are made aware of the policy, and (3) the employees are informed as to the consequences of violating the policy. In his research, Steve also located a decision by the U.S. Court of Appeals for the Ninth Circuit, which held that preventing conflict and ill feelings among employees is a valid business reason to implement an English-language workplace policy.[25]

In accordance with EEOC rules, the Kidmans put their new policy in writing, posted it, and asked each employee to sign it. Nearly every employee, including the most flagrant users of vulgar language, signed the policy. Four employees refused and quit. Later, when they sought unemployment compensation, Arizona ruled that they had quit and not been fired, a ruling that was upheld on appeal.

Those four employees sought the help of the EEOC, which demanded that the Kidmans abandon their English-language workplace policy asserting that, by requiring English in the workplace, the Kidmans were guilty of racial discrimination. The Kidmans refused to abandon the policy, although they did offer to rehire the workers if they would sign the new policy. They got no response to their offer.

In September 2002, the EEOC filed a lawsuit in Arizona federal district court charging that the Kidmans had violated Title VII of the Civil Rights Act of 1964 and Title I of the Civil Rights Act of 1991, which bar discrimination based on "race, color, religion, or national origin," and demanded nearly $200,000 in fines. The EEOC action, which argues that the Kidmans' English-language workplace policy has a "disparate impact" on the Navajo race, is its first language lawsuit involving American Indians, giving the agency, according to the *New York Times*, "a rare chance to flex its muscles on behalf of an Indian group."[26] It appears that "flex[ing] its muscles" is more important than obeying the law because the U.S. Court of Appeals for the Ninth Circuit, whose decisions set precedent for federal courts in Arizona, has rejected the EEOC's equation of language requirements with national origin discrimination.[27]

National talk show host Laura Ingraham declared, "Suits such as this one should be tossed out and ideally the EEOC should be ordered to pay the legal fees of the owners of R.D.'s."[28] Roger Clegg, General Counsel for the Center for Equal Opportunity, went further, asserting that EEOC's lawsuit is the legal equivalent of piling on, suing twice for the same thing, so that the EEOC "can get full compensatory damages, 'including but not limited to, pain and suffering, mental anguish, humiliation, embarrassment, emotional distress, anxiety, inconvenience, and loss of enjoyment of life, in amounts to be determined at trial,' as well as 'punitive damages for [RD's] malicious conduct or reckless indifference.'"[29]

Experts familiar with the EEOC concluded that the agency recognizes that federal law in the Ninth Circuit is against it. Nonetheless, it sued the Kidmans because it expected them to cave under the pressure and sign a consent decree under which they would admit legal liability and abandon their English-language workplace policy. Armed with that signed consent decree or court ordered settlement agreement, the EEOC would be able to threaten other companies and employers, demanding similar settlements from them.

Sure enough, the EEOC placed unrelenting pressure on the Kidmans to sign an agreement. Nevertheless, in September 2003, the court-supervised negotiations failed when the EEOC drafted a consent decree that did not accurately represent the negotiations held by the Kidmans and the EEOC. Moreover, under the terms of the agreement demanded by the EEOC, the agency would become the Kidmans' business partner, involved, for years to come, in day-to-day decision-making. The EEOC was undaunted; in January 2004, it asked the Arizona federal district court to issue a ruling that there had been an agreement and that the Kidmans were bound by it, even though the Kidmans: had never agreed that there had been an agreement; had never affirmed in open court and on the record that there was an agreement to which they were willing to be bound; and had never signed any document of any kind. In fact, the Kidmans had done just the opposite: they said they refused to be bound by any agreement that did not include specific provisions, which the EEOC had failed to include. In September 2004, the Arizona federal district court ruled that, although there was no agreement between the parties as to all material terms of the agreement, there had been agreement on some of the terms, which could be enforced.[30]

Because federal and Arizona law require a "meeting of the minds" on "all material terms" and an intent to be bound before an agreement may have been formed, the Kidmans appealed to the U.S. Court of Appeals for the Ninth Circuit.

The Kidmans know that they have started down the road traveled by Stanley Mann and the Cannons; but they also know that they have no choice in this. The Kidmans do not want the EEOC as their business partner, they know that they have done nothing wrong, and they know that, if they had not adopted their English-language workplace policy, the EEOC would have sued them anyway—this time for sexual harassment.

What is happening to the Kidmans illustrates another outrageous and frustrating reality in dealing with the federal government. The ruling issued by the Ninth Circuit, which rejected the EEOC's approach, was one of those rare occasions when the Ninth Circuit got it right. The most liberal federal appellate court in the land, the one whose decisions most frequently make it to the Supreme Court, and the one most often reversed when its cases get there, sometimes unanimously, had interpreted the law as Congress intended and as the words of federal law provided. That is irrelevant to the EEOC and its agenda-driven lawyers and bureaucrats; apparently it is also irrelevant to the political appointees who purportedly run the agency. Because businesses can ill afford the years of litigation required to challenge an EEOC enforcement action, they are quick to enter into a consent decree or settlement agreement. Thus armed, the EEOC attacks other businesses. Until someone is willing to fight back, federal appellate courts never become involved and the EEOC may ignore their holdings. No wonder so many believe, on viewing what is happening to the

Kidmans, that people have to continue to fight against their government in the courts of the land.

As bad as the federal government can be as a business partner, it is even worse as a neighbor.

CHAPTER 9

FIGHTING THE FEDERAL GOVERNMENT'S BAD NEIGHBOR POLICIES

Love your neighbor, yet pull not down your hedge.

GEORGE HERBERT[1]

You may talk of the tyranny of Nero and Tiberius; but the real tyranny is the tyranny of your next-door neighbor.

WALTER BAGEHOT[2]

In the far western portion of the Upper Peninsula of Michigan, halfway between Iron Mountain and Ironwood, lies Watersmeet.[3] There the Ontonagon River flows north into Lake Superior, the Wisconsin River flows south into the Mississippi River, and the Paint River flows east into Lake Michigan.[4] No wonder locals boast of 302 lakes and 241 miles of trout streams. There is the Cisco Chain comprising fifteen lakes and some 270 miles of shoreline and Lac Vieux Desert at the headwaters of the Wisconsin River, with its abundant and world record fisheries.[5] There is, as well, the million-acre Ottawa

National Forest, with spruce, balsam, maple, birch, and aspen, as well as the Sylvania Wilderness Area.[6] The Ottawa is also the home of Crooked Lake.[7]

It is on the far northern banks of Crooked Lake that, in 1940, Kathy Stupak-Thrall's grandfather and grandmother built a modest cabin to boat and fish in the summer and to recreate in the abundant snows—as much as three hundred inches—in the winter.[8] Today, Kathy and her husband Ben enjoy that cabin and revel in the beauty of Crooked Lake and the forest around it. Crooked Lake is so named because it is, well, crooked; it meanders for more three and one-half miles in and out of inlets, big and small, and along picturesque shorelines. The fishing is not half bad either.[9]

After the land surrounding Crooked Lake were surveyed in the 1850s under the authority of the General Land Office, they were divided and sold to private parties. Crooked Lake itself was never sold; instead, it became the property of the State of Michigan under the Equal Footing Doctrine. In 1966, the United States, under threat of condemnation, purchased, pursuant to the Weeks Law,[10] 14,890 acres of land abutting the southern portion of Crooked Lake, often referred to as "the Sylvania lands."[11] The quitclaim deed the United States received did not transfer any portion of Crooked Lake, or any other lake for that matter, to the United States. All the land the United States received who included in the Ottawa National Forest to be managed, in accordance with multiple use principles, by the U.S. Forest Service. In fact, on the western shore of Crooked Lake, the Forest Service constructed a boat ramp and other water facilities to encourage motorboat use by members of the general public.

Meanwhile, in 1964, Congress passed the Wilderness Act, which established the National Wilderness Preservation System "to be composed of federally owned areas designated by Congress as wilderness areas."[12] Thereafter, beginning in 1972, the Forest Service, at the behest of environmental groups, began a study of the purported roadless area of the Ottawa National Forest. Not surprisingly, folks in Gogebic County, who needed access to the forests, lakes, and rivers for their economic survival and for their own recreational needs, were deeply concerned. Fortunately, within a year, the plan, dubbed "Roadless Area Review and Evaluation (RARE I)," was dead.[13] In 1977, however, at the start of the Carter administration, the Forest Service began RARE II, which concluded in 1979[14] with a report to Congress recommending that certain land in the Ottawa National Forest, including the Sylvania lands, be designated as wilderness.[15] Although the Sylvania lands that the Forest Service had acquired comprised 14,890 acres, when the Forest Service made its recommendation to Congress, it recommended the designation of 18,327 acres as wilderness. This 3,400-acre discrepancy resulted from the Forest Service's assertion, without any legal basis whatsoever, that it owned the lakes, including Crooked Lake. In December 1987, Congress passed the Michigan Wilderness Act in which it designated 18,327 acres of land within the Ottawa National Forest as the Sylvania Wilderness.[16]

Although folks like Kathy Stupak-Thrall were concerned about a highly restrictive land classification being superimposed on the Ottawa National Forest given their needs for access to the land and waters of Gogebic County, they were reassured by the fact that the wilderness statute designated only federal land, did not designate the state-owned lakes inside the national forest, and protected all valid existing rights.[17] Kathy Stupak-Thrall and Ben and their children would be able to use all of Crooked Lake, and her neighbors, one of whom rented out boats for use on Crooked Lake, could stay in business.[18]

Then, in April 1992, the Forest Service issued an order prohibiting the use of sailboats, houseboats, and non-burnable disposable food and beverage containers in the Sylvania Wilderness Area. The Forest Service asserted that it had the right to do this because most of the shoreline of Crooked Lake was now a federal wilderness area. However, the surface of Crooked Lake was not a wilderness area; therefore, in June 1992, Kathy Stupak-Thrall and her husband filed an administrative appeal with the Forest Service challenging the order and arguing, among other things, that their riparian rights on Crooked Lake were valid existing rights that had been destroyed by the Forest Service order. In October 1992, the Forest Service denied the appeal and concluded, astonishingly, that the valid existing rights language in the Michigan Wilderness Act did not apply to the riparian rights of Kathy Stupak Thrall and her husband but applied, instead, only to privately owned mineral rights in the Nordhouse Dunes Wilderness Area. In January 1993, the chief of the Forest Service agreed with and upheld that ruling. Furthermore, volunteered the chief, even if the Thralls' riparian rights were protected valid existing rights, the Forest Service could restrict the use of those rights so long as the restrictions did not effectuate a taking!

In March 1993, Kathy Stupak-Thrall and two of her neighbors filed suit in Michigan federal district court to prevent the Forest Service from interfering with their riparian rights on Crooked Lake.[19] In January 1994, although the district court ruled that Kathy Stupak-Thrall's riparian rights were protected by the valid existing rights language in the Michigan Wilderness Act, it also ruled that the Forest Service's regulation of Crooked Lake was reasonable.[20] The district court held that, because Kathy Stupak-Thrall's use of Crooked Lake was subject to Michigan's reasonable-use doctrine, the question before the court was whether the Forest Service's regulation was reasonable, not whether Kathy Stupak-Thrall's proposed use was reasonable.[21] Of course, this holding turned the reasonable-use doctrine on its head. Kathy Stupak-Thrall and her neighbors appealed.

In November 1995, a three-judge panel of the U.S. Court of Appeals for the Sixth Circuit affirmed the holding of the Michigan federal district court, but on a different basis. The panel reasoned that the Forest Service, like Kathy Stupak-Thrall, was a co-owner of the entire surface of Crooked Lake and thus entitled to reasonable use of that surface. It also held, however, that the Forest Service was a sovereign and therefore could make the rules as to what was a reasonable use. In other words, concluded the panel, Congress had delegated to the Forest Service regulatory powers coextensive with the police powers possessed by local governments in the State of Michigan.[22] The panel's ruling was so outrageously erroneous that Kathy Stupak-Thrall asked the entire Sixth Circuit to rehear the case. Though there had been no dissent from the panel's ruling, the Sixth Circuit quickly granted the petition, vacated the panel's ruling, and reheard the case *en banc.*[23]

Nonetheless, in June 1996, the Sixth Court split 7–7 on the matter thus allowing the Michigan federal district court's ruling to stand.[24] Kathy Stupak-Thrall urged the U.S. Supreme Court to hear her case. Of prime concern to her was that the Michigan federal district court, whose decision now controlled, had held that the Constitution's Property Clause gave Congress, and through Congress, agencies like the Forest Service, the power to regulate private property, citing, in support, a 1976 Supreme Court ruling.[25] However, in that 1976 case, the Supreme Court had declined specifically to rule on that issue. "We . . . leave open the question of the permissible reach of the Act over private lands under the Property Clause."[26] Unfortunately, in 1997, the Supreme Court denied Kathy Stupak-Thrall's petition.[27]

Meanwhile, in May 1995, while Kathy Stupak-Thrall was awaiting the ruling of the Sixth Circuit on the legality of the Forest Service's order regarding sailboats, the Forest Service adopted another order, this one banning gas-powered motorboats. In March 1996, after exhausting their administrative remedies, Kathy Stupak-Thrall and her neighbors sued the Forest Service in Michigan federal district court. At the same time, they sought and, in May 1996, obtained a preliminary injunction enjoining the Forest Service from implementing its ban on gas-powered motorboats. Then, in December 1997, the district court made the injunction permanent when it ruled that the Forest Service's ban on gas-powered motorboats was illegal because it violated the valid existing rights language, which protected property owners like Kathy Stupak-Thrall, that Congress had included in the Michigan Wilderness Act.[28] The Forest Service quickly appealed.

Meanwhile, while reviewing files at the local Forest Service office, Kathy Stupak-Thrall discovered a letter, dated February 15, 1991, from the regional forester's office to the forest supervisor, indicating that the official map and legal description required by the Michigan Wilderness Act were almost complete. However, in March 1998, when she sought to obtain a copy of the official map and legal description, she was told that they "do not exist at this time." Kathy Stupak-Thrall found this incredible; after all, the Michigan Wilderness Act had been passed in 1987.[29]

Kathy Stupak-Thrall believed that a properly prepared map and legal description would end forever the Forest Service's ability to regulate the surface of Crooked Lake because they would reveal that the surface of Crooked Lake belongs to the State of Michigan. Moreover, the documents would demonstrate that riparian owners like Kathy Stupak-Thrall, her neighbors, and the Forest Service all had the right to use the entire surface of Crooked Lake because it was part of their private property. The Wilderness Act of 1964 and the Michigan Wilderness Act of 1987 applied, and could only apply, to federal land; state and private land could not be designated as wilderness or managed as if it was in a wilderness area. A legal map and description would document all this and resolve the matter once and for all.

Kathy Stupak-Thrall further discovered that, on a properly drawn map, survey lines are required to meander around bodies of water such as Crooked Lake. In fact, that is exactly what the General Land Office surveyor did when he surveyed Gogebic County: he meandered his survey lines around Crooked Lake.[30] Because the Forest Service is required to adhere to accepted surveying principles, an official Forest Service map of the Sylvania Wilderness Area would also have boundary lines that meandered around but did not cross Crooked Lake. In May 1998, Kathy Stupak-Thrall and several of her neighbors sued to compel the Forest Service to do what Congress had mandated: prepare a map and legal description for the Sylvania Wilderness Area.

Unfortunately, in April 1999, the Michigan federal district court ruled that Kathy Stupak-Thrall's claims were time barred under the six-year federal statute of limitations. Furthermore, the district court declared, based upon a hand-drawn schematic map used by the U.S. Senate during its consideration of the Michigan Wilderness Act, that Congress intended for the boundary of the Sylvania Wilderness Area to cross Crooked Lake.[31] Kathy Stupak-Thrall appealed to the Sixth Circuit. Finally, more than two years after oral arguments in her case, the Sixth Circuit agreed, in a very brief opinion, with the Michigan federal district court. The map case was at an end; however, even today, eighteen years after passage of the Michigan Wilderness Act, the Forest Service has yet to do an official map and legal description.

While Kathy Stupak-Thrall's map case was on appeal, the Forest Service's appeal of her victory in the motorboat case had been abated. With completion of the map case, the Sixth Circuit was ready to hear the Forest Service's case. Once again, Kathy Stupak-Thrall anticipated that, boundary or no boundary, the Forest Service would argue at the Sixth Circuit that the Michigan federal district court that had ruled in the sailboat case was right: the Forest Service had authority under the Property Clause to regulate state and private land that is adjacent to or affects federal land.

Because the Sixth Circuit had heard her earlier case *en banc*, she planned to ask for immediate *en banc* consideration of the motorboat case, this time from a position of strength. After all, she had won at the federal district court. Perhaps, with one side or the other winning and the Sixth Circuit issuing a definitive ruling on whether the federal government could use the Property Clause to regulate private land, the U.S. Supreme Court would hear the case and resolve the issue it did not resolve in 1976.

It was not to be. In April 2005, the United States announced its intention not to continue with its appeal; instead, it would allow Kathy Stupak-Thrall's motorboat victory to stand. After fifteen years almost to the day, her fight for her property rights and those of her neighbors had ended, not with a triumphant bang, but a whimpering surrender from the Forest Service. Nonetheless, it was a success, albeit an ironic one for the Forest Service and the various environmental groups that had involved themselves in the litigation: Kathy Stupak-Thrall could use a motorboat on Crooked Lake, but not a sailboat.

In this rare instance, the judicial system had worked as it is supposed to work. At the Sixth Circuit, when a three-judge panel issued a ridiculous decision, the other judges on the appellate court voted to rehear the matter *en banc*. That is as it should be, but it happens much, much too rarely. Even the refusal of the Supreme Court to hear Kathy Stupak-Thrall's petition in the sailboat case and finally resolve its 1976 ruling as to the exact relationship between the federal government, as a landowner, and adjacent private landowners has a reasonable explanation.[32] There was no decision from the Sixth Circuit because it had split 7–7; therefore, only the ruling of the Michigan district court was before the Supreme Court and the Supreme Court is not in the business of reviewing holdings of federal district courts. Perhaps some of the justices were awaiting a final ruling from the Sixth Circuit in another Kathy Stupak-Thrall case on whether the federal government may use the Property Clause to regulate her private land. Whatever the reason, the view of the United States that it may regulate private property adjacent to its property must await another day.

Unfortunately for those who work, live, or recreate on state or private land near or adjacent to federal land, the United States's view that it may regulate that land is a dangerous specter. It has been adopted, not merely by the Sixth Circuit as a result of its anomalous 7–7 ruling in Kathy Stupak-Thrall's case, which allowed the Michigan federal district court's expansive view of the Property Clause to stand. The U.S. Court of Appeals for the Eighth Circuit, whose decisions affect seven Midwestern states, has ruled specifically, "Congress may make those rules regarding non-federal land as are necessary to accomplish its goals with respect to federal land."[33]

The United States does not need this overly broad interpretation of the Property Clause to protect the public's land from the type of harm against which all property owners must guard. Like other property owners, the United States may bring a nuisance action against the offending neighbor.[34] Although that would be the epitome of limited and ethical government, it is not the approach that the United States has taken, as the Forest Service demonstrated in its years of litigation with Kathy Stupak-Thrall. The United States does not merely want to share reasonable use with its neighbors; it wants to make the rules as to what is reasonable use and then declare unreasonable use by private landowners to be illegal and punishable by law.

Kathy Stupak-Thrall's encounter with the federal government as a bad neighbor was as a result of land owned by the United States. Sometimes, the federal government becomes a bad neighbor due to its ability to regulate land or even bodies of water adjacent to private property. That was certainly the case with President Clinton's controversial rivers' initiative.

THE AMERICAN HERITAGE RIVERS INITIATIVE

In his 1997 State of the Union address, President Clinton declared, "Tonight, I announce that this year I will designate ten American Heritage Rivers, to help communities alongside them revitalize their waterfronts and clean up pollution in the rivers." In May 1997, the Clinton administration published some scanty information, it could hardly be called details, regarding what it referred to as the American Heritage Rivers Initiative (AHRI).[35] Eleven federal agencies were conveyed as a taskforce to flesh out Clinton's plan, which provided for appointment of a federal overseer, or "River Navigator," for each designated river and for increased federal funding to make the rivers "models of the most innovative economically successful and ecologically sustainable approaches to river restoration and protection."[36] Ironically for westerners, the announcement asserted that, in implementing the program, the federal government sought to assure that "[d]esignated rivers and their communities will also receive a commitment from federal agencies to act as 'Good Neighbors' in making decisions that affect communities."[37] A reading of the fine print revealed that being a "good neighbor" meant only that federal agencies would "inform" and "consult with" local communities.[38]

Westerners and other rural citizens and property owners were not reassured; many had been burned by the condemnation of or the restrictions placed upon private property as a result of the designation of rivers under the federal Wild and Scenic Rivers Act.[39] They feared that Clinton's plan would add yet another layer of federal bureaucracy with authority to stifle economic activity and to restrict the use of private property. Moreover, they questioned Clinton's authority to adopt such a program; assertions by the White House that the purposes section of the National Environmental Policy Act mandated the new program were absurd. After all, under the Constitution's Commerce Clause, it is not the president, but Congress that regulates navigable waters; under the Tenth Amendment, it is not the federal government, but local government that oversees land use planning.[40] In addition, as a result of the vast amount of land owned by the federal government in the West, westerners were concerned about another federal mechanism for limiting land use and local decision-making. On that score as well, Clinton had no power to act unless the power was delegated to him by Congress.[41]

The furor over Clinton's plan forced the administration to extend the comment period for the proposal; nonetheless, in September 1997, Clinton issued an Executive Order creating the new federal program[42] at an annual cost of five million dollars.[43] Yet continuing opposition centered, not only on the money, but also on the fact that the program was duplicitous,[44] smacked of pork,[45] lacked a scientific basis,[46] did not target rivers that were alleged to be "endangered,"[47] and was unconstitutional.[48] It was this final deficiency that sent the Clinton plan into federal court.

In December 1997, Representative Helen Chenoweth (R-1st ID), along with Representatives Don Young (R-AK), Richard W. Pombo (R-11th CA), and Bob Schaffer (R-4th CO), filed a lawsuit in the District of Columbia federal district court challenging the constitutionality of Clinton's AHRI.[49] They asserted that Clinton's decree usurped a host of legislative powers of Congress, including those set forth in the Commerce Clause, the Spending Clause, and the Property Clause, and that it violated several federal statutes, including the Wild and Scenic Rivers Act, the Anti-Deficiency Act, the National Environmental Policy Act of 1969, and the Federal Land Policy and Management Act of 1976.[50]

In March 1998, during oral arguments on the federal government's motion to dismiss for lack of standing, Attorney General Janet Reno's lawyer asserted that Clinton's plan was consistent with federal law and the U.S. Constitution, saying: "We must take the president at his word."[51] To some degree, the District of Columbia district court disagreed, noting that, for the purposes of the federal government's motion to dismiss, the district court assumed that President Clinton's AHRI proposal "unconstitutionally violated the Separation of Powers doctrine and the other constitutional provisions and statutes cited by [the Members]."[52] Nonetheless, the district court held that the Members lacked standing because their injury was "unrelated to passing a specific piece of legislation" and was otherwise lacking in "concreteness or specificity."[53]

Representative Chenoweth and her colleagues immediately appealed. In January 1999, before the U.S. Court of Appeals for the District of Columbia Circuit, their lawyers cited a quarter century of rulings in which that appellate court had held that U.S. Senators and Representatives had standing to challenge various acts of the Executive.[54] Yet, in July 1999, the District of Columbia Circuit ruled that "the portions of our legislative standing cases upon which [the Members] rely are untenable in the light of [the U.S. Supreme Court's decision in] *Raines* [*v. Byrd*]," in which the Supreme Court held that Senator Robert Byrd (D-WV) and others lacked standing to challenge legislation on which they had voted but had lost that vote.[55] "[The Members'] claim to standing on the ground that the president's implementation of the AHRI without congressional consent injured them by diluting their authority as Members of Congress is indistinguishable from the claim to standing the Supreme Court rejected in *Raines*."[56]

Representative Chenoweth believed that the District of Columbia Court of Appeals was wrong for three reasons. First, the Supreme Court had not addressed, directly, the rulings from the District of Columbia court. Instead, it had ruled only on the one instance in which the Supreme Court itself had held that members of a legislative body had standing—a case involving Kansas state legislators.[57] Second, although Senator Byrd had the opportunity to vote regarding the law he sought to challenge in federal court, Representative Chenoweth and her colleagues never had the opportunity to vote because Clinton had implemented the AHRI by fiat.[58] Third, although the District of Columbia court ruled that *Raines* overturned much of its legislative standing jurisprudence and thus applied to Representative Chenoweth's lawsuit, *Raines* did not overturn its 1974 ruling as to Senator Ted Kennedy's right to sue.

Because the Supreme Court addressed only its own rulings on the standing of legislators, Representative Chenoweth asserted that the three-judge panel could not rule that earlier decisions of other three-judge panels had been overruled by the Supreme Court by implication; she asked for *en banc* review. Unfortunately, in September 1999, her petition was denied as was, in March 2000, her petition for Supreme Court consideration of the issue of congressional standing.[59] Apparently, the Supreme Court had said all that it was interested in saying on the subject.[60]

Sometimes the federal government is a bad neighbor, not by way of land it owns or regulates, but as a result of organisms that it imports and releases into an area.

WOLVES IN THE NORTHERN ROCKIES

In November 1994, the U.S. Fish and Wildlife Service published its final rule for the introduction of Canadian wolves into what the federal government euphemistically called the "Yellowstone and central Idaho areas," which it defined as all of Wyoming, all or parts of forty-two of Idaho's forty-four counties, and all or parts of forty of Montana's fifty-six counties.[61] Under its plan, the Fish and Wildlife Service would capture wolves in Canada, import them into the United States, and release them in this vast area of the Northern Rocky Mountains.

The Clinton administration was on the verge of achieving an objective long sought by radical environmental groups: the placement of packs of wild wolves in the rural West so that they could breed and spread throughout the region, under the protection of the Endangered Species Act.[62] Environmentalists in San Francisco, New York, and Boston apparently drew great satisfaction out of knowing that, somewhere out west, in the middle of nowhere, where nobody lives, wolves howl at the moon.[63] One of them called the wolf plan, "the greatest wildlife restoration effort in our nation's history."[64]

Wolves are not a truly endangered species; they are simply a species that did not exist in much of the lower forty-eight. On the other hand, wolves live in great abundance throughout Canada and Alaska. In fact, so abundant is the wolf in Alaska—today there are 7,700–11,200 wolves in the state—that Alaska engages in predator control of the wolf to increase its moose and/or caribou herds.[65] The abundance of wolves in Alaska did not satisfy environmental groups; they wanted the wolf returned to its "historic range" throughout the rural West. In fact, a plan was being developed to place wolves in Arizona after the Yellowstone area plan was implemented.[66]

Days after the Clinton administration announced its plan, the American, Idaho, Wyoming, and Montana Farm Bureau Federations filed a lawsuit in Wyoming federal district court asserting that the introduction of imported Canadian wolves into an area that already had populations of indigenous wolves violated the Endangered Species Act.[67] In fact, there had been hundreds of confirmed sighting of wolves throughout Idaho, Wyoming, and Montana, many by federal employees. Shortly after filing their complaint, the Farm Bureaus sought a preliminary injunction to prevent the planned release of the wolves before the Wyoming district court had the opportunity to hear and rule on the merits of the case. The Farm Bureaus knew that Secretary Babbitt was eager to be photographed by the national media carrying the caged wolves through the snows of Yellowstone National Park.[68]

In January 1995, within hours of the Wyoming district court's order denying the preliminary injunction, environmental groups filed a lawsuit in Idaho federal district court to invalidate the portion of the new rule that permitted ranchers, in the unlikely event that they actually saw a wolf preying on their livestock, to kill the wolf, and that treated both imported and indigenous wolves as endangered under the Endangered Species Act. That case was later transferred to Wyoming federal district court.[69] By April 1995, numerous environmental groups and others had joined in the litigation. Meanwhile, the federal government released thirty-one imported Canadian wolves in the Northern Rockies; in the next two years, another thirty-seven wolves would be released there.[70]

After months of preparation, weeks of briefing, and days of testimony, the Wyoming district court issued its opinion in December 1997.[71] It ruled that naturally occurring gray wolves exist and will continue to exist throughout the Northern Rockies; that introduced Canadian wolves were not "wholly separate geographically" from naturally occurring wolves; and that the federal government had introduced Canadian wolves within the "current range" of naturally occurring wolves. As a result, ruled the Wyoming court, the federal actions had violated the Endangered Species Act. The court ordered the federal government to remove all introduced Canadian wolves and their progeny from the Northern Rockies, and then it stayed its order for the removal of the wolves. By the time the Wyoming court issued its decision, there were 213 wolves through the tri-state area.[72] Environmental groups filed an appeal; they also threw a fit![73]

As a result of the Wyoming federal district court's ruling, the hate campaign put on by wolf advocates—on low boil during the legal proceedings—erupted. As the head of the American Farm Bureau Federation noted, "Wolf stocking program advocates, incited by Defenders of Wildlife, organized a campaign of harassment and intimidation against Farm Bureau with the aim of forcing us to ignore our farmer-written policies and to drop our lawsuit. We have since received several bomb threats and threats against the lives of Farm Bureau officers and their families."[74] That highly visible advocates of a position that some environmental groups regard as morally wrong would draw such a vitriolic response comes as no surprise to the Federal Bureau of Investigation. In May 2005, John E. Lewis, deputy assistant director, Counterterrorism Division of the Federal Bureau of Investigation, testified that the Bureau is greatly concerned about the degree to which "volatile talk turns into criminal activity," and he noted that, "[f]rom January 1990 to June 2004, animal and environmental rights extremists have claimed credit for more than 1,200 criminal incidents, resulting in millions of dollars in damage and monetary loss."[75] While Farm Bureau lawyers prepared for their appearance before the U.S. Court of Appeals for the Tenth Circuit, Farm Bureau leaders and members and individual ranchers throughout the mountain West who had spoken against wolf importation cautiously opened their mail.

In July 1999, oral arguments took place in the Tenth Circuit's largest courtroom before a standing room only crowd; meanwhile, some 337 imported Canadian wolves and their young roamed the Northern Rockies.[76] In April 2000, a three-judge panel issued its unanimous decision: the Wyoming federal district court was wrong; the wolf plan did not violate the Endangered Species Act.[77] By now, five years after the release of the first wolves, there were 437 imported Canadian wolves throughout Idaho, Wyoming, and Montana.[78]

The Farm Bureaus faced several unknowns and highly unlikely eventualities:

- Would the Supreme Court hear their appeal? Only one of every one hundred petitions for Supreme Court review is granted.

- Would the Supreme Court rule in their favor? In cases involving the federal government's interpretation of a statute, the Supreme Court always defers to the agency if its interpretation is "reasonable."
- Would the Supreme Court order the removal of the wolves? By the time the Court might issue its ruling even more wolves would be present in the northern Rocky Mountains. It seemed doubtful that justices from Illinois, New Jersey, New Hampshire, New York, and Massachusetts would require that the wolves be tracked down and trapped or killed.[79]

The Farm Bureaus concluded that an appeal to the Supreme Court would be futile and abandoned their litigation. In early 2005, ten years after the release of thirty wolves, there were believed to be 845 wolves in the tri-state area.[80]

In late 2005, eleven years after the Farm Bureaus filed their lawsuit and three years after the federal government had said the wolf program and the protection of the wolves under the Endangered Species Act would end, both continue. The federal government asserts that it will hand over management of the wolf program to the States of Idaho, Wyoming, and Montana; however, although Idaho and Montana have adopted new rules to permit that management, Wyoming has sued.[81] Meanwhile, an Oregon federal district court invalidated new Fish and Wildlife Service rules that would have eased the burden on ranchers in northern Montana who are suffering from wolf predation.[82] Also suffering are the tiny Montana communities surrounding Yellowstone National Park that depend on elk hunting as their economic mainstay.

A citizens' group asserts, based on its members' observations, that Yellowstone's elk population is about to collapse and that southwestern Montana elk herds are not far behind. "It's going to crash," says Bill Hoppe, president of the group, who lives just north of the park's border. "It won't take much longer." Hunters point out that the number of wolves, imported and indigenous, is way up; elk numbers are way down; and the elk cow/calf ratio, typically twenty to thirty calves per one hundred cows, is now fourteen calves per one hundred cows. Many believe the dramatic decrease in the elk population is the direct result of wolf predation.[83]

Not only are hunters crying wolf, the Montana Fish, Wildlife & Parks Commission is making a similar claim. In December 2004, Montana cut the winter elk hunt in Gardiner from 1,180 hunters to 148 hunters; worse yet, the state's regional wildlife manager predicts the hunt will be discontinued soon. "It's probably going to go away."[84] If the hunters and the local residents in Gardiner, Montana, are upset about their situation, at least two groups are happy about the courtroom victories enjoyed by wolves. Following a recent wolf-related court ruling, a law professor in Vermont crowed that "the wolves are howlin'" and his law students, who "did all the hard labor in the case," are celebrating "a nice victory."[85]

No wonder westerners believe that the federal government is all too often a bad neighbor. Things become even worse when federal bureaucrats arm themselves with badges, summons, and cease and desist orders and go looking for trouble.

CHAPTER 10

FIGHTING THE CRIMINALIZATION OF EVERYTHING

At one time, the sanction of the criminal law was reserved for serious, morally culpable offenders. But during the past 40 years, an unholy alliance of tough-on-crime conservatives and anti-big-business liberals has utterly transformed the criminal law. Today, while violent crime often goes unpunished, Congress continues to add new, trivial offenses to the federal criminal code. With more than 4,000 federal offenses on the statute books, and thousands more buried in the Code of Federal Regulations, it is now frighteningly easy for American citizens to be hauled off to jail for actions that no reasonable person would regard as crimes.

GENE HEALY, *GO DIRECTLY TO JAIL: THE CRIMINALIZATION OF ALMOST EVERYTHING*[1]

It was a beautiful, crystal clear December day on Bobby Unser's ranch near Chama, New Mexico, about one hundred miles northwest of Santa Fe, near the Colorado border. Bobby Unser, sixty-three years old and three-time Indy 500 Winner, had been born and raised in Albuquerque and had lived for years at his ranch. This was one of those days that made him glad that he did. It had snowed recently and the snow in the high country was deep and powdery. It was a perfect day for Bobby Unser to take his brand-new snowmobile and his racecar friend Robert Gayton for a short run in the Jarosa

Peak area in the Rio Grande National Forest just north in Colorado. Bobby Unser knew the area well; he had been snowmobiling there on many occasions. It had spectacular scenery, great snow, and fun and easy terrain; Bobby Unser and his friend would have a pleasant outing and be back in time for dinner.[2]

Robert Gayton had never driven a snowmobile before so Bobby Unser gave him some instructions on operating the machine and while Robert Gayton did several practice runs Bobby Unser hooked up the trailer and got the gear they would need for the quick trip. They made final preparations, Bobby Unser loaded up the machines, and, about noon, they drove the fourteen miles north through 10,022-foot Cumbres Pass. Then, six and a half miles later, they were at the Red Lake Trail parking lot. Robert Gayton practiced some more on the machine to get used to the snow conditions, then they saddled up and were off. Within the hour they were at their destination, a high plateau where they could enjoy the beauty of the day and perfect snowmobile conditions.

Suddenly and unexpectedly, they were swept up in a ferocious ground blizzard. A gale—Bobby Unser would say later it seemed like it was blowing sixty to seventy miles an hour—tore across the powdery new snow and Bobby Unser and Robert Gayton were immediately in whiteout conditions. As they tried to find their way off the plateau and out of the wind, Robert Gayton's machine got stuck; he got onto Bobby Unser's machine and they continued in their attempt to get to safety. But Bobby Unser's machine kept breaking down: in the blowing snow, Bobby Unser and Robert Gayton used their tools and racecar know-how to get the machine running again; but, again and again, it would break down. Finally, darkness fell and Bobby Unser knew that he and his friend had to get to shelter, out of the wind, or they would quickly die.

There was a foldout saw on the snowmobile. They grabbed it and began to hike downhill and out of the wind. Robert Gayton had lost one of his gloves so Bobby Unser dug a snow cave and his friend cut wood to keep their bodies off of the snow. They spent a sleepless night in the snow cave eating candy that Bobby Unser had with him; they were cold but out of the wind at last. The next day they emerged from the snow cave to find their tracks completely obliterated. Bobby Unser knew the general direction that they had to take so they began hiking, alternately breaking trail for each other through waist-deep snow. Unbeknownst to him, Bobby Unser had gotten a virus and he was quickly becoming sicker. He began vomiting until he coughed up blood. Robert Gayton was exhausted and bitterly cold. His clothing, although new, was not as cold-resistant as Bobby Unser's gear, and he did not think he would make it. Several times he wanted to lie down to die, but Bobby Unser refused to let his friend give up. "We're going to make it," Bobby Unser told him. Through that day, that night, and into the early morning hours of the next day, they hiked. Finally they found shelter in a barn, where they also found, of all things, a telephone. Bobby Unser phoned his brother Al, putting into motion a flurry of activity that resulted in their quick rescue. When at last they reached the local hospital, they were treated for exhaustion, frostbite, dehydration, and other related ailments.

Bobby Unser was not aware that the story of his disappearance had made national headlines—in the dangerous conditions near 11,766-foot Jarosa Peak and without food or shelter, Bobby Unser was feared dead by many. But as he was battling against the elements to save his own life, Bobby Unser may have been even more surprised to learn that in the very near future he would be the subject of a U.S. Forest Service criminal investigation into his near-death experience. His alleged offense: operating a motorized vehicle in a federal wilderness area.

On January 7, 1997, still not fully recovered from this nearly fatal experience, Bobby Unser contacted the U.S. Forest Service in Albuquerque, New Mexico, in an attempt to retrieve his lost snowmobiles. He was told to come to the Forest Service office for a meeting designed to help find his snowmobiles. During the meeting, Bobby Unser could not identify any specific area in which the snowmobiles might have been abandoned.

Subsequently, as part of the Forest Service's criminal investigation of Bobby Unser, Forest Service officials requested that Bobby Unser return to the Forest Service office the next day, to review maps and photographs for the purpose of locating his snowmobiles. During Bobby Unser's meeting with the Forest Service officials, one Forest Service employee presented him with a prewritten citation charging that he had unlawfully possessed and operated a motor vehicle within a National Forest Wilderness Area and that he had aided and abetted Robert Gayton in the same violation.[3] Bobby Unser later discovered who was behind the charges. National environmental organizations had demanded that the Forest Service make an example of the famed Indy racecar driver. The Clinton administration's Forest Service and Justice Department were only too happy to oblige.

Bobby Unser was dismayed by the charge. "I nearly died," he fumed, "and my government is prosecuting me!" After some reflection, he began to wonder how he could have ended up in a wilderness area. The place he went to snowmobile—a place he had gone many times in the past—was pure multiple-use national forest. Although there was a wilderness area up there, it was some distance away. If he had accidentally wandered into the wilderness area, he had done so during the height of blizzard conditions when he had no idea where he was.

In March 1997, Bobby Unser pled not guilty to possessing and operating a motor vehicle in a wilderness area and aiding and abetting the possession and operation of a motor vehicle in a wilderness area. Just prior to trial, however, the Colorado federal district court ruled that the violations of which Bobby Unser was charged were strict liability offenses; that is, they were "public welfare offenses." As a result, the United States would not be required to prove that Bobby Unser possessed criminal intent to enter the wilderness area, what lawyers call *mens rea*. Instead, Bobby Unser could be convicted even if he had not intended to be inside the wilderness—even if he were lost when he wandered inside the wilderness or if he got there by accident. Later, the United States dismissed the aiding and abetting charge against Bobby Unser.

In June 1997, Bobby Unser had a two-day trial at the end of which the district court found him guilty and fined him $75, repeating its earlier ruling that the United States did not have to prove criminal intent.[4]

In March 1998, Bobby Unser's case was argued before the U.S. Court of Appeals for the Tenth Circuit, and, in January 1999, the Tenth Circuit affirmed his conviction, ruling, as a matter of law, that violation of the ban on motorized vehicles in wilderness areas is a public welfare offense, one that does not require proof of criminal intent.[5]

In April 1999, Bobby Unser asked the U.S. Supreme Court to hear his case. Obviously, it was not about the $75; it was about the position taken by environmental groups, federal bureaucrats, and now federal appellate judges that a man could be convicted of a felony without proof that he had intended to commit the crime. Even Bobby Unser, someone with no formal legal training, knew in his gut that there was something un-American about all this; his legal team confirmed his beliefs with fact. The Tenth Circuit's ruling directly conflicted with several rulings by the U.S. Supreme Court, including:

- Unless Congress specifies that a crime is a strict liability crime, it is not!
- To be a "public welfare crime," a crime must "seriously threaten a community's health or safety."

- Strict liability crimes are disfavored because they criminalize "a broad range of apparently innocent conduct."
- The United States bears the burden of proof on the necessity defense.

Specifically, as recently as 1994, the Supreme Court, deciding whether provisions in the National Firearms Act were strict liability crimes, concluded that "some indication of congressional intent, express or implied, is required to dispense with *mens rea* as an element of a crime."[6] The Court, although recognizing that mere possession of inherently dangerous items, such as hand grenades, subjects a person to strict liability,[7] refused to apply that rationale to the guns regulated by the National Firearms Act:

> [O]ur holding depends critically on our view that if Congress had intended to make outlaws of gun owners who were wholly ignorant of the offending characteristics of their weapons, and to subject them to lengthy prison terms, it would have spoken more clearly to that effect.[8]

The Supreme Court reached this holding, in part, because of its earlier holdings that, for a crime to be a strict liability offense, it must "seriously threaten a community's health or safety,"[9] and that a failure to require proof of *mens rea* criminalizes "a broad range of apparently innocent conduct."[10] The Tenth Circuit ignored each of these Supreme Court holdings. In addition, the Tenth Circuit violated Bobby Unser's Fifth Amendment rights to due process of law because it made him prove something that must be proved instead by the federal government—that he possessed criminal intent (*mens rea*).[11] The Tenth Circuit did so out of what it called "pragmatic concerns" that Bobby Unser might have better knowledge of where he was than did the Forest Service![12] As if it were not enough that the Tenth Circuit ignored

binding Supreme Court precedent and violated Bobby Unser's constitutional rights, the Tenth Circuit issued a decision in conflict with
decisions of several other federal appellate courts.[13]

Thus, when the nine justices met in the conference room adjacent
to the Chief Justice's chambers to consider Bobby Unser's petition,
they were confronted with a ruling in which the Tenth Circuit:[14]

- Considered an innocuous federal statute written to protect
  national forests from destruction, a statute that contained no
  indication Congress intended to make violation of the statute
  a strict liability crime;
- Concluded that possessing a snowmobile in a wilderness area
  does not "seriously threaten a community's health or safety";
- Knew that, because thousands of miles of wilderness boundaries are unmarked, making the crossing of those invisible
  boundaries strict liability crimes criminalizes apparently innocent conduct, such as crossings that are the result of accident,
  necessity, or emergency; and
- Relieved the United States of its burden to prove criminal
  intent because it would be difficult for the Forest Service to
  prove where Bobby Unser was.

The case seemed ready made for the Supreme Court to exercise its
supervisory function so as to instruct the Tenth Circuit that it meant
what it said as recently as 1994. But, on the first Monday in October
1999, the Court denied Bobby Unser's petition.[15]

WATERS OF THE UNITED STATES

About the same time that Bobby Unser went to the Forest Service
office in Albuquerque to recover his snowmobile, lost somewhere
north of Chama, Larry Squires of Hobbs, New Mexico, was trying to

recover something even more valuable—the use of his land, which had been denied him as a result of an Environmental Protection Agency (EPA) cease and desist order. Larry Squires had just learned that the U.S. Supreme Court would not hear his claim that the EPA's actions were illegal, and he wondered what to do next.

The self-proclaimed environmentalists who targeted Bobby Unser had nothing in common with Larry Squires, a *true* environmentalist. He was also a veterinarian, a rancher, and an entrepreneur; but he was an environmentalist, too. That is why, back in the late 1960s, when folks from the oil patch in the Permian Basin, one of the richest oil fields in the United States, down in Midland, Texas, talked about using the playa lakes—like Laguna Gatuna—around Larry Squires's property to dispose of oil field brine—water injected into oil wells to stimulate recovery and the natural salt that the water picks up when it is brought to the surface—Larry Squires was not concerned. Disposing of brine in the dry, alkaline sink holes—they were not really playa lakes—that covered his land and the land of his neighbors, the Bureau of Land Management (BLM) and the State of New Mexico, made sense to Larry Squires.[16] Because the Hobbs area gets about twelve inches of precipitation a year—some folks say the area is negative wet—the water disposed of there would soon evaporate. Plus, not only was the brine less salty than what occurred naturally in the sink holes, but also the water was trapped there because of the nature of the soils.

In 1969, Larry Squires formed a company, obtained leases from the BLM and New Mexico, and then charged operators to dispose of their brine in Laguna Gatuna. In 1981, he got a permit for an oil treatment plant and, over the next several years, installed facilities for separating oil from the brine after which the water was discharged into holding tanks and then into Laguna Gatuna, where it quickly evaporated. The oil was skimmed off the top of the tanks, treated in the oil treatment plant, and then reconstituted into higher grades of oil by mixing it with condensate from local gas wells. Larry Squires was proud of his operation; it was good for the environment, for the economy, and for energy production.

In November 1986, the EPA, without observing formal rulemaking procedures and without accepting any public comments, published a new rule regarding migratory birds and their impact on "waters of the United States." According to the EPA, waters of the United States included waters that "are or could be used as habitat by... migratory birds that cross state lines."[17] At the time, Larry Squires was unaware of the new rule; however, in early 1987, when he began thinking about constructing a pipeline to various oil companies to transport their brine water to his facilities, one oil company executive wondered out loud about the new migratory bird rule. Could the waters occasionally contained in Laguna Gatuna be considered waters of the United States, covered by the federal Clean Water Act, and subject to EPA regulation and permitting, he asked.

A while later, Larry Squires and his lawyer contacted the regional office of the EPA in Dallas, Texas, and asked about the new rule. Put the request in writing, they were told, and we will let you know. Larry Squires and his attorney did just that. They included in the letter a report from a University of New Mexico hydrologist that Larry Squires had hired. He had confirmed what Larry Squires knew: that there was three feet of impermeable clay beneath the sinkholes, that there was no ground water beneath the sinkholes, and that the nearest navigable stream was forty miles away. Subsequently, in August 1987, the EPA notified Larry Squires that, because "there are no recreational, industrial or other uses that could affect interstate commerce and [] the playa lake is not hydrologically connected to 'waters of the United States,' EPA agrees that Laguna Gatuna would not be considered 'water of the United States.'"[18]

In November 1988, after obtaining the necessary financing for his pipeline, entering into contracts with oil and gas operators, and receiving the required permits, rights-of-way, and leases, Larry Squires began taking waters produced from oil and gas operations through his pipeline and continued receiving brine via truck, engaging in oil recovery operations, and depositing brine into Laguna Gatuna.

In January 1991, the three federal agencies that had some interest in Larry Squires's operation, the EPA, the BLM, and the U.S. Fish and Wildlife Service (FWS), began to question anew whether the occasional waters in Laguna Gatuna were waters of the United States and hence covered by the Clean Water Act and regulated by the EPA's permitting process. Concern was expressed regarding the Aplomado falcon, the snowy plover, and brine shrimp; Larry Squires knew there was no basis for those concerns and, as a veterinarian, advised the federal agencies of that fact. Nonetheless, the drumbeat between and among the agencies regarding Laguna Gatuna grew louder and louder; soon the State of New Mexico had become involved.

Despite the EPA's clear statement in 1987 that it had no Clean Water Act jurisdiction over Laguna Gatuna, EPA officials now were questioning that decision. They did not, however, admit that they were arbitrarily abandoning their earlier position. Instead, they asserted that they had been told, erroneously, in 1987 that Laguna Gatuna "supports no wildlife of any kind" even though it now appeared, based on evidence obtained by the BLM and the FWS, that Laguna Gatuna was "used as a feeding and loafing area by migratory birds" and "as a nesting area during the breeding season." Furthermore, the EPA now asserted, "even potential use by migratory birds is sufficient" to consider Laguna Gatuna "waters of the United States." If Laguna Gatuna were declared waters of the United States, the EPA concluded, Larry Squires could not be given a Clean Water Act discharge permit.[19] Larry Squires was stunned when he received the news; only someone who had never seen Laguna Gatuna could reach those conclusions.

Larry Squires sprang into action. Beginning in April 1991, by way of letters, telephone calls, and meetings as far away as Dallas, Texas, Larry Squires, his lawyers, and his experts sought to persuade the federal and state agencies involved of the facts regarding Laguna Gatuna and his use of it as a brine disposal site.

Larry Squires pointed out that the salt in Laguna Gatuna was not the result of his use of the sink hole for the disposal of brine; instead, the salt in Laguna Gatuna was naturally occurring, the result of evaporation of rainfall and runoff and of inflow from brine springs, which made any water in Laguna Gatuna hypersaline.[20] In fact, all water for agricultural or drinking purposes had to be piped into the area. Furthermore, Larry Squires pointed out, water rarely collects in Laguna Gatuna given annual rainfall in the area of but twelve inches and an annual evaporation rate of seventy-three inches, 600 percent greater than the annual rainfall. Finally, temperatures on the bed of Laguna Gatuna often are in excess of 115 degrees Fahrenheit, thus, any rainfall or runoff evaporates almost instantaneously except during cold weather, the driest time of the year.

Larry Squires pointed out that even if all of the brine that was disposed of in Laguna Gatuna each month were disposed of during a single day it would cover Laguna Gatuna to a depth of only $\frac{1}{32}$ of an inch and would evaporate almost immediately. That amount spread over a thirty-day period would evaporate even faster.

Furthermore, if it were wildlife about which the EPA were concerned, Larry Squires told the federal officials, Laguna Gatuna, its immediate perimeter, and shoreline provide no habitat for any waterfowl, if by habitat the federal government means a place where wildlife naturally or normally lives and grows, in other words, a place that consists of living space, food, water, and cover. In fact, Laguna Gatuna provided no cover, no nesting, no living space, no water, and no food; brine shrimp could not even exist in the infrequent waters of Laguna Gatuna.

As to migratory birds, Larry Squires informed the EPA that migratory birds had never been observed doing anything more than infrequently "loafing" in Laguna Gatuna during the few, short periods that it contains water. Unfortunately, at the extremely high temperatures common in southeastern New Mexico, the water in Laguna Gatuna holds great concentrations of salt and as that material cools, the salt precipitates out, resulting in a slurry. Then, when waterfowl land on Laguna Gatuna, that salt slurry sticks to their plumage, thus preventing flight and causing mortality. Larry Squires informed the EPA that such conditions had always been present at Laguna Gatuna; they had not been exacerbated by his disposal of brine. In fact, his actions mitigated these adverse natural conditions.

Moreover, concluded Larry Squires, Laguna Gatuna is ideally suited to the deposal of brine water from oil field production: doing so is cost effective, facilitates the production of vitally important energy resources, and is an environmentally and ecologically safe method of disposing of a by product of the oil and gas recovery that takes place throughout southeastern New Mexico and west Texas.

At first it appeared that Larry Squires had been successful. After one particular set of meetings, for example, the EPA admitted that further study and thought were necessary and that, in due time, the EPA would reach its decision. In fact, in October 1991, one EPA official wrote, "we regard the limited facts before the agency insufficient for drawing firm conclusions[;] [thus,] after reviewing [Larry Squires's] memorandum and the information attached thereto, we remain undecided." Furthermore, the EPA noted that the FWS had plans to study several playas, including Laguna Gatuna, and would report on its findings.[21]

Then came the deluge, literally. The year 1992 began as an exceedingly wet year and, by the spring, the rains had reached the hundred-year stage. The Hobbs area normally receives twelve inches of rain a year, but that May nearly fourteen inches fell, resulting in substantial flooding and runoff. And, for the first time in many, many years, a lake formed at Laguna Gatuna, attracting a large number of migratory birds.

The combination of high temperatures, large concentrations of salt in the water, rapid evaporation and precipitation of salt, and the resultant production of the salt slurry trapped the ducks. FWS officials, in the process of conducting their study of playa lakes, spotted the dead ducks and, suddenly, the EPA needed no more facts—the dead birds were enough. The EPA immediately issued a cease and desist order against Larry Squires's operation, asserting that, because Laguna Gatuna "provides significant nesting, feeding and loafing area for migratory birds," it was now "waters of the United States." Apparently, the EPA, notwithstanding its letter of a few months before, now had sufficient information—the presence of a few dead ducks at Laguna Gatuna—to reach its decision!

In June 1992, at a meeting with the EPA, Larry Squires sought to replace the furor over the dead ducks with facts on the details of Laguna Gatuna and his operations. The EPA would not hear him out; officials responded with anger and hostility. In fact, when Larry Squires proposed an approach that would allow the EPA to levy a fine so as to permit all evidence to be presented to a federal district court to resolve the matter once and for all, Larry Squires was threatened with criminal charges, resultant jail time, and "the full weight of the federal government." The EPA made it very clear; Larry Squires was out of business. Larry Squires may have been shut down, but the lawyers fighting on his behalf now were very busy.

When Congress adopted the Clean Water Act in 1977,[22] it gave federal bureaucrats authority to regulate waters of the United States, meaning, because Congress's power is limited to things in or significantly affecting interstate commerce, waters that were in interstate commerce. Congress did not define what specific "waters" were in interstate commerce; it left that up to the bureaucrats. For example, although the EPA regulates "wetlands" wherever they may be found, even in the puddles in a shopping mall parking lot, the term wetlands is not included in the Clean Water Act. Thus, for the EPA, brooks, rivers, and streams are within easy reach, but isolated ponds, especially intermittent ponds like those on Larry Squires's property, are something else again. So someone thought up the Migratory Bird Rule.

The rule seemed ripe for challenge. Was the phrase "waters of the United States" so unambiguous that it clearly included Larry Squires's dry sinkholes? Even if the express language of the statute were not totally clear, did Congress intend the phrase "waters of the United States" to include Larry Squires's property? Finally, was the EPA's view of that phrase reasonable? Larry Squires and his lawyers thought the answer to each of these questions was "no" and they wanted a court to agree.

Larry Squires filed a lawsuit in the New Mexico federal district court asserting that the EPA did not have jurisdiction over his land because it contained no waters of the United States and that his due process rights under the Fifth Amendment to liberty and property had been violated. The United States advised the district court that it could not hear the case because:

- The EPA's order was only a "pre-enforcement decision[]";
- The EPA had not yet taken "final" action;
- The United States had not waived its sovereign immunity; and
- Larry Squires's Fifth Amendment rights had not yet been violated.

A short time later, the district court agreed and dismissed Larry Squires's lawsuit. None of it made sense to Larry Squires. The EPA may have argued that what it did to him was "pre-enforcement" and not yet "final" but facing a fine of $125,000 a day for the five years or so it would take to get to the U.S. Supreme Court—in the unlikely event that he would win there—was final enough for Larry Squires. Larry Squires appealed to the U.S. Court of Appeals for the Tenth Circuit.

Although the Tenth Circuit sympathized with Larry Squires's plight, it ruled against him anyway, out of concern for the needs of the EPA:

> [The] policy argument that it should not be necessary to violate an EPA order and risk civil and criminal penalties to obtain judicial review is well taken. Nevertheless, following the reasoning of our sister circuits, we reject [the] conclusion such a situation is "constitutionally intolerable." Judicial review of every unenforced compliance order would undermine the EPA's regulatory authority.[23]

Even though the U.S. Supreme Court had declared, on the very issue presented by Larry Squires, "judicial review of a final agency action by an aggrieved person will not be cut off unless there is persuasive reason to believe that such was the purpose of Congress,"[24] Larry Squires's petition for U.S. Supreme Court review was denied.[25] Amazingly enough, the Supreme Court's decision on Larry Squires's petition would not be its last word on the Migratory Bird Rule.

Denied the right to use his land, Larry Squires sought some measure of recompense; he filed a lawsuit with the U.S. Court of Federal Claims against the United States for the unconstitutional taking of his private property for public use without just compensation.[26] If the

EPA were going to use Laguna Gatuna for bird habitat, Larry Squires wanted to be paid. Over a number of years, the EPA dragged its feet attempting to prevent a ruling in the case. Finally, in early 2001, the matter was ready for trial. Ironically, only a few weeks earlier the U.S. Supreme Court had declared the Migratory Bird Rule unconstitutional.[27] Incredibly enough, the EPA seized upon that decision as the basis for a bold argument to the court as to why Larry Squires's case should be dismissed. Clearly, given the Supreme Court's decision, argued federal lawyers, the EPA had no authority to do what it did to Larry Squires. The closure of his brine disposal operation was *ultra vires* and, therefore, not a compensable act of government; instead, Larry Squires should consider a private suit against the federal employees who had done him wrong. Fortunately, the Court of Federal Claims rejected the government's argument out of hand: "The EPA's withdrawal of its cease and desist order comes nearly nine years too late for plaintiff's purposes... [because] the property lost all its economically beneficial use."[28]

Months later, Larry Squires settled his just compensation case for $2 million,[29] but he would have much preferred to have his business.

Does any of what happened to Bobby Unser and Larry Squires make sense? Are the national forests safer because Forest Service officials may criminally prosecute anyone who crosses an invisible wilderness boundary in a motorized vehicle, even someone who had no intention of being there? Are the waters of the United States—real waters, those that form in bodies on the surface and flow in the interstices beneath—safer because EPA officials may issue a cease and desist order against anyone who tries to use arid and all but useless lands? The answers to all these questions are clearly no.

These two incredible tales from New Mexico demonstrate a fact already known to many who live it every day: environmental statutes, as enforced by federal officials, have nothing to do with protecting the environment. If they did, the Forest Service would have congratulated Bobby Unser on his narrow escape and helped him locate his missing snowmobile and the EPA would have congratulated Larry Squires for finding something beneficial to do with his land, something that produced energy, jobs, and tax revenues while protecting the environment. Furthermore, both agencies would have ascertained the facts, applied the facts to the law, and then concluded that neither Bobby Unser nor Larry Squires had done anything wrong. Then both agencies would have turned to something more important.

What about the answers to another series of questions? Are our liberties less secure because federal bureaucrats are able to turn an innocent violation of an innocuous preserve-the-forest-statute into a strict liability crime or to define terms in a federal statute in such as way as to grant themselves almost unlimited power? Are our liberties less secure when federal agencies respond to the demands of special interest groups, as the Forest Service did in the case of Bobby Unser, or to the emotions of the moment, as the EPA did in the case of Larry Squires, rather than to facts and the law? Are our liberties less secure when federal courts, both trial and appellate, express more concern for the needs of federal agencies than for the constitutional rights of the citizens who seek redress of their grievances? Are our liberties less secure when elected officials—in both the legislative and executive branches of government—refuse to perform their basic duties, including: (1) defining what they mean by the laws they pass, (2) conducting effective and restraining oversight when bureaucrats ignore those meanings, and (3) ensuring that the laws are executed faithfully?

With all these folks, who have taken an oath to the Constitution, so unconcerned about the damage they are doing to the liberties guaranteed by the Constitution and the rule of law, no wonder so many citizens believe that they have to fight for their rights.

The federal government excels at enacting, interpreting, and enforcing laws. One set of laws that the federal government has enacted prohibits distinguishing between and among Americans on the basis of their race and ethnicity. In fact, federal entities and individuals who enforce this prohibition number in the thousands and populate every agency of government. Americans of good conscience do not need the federal government to tell them not to discriminate. After all, Americans know it is morally and ethically wrong to do so; plus, it is in the Declaration of Independence and in the Civil War Amendments to the Constitution. Finally, Americans know that, because blood was shed to make it so, nothing is more important. It is greatly ironic and perplexing therefore, that of the many rules that the federal government ignores, it is the Constitution's equal protection guarantee that it ignores most unabashedly and proudly.

CHAPTER 11

FIGHTING FOR THE EQUAL PROTECTION GUARANTEE

[I]n view of the constitution . . . there is in this country no superior, dominant, ruling class of citizens. There is no caste here.
Our constitution is color-blind, and neither knows nor tolerates
classes among citizens.

U.S. SUPREME COURT JUSTICE JOHN MARSHALL HARLAN, 1896[1]

[U]nder our Constitution there can be no such thing as either a
creditor or debtor race. That concept is alien to the Constitution's
focus upon the individual. . . . In the eyes of government, we are
just one race here. It is American.

U.S. SUPREME COURT JUSTICE ANTONIN SCALIA, 1995[2]

The federal government owns one-third of the nation's land, most
of it in the American West, where at least 50 percent of the land
in many of the eleven western states is owned and managed by
federal government.[3] That land includes national parks, wildlife
refuges, national forests, national recreation areas, and vast tracts of
otherwise not specifically designated public land; that land is managed by the National Park Service, U.S. Fish and Wildlife Service, U.S.
Forest Service, Bureau of Reclamation, Bureau of Land Management,
and other federal agencies.[4] Thus, when highways, roads, and byways

upon that federal land needs to be constructed, improved, or repaired, the contract to do so is let, not by a western state department of transportation, but by a federal agency specifically tasked with that responsibility. That is how a rural, isolated, picturesque bit of asphalt in a national forest became the focal point of a nationwide controversy and the basis for one of the most important U.S. Supreme Court civil rights rulings in history.[5]

Northeast of the Four Corners of New Mexico, Arizona, Utah, and Colorado, lies Cortez, just north of the Ute Mountain Indian Reservation and Mesa Verde National Park. Colorado Highway 145 is the scenic route from Cortez through the San Juan National Forest to the Telluride Ski Resort, a route that follows the Dolores River into pine and aspen forests with one of Colorado's "Fourteeners," a peak in excess of 14,000 feet, Mount Wilson, looming in the distance. Just before reaching the tiny town of Stoner on Highway 145, a Forest Service road heads north along West Dolores Creek and crosses from Montezuma County into Dolores County. It was here, along a five-mile stretch of this two-lane road, that the U.S. Forest Service, in the late 1980s, planned a repaving and guardrail project.

In August 1989, the Central Federal Lands Highway Division (CFLHD) of the Federal Highway Administration and the U.S. Department of Transportation issued a solicitation for bids for the West Dolores project. Subsequently, the winning bidder sought a subcontractor to perform the guardrail portion of the contract. Although Adarand Constructors, Inc., a small, family-owned business located in Colorado Springs, Colorado, and operated by Randy Pech, submitted the lowest bid, it was denied the subcontract.

Instead, the guardrail subcontract was awarded to a minority-owned business certified as a "Disadvantaged Business Enterprise" (DBE) under a federal program that, in this case, provided a $10,000 bonus to the prime contractor for awarding the contract—not to the lowest bidder, but to the lowest *minority* bidder or DBE. For Randy Pech, the loss of the West Dolores Project was the last straw. He decided to fight back against a policy often, but incorrectly, referred to as "affirmative action," which Randy Pech calls "racial discrimination" and which others label "racial preferences" or "racial quotas."[6]

In 1980, the U.S. Supreme Court had upheld the constitutionality of the first congressional program that set aside a portion of federal contracts for businesses owned by racial minorities, ostensibly because the federal program was a "pilot program...limited in extent and duration."[7] In 1989, however, in considering the constitutionality of a similar program adopted by Richmond, Virginia, the Court declared that Richmond's program violated the U.S. Constitution's Equal Protection Clause.[8] It appeared that the Supreme Court's 1980 decision regarding federal race-based contracting was doomed. Then, in June 1990, the Court surprisingly refused to apply its ruling in the Richmond case to race-based decision-making by the federal government.[9] It was against this backdrop that Randy Pech filed his lawsuit two months later, a year to the date from when the federal government issued its solicitation for the West Dolores project.

Randy Pech had started his business in 1976 shortly after leaving college for a more entrepreneurial endeavor. He liked to work hard and he did not mind getting his hands dirty in the process. His father, who had been reading about the guardrail business, brought it to Randy's attention and it seemed like a perfect match. Randy recruited a friend to help and together they sought to obtain the loan they needed to get started. They soon discovered that no bank would loan them the money, not even the bank in which his friend's father was employed, even though the man was one of the bank's bigger customers and served on its board of directors. Finally, Randy Pech's father pitched them an idea: he would put his entire retirement up as collateral for the loan. At last Adarand Constructors, Inc., named using a combination of Randy's first name and his partner's last name, was formed.

Randy did some research to determine what equipment he would need to start, and before long, he bid on his first job, a little guardrail project outside of Golden, Colorado. It turned out to be an enormous challenge! While digging one of his first postholes, Randy Pech hit rock, and a job that should have taken two weeks took two months. As he worked day and night to resolve various problems, he began questioning his decision to go into business for himself. At one point, as he and his father were driving to get another piece of equipment to break through the rock, Randy Pech looked anxiously over at his father, fearing that he was about to lose the life savings of the man who had placed all his trust in him. "I nearly lost it right then and there," Randy said much later. "But Dad never said a thing; he just backed me up."

Randy Pech never gave up. He learned about the business and he worked hard. As other guardrail contractors went out of business, Adarand began to prosper. Randy bid on every job in Colorado and some jobs in Wyoming and New Mexico. More times than not, he was the low bidder and did quality work on the timely basis. Contractors trusted him and wanted to work with him. They knew they could trust Randy to do an excellent job and to treat them fairly and honestly. Randy was living the American dream and nothing should have stood in his way. Then came federal racial preferences.

Randy Pech did not mind losing business to the other guardrail contractors that were owned by racial minorities—that is, when they had submitted the lowest bid, which they were perfectly capable of doing. That was part of the business; next time he would just have to work harder, pinch the pennies tighter, and cut his costs and profits to the bare minimum. What galled Randy Pech was when, after he did all that, he lost the guardrail subcontract to a minority-owned business, not because the minority-owned firm had submitted the lowest bid but because of the federally mandated racial set-asides.

That is what happened on the West Dolores project. Randy Pech had underbid the minority-owned business by nearly $2,000, but that did not make up for the $10,000 the United States gave to the prime contractor to award the job to the minority-owned firm. Defenders of the program called the $10,000 an incentive for contractors to work with minority-owned businesses; the federal government said the $10,000 was reimbursement for costs incurred by the contractor in working with unqualified minority-owned businesses; others simply called the $10,000 what it was, a bribe. Whatever it was called, Randy Pech knew it was wrong and, from what he remembered studying in government class, he thought it was unconstitutional. Randy Pech knew it was a long shot to try to take a case all the way to the U.S. Supreme Court, but he did not think he had any other choice.

Not surprisingly, given the Supreme Court's June 1990 ruling, both the U.S. District Court for Colorado and the U.S. Court of Appeals for the Tenth Circuit made quick work of Randy Pech's lawsuit. In February 1994, the Tenth Circuit, as the federal district court had done earlier, dismissed *Adarand Constructors, Inc. v. Peña*. In May 1994, Randy Pech filed his petition seeking Supreme Court review. For, in Randy Pech's experience, despite the Supreme Court's 1980 prediction that race-based decision-making in federal government contracting would be limited in extent and duration, it was neither. Not only did Congress regularly reauthorize its requirement that a percentage of the work performed in federal highway construction projects be done by firms owned by racial minorities,[10] a percentage that ranged from 5 to 18 percent, Congress defined "socially and economically disadvantaged" business enterprises to include all firms owned by "Black Americans, Hispanic Americans, Native Americans, [and] Asian Pacific Americans" regardless of the owners' social background or economic status. In fact, state agencies were instructed, in certifying businesses as DBEs, to "rel[y] on this presumption" and "not [to] investigate the social or economic status of individuals who fall into one of the presumptive groups."[11] Maybe the Supreme Court, Randy Pech thought, will reconsider what it did in 1980 given what had happened to him.

To the amazement of most legal experts and observers and the delight of Randy Pech, on September 26, 1994, the Supreme Court agreed to hear his case. After the case was briefed throughout the fall of 1994, on January 17, 1995, the day following Martin Luther King Jr. Day, Randy Pech, his wife, and his partner were present when oral arguments began before a standing room only crowd in the Supreme Court Chamber. After the Chief Justice intoned, "We'll hear argument first this morning in Number 93-1841, *Adarand Constructors, Inc., v. Federico Peña,*" oral arguments began. An hour later, the Chief Justice declared, "The case is submitted."

Interestingly enough, in the days following oral arguments, commentators from the Left and Right weighed in on the *Adarand* case. Richard Cohen of *The Washington Post* Writers Group wrote, "[Affirmative action] has outlived its usefulness . . . . [I]t violates the American creed that we must be judged as individuals, not on the basis of race or sex. . . ."[12] Pat Buchanan announced, "[I]t's time to make law in America what it always should have been in the Land of the Free: color blind. Wasn't that the dream?"[13] Then, a mere five weeks after *Adarand* was argued at the Supreme Court, *The Washington Post* reported, on February 24, 1995, that President Clinton had ordered an "intense, urgent review" of affirmative action.[14] Were Clinton and his advisers sensing defeat?

On June 12, 1995, Chief Justice Rehnquist called upon Justice O'Connor to deliver the opinion of the Court in *Adarand Constructors, Inc. v. Peña.* After a brief review of the facts, she announced that the equal protection guarantee protects individuals, not groups. She also set forth the three responses of the Court to the use of race by Congress: skepticism, consistency, and congruence. Then, she dropped the bombshell: *Metro Broadcasting*, decided a mere five years earlier, was overruled. By implication, so too was the Court's 1980 decision in *Fullilove*. The bottom line was, she declared, Congress had to meet the "strict scrutiny" test the Court had imposed fatally on Richmond's race-based contracting program.

The significance of the Court's ruling in *Adarand* cannot be overstated; it was a clear repudiation of much that the federal Executive and Congress had been doing for nearly thirty years. Although it was consistent with what the Supreme Court had ruled often in the past, it was also an open break from the Court's more recent jurisprudence on race-based decision-making by the federal government.[15] Its significance requires a properly thorough analysis.

Justice O'Connor wrote for the Court, "[a]fter reviewing the 'complex scheme of federal statutes and regulations...implicate[d]'" by the "fairly straightforward facts" of the case,[16] determining that Adarand "has standing to bring this lawsuit [for "forward-looking relief"],"[17] and reflecting on the difference between the equal protection language of the Fifth Amendment ("No person shall...be deprived of life, liberty, or property, without due process of law") and the Fourteenth Amendment ("No State shall...deny to any person... the equal protection of the laws"), the Court concluded that it was "necessary to revisit the issue."[18] That review yielded "three general propositions with respect to governmental racial classifications."[19]

First, skepticism: "'[A]ny preference based on racial or ethnic criteria must necessarily receive a most searching examination;'" "[A]ny official action that treats a person differently on account of his race or ethnic origin is inherently suspect;" "[R]acial classifications [are] 'constitutionally suspect;'" "Distinctions between citizens solely because of their ancestry are by their very nature odious to a free people." Second, consistency: "the standard of review under the Equal Protection Clause is not dependent on the race of those burdened or benefited by a particular classification"; all racial classifications reviewable under the Equal Protection Clause must be scrutinized strictly. And third, congruence: "[e]qual protection analysis in the Fifth Amendment area is the same as that under the Fourteenth Amendment"; in other words, the Constitution demands no less of Congress than it demands of state and local governments in their inability to discrimination between and among Americans on the basis of their race.[20]

Justice O'Connor concluded:

> Taken together, these three propositions lead to the conclusion that any person, of whatever race, has the right to demand that any governmental actor subject to the Constitution justify any racial classification subjecting that person to unequal treatment under the strictest judicial scrutiny.[21]

Justice O'Connor then focused her attention on the "surprising turn" taken by the Court in its 1990 decision in *Metro Broadcasting*.[22] In O'Connor's view, the use, by the *Metro Broadcasting* Court, of "intermediate scrutiny" to review congressionally mandated "benign" racial classifications that serve the "important governmental objective" of "enhancing broadcast diversity" departed from prior Court holdings in two important respects.[23]

First, it ignored the Court's 1989 holding in *Croson* that strict scrutiny must be used to "smoke out" "what classifications are 'benign' or 'remedial' and what classifications are in fact motivated by illegitimate notions of racial inferiority or simple racial politics" and to determine that "the means chosen 'fit' th[e] compelling goal so closely that there is little or no possibility that the motive for the classification was illegitimate racial prejudice or stereotype."[24]

Second, *Metro Broadcasting* "squarely rejected" the Court's earlier requirement for "congruence between the standards applicable to federal and state racial classifications. . ."[25] As a result, *Metro Broadcasting* "undermined" the other two propositions that emerge from the Court's equal protection cases: "skepticism of all racial classifications, and consistency of treatment irrespective of the race of the burdened or benefited group."[26]

More importantly, ventured O'Connor, *Metro Broadcasting*'s attack on these three propositions threatens the basic principle of the Fifth and Fourteenth Amendments, that the protection guaranteed is for "*persons*, not *groups*," and that it is a "*personal* right to equal protection of the laws [that may not be] infringed."[27] All of which led the Court to hold:

> [T]hat all racial classifications, imposed by whatever federal, state, or local governmental actor, must be analyzed by a reviewing court under strict scrutiny. In other words, such classifications are constitutional only if they are narrowly tailored measures that further compelling governmental interests. To the extent that *Metro Broadcasting* is inconsistent with that holding, it is overruled.[28]

After addressing aspects of the lead dissent filed by Justice Stevens—primarily by offering up portions of Stevens's powerful attack on race-based decision-making in his dissent in *Fullilove* and his concurring opinion in *Croson*—Justice O'Connor turned to the matter of *stare decisis*.[29] Concluding that *Metro Broadcasting* "itself departed" from the Court's prior holdings, and did so "quite recently,"[30] "we cannot adhere to our most recent decision without colliding with an accepted and established doctrine."[31] Finally, Justice O'Connor concluded "[t]here is nothing new about the notion that Congress, like the states, may treat people differently because of their race only for compelling reasons."[32]

To emphasize that the Court's opinion in *Adarand* is a simple return to "first principles" Justice O'Connor wrote, "Our action today makes explicit what Justice Powell thought implicit in the *Fullilove* lead opinion: federal racial classifications, like those of a State, must serve a compelling governmental interest, and must be narrowly tailored to further that interest."[33] Yet the use of strict scrutiny does not mean that government is "disqualified from acting in response" to "the practice and the lingering effects of racial discrimination against minority groups in this country..."[34] Strict scrutiny "says nothing about the ultimate validity of any particular law."[35] What it does say is that, "whenever the government treats any person unequally because of his or her race, that person has suffered an injury that falls squarely within the language and spirit of the Constitution's guarantee of equal protection."[36]

Noting that the Court's decision in *Adarand* "alters the playing field in some important respects," the Court remanded *Adarand* to the lower courts "for further consideration in light of the principles we have announced."[37] Justices Scalia and Thomas filed concurring opinions,[38] while Justices Stevens, Souter, Ginsburg and Breyer filed various dissenting opinions.[39]

The evening of June 12, 1995, the Supreme Court's decision in *Adarand* was the lead story on all three networks; they reported it as a landmark ruling.[40] The next morning, *Adarand* was at the top of the front page of every major newspaper in the country. *The New York Times* headlined, "By 5–4, Justices Cast Doubts on U.S. Programs That Give Preferences Based on Race—Debate Is Fueled—Rigorous Criteria Set for Court's Approval of Such Programs."[41] Joan Biskupic, beneath a front-page headline in *The Washington Post* that read, "Court Toughens Standard for Federal Affirmative Action," wrote, "The Supreme Court . . . jeopardized a broad range of federal affirmative action programs with a ruling that set a tough new standard."[42] *The Washington Times*, beneath this headline, "Affirmative Action Dealt Blow by Court," reported, "The Supreme Court yesterday imposed strict new limits on politically charged federal affirmative-action programs and required agencies to justify every instance of reverse discrimination."[43]

Indeed, it looked as if federal race-based highway and other federal contracting programs were doomed awaiting only factual findings by the Colorado federal district court to which the case had been remanded before the Supreme Court would invalidate the program as unconstitutional. Nonetheless, the Clinton administration was unrepentant. On July 19, 1995, Clinton announced to a nationwide audience that his approach to affirmative action was to "mend it, don't end it."[44] Clinton's Civil Rights Division at the Department of Justice, however, got Clinton's real message. "It is important for us all not to be intimidated by *Adarand*. We have to take *Adarand* on."[45] So Clinton's lawyers did, first by stonewalling and delaying; then by raising every procedural and substantive argument available, even some that the Supreme Court had rejected in its 1995 *Adarand* ruling.[46]

At last, in June 1997, nearly two years after the Supreme Court issued its landmark decision and after months of lengthy depositions conducted by Clinton lawyers plus briefings and oral arguments, the Colorado federal district court ruled in favor of Randy Pech. The district court ruled that, although the federal program served a "compelling governmental interest," that of redressing past discrimination, it was not "narrowly tailored."[47] The Clinton administration appealed to the Tenth Circuit, which, purportedly because of new regulations adopted by the Clinton administration, declared, in March 1999, that

Adarand Constructors, Inc. v. Slater was now moot.[48] Adarand's petition for rehearing *en banc* was denied summarily. In other words, Adarand's urgings that at least some of the judges on the Tenth Circuit adhere to what the Supreme Court ruled in its 1995 *Adarand* decision fell on deaf ears. Again, Adarand petitioned the Supreme Court to intercede.

On January 12, 2000, the Supreme Court granted Adarand's petition for *writ* of *certiorari*, then, without further briefing, reversed, and remanded the case to the Tenth Circuit after holding, unanimously (*per curiam*), that the case was not moot.[49] Back at the Tenth Circuit, the appellate court ordered supplemental briefing on two narrow questions, one of which was whether the Tenth Circuit could declare the case moot, notwithstanding the Supreme Court's ruling of mere days before! Then, in September 2000, the Tenth Circuit reversed the 1997 ruling of the Colorado federal district court and held that the federal race-based highway contracting program had, at one time, been, but was no longer, unconstitutional.[50] Yet again, Adarand asked the Supreme Court to issue a final ruling in the case. In March 2001, the Supreme Court agreed to hear *Adarand Constructors, Inc. v. Mineta*.

Although the Clinton administration, in its opposition to Adarand's petition for *writ* of *certiorari*, had defended the program's constitutionality, the newly installed Bush administration adopted a different tactic. Solicitor General Ted Olson argued, in the Bush administration's brief and during oral arguments on October 31, 2001, that so much had changed in the federal program since the Court's 1995 *Adarand* ruling that the case had "outlived itself." In fact, Mr. Olson went so far as to withdraw one offending and clearly unconstitutional *Federal Register* document during the oral arguments. On November 27, 2001, the petition was "dismissed as improvidently granted" (called a "dig" by Court insiders) by the Supreme Court.[51] There would be no final ruling by the

Supreme Court on the constitutionality of the federal government's program of awarding federal highway construction contracts on the basis of race.[52] In other words, the Court would not have the opportunity, at least not now, of applying its 1995 ruling in *Adarand Constructors, Inc. v. Peña* to that program.[53]

Thus, the Tenth Circuit had proved itself more implacable and indefatigable than the Supreme Court. Not only did the Tenth Circuit refuse to apply the Supreme Court's 1995 *Adarand* ruling as Justice O'Connor wrote and intended it, the Tenth Circuit turned that ruling on its head using it as a basis for upholding federal racial preferences and quotas. In fact, the Tenth Circuit justified its decision using the very bases set forth by the Supreme Court in *Fullilove* and *Metro Broadcasting*, which the 1995 *Adarand* ruling rejected, as well as the arguments made by the justices who dissented in the 1995 *Adarand* ruling and in *Croson*.[54]

Meanwhile, Marc Lenart who owns and operates tiny Concrete Works of Colorado was deep into his lawsuit against the City and County of Denver for its race-based construction contracting program, which he had filed in 1989, after being denied contracts by Denver.[55] Like Randy Pech, Marc Lenart had been before the Colorado federal district court and the Tenth Circuit, but with different results. In 1994, the Tenth Circuit ruled that the Colorado federal district court had erred when it granted summary judgment in favor of Denver and that the matter should proceed to trial.[56]

In 1999, Judge Richard B. Matsch, who had presided over the Oklahoma City federal building bombing trial, conducted a painstaking three-week trial in which he heard from scores of expert and fact witnesses and considered stacks of expert reports. In March 2000, he ruled that, in accordance with the Supreme Court's 1989 ruling in *Croson*, the Denver program was unconstitutional.[57] Denver appealed to the Tenth Circuit.

At the Tenth Circuit, Marc Lenart argued that the proper test to apply was that set out by the Supreme Court in 1989 in *Croson*, not the perversion adopted by the Tenth Circuit in *Adarand*. Nonetheless, and not surprisingly, the Tenth Circuit applied its own ruling in *Adarand* and held that Denver's program was constitutional.[58] Marc Lenart asked the Supreme Court to review the ruling.

Remarkably, in November 2003, the Supreme Court rejected the case.[59] Justice Scalia filed a stinging dissent, however, in which he was joined by Chief Justice Rehnquist. Justice Scalia called Denver's assertion that its set-aside program was limited to victims of racial discrimination "a sham." In fact, he wrote, the only function of Denver's program is to "channel a fixed percentage of city contracting dollars to firms identified by race."[60] As to the Supreme Court's requirement for a "strong basis in evidence" prior to the use of racial preferences, Justice Scalia declared that the "District Court was correct, and the Tenth Circuit mistaken," that is, "the Tenth Circuit got it exactly backwards."[61]

Justice Scalia found "at least two serious errors" by the Tenth Circuit "that infect [Denver's] statistical evidence." First, Denver "assumed that minority firms were on average as qualified, willing, and able as others." Second, Denver assumed that the minority firms, which were smaller and less experienced, could have won the contracts. The Tenth Circuit was able to reverse the factual findings of the District Court on such matters, notwithstanding that court's detailed and thorough analysis, because the Tenth Circuit views the Supreme Court's requirement for a "strong basis in evidence" as a question of law to be reviewed *de novo* by the Tenth Circuit rather than merely for "clear error."[62] Because the federal appellate courts conflict on this issue, Justice Scalia urged the granting of the petition.[63]

Justice Scalia scolded his colleagues for declining to grant the petition, declaring that their refusal "invites speculation that [the Court's earlier rejection of racial preferences in contracting] has effectively been overruled." "We should grant *certiorari* to make clear that we stand by [our] insistence that '[r]acial classifications are suspect'... and that the courts will employ 'searching judicial inquiry into the justification for such race-based measures ... to [']smoke out['] illegitimate uses of race.'"[64]

Just before the Supreme Court declined to hear Marc Lenart's case, federal appellate consideration of the issue had taken an even more insidious turn. In October 2003, the U.S. Court of Appeals for the Eighth Circuit decided two cases, one out of Minnesota, the other out of Nebraska, challenging the very program contested by Randy Pech. In what some legal experts called an indolent opinion, the Eighth Circuit declined to apply "strict scrutiny" as the Supreme Court had commanded in its 1995 *Adarand* ruling. Instead, the Eighth Circuit referenced the 2000 *Adarand* ruling by the Tenth Circuit and embraced that perversion of the Supreme Court's 1995 *Adarand* ruling.[65] Now two federal appellate courts covering thirteen states in the West and Midwest had upheld the use of racial preferences and quotas in federal highway construction contracting a mere eight years after the Supreme Court apparently had sealed its doom. Incredibly, the Supreme Court declined to hear both cases.[66] This time, Justice Scalia did not bother to file a dissent.[67]

In 2003, *Time*, anticipating the potential resignation of Chief Justice Rehnquist, wrote a lengthy retrospective on his years as Chief Justice of the United States. One of the five cases listed as part of his legacy was *Adarand Constructors, Inc. v. Peña*. "[I]t was Rehnquist's court that ruled in [*Adarand*] in 1995 that preferential treatment based on race in government programs is almost always unconstitutional. This was a legal earthquake, throwing into doubt most of the government's affirmative action programs."[68] *Time* quoted one law professor who proclaimed, "No matter what it decide[d] in the

Michigan cases, [*Adarand*] has made it harder across the board to have affirmative action."[69]

That is all true; however, what happened to the case brought by Randy Pech with the hope that the Court would permanently invalidate race-based highway contracting by governments demonstrates the relative weakness of the Supreme Court when faced with a relentless war of attrition by radical groups, rapacious bureaucrats, and activist judges, all aided by U.S. senators and members of the U.S. House of Representatives who feel no obligation whatsoever to ensure the constitutionality of the laws they pass. That is why people like Randy Pech and Marc Lenart must undertake the battle themselves.[70]

Theoretically, at least, the federal government's use of racial quotas and preferences has the purported objective of achieving equality. Of course, it is not the equality of which most Americans conceive when they hear that word, which is equal opportunity, instead of equal outcome. Nonetheless, the federal government's use of racial quotas and preferences appears absolutely fair and just when compared to the federal government's demand for what one federal judge referred to derisively as "electoral apartheid."[71]

CHAPTER 12

FIGHTING DEMANDS FOR THE RACIAL GERRYMANDERING OF ELECTION DISTRICTS

The conversation soon turned to the topic of Lani Guinier, whose nomination to the Justice Department President Clinton had recently abandoned after the disclosure of her writings on behalf of the idea that American civil rights law requires the election of minorities. At some point, I offered the thought that the story behind the story in the Lani Guinier affair had little to do with civil rights and much to do with communism. The central idea she was advancing—proportional representation—had been tried not only to sorry effect in Europe but also, in the 1940s, in New York City. There it gained only one result, the installation of two Communists on the City Council.

SETH LIPSKY – *WALL STREET JOURNAL* EDITORIAL PAGE[1]

I n the summer of 1999, a government vehicle pulled into the sleepy little north Montana town of Chinook, the county seat of Blaine County, which lies hard up against the Canadian border along what Montanans refer to as "the Highline."[2] The car pulled slowly down Chinook's tiny Main Street and parked at the courthouse, where three lawyers in dark suits emerged, briefcases in hand. Moments later, they were inside sitting across a long conference table from the three Blaine County commissioners.

The suits were from President Bill Clinton's Department of Justice, specifically its Civil Rights Division, which was headed by Acting Assistant Attorney General Bill Lann Lee. Mr. Lee was acting because the U.S. Senate, aware of his radical views, had refused to confirm him; thereupon, Clinton put him in the job anyway.[3] The lawyers from the Justice Department were there to make the commissioners and other Blaine County officials an offer they could not refuse. Not surprisingly, the meeting did not go well.

The U.S. Department of Justice formally advised Blaine County that the manner in which it elected its commissioners—that is, at-large from three residential districts—violated the federal Voting Rights Act because it prevented local American Indians from electing their "candidates of choice." It was irrelevant that Blaine County's system of electing commissioners was state law, that no American Indian in Blaine County had ever been denied the right to register, vote, or run for office, and that the most recent commissioner elected received 98 percent of the American Indian vote. Blaine County was told that, if it did not accede to the Clinton administration's demands, the Justice Department would name each of its officials in a federal lawsuit. With that, the government lawyers left the courthouse and drove quickly out of town.[4]

THE VOTING RIGHTS ACT

There is not just one "Voting Rights Act" or "Civil Rights Act"; indeed, there has been a long series of federal acts adopted with the intention of guaranteeing the rights of all Americans, regardless or race or ethnicity, to register, vote, and run for office. Each was enacted, pursuant to the Constitution's Fifteenth Amendment, in response to the refusal of various state and local officials to allow minorities, at first African-Americans and later Hispanics and American Indians, the right to vote.[5] Thus, Congress enacted the Civil Rights Act of 1870,[6] the Civil Rights Act of 1957,[7] the Civil Rights Act of 1960,[8] the Civil Rights Act of 1964,[9] and, finally, the Voting Rights Act of 1965.[10]

In Section 2 of the Voting Rights Act, Congress codified the Fifteenth Amendment and, in Section 5, required that the U.S. Department of Justice "preclear" any voting changes in "covered jurisdictions," that is, those counties and states with a history of unconstitutional racial discrimination undertaken to deny citizens their right to vote that "has the effect of denying or abridging the right to vote." Not surprisingly, most covered jurisdictions were in the South. In 1970 and 1975, Congress further expanded the Voting Rights Act.

In 1966, the U.S. Supreme Court upheld the constitutionality of Section 5's preclearance requirements and its "effect" test in light of the history considered by Congress of the intransigent, pervasive, and flagrant efforts by certain states to deny African Americans the right to vote.[11] In 1980, however, Court refused to apply the reasoning of Section 5—and its prohibition against adoption of new at-large voting requirements in covered jurisdictions—to Section 2, which contained only the Fifteenth Amendment's voting right guarantee:

> The Fifteenth Amendment does not entail the right to have Negro candidates elected. [It] prohibits only purposefully discriminatory denial or abridgment by government of the freedom to vote "on account of race, color, or previous condition of servitude." Having found that Negroes in Mobile *register and vote without hindrance,*" the District Court and Court of Appeals were in error in [holding that the Fifteenth Amendment had been violated] in the present case.[12]

After all, the Court had held for years that at-large voting is constitutional unless adopted to minimize the voting potential of racial or ethnic minorities.[13] For the Court, violation of the Fifteenth Amendment required a racially discriminatory purpose; a racially disproportionate impact alone was not enough.[14]

Congress responded angrily and, in 1982, amended Section 2 of the Voting Rights Act to overturn the Court's 1980 ruling and to redefine the Fifteenth Amendment.[15] Congress made clear that its "principle immediate target" was "the at-large system of election"[16] and that it objected to the Supreme Court's "intent test" because: "[1] [T]he test asks the wrong question. [W]hat motives were in an official's mind...is of the most limited relevance. [2] [T]he intent test is unnecessarily divisive because it involves charges of racism on the part of the individual officials or entire communities. [3] [T]he intent test will be an inordinately difficult burden for plaintiffs in most cases."[17] By amending Section 2, Congress not only exceeded its authority under the Constitution, it also equated the mere inability of a racial minority to succeed at the polls with a constitutional violation. Moreover, it relieved those who would file Section 2 lawsuits of the obligation to do what litigants must ordinarily do—carry the heavy burden of proving intent.

As amended by Congress, Section 2 now provides:

> No voting...procedure shall be imposed or applied by any State or political subdivision in a manner which *results* in a denial or abridgement of the right of any citizen of the United States to vote on account of race or color...[including that racial minorities] have less opportunity than other members of the electorate *to participate in the political process and to elect representatives of their choice.*[18]

Lawyers in the Justice Department's Civil Rights Division and in organizations like the ACLU and the NAACP Legal Defense Fund now had the ammunition they needed to file lawsuits, not just in the South, but all across the country, including against local jurisdictions that had never denied minorities the right to vote. Use of Section 2's "representatives of their choice" language by the Civil Rights Division began in earnest after Bill Clinton's election. The division soon went after Montana's Blaine County.

BLAINE COUNTY, MONTANA, GOES ON TRIAL

Blaine County is a rural county sixty miles east to west and ninety miles north to south; covering an area of approximately 4,638 square miles, it is the ninth largest of Montana's fifty-six counties. Populated primarily with ranchers and farmers, Blaine County is also the poorest county in Montana, which may be one reason why it was targeted by federal lawyers.[19] In its southeastern quadrant lies the Fort Belknap Reservation, part of which carries over into neighboring Phillips County to the east.

According to the 2000 Census, 7,009 people reside in Blaine County; 52.6 percent (3,685) are White and 45.4 percent (3,180) are American Indians, 83 percent of whom live on the reservation. Although members of the Assiniboine people and the Gros Ventre people reside there, the federally recognized tribe to which members of both groups have been assigned by the federal government is the Fort Belknap tribe. American Indians constitute 38.8 percent of the voting-age population of Blaine County; Whites constitute 59.4 percent.

In accordance with Montana Statute, Blaine County's Board of Commissioners consists of three full-time commissioners, each of whom must live in a different residential district, elected for six-year staggered terms with one commissioner elected every even-numbered year in November, coinciding with federal elections.[20] Though each commissioner must live in a different residential district, each was elected at-large, that is, by a majority all those voting throughout Blaine County.

In November 1999, after Blaine County refused to agree to the demands of the U.S. Department of Justice, the federal government sued Blaine County, Montana, its county commissioners, and its clerk and recorder, in their official capacities, charging that they had violated Section 2 of the Voting Rights Act and asking the Montana federal district court to order creation of a district that would guarantee election of an American Indian commissioner, that is, a "majority-minority-single member district." To succeed, asserted federal lawyers, they need only prove, with voting records and statistical experts, that American Indians in Blaine County vote as a bloc; that non-Indians in Blaine County vote as a bloc; and, that American Indian candidates usually suffer electoral defeat.

That was not enough, responded Blaine County; the Constitution requires much more, as does even the Voting Rights Act. Thus, argued Blaine County, the federal government had to prove: that alleged non-Indian bloc voting was the result of past or present racial hostility and a desire by non-Indians to prevent the election of American Indian candidates; that the socioeconomic and educational status of American Indians, and hence their voting patterns, was the result of racial discrimination by Montana and Blaine County; that there were distinct political issues of importance to American Indians, which the Blaine County Commission had the authority to address; and, that American Indians in Blaine County had been denied, not only the ability to elect American Indian candidates, but also the ability to participate equally in the electoral process.

Not surprisingly, federal lawyers vigorously disputed Blaine County's evidentiary standard; nonetheless, they said, they had evidence that Blaine County had discriminated against local American

Indian voters. For example, they said, there were no voting machines on the Fort Belknap Indian Reservation until 1941. In other words, federal lawyers filed a Voting Rights Act lawsuit in 1999 as a result of what they purported to be racially discriminatory conduct that had occurred nearly sixty years earlier. That was nothing Blaine County would discover. At trial, federal officials would introduce evidence of racism from the late 1800s.

Before the matter could proceed to trial, however, Blaine County moved for summary judgment in its favor arguing that Section 2 of the Voting Rights Act, as amended in 1982, is unconstitutional as a result of a series of U.S. Supreme Court cases that limited Congress's power to enforce the Civil Rights Amendments. As one federal appellate court put it, the Supreme Court "since 1997 introduced an entirely new framework for analyzing the scope of Congress's power under Section 5 of the Fourteenth Amendment."[21] For example, in *City of Boerne v. Flores*, the Supreme Court struck down the Religious Freedom Restoration Act, declaring that the federal government is a "government of enumerated powers."[22]

Although the Constitution specifically limits congressional authority, those limits were waived by the states when they ratified Section 5 of the Fourteenth Amendment and Section 2 of the Fifteenth Amendment, which granted Congress the power to enforce the Civil War Amendments by "appropriate legislation."[23] For congressional legislation to be an "appropriate" means of enforcing those Amendments however, "there must be congruence and proportionality between the means used and the needs to be achieved."[24] In other words, before Congress may enforce the rights guaranteed under the Civil War Amendments by prohibiting conduct heretofore the responsibility of the sovereign states, Congress must have "identified a history and pattern of unconstitutional state transgressions,"[25] including "widespread and persisting deprivation of constitutional rights."[26] The

Supreme Court's "new framework" seemed tailor made for striking down Section 2 of the Voting Rights Act.

Unfortunately, in the meantime, the Montana federal district judge presiding over the case recused himself shortly after the American Civil Liberties Union (ACLU) sought, on behalf of several local American Indians and the tribe, to intervene.[27] A Nevada federal district judge was assigned the case; he quickly brushed aside Blaine County's constitutional arguments and scheduled the matter for trial. Attorneys for Blaine County and the federal government rushed to depose witnesses and to prepare for the battle of the experts that lay ahead.

A two-week trial was held in Great Falls, Montana, in October 2001; scores of fact and expert witnesses were called and hundreds of documents were introduced, which, in Blaine County's view, demonstrated that:

- American Indians had little interest in commissioner elections because there was no distinct political issue unique to them on which the commission could legally take action;
- American Indians had little interest in running for commissioner since 83 percent lived on the Fort Belknap Reservation, which, along with the Bureau of Indian Affairs (BIA), provided all the services there that the County provided elsewhere, plus many more;
- American Indians voted in the Democratic primaries; in fact, their support determined that party's nominee;
- American Indians voted in the general elections; in fact, their support ensured victory for the Democratic nominee;
- American Indians suffered socioeconomically but no more so than non-Indians and perhaps less so given the safety net provided by tribal government and the BIA;

- Non-Indians did not vote as a racial bloc nor were their votes motivated by racial animus or a desire to prevent American Indian candidates from winning election;
- Instances of alleged racial discrimination were anecdotal and not supported by other evidence, badly dated, or not directed at American Indians;
- Montana statutes, going as far back as Montana's territorial days, did not discriminate against American Indians; and
- Any discrimination against American Indians was the result of the policies of, and treatment by, the United States, not Montana.[28]

The United States argued otherwise, of course, but, lacking the best evidence, it had to stretch, resulting in a reach that exceeded its grasp. For example, given only two American Indian candidates for commissioner, one a last-minute write-in candidate, the United States pointed to other elections in which American Indians had been candidates; that evidence was irrelevant.[29] Given the absence of racial discrimination by Blaine County against American Indians, the United States pointed to Montana laws on the books between 1871 and 1949; that evidence was irrelevant.[30] Finally, given the dearth of evidence that Montana had discriminated racially against American Indians, the United States pointed to its own erratic policies toward American Indians; that evidence was irrelevant.[31] As ludicrous as were these last two proffers by the United States, the most outrageous of all was its response to Blaine County's proof of the pudding evidence that Charlie Hay, an American Indian, had been elected, by wide margins with substantial support from the non-Indian community, both as justice of the peace and as county sheriff.[32] Obviously, argued Blaine County, American Indians are able to register, vote, run for, and win election to countywide office in Blaine County. Responded the United States, "Charlie Hay did not run as an Indian."[33]

ALAMOSA COUNTY, COLORADO, COMES CALLING

In the weeks following the trial, lawyers for Blaine County and the United States prepared their proposed findings of fact and conclusions of law, with citations to the record, which, when filed in January 2002 and combined with their pre-trial briefs, would total more than five hundred pages. As Blaine County's attorneys agonized over every word of Blaine County's two hundred-page filing, commissioners from Alamosa County, Colorado, came to visit. They had heard about the Blaine County case while attending National Association of Counties (NACo) and its Western Interstate Region (WIR) meetings.[34] They, like their fellow commissioners in Blaine County, were elected at-large from residential districts; Colorado law mirrored the Montana statue. And they, like the Blaine County commissioners, had heard recently from the U.S. Department of Justice.

In fact, days after the attack on the United States by radical Islamic terrorists on September 11, 2001, the commissioners had received a telephone call from the Bush administration's Justice Department. The federal lawyers on the other end of the line said that they were reluctant to fly given the recent attacks but did want to put Alamosa County on notice. The Civil Rights Division had concluded that Alamosa County had violated the Voting Rights Act due to its failure, over the years, to election a sufficient number of Hispanics as county commissioners. The commissioners believed that they had done nothing wrong; nonetheless, their plea to Colorado's attorney general had fallen on deaf ears. He refused to defend them and the Colorado statute that was the cause of their trouble. Their situation was unique, he said; they were on their own. Would Blaine County's lawyers represent Alamosa County? Of course!

On November 27, 2001, the Justice Department issued a press release announcing that it had filed a Voting Rights Act lawsuit against Alamosa County, Colorado. In January 2002, as Blaine County's lawyers put the finishing touches on Blaine County's brief, the County Attorney for Alamosa County filed the County's answer. Days later, Blaine County's attorneys prepared for another Voting Rights Act lawsuit.

A few months later, the federal judge from Nevada issued his opinion in *United States v. Blaine County*. Notwithstanding the complexity of the case, the number of witnesses, the days of testimony, the stacks of expert reports, the plethora of evidentiary, legal, and constitutional issues, not to mention the five hundred pages of pre-trial briefs and post-trial findings of facts and conclusions of law, the district court issued a slender opinion, which ran a scant twenty-one pages of which fourteen were a recitation of the facts. The district court ruled:

- American Indians have heightened concern regarding a distinct political issue; however, the court did not identify the issue or where it was found in the record;
- American Indians vote as a politically cohesive block; however, the court did not identify in what elections that cohesive voting occurred;
- American Indians have been victimized by racial discrimination by the United States, Montana, and Blaine County; however, the court did not indicate what facts support that finding; in fact, the court relied on the unpublished findings of another Montana federal district court in an earlier case involving a different county and different plaintiffs;[35] and
- American Indians are socioeconomically depressed and that status prevents them from equal participation in the election process; however, the court made no findings that the present effects of past discrimination caused that socioeconomic disparity.[36]

It was the worst of all possible rulings: the district court had made broad general findings that supported its conclusion that the Voting Rights Act had been violated but did not tie those findings to specific evidence upon which the district court relied. Complicating matters further, the district court did not issue any rulings on Blaine County's objections to improper evidence, which it had taken under advisement; therefore, it was unknown what evidence was before the court when it ruled. An appeal to the most difficult federal appellate court in the country—cases out of the U.S. Court of Appeals for the Ninth Circuit are the most likely to be reviewed by the Supreme Court and the most likely to be reversed, many unanimously—now looked almost impossible.

Blaine County's commissioners saw the handwriting on the wall. Although they hoped for the best at the Ninth Circuit, they prepared for the worst by creating the minority-majority single-member voting district that the United States had demanded. Located primarily on the Fort Belknap Reservation, the district had a voting-age population of 87.19 percent American Indian and 11.8 percent non-Indian; as expected, the district court approved the plan.[37] Thereupon, Blaine County filed its appeal to the Ninth Circuit and subsequently filed a motion urging the Ninth Circuit to grant a stay of the district court's ruling on Blaine County's case to keep the commission districts as they were before the federal government filed its lawsuit. The Ninth Circuit refused to grant the stay; Blaine County finalized the new district; and, in November 2002, one of the American Indian activists who had testified for the United States was elected commissioner.

Nevertheless, Blaine County's commissioners consoled themselves, there was a sliver of hope. A handful of judges on the Ninth Circuit were thoughtful jurists with a commitment to the Constitution and a willingness to dissent from the Ninth Circuit's oft-time radical decisions. Regardless of the three judges assigned to Blaine County's panel, perhaps the Ninth Circuit's conservative judges would dissent when the Ninth Circuit refused to reconsider the case *en banc*.

Meanwhile, Blaine County's attorneys proceed on two tracks: they prepared a lengthy opening brief at the Ninth Circuit in the Blaine County case and they drafted a motion for summary judgment in the Alamosa County case asserting that Section 2 of the Voting Rights Act is unconstitutional. In January 2003, the attorneys filed both documents. As they awaited the filing of their reply brief in the Blaine County case, they prepared for trial in the Alamosa County case.

ALAMOSA COUNTY, COLORADO, GOES ON TRIAL

Alamosa County is located in south-central Colorado west of the San-gre de Cristo Mountains in the San Luis Valley, the world's largest alpine valley, some 170 air miles south, southwest of Denver; the Great Sand Dunes National Park lies in its northeast corner.[38] The county is primarily rural with farming and ranching as its major industry.[39] Alamosa County is one of sixty-four counties in Colorado and, like all other Colorado counties, elects its commissioners at-large from residential districts, a system that has been in place since Alamosa County was formed in 1913.[40]

Alamosa County's population, according to the 2000 Census, is 14,966, of whom 54 percent (8,089) are White, 41 percent (6,197) are Hispanic, and 4.5 percent (680) are of other races or ethnicities.[41] The County's voting-age population is 57.9 percent White and 37.6 percent Hispanic.[42] Hispanics and Anglos have lived in Alamosa County for more than a century; more than 70 percent of local Hispanics were born in Colorado, many in Alamosa County or elsewhere in the San Luis Valley.[43]

As it had in the Blaine County case, the United States asserted that in Alamosa County Anglos voted as a bloc; Hispanics voted as a bloc;

and Hispanics were not able to elect their candidates of choice. As proof, the United States pointed out that only two Hispanics had been elected commissioner in the last quarter century. Alamosa County countered that the United States had to prove, and could not prove:

- That racial discrimination, past and present, prevented Hispanics from equal participation in the election of commissioners;
- That Hispanics lacked an equal opportunity both to participate in the political process and to elect their candidates of choice; and
- That Hispanic voters have distinct political issues of concern to them on which the Commission could legally take action.

After the depositions of fact and expert witnesses and the preparation of expert reports, a seven-day trial was conducted in May 2003 in Denver, Colorado, after which the United States and Alamosa County filed post-trial briefs. Then the wait began.

The day before Thanksgiving 2003, the Colorado federal district court issued its ruling: a complete victory for and vindication of the Alamosa County commissioners and other elected officials named in the federal lawsuit. Concluded the district court, "The ability of Hispanic voters to participate or elect candidates of their choice in county commissioner elections has neither been abridged nor curtailed in violation of Section 2 of the Voting Rights Act."[44] The district court found proof of that finding in "the successful nomination of Hispanic candidates through both the Democratic and Republican parties and the election of Hispanic candidates to the Board in three out of the five races in which Hispanic candidates competed."[45]

As to any split in Alamosa County, "[the] most notable divergence in interest is tied to socioeconomic need, with the interests of impoverished Hispanic residents being similar to those of impoverished

Anglo residents."[46] Moreover, "educational, socioeconomic, and geographic diversity within the Hispanic population is also reflected in social political views [with some seeing] the cup as half-empty [and others seeing] the cup as half full."[47] Regardless of any such split, there was one "fundamental electoral truth," declared the court. "[T]o be elected in Alamosa County, a candidate must appeal to both Anglo and Hispanic voters." "Subtle or overt ethnic appeals have been made in some elections . . . and have resulted in failure at the polls."[48]

The district court mentioned, in particular, a commissioner election held in November 2002, six months before the trial. The Republican nominee was Hispanic; the Democratic nominee was Hispanic; and the write-in candidate was Anglo. The Republican nominee was elected. When Alamosa County's attorneys pointed to the results as giving lie to the United States's claim, the United States responded that only a Hispanic Democrat could represent Alamosa County Hispanics! The district court labeled that suggestion "convenient" and "disingenuous." "The evidence is to the contrary, Hispanic voters belong to both parties and support Anglo as well as Hispanic candidates."[49]

When the United States declined to appeal the Alamosa County case to the U.S. Court of Appeals for the Tenth Circuit in Denver, the county's victory was complete.[50] Furthermore, Alamosa County residents would be spared the court-imposed racial divisiveness that was visited upon Blaine County and other jurisdictions victimized by litigation under Section 2 of the Voting Rights Act.

BLAINE COUNTY AIMS AT THE SUPREME COURT

Days before the Colorado federal district court's ruling in the Alamosa County case, Blaine County's worst fears were realized during oral arguments at the Ninth Circuit. The panel assigned to hear the case could not have been worse: all three were appointed by President

Clinton. When oral arguments took place in Seattle, Washington, Blaine County's attorney was greeted with open hostility from the panel. Thus, it was no surprise when, in April 2004, the panel ruled against Blaine County. There was one positive feature to the Ninth Circuit's ruling: the lack of specificity that had characterized the district court's ruling was gone; the Ninth Circuit panel knew what it believed both as to the constitutionality of Section 2 of the Voting Rights Act and what was required to prove a violation of that statute. It set out those beliefs clearly and forthrightly. Unlike the district court's deficient ruling, the panel's decision framed the issues for the further appeal that Blaine County wanted.

Blaine County petitioned for all active judges on the Ninth Circuit to rehear the case—that is, a petition for rehearing *en banc*—pointing out that the panel had disregarded the Supreme Court's new framework for considering the constitutionality of legislation like Section 2 of the Voting Rights, putting the panel in conflict, not just with the Supreme Court, but also with other federal appellate courts. Moreover, Blaine County argued that, in conflict with the Supreme Court and other circuits, the panel, to uphold a finding of a violation of the Voting Rights Act, had failed to require proof that:

- American Indians had been denied an equal opportunity both to participate in elections and to elect their candidates of choice;[51]
- Non-Indians had voted as a bloc out of racial animus and a desire to prevent the election of American Indian candidates;[52] and
- American Indians had identified distinct political issues that could be addressed by the Blaine County Commission.[53]

It came as no surprise when, in September 2004, the Ninth Circuit declined to rehear the case *en banc*. What was shocking was that, despite dissents filed in the past regarding related denials, no judge dissented in the Blaine County case.[54] Nonetheless, when Blaine County's attorneys filed their briefs urging the Supreme Court to review the ruling of the Ninth Circuit, they were optimistic. After all, the Ninth Circuit had rejected out of hand the Supreme Court's recent jurisprudence on testing the constitutionality of Section 2 of the Voting Rights Act;[55] moreover, four Supreme Court justices had made very clear their view that the constitutionality of that statute was very much in doubt.[56] It was not to be. In April 2005, the Supreme Court, without dissent, declined to hear the case.

Blaine County officials had fought a brave fight for some of the most important principles of the Constitution, including dual sovereignty, federalism, and the equal protection guarantee. Moreover, they had never lost their courage or commitment to final victory notwithstanding vitriolic and vicious attacks some of which included racial demagoguery. Nonetheless, battling the world's largest law firm—the U.S. Department of Justice—they had paid a steep financial price.[57]

CONCLUSION

The as yet unfinished tragedy of Section 2 of the Voting Rights Act and its application to tiny, rural, western counties is an instructive tale of what happens when officials fail to perform their constitutional duties:[58]

- Congress, in a sop to a radical race-based agenda, "repeals" a Supreme Court opinion and "amends" the Constitution, an action that fails to draw a presidential veto.
- Agenda-driven lawyers in both the U.S. Department of Justice and radical groups, with the assistance of local activists and agitators, scour the country for underlawyered units of local government to hit with Congress's lawyer-friendly statute.

- Activist judges, sympathetic with the issue, or apathetic judges, overwhelmed by the factual and legal issues involved, rule in favor of the litigants who demand racial gerrymandering.

- Judges on appellate courts defer to their colleagues by not dissenting, either when serving on three-judge panels or when asked to consider a petition for *en banc* review.

- Judges on appellate courts, recognizing that the odds are against a Supreme Court rebuke even if they thumbs their noses at clear Supreme Court precedent, ignore that precedent.

- The Supreme Court, eschewing a heavier caseload, allows appellate decisions that give great offense to the Court's on-point rulings to go unreviewed and unreversed.

These officials all have taken an oath to support and defense the Constitution. No wonder people are cynical. No wonder confidence in political institutions—Congress, the Executive, the Judiciary—is at an all time low. No wonder those who truly care must fight on![59]

The fight for the rights guaranteed by the Constitution must take place, not just on a national level, regarding liberty-stripping legislation like Section 2 of the Voting Rights Act. It must take place, not just on a local level, regarding attempts by government to rob people of their freedom in the name of politically correct, feel-good, "for the children" ordinances. It must occur lot-by-lot and house-by-house as people demand their rights under the Constitution's Fifth Amendment.

CHAPTER 13

FIGHTING "TAKINGS" COMMITTED "WITHOUT JUST COMPENSATION"

[W]hile property may be regulated to a certain extent, if regulation goes too far it will be recognized as a taking.... We are in
danger of forgetting that a strong public desire to improve the
public condition is not enough to warrant achieving the desire by
a shorter cut than the constitutional way of paying for the
change.

U.S. SUPREME COURT JUSTICE OLIVER WENDELL HOLMES[1]

The Fifth Amendment's guarantee that private property shall not
be taken for a public use without just compensation was
designed to bar Government from forcing some people alone to
bear public burdens which, in all fairness and justice, should be
borne by the public as a whole.

U.S. SUPREME COURT JUSTICE HUGO L. BLACK[2]

Maurice and Dolores Glosemeyer live near Marthasville, Missouri, some fifty miles southwest of St. Louis, in Warren
County. Like many folks situated in the rolling farmland just
north of the Missouri River, they used to raise hogs but that was before
all the people started to come visiting every weekend. Seems that hogs
just will not put on the weight when people think they are part of a
petting zoo. Times have been especially tough—the Glosemeyers have
been operating mostly in the red—since the floods of 1993, when all
of Iowa to the north and much of Missouri was a disaster area. The

floodwaters receded, but the thing that brings the people to their farm and that forced the Glosemeyers to sell their hogs has not gone away—that is, the hiking, jogging, and biking trail that pulses each weekend with twenty thousand people, people who pet the Glosemeyers' hogs, borrow their tools and other possessions, and explore or seek shelter in their barns and outbuildings.

In the late 1800s, a railroad was built through twelve acres of their predecessor's property. For "a dollar in hand and other consideration," the family that owned the farm before the Glosemeyers sold the railroad a right-of-way, or easement, across the flat part of their land, the part that was flooded in 1993 when the Missouri River left its banks. Over the years, the Missouri-Kansas-Texas (MKT) did a fair amount of business, but the Glosemeyers' stretch was not the only place that flooded out. Other places along that bottom land that made good farming and, when dry, a good flat piece to run a railroad, flooded even more often. Plus, the railroad bridges were old and in need of replacement.[3] Finally, in September 1986, the MKT had enough; it closed down, and, although it took its track with it, it left its right-of-way behind; after all, it had no more use for it.[4] The Glosemeyers were pleased because, under the terms of their contract with the railroad, when the railroad abandoned the right-of-way, which was for "railroad use and no other purposes," the Glosemeyers would get it back[5]—or so they thought. Instead, back in 1983, covetous politicians and bureaucrats and the your-land-ought-to-be-my-land crowd had other ideas, and Congress enacted amendments to the National Trails System Act in what was known popularly as the federal Rails-to-Trails Act.[6]

When Congress wrote the Rails-to-Trails Act, it knew that easements like the one the Glosemeyers' predecessors had conveyed, were for railroad purposes. Congress also knew that, once abandoned by the railroad, under contracts that folks like the Glosemeyers held, under the common law, under, in fact, the U.S. Constitution, the land would revert to the holder of the primary estate and that contract. So to prevent that abandonment and the reversion that, under the law, would naturally follow, Congress created a legal fiction. The fiction was that, someday, though that day might never come, the railroad would need to come back. Therefore, out of its desire "to preserve" railroad rights-of-way, "to protect" railway corridors, and "to encourage" energy-efficient transportation, Congress would not permit the right-of-way to be abandoned. (The only feel-good language missing was "for future generations" and "for the children.") Thus, when a railroad proposed to abandon its right-of-way, if "a state, political subdivision, or qualified private organization" agreed to assume responsibility for the right-of-way, the land would be transferred to that entity "for interim use." As a result, wrote Congress, the railroad's abandonment of the right-of-way "shall not be treated, for purposes of any law or rule of law, as an abandonment." Congress knew what it was doing; it was voiding the contract that the Glosemeyers had with the MKT!

Maurice Glosemeyer knew that, as far as the MKT was concerned, the interim use thing was a joke; neither the MKT nor any other railroad was coming back along the right-of-way through his property. Congress might just as well be preserving dirigible landing spots to be used when everyone forgot about the 1937 Hindenburg disaster.[7] So, after the Missouri Department of Natural Resources stepped forward to take over the right-of-way for "interim" trail use, which it labeled the Katy Trail, and to prevent the abandonment that would have given the land back to the Glosemeyers, Maurice and Dolores Glosemeyer, in December 1986, filed a lawsuit, first in state court, then in Missouri federal district court. The case attracted a great deal of interest: the United States and eleven environmental groups quickly jumped into the lawsuit as defendant-intervenors.

In May 1988, the Missouri federal district court ruled against the Glosemeyers, holding that Congress had the constitutional authority to adopt the Rails-to-Trails Act and that the Glosemeyers were entitled only to just compensation for which they could file suit after the taking of their private property was complete.[8] In July 1989, the U.S. Court of Appeals for the Eighth Circuit affirmed the Missouri federal district court's ruling; all the Glosemeyers could do, the appellate court ruled, was to file a lawsuit to obtain just compensation.[9] As lawyers for the Glosemeyers prepared their petition to obtain U.S. Supreme Court review, lawyers for yet another family affected by the Rails-to-Trails Act were preparing for oral arguments before the Supreme Court.

J. Paul Preseault and Patricia Preseault own property near the shore of Lake Champlain in Burlington, Vermont. In 1975, the Vermont Railway, which operated trains on the right-of-way that passed through the Preseaults' property, ceased operations and removed all railroad equipment from the property.[10] Like the Glosemeyers, the Preseaults sought to get their property back; instead, in 1986, the Interstate Commerce Commission (ICC) authorized the use of the right-of-way as a public recreational hiking and biking trail.[11] The Preseaults challenged the ICC's order, first before the ICC and then at the U.S. Court of Appeals for the Second Circuit. The Second Circuit upheld the authority of Congress to preserve rail corridors and to permit recreation on public trails.[12] In November 1989, the Supreme Court heard arguments in the Preseaults' case.

In February 1990, the Supreme Court unanimously upheld the authority of Congress to enact the Rails-to-Trails Act, rejecting, among other arguments, the Preseaults' contention, like that of Maurice Glosemeyer, that interim use was a charade:

> Congress apparently believed that every line is a potentially
> valuable national asset that merits preservation even if no

future rail use for it is currently foreseeable. Given the long
tradition of congressional regulation of railroad abandon-
ments...that is a judgment that Congress is entitled to
make.[13]

Justice O'Connor filed a concurring opinion, in which she was joined
by Justices Scalia and Kennedy, to opine that, contrary to the conclusion of the Second Circuit, a taking for which just compensation
could be owed had occurred already and did not require any further
federal action.[14] Five days later, the Supreme Court denied the Glosemeyers' petition for Supreme Court review.[15]

So, in March 1993, the Glosemeyers filed a lawsuit in the U.S.
Court of Federal Claims in Washington, D.C., to obtain the just compensation to which Justice O'Connor, and implicitly the other eight
justices, believed they were entitled. They would have to wait, however, because the Preseaults had beat them to the courthouse and the
federal government wanted to wait to see what would happen in the
Vermont case.

In November 1992, the Court of Federal Claims ruled against the
Preseaults,[16] and, in 1995, a three-judge panel of the U.S. Court of
Appeals for the Federal Circuit heard the Preseaults' appeal and
affirmed the ruling of the Court of Federal Claims, ruling in favor of
the United States.[17] Thereupon, the entire Federal Circuit agreed to
rehear the case *en banc*, vacated the earlier decision, and ordered additional briefing and argument.[18]

In November 1996, the Federal Circuit, in a thoughtful and thorough opinion, ruled in favor of the Preseaults and, in the process,
rejected a series of arguments raised by the United States and the State
of Vermont.[19] For example, the United States had asserted that,
because Congress has complete control over railroad operations, the
Preseaults should have expected that, in time, Congress would deprive

them of their property rights in legislation regarding railroads. Thus, either the Preseaults had no "reasonable expectation" that they would have the use of their property; or they acquired their property with knowledge of "background principles" regarding Congress's regulation of railroads and their rights-of-way.[20] Nonsense, ruled the Federal Circuit.[21] Equally absurd was the claim by the United States that it had not taken the Preseaults' property, the State of Vermont had taken it. No, ruled the court, Vermont entered upon the Preseaults' land under the authority granted by Congress in the Rails-to-Trails Act.[22] The Federal Circuit sent the Preseaults back to the Court of Federal Claims for a determination of the amount owed by the United States in just compensation and, nearly as important, given the years of litigation, for attorneys' fees.[23] Left unanswered by the Federal Circuit was whether there is a taking when, upon proposed abandonment by a railroad, the federal government orders the right-of-way "railbanked" for possible future railroad use and allows for interim present use as a trail.[24] That was the issue facing the Glosemeyers as they headed to the Court of Federal Claims.

In January 2000, after years of foot-dragging by attorneys for the Clinton administration, what with their demands for more and more fact-finding and discovery depositions, the matter was finally decided. "Congress has the power to impose its will [by adopting the Rails-to-Trails Act]; if it extinguishes a property interest in the process, however, the Government must pay," the Court of Federal Claims began its analysis.[25] To decide if a property interest had been extinguished, the Court of Federal Claims analyzed three arguments offered by the United States.

First, the United States argued that the right-of-way had not been abandoned. The court ruled that "the railroads intended to abandon, and in fact did abandon, their easements." Thus, under Missouri law, but for the Rails-to-Trails Act, the Glosemeyers would have had immediate access to their property.[26] Second, the United States argued that use of the former rail line as an interim trail was a railroad purpose. The court ruled that, under Missouri law, "[r]ecreational hiking, jogging and cycling are not connected with railroad use in any meaningful way."[27] Finally, the United States argued that "potential future rail service over the same route[]," that is, "railbanking," is a railroad purpose. The court ruled that, under Missouri law, "railbanking [is] a non-railroad purpose."[28] Therefore, ruled the court, under Missouri law, because the easement on the Glosemeyers' property was exclusively for railroad purposes, the Glosemeyers "would have been secure in the knowledge that Missouri law guaranteed that . . . [w]hen the railroads ceased operations, [the Glosemeyers] would own the land free of any easements. Those expectations have been thwarted[,] [s]olely because of the operation of the Rails-to-Trails Act."[29]

Without the Rails-to-Trails Act, wrote the Court of Federal Claims, the Glosemeyers "could exclude all but the railroad[] from use of the right-of-way[], [but] now the public at large has access. This is a physical taking of the [Glosemeyers'] property."[30] The Glosemeyers had been denied the power to exclude, "traditionally [] considered one of the most treasured strands in an owner's bundle of property rights."[31] The court ended its decision with this:

> The likelihood that the Rails-to-Trails Act was motivated by
> a commendable interest in public recreation or was an exercise in great foresight is immaterial. Rights in private property are more durable than the current majority's notion of
> what constitutes a worthy cause. As Justice Holmes said . . . ,
> "a strong public desire to improve the public condition is not
> enough to warrant achieving the desire by a shorter cut than
> the constitutional way of paying for the change."[32]

Given the lopsided ruling by the entire Federal Circuit Court of Appeals in the *Preseault* case, the United States declined to appeal. In December 2002, almost sixteen years to the day from when the Glosemeyers first went to the courthouse, the Glosemeyers and the United States agreed to the award of $200,000 as just compensation. In March 2004, the Glosemeyers' attorneys were awarded $150,000 for winning the Glosemeyers' case.

TAKING YEARS FOR TAKINGS CLAIMS

The battle for just compensation for the victims of the Rails-to-Trails Act continues, seemingly unabated, due in part to the demand by urban dwellers for paths through the backyards of others.

For example, in farming country in Weld County near Windsor, Colorado, there lies an 80-foot-wide railway easement, dating from 1905, once occupied by the Great Western Railroad. In October 2003, the Great Western Railway Company filed an application with the federal government for permission to abandon an 11.7-mile stretch of track near the cities of Severance, Windsor, and Eaton, Colorado, which, it admitted, for "more than ten years, rail service has not operated thereon." In November 2003, the cities of Windsor, Severance, and Eaton filed a request, under the Rails-to-Trails Act, to "rail bank" the right-of-way for use as recreational trail.

Local farmers, as well as the Colorado Farm Bureau, the Weld County Farm Bureau, and a newly formed organization of property owners, believe that the property has been abandoned and now belongs to the landowners. At the very least, they believe, the landowners, just like the Preseaults and Glosemeyers before them, are entitled to just compensation. They only hope it does not take sixteen years.

Of course, it should not. The *Preseault* and *Glosemeyer* cases, at least in their very early stages, were breaking new ground and perhaps zealous litigation on the part of federal government lawyers was understandable. Once the precedents were made and the issues became more mundane and straightforward, the federal government should have picked up the checkbook. In fact, that is what the U.S. Department of Justice during the Clinton administration asserted that it was doing when Congress, after Republicans had taken control of the U.S. House of Representatives, tired of the delays and duplicity of Catch-22 rules regarding the recovery of just compensation and proposed legislative relief for property owners. The Clinton administration opposed the fast track bill, asserting that it was always eager to pay property owners for illegal takings.

Nonetheless, when one of the federal government's imported wolves killed a $500 calf that belonged to an Idaho rancher, the check was months getting to him: it had to be approved by the third-ranking official at the U.S. Department of Justice.[33] Jim and Fred Purcell and Jim George, who own Texas property declared off-limits to use because it is the home of federally protected cave bugs, expect that, if they are lucky, it will take years, not months to recover the millions of dollars in just compensation they believe they are owed by the federal government.[34]

HOW MANY STICKS IN THE BUNDLE

Lawyers often compare property rights to "sticks in a bundle," meaning that the right to own and use property consists of numerous rights tightly bound together. For example, the Supreme Court has declared that "the right to exclude [others is] 'one of the most essential sticks in the bundle of rights that are commonly characterized as property.'"[35] Nonetheless, the landowner's right to exclude is the stick most frequently targeted by radical groups and covetous bureaucrats.

For example, in South Dakota, urban legislators were infuriated after the South Dakota Supreme Court upheld the trespass conviction of a hunter who had entered onto a landowner's private property without permission. They quickly passed a law that authorized such entry, a law that brought a constitutional challenge from ranching families.[36] Earlier, in Montana, urban residents, environmental groups, and fishing guides demanded the right to enter onto private property without permission to fish and recreate; the Montana Supreme Court gave them that right, which the state legislature soon codified. A constitutional challenge to that law suffered an early defeat and then was abandoned; a later challenge, dismissed on procedural grounds, failed to reach the U.S. Supreme Court.[37] Most recently, urban residents of Coeur d'Alene, Idaho, demanded the right to cross private property to enjoy Lake Coeur d'Alene. Thereupon, the city not only barred the landowner from maintaining a fence to prevent entry, it told its police officers not to arrest anyone trespassing there. The landowners' challenge is now at the Idaho Supreme Court and may be headed for the U.S. Supreme Court.[38] Ironically, a similar demand to cross private property to see the Pacific Ocean brought the Supreme Court's famous and forceful rebuke in 1987 in *Nollan v. California Coastal Commission*.[39]

Typically, one stick that is included always in any description of the property rights' bundle is the right to sell or otherwise dispose of property. Incredibly, however, Congress and the federal courts, on occasion, have taken that right; consider, for example, the strange case of Timothy Kornwolf of Stillwater, Minnesota.

In November 1999, Timothy Kornwolf opened the door of his home to one Ivar Husby, who introduced himself as a Norwegian collector of Laplander artifacts interested in Indian paraphernalia. In reality, Husby was a Norwegian police chief working undercover for the U.S. Fish and Wildlife Service. Carrying a briefcase filled with cash and a hidden audio and video recorder, Husby intended to purchase an eagle feather headdress and a Sioux dance shield. After Husby got what he wanted, Timothy Kornwolf was arrested and charged in an eight-count federal indictment.

Timothy Kornwolf had violated the Bald and Golden Eagle Protection Act and the Migratory Bird Treaty Act, known together as the Feather Act, which prohibits the sale of golden eagle feathers.[40] The headdress and shield had been in Timothy Kornwolf's family since 1904, when his mother's mother's brother, "Uncle Nick," Nicholas J. Klein, a member of Buffalo Bill's Wild West Show, had acquired the headdress and shield, which he later gave to Timothy Kornwolf, his favorite grand nephew.

Before the Minnesota federal district court, Timothy Kornwolf's attorney argued that, because the Feather Act permitted Timothy Kornwolf to possess the golden eagle feathers but prohibited him from selling them, the Feather Act violated the Constitution's Fifth Amendment. The Minnesota district court rejected that argument, relying on a 1979 U.S. Supreme Court decision in which the Court, focusing on the property rights the Feather Act allowed owners to retain rather than on the rights the law removed, ruled that the Feather Act was constitutional. "At least where an owner possesses a full 'bundle' of property rights, the destruction of one 'strand' of the bundle is not a taking, because the aggregate must be viewed in its entirety."[41]

In 1987, the Supreme Court again faced much the same issue regarding a federal law that denied tribal members the right to pass their property on to their heirs. In that case, the Court declared that, although the law took but one stick in the bundle of sticks, that stick is similar to the right to exclude others, "one of the most essential sticks in the bundle of rights that are commonly characterized as property." "In one form or another, the right to pass on property—to one's family in particular—has been part of the Anglo-American legal system since feudal times."[42] The significance of the Court's ruling regarding its earlier decision on the same issue was not lost on three members of the Court. Justice Scalia, joined by Chief Justice Rehnquist and Justice Powell, wrote, "In my view the present statute, insofar as concerns the balance between rights taken and rights left untouched, is indistinguishable from the [Feather Act, which was] at issue in [our 1979 ruling]. Because that comparison is determinative of whether there has been a taking ... in finding a taking today our decision effectively limits [that 1979 decision] to its facts."[43]

Remarkably, the Minnesota district court did not ask what was left of the Supreme Court's 1979 ruling, on which the district court relied, after the Supreme Court's 1987 decision, which all but overruled its 1979 ruling. Nor did the district court accept Justice Scalia's invitation to compare the facts of the 1979 ruling with the facts in Timothy Kornwolf's case. Had it done so, it would have found that, although those prosecuted in 1979 had not presented any evidence of preexisting ownership, Timothy Kornwolf had done just that! After the Minnesota district court ruled against him, Timothy Kornwolf entered a plea of guilty to four counts of the indictment, reserving his right to withdraw that plea if the U.S. Court of Appeals for the Eighth Circuit declared the Feather Act unconstitutional.

Timothy Kornwolf had hopes that the Eighth Circuit would do what the Minnesota federal district court did not do: hold that the Supreme Court had abandoned its 1979 holding that it is constitutional for the federal government to deny an owner the right to sell his property. His hopes were dashed when the Eighth Circuit failed to apply the Supreme Court's 1987 and 1997 analyses regarding the right to sell or pass on one's property and, instead, focused only on the rights that Timothy Kornwolf still possessed. The Eighth Circuit ruled that there had been no unconstitutional taking of Timothy Kornwolf's property.[44] Unfortunately, the Supreme Court declined to hear his appeal.[45] Had the Court heard his case, it might have overturned its 1979 decision, declared unconstitutional the Feather Act's prohibition on the right of owners to sell what they lawfully possess, and put a serious crimp in the Fish and Wildlife Service's practice of sending foreign undercover agents, with suitcases full of cash, into the homes of American citizens to urge them to break the law![46]

Yet another stick in the bundle of sticks concerns whether landowners really own their property if they must ask permission to access that property. Take, for example, the right of a company to mine coal that it owns in McCreary and Wayne Counties, Kentucky, coal that lies beneath land that was purchased from the company by the United States, under threat of condemnation, and that is now managed by the federal government as the Daniel Boone National Forest.[47]

Because of the long history of mining in Kentucky, there is a well-established body of state law governing severed mineral estates such as these; specifically, Kentucky recognizes that one party may own minerals in a tract of land and someone else may own the surface above those minerals. Moreover, Kentucky recognizes that, for mining purposes, the owner of the minerals has the right to use the surface in order to remove the minerals, referred to as an "implied easement of necessity." Plus, because the mineral owner has an easement in the surface, his mineral estate is the dominant estate. As a result, his rights include: the right to reasonable ingress and egress both across and through the surface; the right to make mine openings; the right to build appurtenant structures; and the right to run power lines over the surface. In other words, the mineral owner has the right to occupy and use the surface to the extent reasonable and necessary to extract the minerals.

These property rights, as defined by the Commonwealth of Kentucky, are entitled to the protection of the U.S. Constitution. In fact, as early as 1910, Justice Oliver Wendell Holmes ruled that an easement is a property interest protected by the Takings Clause of the Fifth

Amendment.[48] Moreover, these rights have been applied against the United States. For example, in 1911, the Supreme Court ruled that a cattleman did not have to obtain the permission of the Yosemite National Park Superintendent to drive his cattle through the park to land that he owned inside the park.[49] The Supreme Court reached an analogous ruling regarding easements in 1987 when the State of California demanded a "public easement across a landowner's premises."[50]

In 1977, Congress passed the Surface Mining Control and Reclamation Act, which barred surface coal mining within any national forest that was incompatible with various other values of the forest, subject to valid existing rights.[51] When the Stearns Coal and Lumber Company sought to mine a portion of the 35,611 acres of coal that it owns, the Office of Surface Mining (OSM), and subsequently the federal courts, ruled that the mining activity would take place on federal land and was thus barred. After the OSM ruled that the company did not have valid existing rights to mine, the company sought just compensation.

In August 2002, the Court of Federal Claims ruled that the federal law had effectuated a "physical taking by operation of law" because it "eliminated [Stearns'] traditional property rights," that is, the company's surface easement and, therefore, its "right to mine."[52] The company was awarded $10,057,000, plus interest, as just compensation. In January 2005, the U.S. Court of Appeals for the Federal Circuit reversed that decision and held that no "physical taking" had occurred and that, if a regulatory taking had occurred, it would not be ripe until the OSM had made compatibility determinations as to each of the hundreds of mining parcels in the company's 35,611 acres.[53] In other words, held the Federal Circuit, barring a property owner from entry onto his own land was not the type of physical occupation that is considered a *per se* taking for which just compensation must be paid.

Despite the clear conflict between the Federal Circuit's ruling and U.S. Supreme Court precedent, not to mention the importance of the issue presented,[54] the Supreme Court refused to review the case.[55]

PUBLIC USE HEARTBREAK

The Constitution's Fifth Amendment does not simply guarantee that a property owner deprived of his private property will receive just compensation when his property is taken.[56] The Fifth Amendment also provides that his property will only be taken for "public use."[57]

Traditionally, public use had been viewed as those activities commonly associated with public works, roads, schools, and hospitals. In 1954, however, the U.S. Supreme Court addressed the case of a landlord, whose department store was neither blighted nor constituted a public nuisance, yet his property was condemned because the area in which his store was located was classified as undesirable and the federal government declared that it would serve the public interest if that area were sold to private entities who would redevelop the land. The landlord lost his suit when the Supreme Court granted Congress a blank check upon which to write its own brand of urban redevelopment.[58]

Then, in 1984, the U.S. Supreme Court took the next, disturbingly logical step in broadening the definition of public use when it upheld a Hawaii state court decision that allowed Hawaii to take, by eminent domain, the property of landlords solely for the purpose of sale to those landlords' current tenants. Justice O'Connor declared:

> The mere fact that property taken outright by eminent domain is transferred in the first instance to private beneficiaries does not condemn that taking as having only a private purpose. The Court long ago rejected any literal requirement that condemned property be put into use for the general

public. It is not essential that the entire community, nor even any considerable portion, directly enjoy or participate in any improvement in order for it to constitute a public use.[59]

More recently, and in one of the more hopeful indications that the courts were moving in the other, right direction in defining public use, a California federal district court barred the city of Lancaster and its redevelopment agency from condemning property "where Lancaster's condemnation efforts rest[ed] on nothing more than the desire to achieve the naked transfer of property from one private party to another."[60] Then, in July 2004, one of the strongest indications yet came from a most unexpected source. The Michigan Supreme Court reversed one of its most notorious decisions, issued a resounding *mea culpa*, and breathed new life into the public use doctrine as a serious constraint on the power of government to condemn private property. Twenty years earlier, the Michigan Supreme Court had permitted Detroit to wipe out an entire neighborhood and hand the land over to the General Motors Corporation for a new plant because the new facility would create jobs. At that time, the Michigan Supreme Court had ruled that Detroit's plan was for a public use.[61] Declared the Michigan Supreme Court in overturning its 1981 ruling:

> *Poletown*'s economic benefit rationale would validate practically any exercise of the power of eminent domain on behalf of a private entity. After all, if one's ownership of private property is forever subject to the government's determination that another private party would put one's land to better use, then the ownership of real property is perpetually threatened by the expansion plans of any large discount retailer, "megastore," or the like.[62]

The decision of the Michigan Supreme Court was read eagerly at Skyland Shopping Center at Good Hope Road and Alabama Avenue in southeast Washington, D.C., in Anacostia, a neighborhood named for the river that separates it from the rest of the Capital. Skyland is a non-contiguous collection of 170,000 square feet of retail properties with fifteen different owners that sprawls across twelve acres next to five acres of woodland. Although it lies in a city that has seen some tough times, Skyland is a place of hope.

One of the Skyland's owners is an African-American couple whose business in northeastern Washington was burned down in the 1968 riots. They moved to Skyland a short time later, worked hard, and prospered. Another family bought its share of the shopping center in the 1940s and, through the bad days since, held on, pouring millions into its property. Two men, long-time employees of a liquor store proprietor, are more recent owners: they mortgaged their homes and bought the store, pursuant to the former proprietor's will, after his death. Then there are Skyland's tenants, each of whom demonstrates that the American dream is vibrantly alive!

Moreover, Skyland is a thriving retail operation. Each day, the parking lot that meanders among the buildings is a river of traffic. Vendors arrange their wares on the streets of Skyland rather than before the upscale and multimillion dollar redevelopment project across Good Hope Road. Residents, 49 percent of whom are from households that earn less than $35,000 a year, ride the bus to Skyland, shop at the post office, grocery store, beauty shop, drug store, check cashing store, and other outlets, then barter with freelance taxis to deliver them and their wares home. Tellingly, the grocery is reputed to be the highest grossing outlet of its regional chain.

To most folks, Skyland is a great success. A cross-section of Americans own and invest in property. Tenants, some newly arrived in this country, run businesses. Employees believe they may one day own the boss's business. And, local residents shop for an array of reasonably priced goods and services.

But to the D.C. Council, Skyland is a slum that must be condemned, razed, and, at a cost of $27 million, turned over to a private developer for an unnamed retailer. In May 2004, after the D.C. Council passed emergency legislation, its members and staff jetted off to a Las Vegas "big box" convention to shop the property, but there were no takers. Experts say that the numbers make no sense and that an economic disaster awaits if the proposed redevelopment plan goes forward, which is nothing compared to what will befall those who have poured their lives into Skyland. So when they read the good news that the Michigan Supreme Court had changed its mind on what constitutes public use, they were given new hope about the prospects for their fight against a government that cares not a whit about them.

Unfortunately, the good news on public use lasted less than a year. In one of its final decisions of the October 2004 term, whose name, *Kelo v. City of New London*, became instantly infamous, the Supreme Court declared that the seizure of private, well-maintained homes to convey to another private owner for new development that would arguably increase tax revenues was a public use.[63] As the bases for its ruling, which inflamed the nation, the Court cited the *stare decisis* effect of its 1954 and 1984 public use rulings, its broadened view that public use actually means public purpose, and its required deference to the decision-making of a local unit of government.[64] Ironically, for she had authored the Court's 1984 decision, Justice O'Connor cried foul: "[The Court has] effectively... delete[d] the words 'for public use' from the Takings Clause of the 5th Amendment" and thereby "refus[ed] to enforce properly the federal Constitution."[65] As a result, "Nothing is to prevent the state from replacing any Motel 6 with a Ritz-Carlton, any home with a shopping mall, or any farm with a factory."[66] Added Justice Thomas:

> If such "economic development" takings are for a "public use,"
> any taking is, and the Court has erased the Public Use Clause
> from our Constitution. . . . The most natural meaning of the
> Clause is that it allows the government to take property only
> if the government owns, or the public has a legal right to use,
> the property, as opposed to taking it for any public purpose.[67]

Notwithstanding the Supreme Court's ruling in *Kelo*, the Michigan Supreme Court's 2004 ruling is still good law—in Michigan! Thus, the battle now shifts to the highest appellate court in each of the sovereign states where, perhaps, the state's constitution more explicitly and strictly defines public use or the court finds the Michigan ruling more persuasive than *Kelo*. For example, along the south Santa Fe corridor in the southern part of the greater Denver, Colorado area, the City of Sheridan plans a three hundred-acre condemnation action that is little more than forced redistribution of that property to a private developer.[68] Whether, ultimately, the Colorado Supreme Court follows *Kelo* or the Michigan Supreme Court is eagerly awaited.

In the American West, a handshake is enough of a commitment; a person's word is truly his bond. He stands by what he says, the deals that he makes, and the agreements that he enters into no matter how much time goes by or things change. Not so the federal government. A deed signed by President Wilson, an act adopted by the 39th Congress, a case decided by Justice Oliver Wendell Homes are as new and fresh and adaptable as the baby-faced lawyer who represents the U.S. Department of Justice and hence the United States. As a result, property owners in the West are unable to rely on anything; regardless of how old, venerable, and unassailable it may seem.

CHAPTER 14

FIGHTING FOR ACCESS TO PRIVATE PROPERTY

Despite current hype from Senate Democrats, the landmark cases of the next five years probably won't concern civil rights, abortion or other issues that have liberals so worked up... Instead, I believe some of the biggest cases will deal with property rights[, for example] one of the most ancient principles in property law, that ownership includes an absolute right of access (what the law calls an "easement") and lawful use.

EDWIN MEESE III[1]

I n 1983, Raymond and Nancy Fitzgerald purchased the O'Haco Cabins Ranch in Coconino County, Arizona, fifty-five miles south of Winslow.[2] Historically, and at the time the Fitzgeralds bought their ranch, the only way to get to the ranch was to cross land owned by the United States; specifically, a Forest Service road across the Apache-Sitgreaves National Forest. In fact, shortly after the Fitzgeralds purchased their ranch, the Forest Service obliterated all access routes to the ranch except that one road.

Until the spring of 1986, the Fitzgeralds had no problem getting to their ranch; they had a good relationship with Forest Service personnel and the agency never interfered with their use of the Forest Service road to get to their property. As far as the Fitzgeralds knew, none of the people who had owned the ranch before them had ever had any trouble with the Forest Service on that score.

However, in the spring of 1986, the Forest Service informed the Fitzgeralds that they had to apply for a special-use permit to continue to use the Forest Service road to get to their ranch. In June 1986, the Fitzgeralds complied with the Forest Service demand and applied for a special-use permit. In late 1986, the forest supervisor gave the Fitzgeralds a special-use permit, which they had to sign in order to continue using the Forest Service road to access their ranch.

The Fitzgeralds were astonished to discover, after examining the special-use permit, that in it the Forest Service insisted it had the right: to limit the uses the Fitzgeralds could make of their property, to cancel the use of the Forest Service road at any time, and to refuse to grant to anyone who purchased the ranch from the Fitzgeralds the same right of access to the property that the Fitzgeralds had. The Fitzgeralds believed that those restrictions deprived them of the rights they were guaranteed by the patent (title) they held to their land, by the common law, and by laws enacted by Congress. They refused to sign the Forest Service's special-use permit and told the Forest Service official why. As a result, in May 1988, the Forest Service issued an order closing the Forest Service road to all motorized vehicles.

In September 1988, the forest supervisor gave the Fitzgeralds a new document, entitled private road easement, and again told them they could not access their ranch by way of the Forest Service road unless and until they signed the document. Once again, the Fitzgeralds notified the regional forester they would not sign the document because it was illegal and deprived them of their rights and their right of access.

In March 1994, after appealing the decision to various Forest Service officials and thus exhausting their administrative remedies, the Fitzgeralds filed a lawsuit in Arizona federal district court "to quiet title to an easement for access" over the Forest Service road.[3] In May 1996, the district court ruled against the Fitzgeralds, holding that they did not own any easement for access over the Forest Service road and that, although they owned statutory rights of access, the private road easement that the Forest Service demanded that the Fitzgeralds sign did not violate those rights.[4] The Fitzgeralds appealed to the U.S. Court of Appeals for the Ninth Circuit; however, on New Year's Eve 1996, the Forest Service document expired, and the Fitzgeralds had to start over!

In July 1999, the Fitzgeralds again requested an application for a special-use permit, which the Forest Service claimed the Fitzgeralds had to sign before they could use the Forest Service road to get to their ranch. In January 2000, the Fitzgeralds completed the application and submitted it to the Forest Service. Now, however, the Forest Service wanted the Fitzgeralds to perform a survey of the Forest Service road, which the Fitzgeralds completed by August 2000. Late that month, the forest supervisor delivered to the Fitzgeralds a new document that he said the Fitzgeralds would have to sign if they wanted to use the Forest Service road to get to their property.[5] The document had the same unacceptable terms that the Forest Service had demanded of the Fitzgeralds fourteen years before. They again refused to sign and, in January 2002, filed a lawsuit in Arizona federal district court.

In their lawsuit, the Fitzgeralds argued, first, that they had an "easement by necessity" because: the land that included their ranch was owned by the United States; the United States severed the ranch from property that it owned; and the original owners and the Fitzgeralds had to cross land owned by the United States to get to their property.[6] The Fitzgeralds argued, second, that, in passing the Homestead Act

Congress gave homesteaders the right to enter public land in order to reside on and cultivate the land and that Congress sought to induce Americans to settle and cultivate the West. Both of these purposes would be frustrated if homesteaders did not have an implied easement to access their land.[7] The Fitzgeralds argued, finally, that the patent signed by President Wilson expressly conveyed the land "with the appurtenances thereof," which means those items without which the land may not be enjoyed, such as an easement for access.[8]

Unfortunately, the Arizona federal district court ruled against the Fitzgeralds in March 2004, concluding that the United States could not be sued to enforce an easement of necessity and that the Fitzgeralds had other, federal statutory rights that they could use.[9] It was clear to the Fitzgeralds' attorneys that the district court was wrong; other federal courts, including federal appellate courts had ruled exactly the opposite.[10] An appeal was planned.

Sadly, in the years since the Forest Service first decided to prevent Raymond and Nancy Fitzgerald from using their ranch, both had become elderly and infirmed. It is now up to their children to continue the fight on behalf of their parents and the ranch that they love. What happened to the Fitzgeralds is an all too common occurrence for property owners. There is a reason, when victory does come after years of litigation against the world's largest law firm—the U.S. Department of Justice—that the victor is too often referred to as, for example, "the Widow Dolan."[11]

FORD OR SKATE THE RIVER

Over one thousand miles due north of the Fitzgerald ranch, just north of Polebridge, Montana, another family is having trouble getting access to its private property. This time, it is the National Park Service that is refusing to abide by the express terms of patents issued, statutes adopted, and cases decided. Jack McFarland, however, may be young enough to win his fight and ultimately enjoy his property.

In the early 1890s, the land in the northwest corner of Montana, just like the land near Winslow, Arizona, and elsewhere throughout the West, was settled by homesteaders pursuant to the Homestead Act. In 1901, access to those Montana homesteads was assured by the creation of a road, known today as Glacier Route 7, which runs forty miles from Lake McDonald, in the south, to Kintla Lake, less than five miles from the Canadian border, in the north. In 1910, Congress created Glacier National Park, placing within its borders all land, including homesteaded land, east of the North Fork of the Flathead River, an area called North Fork.[12] In 1916, President Woodrow Wilson signed a patent granting title to some of those North Fork lands, including land that, in 1984, was purchased by Jack McFarland from his grandmother.

The Homestead Act granted the public the right "to enter" federal land and to stake claims to that land so as "to reside upon" it. Later, recognizing that it was including within Glacier National Park land that had been homesteaded, Congress took steps to protect the rights of all homesteaders, providing: "Nothing [in the Glacier National Park Act] shall affect any valid claim, location, or entry existing under the land laws of the United States . . . or the rights of any such claimant, locator, or entryman to the full use and enjoyment of his land."[13] Finally, the patent signed by President Wilson provided, "TO HAVE AND TO HOLD the said tract of land, with the appurtenances thereof, unto the said claimant and to the heirs and assigns of the said claimant, forever."

With such ironclad assurances, the homesteaders, their heirs, and assigns enjoyed full use and enjoyment of their private property in North Fork, including during the winter when portions of Glacier National Park were closed to the general public. Even after the

National Park Service installed a gate at the Polebridge ranger station, property owners like Jack McFarland's grandmother were free to drive north on Glacier Route 7 to reach their private property; her property was just three miles north of the station. Plus, the National Park Service went to great pains to guarantee that access by providing the property owners the means necessary to come and go as they pleased.

Fact of the matter is, the National Park Service knew that, by law, it could do no less. In its 1985 *Land Protection Plan* for Glacier National Park, the National Park Service wrote: "Private land owners [in Glacier National Park] have certain rights that must be respected[.]" Although "[p]ublic access and use may conflict with private ownership," because "private property owner rights [are] guaranteed in the enabling legislation for the park" and because "private property owner[s] retain[] reasonable and adequate use and enjoyment of [their] property[,]" the National Park Service has no power to deny access to that property.[14]

Thus it was that, ever since 1910, landowners like Jack McFarland were able to use their property in all seasons, coming and going as they pleased. In time, Jack McFarland restored his grandmother's home, intending to live there permanently. As it always had, the National Park Service facilitated and encouraged Jack McFarland's use of Glacier Route 7. Then, in late 1999, the National Park Service sent Jack McFarland an e-mail; it had changed its policy, the National Park Service wrote, as of now, "no one will drive park roads once they are closed to the public." Jack McFarland's requests for authorization to continue to access his property year-round were in vain.

In February 2000, Jack McFarland sued in Montana federal district court, demanding that the National Park Service adhere to all the promises made by Congress and President Wilson. He sued under the Quiet Title Act, claiming an easement to use Glacier Route 7, and under the Administrative Procedure Act, claiming that the National

Park Service arbitrarily and capriciously denied him access to his property.[15]

In July 2003, the district court dismissed Jack McFarland's case, not because Jack McFarland did not own an easement in Glacier Route 7 or because, in denying his request for access, the National Park Service acted properly. Instead, the district court ruled that Jack McFarland had waited too long to file his complaint, that is, beyond the Quiet Title Act's twelve-year statute of limitations, which, according to the district court, began to run in 1976 when the National Park Service restricted the general public's ability to use Glacier Route 7 north of Polebridge ranger station. Though the National Park Service had continued to give Jack McFarland complete access to Glacier Route 7 until late 1999, he should have known in 1976, ruled the district court, that the National Park Service believed it could deny him that right.[16]

Incredibly, the district court reached this conclusion notwithstanding what the National Park Service had put in writing in 1985, which is that it could not deny people like Jack McFarland access to their property. How could Jack McFarland have been put on notice that the federal government's property interest was adverse to his when the National Park Service itself did not believe that to be the case?

In October 2003, Jack McFarland appealed to the U.S. Court of Appeals for the Ninth Circuit. Fortunately, the Ninth Circuit reversed the Montana federal district court, ruling that the federal government's claim of ownership of Glacier National Park did not mean that Jack McFarland did not have an easement.[17] Jack McFarland will now be able to return to federal district court to face the federal government's most audacious claim of all: that even though the National Park Service road to his house is closed in the winter, he still has reasonable access to his house because he may park next to and hike across private property on the west side of the North Fork River and wade through or ski across the river to his land on the east side!

THE RIGHT TO ACCESS WATER FACILITIES

Jack McFarland may not want to cross treacherous waters to reach his private land, but a number of westerners want to cross federal land to get to their private water. Specifically, the descendants and devisees of homesteaders want access to the dams, reservoirs, and ditches that their predecessors built on federal land to ensure that the land would be capable of productive use. Two specific federal statutes authorized landowners to enter upon federal land and, under certain circumstances, to construct the facilities that would allow them to apply waters to "beneficial use" and thereby acquire water rights, perhaps the most important property right that a person could own in the arid West. Once constructed and maintained, those facilities constitute a valuable property right, access to which may not be denied.

Nonetheless, the U.S. Forest Service, particularly in far western Montana, has embarked upon a policy of refusing to recognize these rights and of barring landowners from getting to their dams, reservoirs, and ditches. The Forest Service, just as it did with the Fitzgeralds, is willing to grant these landowners a special-use permit, restrictive and revocable, or a fee Ditch Bill Easement, which is free; however, such limited access is consistent neither with federal law nor the interests of the landowners. If the landowners want to ensure the value of their land to convey to others, they must have the water rights that go with the land.

A classic example involves Stephen and Jean Roth and their Trapper Peak Ranch near Darby, Montana. In 1988, they purchased 750 acres in Ravalli County, and, in 1990, they bought fifty adjacent acres; both purchases included water rights to operate their ranch, including Tamarack Lake Dam and Reservoir and four ditches. The Roths asserted that, under congressional acts adopted in 1866 and 1891,[18] they held easements for these facilities, easements the Forest Service could not prevent them from using. When the Forest Service denied them access to those facilities, the Roths sued the United States under the Quiet Title Act in Montana federal district court. The Roths asserted that they owned an easement in the Bitterroot National Forest, created in 1897, and the Selway-Bitterroot Wilderness Area, created in 1964, by which to access their water facilities. A little more than a year later, the Roths and the Forest Service had exchanged briefs. Days after oral arguments in the case, the district court, in December 2003, ruled in favor of the Roths.[19]

In opposing the Roths' lawsuit, the United States had asserted first that the twelve-year statute of limitations for filing a Quiet Title Act suit had expired because the Forest Service had always disputed their claim. The court rejected the argument pointing to a 1998 document in which the Forest Service admitted that the Roths did indeed own an easement for the Tamarack Lake Dam and Reservoir. On the merits, the Roths argued that, once their predecessors had constructed the Tamarack Lake Dam and Reservoir on federal land, pursuant to the Act of 1891, the easement authorized by Congress vested automatically. The United States countered that those rights did not vest automatically; instead, the Secretary of the Interior had to approve the easement. The court rejected that argument because it was at odds with the position espoused by the U.S. Department of the Interior beginning in 1910, a position embraced twice by the U.S. Supreme Court.[20] The court also concluded that to accept the United States's new position would be to condemn the 1891 Act of Congress to "a sort of legal purgatory."[21]

As to the Roths' ditches, which the Roths asserted were protected rights-of-way under both the 1866 Act and the 1891 Act, the United

States argued that the Roths had "not carried their burden of proof" without explaining what statutory requirements the Roths had failed to meet or citing anything in the record to support its position. The district court flatly rejected the United States's argument concluding that the Roths had "indeed met their burden...."[22] The court did so in part because, in 1975, a Forest Service district ranger wrote "[a] review of old records reveals the ditches... were in place prior to [creation of Bitterroot National Forest]; [thus,] no special use permit will be required."[23]

As to every claim made in its case with the Roths, the Forest Service knew better. The Forest Service knew it had acted adversely to the Roths' rights only recently; the Roths' case was not time barred. The Forest Service knew the Roths' rights to the dam and reservoir had vested automatically; the United States had taken that position for nearly one hundred years. The Forest Service knew the Roths' ditch rights predated creation of the Bitterroot National Forest; it admitted that in 1975.

For those who litigate often against the United States and its attorneys, nothing is surprising about the federal government's arguments in the Roths' case. Of course, federal lawyers would assert that what the federal government said in the past no longer applies; that documents do not mean what they say; and that legal precedents do not stand for the propositions for which they have been cited for decades. What is surprising is that a federal district court would so quickly and thoroughly dispense with those deceptive legal slights-of-hand. Despite the significance of the victory, and it is greatly encouraging to those with similar easement throughout the West, it is only the decision of a federal district court. Of course, the United States appealed to the always unpredictable, but all too often left-leaning, U.S. Court of Appeals for the Ninth Circuit.

Meanwhile, scores of others have lined up in Montana federal district court awaiting final resolution of the victory won by the Roths, including Thomas H. Dunbar, trustee for the Thomas and Margaret Dunbar Trusts; Big Creek Lakes Reservoir Association of Victor, Montana; and Carlton Creek Irrigation Company of Florence, Montana.[24]

THE NEED TO LAWYER UP

Some of these ranchers will have a harder time proving up their rights than others, not because they do not possess those rights but because they listened to, relied upon, and trusted the words of federal bureaucrats. Consider, for example, the situation facing ranchers in extreme western Montana near the Idaho border who belong to the Big Creek Lake Reservoir Association, which owns 2,500 acre-feet of water rights stored in Big Creek Dam and Reservoir and 200 acre-feet of water stored in the South Fork Dam and Reservoir.

In August 1897, L. Lacoursier, M.M. Williams, and Arthur Beckwith created the South Fork Dam and Reservoir by damming up and placing a headgate on a lake located on public land in Ravalli County, Montana. As a result, Messrs. Lacoursier, Williams, and Beckwith claimed and appropriated, in accordance with Montana law, the surplus water created by their dam, which they used to irrigate their ranches. Over the next fifteen years, the South Fork Dam and Reservoir was deeded and transferred to individuals who, subsequently, received permits from the U.S. Forest Service, which authorized location of the South Fork Dam and Reservoir within the Bitterroot National Forest and, as of 1964, the Selway-Bitterroot Wilderness Area.

Meanwhile, in June 1931, three of Big Creek Lake Reservoir Association's predecessors, John R. Smith, Herb Chilson, and Lee Gibson, applied for a permit to store irrigation water in the South Fork Dam and Reservoir by reconstructing the dam on the South Fork Lake and by making repairs to the headgate and cut. Finally, in August 1942, Messrs. Smith, Chilson, and Callender[25] were issued a permit to store water in the South Fork Dam and Reservoir. According to the permit, they "agree[d] to build a dam...." Over the next several years, the permit holders notified the Forest Service that they had sold and transferred their interests in the South Fork Dam and Reservoir and their permits to the Big Creek Lake Reservoir Association.

Like the Roths, the ranchers who belong to the Big Creek Lake Reservoir Association have met all the requirements necessary to establish an easement to their dam, reservoir, and ditches that Congress established, in accordance with the consistent and continuing application of those requirements by the U.S. Department of the Interior and the interpretation of those requirements by the U.S. Supreme Court over the last one hundred years. Even though the federal district court in which the ranchers are appearing has ruled already, in *Roth*, on the nature of these requirements and how they are to be met, federal government lawyers dispute that ruling in challenging the ranchers' efforts to quiet title to their water facilities. No doubt the federal government will keep on doing so in the Big Creek Lake Reservoir Association case and in the other cases lined up behind the Roths, at least until a definitive ruling from, at least, the U.S. Court of Appeals for the Ninth Circuit and maybe even the U.S. Supreme Court.

In the Big Creek Lake Reservoir Association case however, the federal government has raised a new legal issue. The Forest Service is asserting that the ranchers have abandoned their water rights and, with them, their right to an easement to the dam and reservoir their predecessors constructed back in the late 1800s. In fact, the United States sued the ranchers in Montana water court to deny them the rights that were acquired nearly 110 years ago and either sold or passed down to them over the decades. The tack taken by the Forest Service and its attorneys is a cautionary tale in dealing with the federal government and illustrates the ever-present necessity—even though the bureaucrat across the table may be one's neighbor and the federal agency a part of the physical embodiment of the flag that one salutes—to "lawyer up." Failure to do so, as is said in the police dramas, "may be held against you."

Big Creek Lake Reservoir Association and its predecessors always intended to use the South Fork Dam and Reservoir; however, they met with constant resistance from the Forest Service in their efforts to do so. Beginning in the early 1940s, the Forest Service rejected pleas by the ranchers that they be allowed to repair and to maintain the South Fork Dam and Reservoir; instead, demanded the Forest Service, the ranchers should focus their attention and resources on the repair and maintenance of the Big Creek Dam and Reservoir. Even after, in the mid-1960s, the headgate on the South Fork Dam and Reservoir "disappeared," the Forest Service refused the ranchers access.[26] Only after the Big Creek Lake Reservoir Association repaired and maintained the Big Creek Dam and Reservoir, said Forest Service officials, would the Forest Service allow the ranchers to work on the South Fork Dam and Reservoir. This was not an insignificant demand and the Forest Service knew it.

Over the years, work on the Big Creek Dam and Reservoir took all of the ranchers' time, energy, and money; in fact, reconstructing the dam as the Forest Service demanded, which cost $132,000, depleted the association's treasury. Moreover, work on the dam and reservoir was not enough, the ranchers had to perform major maintenance work on their ditches, which they did during the 1970s and 1980s. Furthermore, the Forest Service knew that, because of the unique nature of the Big Creek Dam and Reservoir, a great deal of work would be required to maintain the facilities, each and every year. The Forest Service increased the difficulty of performing that work, for example, by ordering that chainsaws could not be used because the dam and reservoir were in a wilderness area. Sisyphus-like, the ranchers kept at the work on Big Creek Dam and Reservoir.

The ranchers needed more than the permission of the Forest Service to access their dam and reservoir and do the reconstruction work that they knew was necessary. They needed a way to get there. Over the years, the South Fork Trail, which led to the South Fork Dam and Reservoir, had fallen into disrepair; it was now almost impassable. Ironically, given the Forest Service's persistent insistence that the ranchers do time-consuming and expensive reconstruction and maintenance of the Big Creek Dam and Reservoir, the Forest Service simply refused to do the same thing on its land with regard to the South Fork Trail.

Thus, beginning in the mid-1950s, the ranchers entreated Forest Service officials to do the reconstruction work that had to be done on the South Fork Trail to permit the ranchers to reach their property. Every year, the Forest Service asserted that repair of the South Fork Trail was not on the agency's list of projects to be undertaken or that no funds were available to do the work. The Forest Service continued to take that position even after 1977, when the ranchers completed the major reconstruction of the Big Creek Dam that the Forest Service had maintained was a precondition to the Forest Service allowing them to work on the South Fork Dam and Reservoir. Every time the ranchers urged the Forest Service to do the repairs necessary to the South Fork Trail to permit the ranchers to get to the South Fork Dam and Reservoir, the Forest Service declined because the project was not a priority and it lacked the funds necessary to do the work.

For example, in 1990, when the ranchers pleaded with the Forest Service, once again, to do the necessary repairs, the Forest Service responded, "[m]aintenance of the South Fork Trail is not in our trail maintenance plan for this year. We may be able to do this next summer if funding is available." Yet another excuse devised by the Forest Service was that it was developing regulations regarding the repair of dams in wilderness areas, which it completed, at last, in 1996. Finally, in January 1998, the Forest Service boldly proclaimed that the Big Creek Lake Reservoir Association did not owe an easement in the dam, reservoir, and ditches that its predecessors had constructed on public land.

As a result, in March 2004, in full compliance with the federal statute limiting when a lawsuit could be filed (statute of limitations), the Big Creek Lake Reservoir Association filed a lawsuit in Montana federal district court asserting that it owned a property right, an easement, in the South Fork Dam and Reservoir, and had the right to access and maintain its property.[27] The ranchers' lawsuit was similar to the ones filed by the Roths and others. In response, the Forest Service's attorneys not only filed an answer to that lawsuit, they also challenged the ranchers' water rights in Montana water court.[28] Incredibly, the Forest Service asserted that, because the ranchers had not repaired the South Fork Dam and Reservoir—an effort that the Forest Service had barred them from undertaking—the ranchers had abandoned the water rights and those rights now belonged to the Forest Service!

The ranchers of the Big Creek Lake Reservoir Association now found themselves in two courts. Before the water master, the ranchers argued that they had never abandoned either their water rights or their claims to the dam and reservoir. They pointed out that, even though the manmade dam had disappeared during the 1960s, a natural dam had formed that ensures an appreciable amount of water to flow annually, water the ranchers put to beneficial use. In fact, water from this natural dam has increased the irrigation season for several of the ranchers by up to a week. Furthermore, the ranchers provided specific evidence of the economic, financial, and legal difficulties that had prevented them from greater use of the water they claimed in the South Fork Reservoir.

Specifically, they demonstrated that actions of the Forest Service had prevented them from repairing and operating the South Fork Dam and Reservoir since the 1960s to the degree that they had desired. Not only had the Forest Service made repair prohibitively expensive as a result of its regulations, but also the Forest Service had obstructed their access to their dam and reservoir, both by denying them permission to enter the land and by refusing to maintain the trail by which they would reach their dam and reservoir. Furthermore, the ranchers continued to operate parts of their irrigation system with expenditures of money and time and continued to attempt to repair the dam, reservoir, and ditches. With testimony from Big Creek Lake Reservoir Association members and other witnesses and in a post-hearing brief, the ranchers sought to prove that they had no intention of abandoning, and had not abandoned, their water rights.

It was not enough. In July 2005, the water master ruled that the Association had abandoned its water rights; the ranchers immediately appealed.[29] Meanwhile, the Forest Service rushed to Montana federal district court asserting that the water master's ruling as to the Association's water rights demonstrated that the Big Creek Lake Reservoir Association did not own a property right to the South Fork Dam and Reservoir. In response, the ranchers maintained, first, that the water master's ruling is on appeal and therefore not dispositive and second, that even the loss of the water right does not preordain the loss of the Association's right to its dam and reservoir. Nonetheless, they face a long battle.

Sophisticates might assert that the ranchers should have lawyered up years ago. But why should they have done that? After all, they were dealing with, if not friends, then at least neighbors. Plus, the people they were dealing with worked for the United States Government, the embodiment of, as maudlin as it sounds, millions believe it, their country. They might not like all that their government does but it would not purposefully attempt to deceive them, would it?[30] Finally, lawyers cost money and already they had spent more than a hundred thousand dollars.

Furthermore, there is a serious question whether, even if they had lawyered up, it would have done any good. The federal government's lawyers would have told their lawyers the same thing that the non-lawyer bureaucrats at the Forest Service were telling them, only it would have been written in convoluted legalese and it would have cost them a hundred and some dollars an hour. In addition, if their lawyer had filed a lawsuit, it would have been dismissed as not ripe; a federal judge would be unlikely to second guess the Forest Service's assertion that there were things that had to be done before the Forest Service could allow the ranchers access to the South Fork Dam and Reservoir. "These things take time," federal lawyers would argue. "Of course, they do," the judge would respond. "Come back when the Forest Service absolutely forbids your access." Would hiring a lawyer have made a difference with the water master? Maybe, but why should it? Was it not enough that, year after year, the ranchers sought permission to do what had to be done? Since when does a person have to hire a lawyer to give his words meaning, substance, and heft? Apparently, it seems, given the fate that has befallen the ranchers of the Big Creek Lake Reservoir Association, at least for now, anytime one deals with the federal government, its agencies, bureaucrats, and lawyers!

Many legal issues in the West are judgment calls: whether a species is "endangered"; whether a sinkhole may be labeled "waters of the United States"; or whether an environmental study constitutes the necessary "hard look." However, the rights of those who own property originally settled by homesteaders to access—across federal land—to their property, whether it is their ranch, their grazing allotment, or their water facilities, are beyond dispute. Congress could not have been more explicit in the laws it wrote on the subject and the legislative history of those laws is incontrovertible. Furthermore, the patents issued to those homesteaders conveyed to them every right they would need for the full enjoyments of that land. And if that were not enough, and it should be enough, the common law—the law the United States inherited from England—provides the rights the homesteaders believed they were receiving.

It is unconscionable, therefore, for lawyers in the employ of the United States of America to argue otherwise in the courts of the land. Someone should put a stop to it; perhaps one day, someone will.

Westerners' fights for their rights are not limited to matters of history or antiquity or to battles with federal and state governments and the usual suspects. In a volatile and dynamic world, there are new challenges, new adversaries, and new fronts. But not all is changing; there are immutable truths: the vision of the Founding Fathers; the sacrifice of the nation's heroes; and the ideal that America holds out to the world.

CHAPTER 15

FIGHTING ILLEGAL IMMIGRATION AND OTHER ABUSES

> Mexican officials here and abroad are involved in a massive and almost daily interference in American sovereignty. . . . [T]he millions [of illegal aliens] across the country [] are not a naturally occurring phenomenon, like the tides. They are there thanks in part to Mexico's efforts to get them into the U.S. in violation of American law, and to normalize their status once here in violation of the popular will. Mexican consulates are engineering a backdoor amnesty for their illegal migrants and trying to discredit American immigration enforcement—activities clearly beyond diplomatic bounds.
>
> HEATHER MACDONALD, *MEXICO'S UNDIPLOMATIC DIPLOMATS*[1]

> "Congress shall make no law . . . abridging freedom of speech." What part of "no law" does Congress not understand?
>
> DAVID R. HENDERSON – HOOVER INSTITUTION[2]

Randy Pullen of Phoenix, Arizona, was frustrated. As he drove down the streets of his hometown, read the newspapers, and listened to the radio, he could tell that the problem of illegal immigration was getting worse, if that were even possible. As many as five hundred thousand illegal aliens were already living in Arizona. As far as he was concerned, illegal immigration was the single biggest issue facing not just his town, but all of Arizona. No other issue casts such a long shadow over the state's future.

He knew from the articles that he had read that welfare and other safety-net payments were being paid illegally to "undocumented immigrants," as they were euphemistically called. This was costing Arizona at least $1 billion annually, or about $700 a year for every Arizona household, though from personal experience he imagined the number was much higher. He also knew that Congress, with its enactment of the federal welfare reform act in 1996—the one Clinton signed on the third try—had mandated that state employees not be barred from receiving from or sending to the Immigration and Naturalization Service (INS), or, as it became in 2003, the Department of Homeland Security, information regarding the immigration status of anyone. Yet, he knew that no one in Arizona's social service agencies was performing what lawyers call due diligence on the people to whom Arizona was handing taxpayer money and other benefits. In fact, from his investigations of state agencies and those of others, he knew that the agencies were assisting illegal aliens in obtaining social service benefits.

Plus, there was the issue of voting. To vote, a person must be a citizen, have sworn allegiance to the United States, and have borne at least some of the burden for providing the benefits that the politicians promised, benefits that people like Randy Pullen and his friends had to pay for with their tax dollars. What, if anything, were election officials doing to make sure that those in line at the polling booths had the right to be there? Nothing, Randy Pullen expected.

Every day it seemed as if there was yet another story in the media about the porous United States–Mexico border, particularly in southern Arizona. Randy Pullen knew that the United States had tightened up America's southern border elsewhere—in Texas, New Mexico, and California; however, the federal government had purposefully left the Arizona border unchanged. The plan, he had learned, was to direct immigration traffic from Mexico into Arizona, where, purportedly, it could be targeted by the Bureau of Customs and Border Protection. Maybe that was a good theory in Washington, D.C., but out in the middle of nowhere, in the wide-open spaces of Cochise, Santa Cruz, Pima, and Yuma Counties, that idea was ridiculous.

Some ranchers, whose property was near or adjacent to the Mexico border, compared the hordes crossing their land to "rush hour traffic in downtown Phoenix." That was nothing compared to the fear, for their wives, children, livestock, buildings, and yes, even their own personal safety, that these citizens faced every day. The people coming across the border were ill-prepared for the journey, and, as a result, they were dehydrated, hungry, and frightened. They were *desperate*, which, in the ranchers' minds, made them very dangerous. "Why won't someone do something?" they asked time and again at their meetings. Federal officials just shrugged and said they did not have the resources to deal with the problem.

That is exactly the same thing the politicians in Washington, D.C., are doing, thought Randy Pullen. They shrug their shoulders and say it's not their problem. And the state and local bureaucrats were just as uninterested in solving the problem—it was always someone else's responsibility. But Randy Pullen refused to see that as the end of the line. If the government was not going to fulfill its role and protect its citizens, then Randy Pullen would just have to do it himself.

Randy Pullen teamed up with his friends, State Representatives Randy Graf and Russell Pearce, Gene Reed, and Willa Key, all of Phoenix, Sue Voss and Marcia Ridgely of Tucson, and Iris Lynch and Kathryn Harvey of southern Arizona, and they began their efforts to put something on the ballot: something simple that people could easily get their heads around. They came up with four such ideas. First, Arizona public employees who handed out "benefits" would be required to ask for proof positive that the person applying for benefits was entitled to receive them.[3] Second, Arizona public employees who learned that a person who applied for public benefits was not entitled, as a result of his immigration status, to receive those benefits would be required to report that information to the federal government. Third, Arizona poll officials would be required to obtain proof positive that all prospective voters had the right to vote in the election for which they were presenting themselves. Fourth, Arizona citizens would have the right to file lawsuits to force bureaucrats to do their job and obey these directives.[4]

Over the course of several months, Randy Pullen, Kathy McKee, and others collected signatures to get their initiative on the ballot. The Federation for American Immigration Reform (FAIR), the leading immigration policy organization in the country, in Washington, D.C., and its executive director Dan Stein and staff counsel Michael Hethmon, agreed to weigh in with financial, legal, and moral support. Finally, in July 2004, Randy Pullen and his friends presented more than 190,000 signatures—what they believed was easily the number of requisite signatures—to the Arizona secretary of state and demanded a place on the November 2004 ballot. That is when the real fireworks started.[5]

Almost immediately, opponents began a campaign of disinformation, distorting both the language and the objectives of the "Arizona Taxpayer and Citizen Protection Act," ballot issue Proposition 200, as well as impugning the motives and character of people like Randy Pullen.[6] The mainstream media could not get enough of the rash rhetoric, which it quickly reported, but it was less thorough when it came to informing prospective voters of the exact language of Proposition 200. Moreover, although a host of Arizona State Senators and Representatives joined with Randy Pullen in calling for passage of Proposition 200, the governor, attorney general, and entire Arizona congressional delegation weighed in against it.[7] Then, days before the election, even as absentee ballots were being marked, returned, and accepted, opponents filed yet another lawsuit to kick Proposition 200 off the ballot; it was the third such legal challenge to the ballot initiative. As had the others, that ploy failed; the votes would be counted.

Randy Pullen remained confident. All along, public opinion polls had been showing broad and deep support for his initiative,[8] but he had watched enough elections to know that polls are one thing, the results at the polls are something else again. At the end of the day, it was not even close. Proposition 200 passed, 56 percent for and 44 percent against. The mainstream media were especially amazed at one statistic that reflected what Randy Pullen had known all along: 47 percent of Hispanic voters and 65 percent of African American voters had voted in favor of Proposition 200!

Even before the signatures had been turned in to the Arizona Secretary of State, Randy Pullen had heard rumors that the ACLU and the Mexican American Legal Defense and Education Fund (MALDEF) would file a lawsuit to stop the initiative from becoming law if it were approved by the voters. Sure enough, on November 29, 2004, both groups went to the Arizona federal district court in Tucson and filed their complaint: the ballot initiative was unconstitutional because it impermissibly invaded an area that had been preempted by Congress, they asserted. The next day, the ACLU and MALDEF sought a temporary restraining order (TRO) to prevent Proposition 200, signed just days before by the governor, from taking effect. Not surprisingly to Randy Pullen, the Arizona attorney general raised no objection to the imposition of the TRO: Arizona would not suffer any irreparable injury if enactment were delayed, state lawyers demurred. Randy Pullen wondered about the $2.7 million a day that Arizona would lose in the payment of illegal benefits.

Randy Pullen, his Yes on Proposition 200 Committee, and FAIR obtained legal counsel and quickly moved to intervene in the case. Someone has to be there to ensure that the will of the voters of Arizona is protected, they all decided. On December 8, 2004, their motion was granted, and, on December 22, 2004, after the filing of stacks of briefs, they were in Arizona federal district court in Tucson. When the hearing ended, the district court denied the opponents' motion for a preliminary injunction and lifted the earlier TRO. According to the court, the opponents had failed to demonstrate that they would win on the merits in the claim that Proposition 200 was unconstitutional.[9] Just moments later, in front of the television news cameras arrayed before the Tucson courthouse, lawyers for MALDEF said they would appeal immediately.

The ACLU and MALDEF sought an emergency stay from the U.S. Court of Appeals for the Ninth Circuit, which was denied on January 14, 2005. Then, ten days later, the ACLU and MALDEF got their third piece of bad news in little more than a month when the U.S. Department of Justice's Civil Rights Division informed the Arizona attorney general that the voting provisions of Proposition 200 did not violate the federal Voting Rights Act.[10]

Apparently, this was too much for the opponents of Proposition 200, including Mexico! In what appears to have been an act of desperation, Mexico's top diplomat made a shocking announcement: Mexico was working with the groups fighting Proposition 200, and, if they did not win in federal court, Mexico would haul the United States before the United Nations Human Rights Commission![11]

As outrageous as this was, it was no idle threat; Mexico has a history of dragging the United States before international tribunals. Consider, for example, the case of the infamous Jose Medellin! In June 1993, Mexican citizen Jose Ernesto Medellin and his gang raped, tortured, and murdered two teenage girls in Houston, Texas. Medellin and four others were convicted of capital murder and sentenced to death.[12]

In April 1997, when Mexico discovered that Medellin was a Mexican citizen, it immediately provided him a top-flight New York City lawyer who argued that, under the Vienna Convention, Medellin's rights had been violated. In January 2003, Mexico sued the United States in the International Court of Justice (ICJ) on behalf of Medellin and fifty-three other Mexican nationals on Texas's death row. In March 2004, by a vote of fourteen to one, the ICJ ruled that the United States had violated the Vienna Convention as to Medellin and fifty other Mexican nationals!

In May 2004, the U.S. Court of Appeals for the Fifth Circuit ruled, based on U.S. Supreme Court precedent, that Medellin had waived his Vienna Convention rights, just as a U.S. citizen might waive his constitutional rights.[13] Mexico brushed the Fifth Circuit's ruling aside, and, after the U.S. Supreme Court, in December 2004, agreed to hear the case, told the U.S. Supreme Court during oral argument in March 2005, that Mexican citizens who kill in the United States have more rights than do U.S. citizens who commit murder.[14] Fortunately, the U.S. Supreme Court declined to rule in the case and, in May 2005, dismissed Medellin's case as improvidently granted.[15] Medellin's case is not over, however; Mexico will send its New York City lawyer back to the U.S. Supreme Court on Medellin's behalf. Clearly, Mexico would not think twice about taking the United States before the despots who sit on the U.N. Commission on Human Rights over Arizona's Proposition 200. That is especially the case if Randy Pullen and his friends win in federal court and other states adopt their own versions of Proposition 200.

A few weeks after the Mexican diplomat made his threat, Mexico upped the ante even further in its war on Arizona's Proposition 200. Shortly after visiting Arizona, seven Mexican senators issued a report in which they called Arizona a hotbed of "xenophobia and discrimination" and demanded that the Mexican government give even more support to groups, like the ACLU and MALDEF, in their fight to defeat Proposition 200 in court.[16]

Nonetheless, Randy Pullen fought on and, in June 2005, his attorneys appeared before the U.S. Court of Appeals for the Ninth Circuit. Days prior to their arrival in San Francisco for the argument, the Ninth Circuit panel had asked them to address whether the clients represented by the ACLU and MALDEF had standing to file their lawsuit, that is, had they been injured, and whether the matter was ripe for judicial review, that is, had final decisions been made as to how Proposition 200 was going to be applied or was it still a moving target. Randy Pullen's lawyers argued that the plaintiffs had failed to demonstrate an injury and that their case should be dismissed.

Moreover, argued Randy Pullen's lawyers, Proposition 200 was clearly constitutional because it did not invade an area that had been preempted by Congress; instead, it merely did the very thing that Congress, in adopting the welfare reform act in 1996,[17] had urged states to do. Under that law, states were prohibited from paying "state and local benefits" to illegal aliens,[18] a provision adopted by Congress "to remove the incentive for illegal immigration provided by the availability of public benefits."[19] Furthermore, Congress barred states from restricting the ability of governments, whether state or local, to communicate with federal officials regarding an individual's immigration status,[20] and states were "authorize[d] to require an applicant for state or local public benefits ... to provide proof of eligibility."[21] In addition, argued Randy Pullen's attorneys, if Congress seeks to preempt action by states, it must do so in clear and manifest language because, under the Constitution. states are sovereigns as well. Finally, the regulation of immigration, which Congress has preempted for itself, consists solely of deciding who may enter the country and under what conditions they may be allowed to stay.[22] Arizona, with its adoption of Proposition 200, is not addressing either issue; instead, Arizona is fulfilling the objectives set forth by Congress in the welfare reform act. Therefore, Proposition 200 is constitutional.

In August 2005, a Ninth Circuit panel ruled that the plaintiffs represented by the ACLU and MALDEF lacked standing to challenge Proposition 200, denied the appeal, and remanded the case to the Arizona federal district court where it was dismissed.[23] Nonetheless, Randy Pullen believes that the ACLU and MALDEF, with the backing of Mexico, will continue to file lawsuits to get Proposition 200 declared unconstitutional or otherwise to prevent its implementation.

In the meantime, there are other battles to fight. Notwithstanding that, as a scare tactic in the campaign before the election, opponents of Proposition 200 defined the term benefits in the initiative quite broadly, after the election they changed their tune and have sought since to define the term as narrowly as possible to reduce its impact. On November 12, ten days after the election, the Arizona attorney general issued an opinion giving the term benefit the narrowest possible application.[24] Randy Pullen and others filed a challenge to that opinion.[25] In addition, the governor vetoed a number of bills, including legislation that would have provided regulations for the voting fraud provisions of Proposition 200. Only recently was an agreement reached that allows the secretary of state to implement those key sections of Proposition 200.[26]

Randy Pullen believes he has brought national attention to the issue of illegal immigration. Today, even the mainstream media is filled with stories of the problems caused by illegal immigration—soaring benefits costs, increases in infectious diseases, including some not seen in hospitals for decades, out of control crime rates and dangerous gangs, and the risk of terrorist infiltration. Even cities far from the U.S.-Mexican border have been touched by the controversy and even tragedy.

In Denver, Colorado, on Mother's Day, May 8, 2005, a Denver detective, Donald Young, was murdered and his partner, Detective Jack Bishop, was wounded by Raul Garcia-Gomez, a nineteen-year-old illegal alien, who fled to Mexico. Incredibly, Garcia-Gomez had been stopped several times by Denver police, but Denver has restricted the ability of its police to investigate the status of potential illegal immigrants in the Mile High City. This policy, adopted by the current mayor's predecessor, Wellington Webb, may be in direct conflict with the federal law that Randy Pullen used to such good effect in adopting Proposition 200, a law that bars any limits on the ability of state and local officials to communicate freely regarding immigration status.[27] No doubt, Randy Pullen's example may have inspired another person to conclude that he is the someone who can do something about such senseless tragedies.

FIGHTING FOR THE RIGHT TO SPEAK AND TO BE HEARD

Groups like the ACLU and MALDEF, as Randy Pullen discovered, have their own unique view of the commands of the U.S. Constitution. A thousand miles away, some rural folks in Montana learned the same lesson regarding Common Cause.

Common Cause and its allied groups in Montana, primarily in Missoula, maintain that voting on Montana ballot initiatives has been undemocratic because, on occasion, corporations participate. Notwithstanding that those corporations may become involved because of their economic interests; the economic interests of their stockholders, some of whom live in Montana; and the economic interests of their employees, many of whom live and, thanks to the corporations, work in Montana; Common Cause believes that such involvement skews the outcomes and should not be permitted.

As a result, in the fall of 1996, while much public controversy and interest was focused on other more economically harmful ballot initiatives, Common Cause succeeded in gaining voter approval of a proposal, I-125, which barred corporations and groups that received more than a limited amount of financial support from corporations from participating meaningfully in ballot initiatives. Trade associations, like the Montana Mining Association and the Northwest Mining Association, which exist, in part, for the purpose of communicating with their members and the public on issues that affect the economic well-being of their member companies, were thus barred from doing what they had done for years. Moreover, a tiny grassroots group, Communities for a Great Northwest, which operates out of a double-wide trailer in Libby, Montana, and exists only as a result of the tiny contributions of its rural members and the sometimes generous support of corporations that see merit in its public advocacy regarding environmental issues, would be shut out of the public debate on ballot initiatives for good. Not surprisingly, with corporations and the groups that sometimes, although not always, agree with them barred from participating in ballot initiatives, Common Cause, with an annual $10 million budget,[28] had the ballot initiative field pretty much to itself.

In 1998, after what some referred to as the gag law went into effect, those three groups and a handful of others filed a lawsuit in Montana federal district court.[29] They asserted that the gag law denied them their First Amendment right of speech, which includes not only the right to speak on matters of public importance but also the right to be heard. They were particularly concerned because, shortly before they filed their lawsuit, various environmental groups, knowing of the enforced silence of the very entities that had opposed them so effectively in the past, placed an anti-mining initiative on the ballot that would kill new Montana mines and the high paying jobs that went with them. The trade associations and grassroots group feared that, if the gag law remained in effect and they were barred from speaking out, the anti-mining initiative would prevail easily. Thus, they urged the Montana federal district court to move speedily in its consideration of the constitutionality of the gag law so that they might be free to enter the fray.

In October 1998, at the conclusion of the trial, the Montana federal district court ruled from the bench that the gag law was unconstitutional on its face. In a written ruling, the court held that "the corporate voice [was] silenced" because the gag law deprived "corporations of the ability to communicate their political views during ballot issue campaigns" and "to communicate political ideas directly to the electorate":

> [The gag law] precludes corporations from directly resisting potential laws that could put them out of business.... Perhaps almost as important, [the gag law] prevents the electorate from being exposed to diverse viewpoints on public policy issues.[30]

The associations and grassroots group moved for an injunction barring voting on the anti-mining initiative, which was days away, because the gag law had barred them from participating in the election campaign. The district court rejected the motion as premature,[31] and, from the bench, mused, "[W]ho knows, [you] may be able to persuade the people that [the initiative] ought not be adopted" after all and, if so, "then there is nothing for the courts to rule on."[32]

It was not to be. The richly financed non-profit proponents of the anti-mining initiative had been campaigning aggressively for several months, unfettered by the gag law, unchallenged by any coordinated opposition, and unopposed in their advocacy. The trade associations and grassroots group, on the other hand, had been muzzled, unconstitutionally, for all that time. They now had only eleven days to counteract the effects of their prolonged, state-coerced silence; to provide the voters of the entire State of Montana with the suppressed, complex facts about the anti-mining initiative; and to sway the opinions of voters who had heard but one voice on the subject for months. That was impossible.[33] It came as no surprise to anyone, therefore, that the anti-mining initiative passed by a margin of 52 to 48 percent.[34] After their narrow defeat, the trade associations and grassroots group returned to the Montana federal district court seeking to enjoin the election results, but the court refused to do so.[35]

In December 1998, an appeal was made to the U.S. Court of Appeals for the Ninth Circuit, arguing that the Montana district court erred by not enjoining the election. In September 2000, a panel of the Ninth Circuit ruled that the gag law was unconstitutional; however, the panel refused to address whether the election should have been enjoined to permit those who had been barred from speaking due to the gag law to participate fully, calling that issue moot. The Ninth Circuit implied that there had been no evidence:

- That being barred from participation for all but eleven days of an election campaign had affected the ability of the trade associations and grassroots group to campaign;
- That, if the gag law had such an effect on their ability to campaign, eleven days were not enough time for them to recover from that effect; or
- That, if eleven days were not enough time for them to recover, holding a special election would not be "too expensive."[36]

In May 2001, the associations and group sought review by the U.S. Supreme Court, citing to the Court its definitive ruling on the subject:

It is the viewers and listeners, not the right of [speakers,] which is paramount. It is the purpose of the First Amendment to preserve an uninhibited marketplace of ideas in which truth will ultimately prevail...It is the right of the public to receive suitable access to social, political, esthetic, moral, and other ideas and experiences which is crucial here. That right may not constitutionally be abridged either by Congress of by [other lawmakers].[37]

Nonetheless, in October 2001, the Supreme Court declined to hear the case.[38] Thus, the associations and group were vindicated: the law had unconstitutionally barred them from participating in a ballot initiative campaign and, hence forth, they would not be so barred. However, for whatever reasons, the district court refused to set the election results aside. Worse yet, the Ninth Circuit declined to do so because it would be too expensive. Although the Supreme Court's holdings on this issue and its remedy were clear, the Ninth Circuit was able to ignore those rulings with the knowledge that, odds were, the Supreme Court would not review and reverse the Ninth Circuit's opinion.

There is one cautionary note for the associations and likeminded entities in other states. Attorneys for the State of Montana were approached just before argument by several people who said they were eager to learn the outcome of the case because they wanted to adopt similarly restrictive legislation in their states. In an ironic twist, if those unidentified activists are of the same frame of mind today, they need not go to the trouble. In 2002, with adoption of the McCain-Feingold bill, Congress did much of their work for them.[39] What about the Supreme Court? In 2003, the Court upheld the constitutionality of that legislation brushing aside many of the cases that the Montana associations and group had cited to the Court back in 2001 when they sought *certiorari*.[40]

USING THE FIRST AMENDMENT AS A SHIELD NOT A SWORD

Federal appellate courts are not always so reluctant to find that, because a favored litigant's First Amendment rights have been violated, they must grant an extraordinary remedy, such as declaring unconstitutional an Act of Congress, even on a matter uniquely within the expertise of Congress such as national defense.

Late in 2004, as the nation celebrated the holidays, Americans reached out to others. Across the country, gifts were purchased, packaged, and sent off to uniformed men and women serving in Iraq and Afghanistan. Visits were made, care given, and prayers raised for the hundreds injured in combat. And, as families gathered to welcome in the New Year, America remembered those who had made the ultimate sacrifice for their country. Confronted by such selflessness, humbled millions ask, what can we do?

Meanwhile administrators, professors, and students at America's elite law schools were in a celebratory mood as a result of a victory they had won in late November, at the U.S. Court of Appeals for the Third Circuit. These law schools and their professors, faced with a federal law mandating that they allow military recruiters onto their campuses or lose federal funding, had complained that they should not be required to make any sacrifice whatsoever, even something as insignificant as scheduling appointments or reserving a room for interviews. In fact, asserted these law schools and their professors, being required to allow military recruiters on campus violates their freedoms of speech and association. Incredibly, the Third Circuit agreed, and declared that federal law, the Solomon-Pombo Amendment unconstitutional.

The case, *Forum for Academic & Institutional Rights, Inc. (FAIR) v. Rumsfeld*, had been filed in September 2003 in New Jersey federal district court against Secretary of Defense Donald H. Rumsfeld and five other Cabinet secretaries. After the district court dismissed FAIR's case, FAIR appealed to the Third Circuit, which ruled, on November 29, 2004, by a two to one margin, that the law is unconstitutional![41]

FAIR says it is an "association of twenty-four law schools and law faculties whose mission is to promote academic freedom and to support educational institutions is (sic) opposing discrimination" whose "first project is a legal challenge to the Solomon Amendment." FAIR, which has refused to disclose its members, except *in camera* to a federal judge, says that, because law schools have anti-discrimination policies and the military bars homosexual activity, being forced to host military representatives on campus suppresses their speech and compels them to associate with a message they abhor.

One Third Circuit judge, a World War II U.S. Marine Corps Major, dissented,[42] first discrediting the panel's reliance on two U.S. Supreme Court rulings where the Court held that parade organizers need not accept gay pride marchers and that the Boy Scouts may expel a homosexual scoutmaster. Then, the dissent disclosed that the Third Circuit had rejected FAIR's arguments in an earlier case, barring the panel's ruling. Next, noting the sophistication of law schools faculties and students, the dissent declared that they were capable of disassociating themselves from the military's message when recruiters came. Finally, speaking for most Americans, the dissent rejected:

> [t]he subjective idiosyncratic impressions of *some* law students, *some* professors, or *some* anti-war protesters [that recruiters bring discredit to campus, because] men and women in uniform are almost universally considered as heroes, sacrificing not only their lives and well-being, but living separate from all the comforts of stateside living. . . . [43]

If this case were about principle, elite law schools would be demanding that recruiters come to their campuses. As the abuses at Abu Ghraib prison and the alleged shooting of an unarmed Iraqi in Fallujah demonstrate, there is a vital need for highly qualified lawyers to serve as military trial and defense counsel and as judges on military tribunals. America's credibility in the world community and the confidence of uniformed Americans in the fairness of military justice depend on skilled lawyers from the nation's best law schools.

The case brought by the law schools is not about principle! That is obvious because the ethical sensitivity on which it is based does not extend to those hired by colleges (former weatherman Bernadine Dohrn is the director of a legal clinic at Northwestern University) or those invited to speak there (Laura Whitehorn, who spent fourteen years in prison for plotting a 1983 bomb attack on the U.S. Capitol, spoke last year at Duke). Furthermore, elite law schools, while demanding the right to discriminate on the basis of the race of the students applying for acceptance in order to ensure classroom diversity, decry the military's claim that it must discriminate on the basis of sexual activity so as to ensure unit cohesion.

No, this case is the result of the cultural divide that separates college professors from the vast majority of Americans who are proud of and support our troops. Simply stated, it is not the military recruiters' message that these professors abhor; it is the military recruiter in uniform! The conceit of these colleges, their law schools, and their professors—they want millions in taxpayer dollars but they do not want the military, the sons and daughters of taxpayers, on their campuses to hire JAG officers.

Congressman Richard Pombo (R-CA-11th) and three law students from New Jersey and Pennsylvania filed a brief with the U.S. Supreme Court,[44] which agreed to hear this important case, asserting that Congress, given its power to "provide for the common Defense, "[t]o declare War," and "[t]o raise and support Armies [and] a Navy,"[45] may condition its grant of money, and that law students have the right to hear the speech of the military recruiters, a right superior to that of the law schools and their professors to suppress speech with which they disagree. As this book went to print, the Supreme Court heard arguments in this case on December 6, 2005.

It is time, believe people like Randy Pullen, the miners of Montana, and the politically incorrect students at the nation's law schools, that their rights of speech and access to the courts be treated with as much solicitude as the courts treat those of the ACLU, MALDEF, Common Cause, and left-wing professors.

EPILOGUE

And the beat goes on.[1]

It ain't over 'til it's over.[2]

The fundamental things apply, as time goes by.[3]

Thus it is that Warriors for the West continue to wage their battles against legislation, either as written or as interpreted; bureaucrats, whether unscrupulous, covetous, incompetent, or simply wrongheaded; and elected and appointed politicians, driven by their personal or professional agendas. In doing so, these Warriors fight wealthy special interest groups and huge bureaucracies and their seemingly inexhaustible supply of lawyers, time, and money, largely unaided by officials in the Legislative, Executive, and Judicial branches. Against such odds, more often than one would expect, the

Warriors win. Even when they lose, they ready themselves for the next battle. For, notwithstanding the nation's fascination with the Supreme Court as the ultimate and final arbiter, states supreme courts and three-judge panels of federal appellate courts are the ones that, most of the time, have the last word. Nonetheless, Warriors for the West know that, in time, change is possible before those courts and ultimately before the Supreme Court. They know that because of the paths these courts have trod over the decades. Thus, for them hope abounds.

In 1922, Supreme Court Justice Oliver Wendell Holmes declared that government takes private property contrary to the Constitution not only when it seizes the property outright, but also when it regulates it out of use.[4] It was not until 1987, however, that the Supreme Court gave real meaning to Justice Holmes's words by allowing property owners to challenge the regulatory takings of which he had written.[5] And, if the Court's recent rulings are any indication, the Court still has not got it right.[6]

Similarly, the Supreme Court sanctioned "separate but equal" treatment of citizens based on their race in 1896;[7] held that separate was never equal when it came to race in 1954;[8] authorized racial distinctions by the federal government when awarding federal contracts in 1980;[9] and then, in 1995, held that racial distinctions between and among Americans are almost never constitutional.[10] One hundred years to reach the position espoused by a dissenting justice in 1896![11] Nonetheless, to end race-based governmental decision-making, the Court still has work to do.[12]

Likewise, for decades, the Supreme Court held that the Commerce Clause barred federal legislation—almost no commerce was interstate—a view that reached its high-water mark in 1935.[13] Beginning in 1937, the Court sharply reversed course and, for decades, everything somehow affected commerce, either directly or indirectly.[14] In

1995, however, the Supreme Court appeared to put an outer limit on the Commerce Clause, holding that a federal law regarding guns in school yards was unconstitutional.[15] Hopes for a complete reversal of the Court's post-New Deal refusal to give substance to the Commerce Clause were short lived; that battle is far from over.[16]

If there is a lesson here, it is that preserving the rule of law, constitutional liberties, and a republican form of government is a work in progress. America's Founding Fathers knew this, of course. Patrick Henry argued, "The battle, sir, is not to the strong alone; it is to the vigilant, the active, the brave."[17] Wrote Alexander Hamilton, "[T]he passions of men will not conform to the dictates of reason and justice, without constraint."[18] James Madison warned, "[T]here are more instances of the abridgment of the freedom of the people by gradual and silent encroachments of those in power than by violent and sudden usurpations."[19] Declared Thomas Jefferson, "If a nation expects to be ignorant and free, in a state of civilization, it expects what never was and never will be."[20] John Adams counseled, "There is danger from all men. The only maxim of a free government ought to be to trust no man living with power to endanger the public liberty."[21] More than fifty years later, Andrew Jackson cautioned, "Eternal vigilance by the people is the price of liberty, and that you must pay the price if you wish to secure the blessing. [B]e watchful in your States as well as in the Federal Government."[22] Most recently, Ronald Reagan declared, "The future doesn't belong to the faint-hearted. It belongs to the brave."[23]

Thus, those who wish to "secure the blessing of liberty to [themselves] and [their] posterity,"[24] must bravely become engaged, step forward, and bear the burdens that are asked of those who, like generations of Americans before them, believe that America is, as Ronald Reagan expressed it, "the last best hope of man on Earth."[25] These burdens are not inconsequential. It is not easy confronting one's own government, being the subject of *ad hominem* attacks by radical groups and the mainstream media, and expending financial or scarce human resources on exhausting and seemingly never-ending battles. Nonetheless, it must be done. Moreover, knowing that victory is possible and that one's battle will embolden others to fight as well, makes it all worthwhile. After all, as Ronald Reagan put it, "If not us, who? If not now, when?"[26]

Since 1977, Mountain States Legal Foundation has been saying, "Us!" and "Now!" On behalf of the heroic individuals and entities of these pages—true Warriors for the West—Mountain States Legal Foundation has been "in the courts for good," fighting for individual liberty, the right to own and use property, limited and ethical government, and the free enterprise system. That fight continues. Join us there; today!

ENDNOTES

Chapter 1: Fighting the "Pit Bull of Environmental Laws"

1. *Christy v. Lujan*, 490 U.S. 1114, 1116 (1989) (White, J., dissenting). Richard P. Christy grazed his sheep near Glacier National Park in Montana. In July 1982, grizzly bears protected under the Endangered Species Act killed 20 of his sheep. After his requests for assistance from the federal government and his attempts to scare the bears away were unsuccessful, he killed a grizzly bear that attacked his sheep. He was fined $2,500, which he challenged as a violation of the Due Process Clause and as an uncompensated taking of his property. When the Montana federal district court and the U.S. Court of Appeals for the Ninth Circuit rejected his claims, he sought Supreme Court review.

2. http://www.montanascenicloop.com/dupuyer.htm

3. Endangered Species Act (ESA), 16 U.S.C. § 1531, *et seq*. The ESA is implemented by the U.S. Fish and Wildlife Service in the U.S. Department of the Interior and by the National Marine Fisheries Service in the U.S. Department of Commerce.

4. 16 U.S.C. § 1540(a)(3). The Fish and Wildlife Service maintains that, even when a grizzly charges a person, it is not the sign of an imminent attack; it may be merely a "false charge."

5. Of course John Shuler was "glad"; if he had not killed the grizzly, he would be dead!

6. The witness also testified that, in response to his statement that the "cheapest" way to prevent grizzly-bear predation was the $3,000 electric fence, John Shuler said that the "best" way was to provide Shuler with a box of .375 shells. The ALJ recognized that by "best" Shuler meant "cheapest."

7. *FWS v. Shuler*, Docket No. Denver 91-2, slip op. (1993).

8. *Id.*

9. *Id.* The basis for the Fish and Wildlife Service's fine was curious. After all, the Fish and Wildlife Service had concluded that the bear Shuler killed was a "nuisance bear" and that, if it were caught preying on livestock, it would be killed. Thus, it would appear that Shuler had done what the Fish and Wildlife Service planned to do and the value of the grizzly was zero. The Fish and Wildlife Service came up with the $5,000 because that is the cost for an easterner to hire an outfitter and come west to kill lawfully a grizzly.

10. *Beard v. United States*, 158 U.S. 550, 563 (1895); *State v. Swan*, 165 P. 627, 631 (Okla. 1917).

11. It is not unusual for a case before the Ad Hoc Board or its sister panel, the Interior Board of Land Appeals (IBLA), to take four years to get a decision. In fact, one case took more than five and a half years. *Julie Dimitrov, et al.*, 164 IBLA 278 (2005).

12. *FWS v. Shuler*, 13 OHA 67 (FWS App. 1996).

13. "In Suits at common law, where the value in controversy shall exceed twenty dollars, the right of trial by jury shall be preserved, and no fact tried by a jury shall be otherwise re-examined in any Court of the United States, than according to the rules of the common law." U.S. Const. amend. VII. The Supreme Court ruled that the fines assessed by federal agencies are "administrative" and not covered by the Seventh Amendment. *Atlas Roofing Co. v. Occupational Safety and Health Review Commission*, 430 U.S. 442 (1977).

14. *Shuler v. Babbitt*, No. 96cv110 (D.Mont. Dec. 8, 1998).

15. *Shuler*, 243 F.3d 549 (9th Cir. 2000) (unpublished decision).

16. David Simpson, *Man survives 'violent' grizzly encounter*, Jackson Hole Guide, Sept. 30, 1998, at A1.

17. Author's recollection from a telephone conversation in early 1999.

18. Radical environmental groups call the Endangered Species Act the "pit bull of environmental laws" because, unlike almost every other federal statute, it does not permit, in most of the decisions that it compels officials to make, consideration of cost or a balancing of competing interests. As the Supreme Court declared famously in *Tennessee Valley Authority v. Hill*, 437 U.S. 153, 184 (1978), not a single one of a species may go out of existence "whatever the cost."

19. *See, e.g.*, William Perry Pendley, *War on the West, Government Tyranny on America's Great Frontier* 85-98 (Regnery 1995).

20. Jack Ward Thomas, a biologist, President Clinton's Chief of the U.S. Forest Service and the expert regarding the protected northern spotted owls, said, "There isn't a magic number [of owls] as far as I know in science. All of these decisions in the end turn out to be moral decisions...." Quoted by Associated Press reporter Robert Greene. A former regional director of the Fish and Wildlife Service admitted that his agency did not make decisions based on biological science but instead based on political science, which he called the "balancing of competing demands." Endangered Species Law and Regulation Conference, Sacramento, Calif., Feb. 10, 1994.

21. In southern Wyoming and northern Colorado, the U.S. Forest Service refused to harvest more timber in the national forests there so as to increase the water levels in the North Platte River. Instead, to aid protected species at risk due to low water levels, the Fish and Wildlife Service demanded that ranchers give up their water rights. When the ranchers sued to compel the Forest Service to comply with the Endangered Species Act, the case was dismissed on procedural grounds. *Coalition for Sustainable Resources v. Forest Service*, 48 F.Supp.2d 1303 (D.Wyo. 1999), 259 F.3d 1244 (10th Cir. 2001).

22. *Babbitt v. Sweet Home Chapter of Communities for a Great Oregon*, 515 U.S. 687 (1995).

23. The Endangered Species Act prohibits the "taking" of species; "take" is defined to include "harm"; and "harm" defined to include "habitat modification." 16 U.S.C. §§ 1531, 1532.

24. *U.S. Fish and Wildlife Service v. Drake*, Docket No. Denver 99-1, 999 Int. Dec. 999, 2001 WL 1769732, at **34 (Dec. 21, 2001).

25. *Id.* at **21.

26. *Id.* Only one other ALJ ruling is posted or, without being upheld by the IBLA, cited to as authoritative precedent.

27. *U.S. Fish and Wildlife Service v. Drake*, 29 OHA 71 (2004).

28. Endangered and Threatened Wildlife and Plants: Final Rule to List the Preble's Meadow Jumping Mouse as a Threatened Species, 63 *Fed. Reg.* 26,517 (May 13, 1998) (to be codified at 50 C.F.R. Part 17).

29. http://www.census.gov/Press-Release/www/1999/cb99-50.html

30. Letter from Fish and Wildlife Service to Mr. Robert B. Hoff (Oct. 12, 2000).

31. *Hoff v. Norton*, No. 03cv01011 (D.Colo. Dec. 22, 2003).

32. *Mountain States Legal Foundation v. Norton*, No. 03cv0250 (D.Wyo. filed Dec. 9, 2003); http://www.eswr.com/f012803a.htm

33. After MSLF filed its lawsuit on December 9, 2003, on December 17, 2003, the State of Wyoming's Office of the Governor and Coloradoans for Water Conservation and Development filed petitions to delist the PMJM based on "data error" (*i.e.*, new information discovered) and "taxonomic revision." http://mountain-prairie.fws.gov/preble/

34. Gary Gerhardt, *Doubt about mouse: Preble's species' protected status in limbo after scientist wavers on own research*, Rocky Mountain News, Apr. 30, 2004, 1A. Endangered and Threatened Wildlife and Plants: 12-Month Finding on a Petition To Delist the Preble's Meadow Jumping Mouse (*Zapus hudsonius preblei*) and Proposed Delisting of the Preble's Meadow Jumping Mouse, 70 *Fed. Reg.* 5,404 (Feb. 2, 2005) (to be codified at 50 C.F.R. Part 17). http://mountain-prairie.fws.gov/pressrel/05-05.htm; http://mountain-prairie.fws.gov/preble/HOME/FRnoticefinal02022005.pdf

35. North Central Montana Working Group, North Central Montana Black Footed Ferret Reintroduction and Management Plan 19 (April 1992), unpublished manuscript available from Montana Department of Fish, Wildlife and Parks, Helena, Montana.

36. *Id.* at 19.

37. Endangered and Threatened Wildlife and Plants: Establishment of a Nonessential Experimental Population of Black-footed Ferrets in North-Central Montana—Final Rule, 59 *Fed. Reg.* 42696, 42696 (Aug. 18, 1994) (to be codified at 50 C.F.R. Part 17).

38. *Friends of the Earth, Inc. v. Laidlaw Environmental Services, Inc.*, 528 U.S. 167 (2000); *accord Adarand Constructors, Inc. v. Slater*, 528 U.S. 216 (2000) (*per curiam*).

39. *Montana Sport Shooting Ass'n, Inc. v. Norton*, 355 F.Supp.2d 19 (D.D.C. 2004).

40. *Montana Sports Shooting Ass'n*, No. 04-5434, 2005 WL 281086 (D.C. Cir. June 14, 2005) (*per curiam*), *en banc denied*, 2005 WL 2810686 (Sept. 28, 2005), *petition for cert. filed* (U.S. Dec. 21, 2005).

41. The operative phrases on the issue are "voluntary cessation of a challenged practice," *Friends of the Earth, Inc. v. Laidlaw Environmental Services, Inc.*, 528 U.S. 167, 169 (2000), and "capable of repetition while evading review," *Rex v. Owens, ex rel. State of Oklahoma*, 585 F.2d 432, 434 (10th Cir. 1978).

42. *McCulloch v. Maryland*, 17 U.S. (4 Wheat.) 316, 405 (1819). "The powers not delegated to the United States by the Constitution, nor prohibited by it to the States, are reserved to the States respectively, or to the people." U.S. Const. amend. X.

43. U.S. Const. art. I, § 8, cl. 3.

44. *A.L.A. Schecter Poultry Corp. v. U.S.*, 295 U.S. 495, 550 (1935).

45. *NLRB v. Jones & Laughlin Steel Corp.*, 301 U.S. 1 (1937).

46. *U.S. v. Lopez*, 514 U.S. 549 (1995).

47. *GDF Realty Investments, Inc. v. Norton*, 169 F.Supp.2d 648, 664 (S.D. Tex. 2001) ("The regulated activity at issue here substantially affects interstate commerce.").

48. *GDF Realty*, 326 F.3d 622, 640-641 (5th Cir. 2003).

49. *GDF Realty*, 362 F.3d 286 (5th Cir. 2004) (*en banc*). The dissent was written by Judge Edith Hollan Jones, often mentioned as a potential Supreme Court nominee. http://washingtontimes.com/national/20050520-121231-2088r.htm

50. *GDF Realty*, 362 F.3d at 287.

51. One of the ironies for conservatives, libertarians, or others on the right side of the political spectrum is that the left demands slavish adherence to Supreme Court precedent that is favored by the left. For example, any judge who questions *Roe v. Wade*, 410 U.S. 113 (1973), is "outside the mainstream" and not fit for service on the federal judiciary. However, rulings like *Lopez, supra*, are not entitled to that type of devotion.

52. *GDF Realty, cert. denied*, ___ U.S. ___, 125 S.Ct. 2898 (2005).

53. After the Supreme Court's most recent decision holding that Congress may regulate the growing of medical marijuana under California law, many believe that nothing remains of the limits imposed by *Lopez*, even though the majority asserts that its ruling does not overturn *Lopez. Gonzales v. Raich*, ___ U.S. ___, 125 S.Ct. 2195 (2005).

Chapter 2: Fighting Lyin' Cheatin' Bureaucrats

1. http://dcnr.nv.gov/markers/mark_69.htm

2. http://hometown.aol.com/Gibson0817/jarbidge.htm; http://www.ghosttowns.com/states/nv/jarbidge.html; http://www.nevadaweb.com/cnt/cc/jrbg.html

3. Act of May 10, 1872, 17 Stat. 91, 30 U.S.C. § 21, *et seq.*

4. *Castle v. Womble*, 19 L.D. 455 (1894). Maley, *Handbook of Mineral Law* 212-219 (MMRC Publications rev. 2d ed. 1979).

5. Specifically, the BLM records were the Master Title Plat (MT Plat) and Historical Index (HI); officially, the land was "segregated from mineral entry."

6. *John D. Bernt*, 147 IBLA 352, 355 (1999).

7. *Id.* at 354.

8. 5 U.S.C. § 701, *et seq.*

9. 28 U.S.C. § 2680(h).

10. The FTCA has a two-year statute of limitations; that is, a claim must be filed within two years of the facts that gave rise to that claim. Because of the time that John Bernt's case was before the IBLA, that two-year period, had it applied, had expired. The Nevada district court ruled that the FTCA was John Bernt's only cause of action and its two-year statute of limitations had expired. *Bernt v. Babbitt*, No. 00cv-0571 (D.Nev. Mar. 9, 2001).

11. Remarkably, the certification was based upon conversations with individuals who were not involved in the events alleged by John Bernt. Moreover, there is no indication that, in making their certification, the federal lawyers spoke to the employees who were involved.

12. *NEC Corp. v. United States*, 151 F.3d 1361, 1371 (Fed. Cir. 1998).

13. *Id.*

14. *Haley v. Department of the Treasury*, 977 F.2d 553, 558 (Fed. Cir. 1992).

15. "If there is wrongdoing in government, it must be exposed. . . . [The government lawyer's] duty to the people, the law, and his own conscience requires disclosure . . . . " Jack B. Weinstein, *Some Ethical and Political Problems of a Government Attorney* 18 Maine L. Rev. 155, 160 (1966).

16. H.R. 2074, 104th Cong. (1995).

17. One of the purported reasons for the withdrawal was to "protect . . . areas of traditional religious importance to Native Americans." This reason violates the Establishment Clause of the First Amendment to the Constitution.

18. So controversial were Secretary of the Interior Bruce Babbitt's actions that Senator Orrin Hatch advised President Clinton that getting him confirmed for a seat on the U.S. Supreme Court would be "a tough, political battle." Orrin Hatch, *Square Peg: Confessions of a Citizen Senator* 180 (Basic Books 2002).

19. *United States v. Midwest Oil Co.*, 236 U.S. 459 (1915).

20. "Effective on and after the date of this Act, the implied authority of the President to make withdrawals and reservations resulting from acquiescence of the Congress (*U.S. v. Midwest Oil Co.*, 236 U.S. 459) and the following statutes and parts of statutes are repealed." Pub. L. No. 94-579, § 704(a), 90 Stat. 2744, 2792 (1976).

21. U.S. Supreme Court Justice George Sutherland's description of the U.S. Attorney's role is instructive: "[W]hile he may strike hard blows, he is not at liberty to strike foul ones. It is as much his duty to refrain from improper methods calculated to produce a wrongful conviction as it is to use every legitimate means to bring about a just one." *Berger v. United States*, 295 U.S. 78, 88 (1935). Although Justice Sutherland was writing regarding criminal prosecution, his instructions should apply to civil proceedings as well.

22. *Mount Royal Joint Venture v. Norton*, No. 99cv2728 (D.D.C. Aug. 26, 2005).

23. http://www.usatoday.com/news/washington/2001-04-04-irs.htm

24. In passing the Equal Access to Justice Act, 28 U.S.C. § 2412, Congress expressed concerns that persons "may be deterred from seeking review of, or defending against, unreasonable governmental action because of the expense involved in securing vindication of their rights." Pub. L. No. 96-481, § 202(a), 94 Stat. 2321. Explained the House Report:

For many citizens, the costs of securing vindication of their rights and the inability to recover attorney fees preclude resort to the adjudicatory process. When the cost of contesting a government order, for example, exceeds the amount at stake, a party has no realistic choice and no effective remedy. In these cases, it is more practical to endure an injustice than to contest it.

H.R. Rep. No. 96-1418 (1980), *reprinted in* 1980 U.S.C.C.A.N. 4984, 4988.

25. There are scores of such statutes including: the Equal Access to Justice Act, 28 U.S.C. § 2412(b); Endangered Species Act of 1973, 16 U.S.C. § 1540(g)(4); Freedom of Information Act, 5 U.S.C. §§ 552(a)(4)(E), (F); and Uniform Relocation Assistance and Real Property Acquisition Policies Act, 84 Stat. 1906, 42 U.S.C. §§ 4654(a), (c).

26. For example, contrast *Kenseth v. Commissioner*, 259 F.3d 881 (7th Cir. 2001), with *Estate of Clarks v. United States*, 202 F.3d 854 (6th Cir. 2000).

27. *Comm'r. v. Banks*, 543 U.S. ___, 125 S.Ct. 826 (2005). The Court based its ruling on the following:

> A taxpayer cannot exclude an economic gain from gross income by assigning the gain in advance to another party. *Lucas v. Earl*, 281 U.S. 111 (1930); *Commissioner v. Sunnen*, 333 U.S. 591, 604 (1948); *Helvering v. Horst*, 311 U.S. 112, 116-117 (1940). The rationale for the so-called anticipatory assignment of income doctrine is the principle that gains should be taxed "to those who earn them," *Lucas, supra*, at 114, a maxim we have called the "first principle of income taxation," *Commissioner v. Culbertson*, 337 U.S. 733, 739-740 (1949).
>
> *Id.* at 831.

28. "[T]he concern for many, perhaps most, claims governed by fee-shifting statutes" was redressed by "the amendment added by the American Jobs Creation Act." *Id.* at 834. The Court is in error because numerous federal fee-shifting statutes, for example, the Equal Access to Justice Act, 28 U.S.C. § 2412, and the Uniform Relocation Assistance and Real Property Acquisition Policies Act, 42 U.S.C. §§ 4601-4655, were not included in that amendment.

29. *Id.* at 831 (citing *Culbertson*, 337 U.S. at 739-740).

30. *E.g., Krecioch v. United States*, 316 F.3d 684, 688 (7th Cir. 2003).

31. Rev. Proc. 93-59.

32. *Banks*, 125 S.Ct. at 829.

33. Rev. Rul. 80-364. The situation with the union and the client of a PILF are the same. In both situations: (1) attorneys provided legal services to their clients "free of charge"; (2) there was a labor agreement or federal fee-shifting statute that provided for an award of attorneys' fees; (3) the court awarded attorneys' fees pursuant to a labor agreement or a federal fee-shifting statute; and (4) the attorneys' fees were paid to the attorneys.

34. The IRS considers attorneys' fees paid by a defendant to a plaintiff's attorney to be a discharge of a debt and, thus, required to be included in the plaintiff's gross income. IRC § 61(a)(12) ("gross income" includes "[i]ncome from discharge of indebtedness"). PILFs may not charge their clients attorneys' fees. Instead, in accordance with their charitable nature and Rev. Proc. 92-59, PILFs provide their services "free of charge." As a result, a PILF's client does not incur a debt to the PILF with respect to attorneys' fees. Without a debt, the award of attorneys' fees to a PILF under a federal fee-shifting status is not a discharge of the client's indebtedness and, therefore, the receipt of attorneys' fees by the PILF is not a taxable event to the client.

35. *Faulkner v. Jones*, 10 F.3d 226 (4th Cir. 1993).

36. Press Release, ACLU, Legal fees from the battle to admit Shannon Faulkner will go to Women's Rights Project, (Oct. 4, 2000), *available at* http://www.aclu.org/WomensRights/WomensRights.cfm?ID=8143& c=172. It could have been worse. Her lawyers originally asked for $6.7 million. Patrick J. Buchanan, *Triumph of the Scalawags* (Aug. 25, 1997), *available at* http://www.buchanan.org/pa-97-025.html

Chapter 3: Fighting Racial Preferences Disguised as Trust Responsibilities

1. Fergus M. Bordewich, *Killing the White Man's Indian: Reinventing Native Americans at the End of the Twentieth Century* 330 (First Anchor Books 1997).

2. The 1997 Montana Big Game Hunting Regulations provide that hunters must have permission of the landowner, lessee, or his agent before hunting big game animals, including deer, on private property, regardless of whether the land is posted.

3. Mont. Code 87-1-304.

4. In 1997, the Montana Fish, Wildlife and Parks Commission promulgated its Big Game Hunting Regulations, which provide that "[b]ig game hunting privileges on Indian Reservations are limited to tribal members only."

5. Eventually, Sandra Shook pled guilty after reserving her right to challenge the constitutionality of the Montana law. Ms. Shook was sentenced to five days in the Sanders County Jail, which was suspended, ordered to pay a fine in the amount of $500.00, and ordered to forfeit all privileges to hunt in the State of Montana for a period of 24 months from the date of conviction.

6. *State of Montana v. Shook*, 313 Mont. 347, 67 P.3d 863 (Mont. 2002), relied on *Morton v. Mancari*, 417 U.S. 535 (1974). In *Mancari*, the Supreme Court upheld an employment preference for American Indians seeking positions in the Bureau of Indian Affairs. The Court did so because the Indians who qualified for the preference were "members of quasi-sovereign tribal entities whose lives and activities are governed by the BIA in a unique fashion." *Id.* at 554. Moreover, the preference was an essential aspect of the Indian Reorganization Act of 1934, 25 U.S.C. § 461, *et seq.*, the "overriding purpose [of which] was to establish machinery whereby Indian tribes would be able to assume a greater degree of self-government, both politically and economically." *Id.* at 542. Therefore, the Court held that federal legislative classifications would merit rational-basis scrutiny, "as long as the special treatment can be tied rationally to the fulfillment of Congress's unique obligation toward the Indians."

7. *Shook*, 67 P.3d at 863.

8. *Id.*

9. *Id.*

10. *Id.* at 866-67.

11. *Adarand Constructors, Inc. v. Peña*, 515 U.S. 200 (1995). See Chapter 11.

12. *Id.* at 244-45 (Stevens, J., dissenting). Legal commentators have joined with Justice Stevens. David C. Williams, *The Borders of The Equal Protection Clause: Indians as Peoples*, 38 U.C.L.A. L.Rev. 759 (1991); Wayne R. Farnsworth, *Bureau of Indian Affairs Hiring Preferences After Adarand Constructors, Inc. v. Peña*, 1996 B.Y.U. L. Rev. 503, 509-510 (1996) ("To say, as the *Mancari* Court did, that the criteria was 'not even a racial preference' stretches the imagination, and is comparable to suggesting that discriminating on the basis of pregnancy is not the same as discrimination on the basis of gender."); Patricia A. Kaplan, *When States' American Indian Teacher Preferences in Public Schools Violate the Fourteenth Amendment*, 17 Hamline L. Rev. 477, 494 (1994) ("[T]he Supreme Court's justification of a lower level of review of federal action affecting Indians based on a distinction between Indians as a political group versus a race...has been heavily criticized.").

13. The Indian Commerce Clause, U.S. Const. art. I, § 8, cl. 3, provides, "The Congress shall have Power... To regulate Commerce with foreign Nations, and among the several States, and with the Indian Tribes." Also often cited is the presidential power to make treaties, U.S. Const. art. II, § 2, cl. 2, and Congress's power to make regulations respecting territory belonging to the United States, U.S. Const. art IV, § 3, cl. 2. Based upon these provisions, the Supreme Court recognized a trust relationship between the federal government and American Indians in *Cherokee Nation v. Georgia*, 30 U.S. 1 (1831). Justice Marshall characterized Indian tribes as "domestic dependent nations" with a relation to the United States that "resembles that of a ward to his guardian." *Id.* at 17.

14. *Washington v. Confederated Bands and Tribes of the Yakima Indian Nation*, 439 U.S. 463, 501 (1979). "*Mancari* held only that when Congress acts to fulfill its unique trust responsibilities toward Indian tribes, such legislation is not based on a suspect classification. [] Indeed, in its more recent case of *Rice v. Cayetano*, 528 U.S. 495 (2000), the Supreme Court expressly stated that the *Mancari* 'opinion was careful to note... that the case was confined to the authority of the BIA, an agency described as ["]sui generis.["].'" *Malabed v. North Slope Bureau*, 335 F.3d 864, 868 (9th Cir. 2003). *See also Lac Court Oreilles Band of Lake Superior Chippewa Indians of Wisconsin*, 367 F.3d 650, 667 (7th Cir. 2004).

15. Article I of the Montana Constitution provides only that land held by Indians or Indian tribes remains under the "jurisdiction and control" of the United States.

16. The Flathead Treaty, concluded at Hell Gate in the Bitter Root Valley of Montana on July 16, 1855, was ratified by the Senate on March 8, 1859, and signed by the President of the United States, James Buchanan, that same year. Montana did not join the Union as the 41st State until 1889. Moreover, the Flathead Treaty granted hunting privileges, within the reservation, to all "citizens of the Territory." Flathead Treaty art. III.

17. *See City of Richmond v. J.A. Croson Company*, 488 U.S. 469 (1989). *Adarand Constructors, supra*, which addressed the use of racial preferences by Congress, noted that the Court was adopting the same test that it had applied earlier to Richmond.

18. The degree of blood quantum required for each tribe may be referenced through their respective constitutions and bylaws: Blackfeet Constitution & Bylaws, http://www.tribalresourcecenter.org/ccfolder/blackfeet_constandbylaws.htm; Crow Tribal Constitution, http://www.tribalresourcecenter.org/ccfolder/crow_const.htm; Salish and Kootenai Constitution and Bylaws, http://www.tribalresourcecenter.org/ccfolder/salishandkootenai_constandbylaws.htm; Fort Peck Comprehensive Code of Justice 2000, http://www.ftpeckcourts.org/CCOJ/Title004.htm; Constitution of the Fort Belknap Indian Community, www.tribalresourcecenter.org/ccfolder/fort_belknap_const.htm; Northern Cheyenne tribe Constitution and Bylaws, http://www.mt.blm.gov/mcfo/cbm/eis/NCheyenneNarrativeReport/AppB.pdf

19. In *Rice v. Cayetano*, 528 U.S. 495, 522 (2000), the Supreme Court struck a Hawaii law that limited certain voting rights to either "Hawaiian" or "native Hawaiian," holding that "[t]o extend *Mancari* to [authorize the Hawaii law] would be to permit a State, by racial classification, to fence out whole classes of its citizens from decision-making in critical state affairs."

20. In *Williams v. Babbitt*, 115 F.3d 657 (9th Cir. 1997), the Ninth Circuit held the federal government's interpretation of the Reindeer Act of 1937, 25 U.S.C. § 500, *et seq.*, which prohibited non-Natives from herding reindeer in Alaska, unconstitutional. The Ninth Circuit surmised that "*Mancari's* days are numbered" if *Adarand* controls. In *Williams*, the Ninth Circuit further interpreted *Mancari* "as shielding only those statutes that affect uniquely Indian interests." *Id.* at 665.

21. U.S. Department of the Interior, Bureau of Land Management, *Public Land Statistics 1992* at 5. U.S. Department of the Interior, National Park Service, *Briefing Statement* 5 (Feb. 9, 1994) *available at* http://www.nps.gov/grca/index.htm. Grand Canyon was designated a national monument in 1908; it became a national park in 1919.

22. 16 U.S.C. § 1a-1; note Sec. 3, Pub. L. No. 100-91 (Aug. 18, 1987).

23. Regulatory Flexibility Act, 5 U.S.C. §§ 601-612. Section 603(a) requires an analysis if a proposed rule will have "significant economic impact on a substantial number of small entities."

24. *65 Fed. Reg.* at 17,720.

25. *Id.* at 17,723.

26. *Id.* at 17,708.

27. *Id.*

28. *Id.* at 17,707-33.

29. *Id.* at 17,718.

30. *Id.* at 17,707-33.

31. Because the challenge was to an FAA rulemaking, the case began, not at the district court, but at the federal court of appeals. 43 U.S.C. §46110(a).

32. *U.S. Air Tour Ass'n v. FAA*, No. 00-1201, slip op. at 21-22 n.8 (D.C. Cir. Aug.16, 2002).

33. *U.S. Air Tour Ass'n, supra*; *Mancari*, 417 U.S. at 555.

34. *U.S. Air Tour Ass'n, supra*, quoting *Narragansett Indian Tribe v. National Indian Gaming Comm'n*, 158 F.3d 1335, 1340 (D.C. Cir. 1998).

35. *U.S. Air Tour Ass'n, supra*, citing *Agostini v. Felton*, 521 U.S. 203, 237 (1997).

36. "When we got a call that Americans were down, we didn't ask their race; we went to get them out," said Ron Williams. http://www.jeffersonreview.com/articles/2003/050503/doesthe.htm

37. *U.S. Air Tour Ass'n*, 298 F.3d 997 (D.C. Cir. 2002), *petition for cert. filed sub nom AirStar Helicopters, Inc. v. FAA*, 71 U.S.L.W. 3430 (Dec. 13, 2002). Air Star Helicopters was represented in the filing of its petition for Supreme Court review by Sharon Browne of the Pacific Legal Foundation, Sacramento, California.

38. The two cases, in which scores of friend of the court briefs had been filed, were *Gratz v. Bollinger*, 539 U.S. 244 (2003), and *Grutter v. Bollinger*, 539 U.S. 306 (2003), litigated by the Center for Individual Rights in Washington, D.C.

39. Professor Francis Paul Prucha concludes:

Jefferson (like most of his contemporaries) explained the difference [between Europeans and Indians] by the environment. If the circumstances of their lives were appropriately changed the Indians would be transformed. In that happy event, Jefferson asserted, "we shall probably find that they are formed in mind as well as in body on the same module with Homo sapiens Europeaus." So convinced was [Jefferson] of racial equality or uniformity that he urged physical as well as cultural amalgamation of the Indians with the whites. "In truth," he wrote to the Indian agent Benjamin Hawkins, "the ultimate point of rest and happiness for them is to let our settlements and theirs meet and blend together, to intermix and become one people." [] Since the Indian by nature possessed the capacity for civilization, Jefferson admitted the responsibility of the whites to aid the natives in attaining that great goal... [T]he movement toward civilization he held to be inexorable, and unless the Indians moved with the tide, they would surely be destroyed... Jefferson [held to] the "stages of society" theory that dominated the minds of the nineteenth century, the idea that the set stages of savagery, barbarism, and civilization followed one another inevitably, as the history of all human societies had shown. If the whites had gone through that process over the centuries, there's no reason to doubt that the Indians would follow the same route.

Francis Paul Prucha, *The Great Father: The United States Government and the American Indians* 137-138 (University of Nebraska Press 1984).

40. Prucha, *supra*, explains at 317:

[R]eservations – in most cases small parcels of land "reserved" out of the original holdings of the tries or bands – developed as an alternative to the extinction of the Indians. The reservations, however, were thought of as a temporary expedient, for whites dealing officially with the Indians in the 1850s all accepted the idea that the nation within its new continental limits would become the abode of enterprising and prosperous American citizens. They had no notion of a pluralistic society or a divided land occupied in part by European immigrants and their descendants and in part by American Indians adhering to their own customs. The goal was to ease the immediate conflicts between the two cultures and to prevent, as far as it was in their power to do so, the utter destruction of the weaker party.... But beyond protection and preservation there was the ultimate goal of transformation to induce the Indians all to become cultivators of the soil, to adopt the white man's language, customs, and religion, and, finally, to be self-supporting citizens of the commonwealth, a goal that all but a few believed was entirely practicable if only the proper means were applied.

41. The General Allotment Act of 1887, known as the Dawes Act, 24 Stat. 388, authorized allotments of 160 acres to each head of a family and 80 acres to others, which could be doubled if the land was suitable for grazing. Title was to remain in the United States in trust for 25 years, after which it was to be conveyed to the Indian allottee. Upon receipt of an allotment (or, after amendment in 1906, receipt of title) the allottee became an United States citizen subject to state criminal and civil law. In 1924, Congress made all American Indians born in the United States citizens, irrespective of land ownership.

42. 25 U.S.C. § 461, *et seq.*

43. 67 Stat. B132 (1953).

44. 116 *Cong. Rec.* 23258.

45. Congress did so with the Indian Financing Act of 1974, 25 U.S.C. § 1451, *et seq.*, which established a revolving loan fund to aid the development of Indian resources, and the Indian Self-Determination and Education Assistance Act of 1975, 25 U.S.C. § 450, *et seq.*, which authorized the Secretaries of the Interior and of Health, Education and Welfare to enter into contracts under which the tribes themselves would assume responsibility for the administration of federal Indian programs.

46. 26 U.S.C. § 1781, *et seq.*

47. 25 U.S.C. § 450a(b).

48. 59 *Fed. Reg.* 22951'(1994).

49. In *California v. Cabazon Band of Mission Indians*, 480 U.S. 202 (1987), the Supreme Court held that California, even though it had criminal jurisdiction over reservation land, did not have jurisdiction to enforce its gambling laws regulating bingo since such laws were regulatory, rather than criminal. The Court held further that Congress had not seen fit to share its jurisdiction regarding gambling on Indian reservations with the States. In 1988, Congress adopted the Indian Gaming Regulatory Act (IGRA). Pub. L. No. 100-497 (Oct. 17, 1988), 102 Stat. 2467, 25 U.S.C. § 2701, *et seq.* In its findings, Congress declared, "Indian tribes have the exclusive right to regulate gaming activity on Indian lands if the gaming activity is not specifically prohibited by Federal law and is conducted within a State which does not, as a matter of criminal law and public policy, prohibit such gaming activity." 25 U.S.C. § 2701(5). The IGRA was an attempt by Congress to share its power over gaming in Indian Country with the states, striking a balance between the rights of Tribes to engage in activities generally free of state jurisdiction and the interests of states in regulating gaming activities within their boundaries.

50. http://playermagazine.com/managearticle.asp?C=280&A=14545

51. *Id.* William N. Thompson, Professor of Public Administration at the University of Nevada at Las Vegas, cautions that the earnings of tribal casinos are almost impossible to verify independently.

52. The U.S. Department of Interior grants recognition, for eligibility for federal services and other benefits of tribal status, to Indian groups that have maintained a "substantially continuous tribal existence and which have functioned as autonomous entities throughout history until the present." 25 C.F.R. Par 83.3. *See* Indian Entities Recognized and Eligible to Receive Services from the United States Bureau of Indian Affairs, 65 *Fed. Reg.* 13,298 (Mar. 13, 2000).

53. 25 U.S.C. § 2719.

54. http://www.rockymountainnews.com/drmn/state/article/0,1299, DRMN_21_3536014,00.html

55. William N. Evans and Julie H. Topoleski, *The Social and Economic Impact of Native American Casinos*, National Bureau of Economic Research Working Paper 9198, 46.

56. *Id.* at 49.

57. What about, for example, "the costs of lost productivity, child neglect, bankruptcy, divorce, addiction, suicide, and the myriad other social consequences of gambling." Jan Golab, *Arnold Schwarzenegger Girds for Indian War*, in *Warriors, Messiahs, Governors, and Generals*, The American Enterprise, January/February 2004, at 38.

58. One writer suggested, in 1997, that those answers do not exist because of the newness of Indian gaming; that local governments have not studied it because it is beyond their jurisdiction, and that casino earnings are difficult to trace. Roger Dunstan, *Gambling in California*, California Research Bureau, January 1997, at 12.

59. Golab, *supra*, at 36.

60. *Id.* at 37. *Johnson v. Bustamante*, 2003 WL 23782188 (Cal.Sup. Sept. 22, 2003).

61. Golab, *supra*. at 40.

62. Bipartisan Campaign Reform Act of 2002, Pub. L. No. 107-155 (Mar. 27, 2002), amending Federal Election Campaign Act of 1971, 2 U.S.C. § 431, *et seq*. The Federal Election Commission wrote on May 15, 2000, "Although [an American Indian tribe] is a person under the [Federal Election Campaign] Act, it is not an individual and is therefore not subject to the $25,000 limit on its annual total of contributions.[] [A tribe] may make contributions that are otherwise lawful under the Act and Commission regulations."

63. Darryl Wold, the FEC's Republican chairman, said "that, under the new advisory, a tribe could give $20,000 annually to each of a political party's national committees, plus $5,000 to each of 50 state parties, for a total of $310,000 per year in hard money contributions." BNA Money & Politics Report, May 20, 2000. That is not the half of it:

> [T]he FEC's opinion could introduce approximately $835 million worth of "political wampum" during a two-year election cycle. [L]ike "any other person," an Indian tribe can contribute $20,000 during a calendar year to a national party committee and to each of its affiliated campaign committees, $5,000 per calendar year to a state party committee, $5,000 per year to a PAC, and $1,000 per election to a federal candidate.

> Without the $25,000 annual limit on total contributions, though, an Indian tribe can now contribute $240,000 during a two-year election cycle to the Democratic and Republican national parties and their affiliated House and Senate campaign committees, up to $1 million during an election cycle to the 50 Democratic and Republican state party committees, and distribute as much as $1,872,000 among every Democratic and Republican candidate for election to the House and Senate.

> [I]f each of the 200 casino-owning tribes establishes a PAC, then all of the tribes could exchange maximum $5,000 per year contributions, resulting in $2 million for each PAC during a two-year election cycle.

> Thus for the 200 casino-owning tribes, a single election cycle could yield $48 million for the national parties and their affiliated campaign committees, $200 million for the state party committees, $400 million for their own PACs, and $374.4 million for federal candidates-a grand total that exceeds $1 billion!

Edward Zuckerman, *FEC lets Indian tribes convert government funds to political contributions*, Political Finance & Lobby Reporter, June 14, 2000.

64. *Oklahoma Tax Commission v. Citizen Band Potawatomi Indian Tribe of Oklahoma*, 498 U.S. 404 (1991).

65. The second ruling was *Oklahoma Tax Commission v. Chickasaw Nation*, 515 U.S. 450 (1995).

66. Research reveals that consumers will shift the outlet they use to purchase motor fuel based on price differentials of one to two cents per gallon. Energy Analysts International, *The Convenience Store Industry vs. Hypermarkets: Strategies for Competition* 15-1 (2002).

67. Several tribes also filed friend of the court briefs. http://www.supremecourtus.gov/docket/04-631.htm. Oral arguments in the case took place on October 3, 2005.

68. *Wagman v. Prairie Band Potawatomi Nation*, ___ U.S. ___, 2005 WL3285050 (Dec. 6, 2005)

69. http://www.factalliance.org/facts.html. "According to a study conducted by economist Brian O'Connor, owner of New Jersey-based Ridgewood Economic Associates Ltd., between $526 million and $609 million was lost in 2001 because of the state's failure to collect taxes on these sales. Early 2002 data suggests as much as $895 million was lost last year, O'Connor said." http://www.bizjournals.com/albany/stories/2003/01/13/daily14.html

70. *Citizen Band Potawatomi Indian Tribe*, 498 U.S. at 514 (Stevens, J. concurring).

71. "How much blending can occur before Indians finally cease to be Indians...The question is sure to loom ever larger in the coming generations as the Untied States increasingly finds itself in 'government to government' relationships with 'Indian tribes' that are, in fact, becoming less ethnically Indian by the decade. Within two or three generations, the nation will possess hundreds of semi-independent 'tribes' whose native heritage consists mainly of autonomous governments and special privileges that are denied to other Americans." Fergus M. Bordewich, *supra*, at 330.

72. Jeff Testerman, *Tribe faulted for not warning its casino patrons: A judge says few know that state legal protections don't apply there*, St Petersburg Times, July 5, 2005. Those frustrated by the tribe's sovereign immunity include "one woman who alleged she had been deprived of a $64,000 bingo jackpot by casino employees who unfairly disqualified her."

73. "Both Title VII [of the Civil Rights Act] and the Americans with Disabilities Act (ADA) expressly exclude Indian tribes. Similarly, the Ninth Circuit has held that tribes are immune from suit under the Age Discrimination in Employment Act (ADEA). Tribes are also immune from suit under 42 U.S.C. 1983. Likewise, state discrimination laws do not apply to tribal employers." Gabriel S. Galanda, *Reservation of right: A practitioner's guide to Indian Law in Montana*, The Montana Lawyer, January 2003.

74. http://www.cnn.com/2004/LAW/01/02/banishing.indians.ap/

75. *See, e.g., Talton v. Mayes*, 163 U.S. 376 (1896); *United States v. Wheeler*, 435 U.S. 313 (1978).

76. *See Morris v. Tanner*, No. 99-CV-82 (D.Mont. June 15, 1999); *Morris v. Tanner*, 288 F.Supp.2d 1133 (D.Mont. 2003) (on remand).

77. The United States was there, not to defend Mr. Morris' civil rights, but to defend the 1990 Amendments and the authority of a foreign tribe to prosecute Mr. Morris criminally.

78. 25 U.S.C. § 1301(2).

79. *Morris v. Tanner*, 16 Fed.Appx. 652 (9th Cir. 2001).

80. *Morris*, 288 F.Supp.2d at 1141.

81. *Adarand v. Peña*, 515 U.S. 200 (1995); *Rice v. Cayetano*, 528 U.S. 495 (2000).

82. *Morris*, 288 F.Supp.2d at 1142, n. 7.

83. *Means v. Navajo Nation*, 420 F.3d 1037 (9th Cir. 2005); *Morris v. Tanner*, 141 Fed. Appx. 696 (9th Cir. 2005).

84. *Roberts v. Hagener*, No. 05cv153 (D. Mont. filed Nov. 30, 2005).

Chapter 4: Fighting Clinton's Abuses of the Antiquities Act

1. White House Press Release, Establishment of the Grand Staircase-Escalante National Monument (Sept. 18, 1996).

2. More than nine months later, in conditions worthy of a James Bond movie, Senator Robert Bennett (R-UT) was allowed to see previously withheld White House documents on the creation of the Utah monument. Declared Bennett: "[T]he documents confirmed absolutely the long-standing belief that the administration misled the Utah delegation and the general public... After reviewing the documents, I'm satisfied that the primary motivation in creating the monument was politics." *Bennett: Papers Prove Clinton 'Misled' Utahns*, Salt Lake City Tribune, June 24, 1997, at A4.

3. 16 U.S.C. § 431 provides, in part:

   The President of the United States is authorized, in his discretion, to declare by public proclamation historic landmarks, historic and prehistoric structures, and other objects of historic or scientific interest that are situated upon the lands owned or controlled by the Government of the United States to be national monuments, and may reserve as a part thereof parcels of land, the limits of which in all cases shall be confined to the smallest area compatible with the proper care and management of the objects to be protected.

4. *Merriam-Webster's Collegiate Dictionary* (2003). *See* H.R. Rep. No. 2223, 59th Cong., 1st Sess. 1-8 (1906); S. Rep. No. 3797, 59th Cong. 1st Sess. 1 (1906).

5. *See* R. Lee, *The Antiquities Act of 1906* 47-77 (1970); Comment, *Public Land Withdrawal and the Antiquities Act of 1906*, 56 Washington Law Review 449 (1981).

6. H.R. Rep. No. 2224, 59th Cong., 1st Sess. 1 (1905).

7. Act of June 29, 1906, ch. 3607, §§ 1-2, 34 Stat. 616 (1906), codified at 16 U.S.C. §§ 111, 112.

8. R. Lee, *supra*, at 81, agrees. If 216,960 acres is too large for a national monument, what is 1,700,000 acres?

9. Frank Bond, Chief Clerk of the General Land Office, speaking at the first National Park Conference, held at Yellowstone National Park in 1911. R. Lee, *supra*, note 76, at 109 (quoting F. Bond, *The Administration of National Monuments, in Proceedings of the National Park Conference, held at Yellowstone National Park, September 11-12, 1911* 80-81 (1912)).

10. http://www.nps.gov/deto/home.htm

11. 43 U.S.C. § 1701, *et seq.*

12. 42 U.S.C. § 4332, *et seq.*

13. *Monumental Abuse: The Clinton Administration's Campaign of Misinformation on the Establishment of the Grand Staircase-Escalante National Monument*, H.R. Rep. 105-824, 105th Cong., 2nd Sess. 6 (1998). The U.S. Geological Survey estimates that the Plateau contains 62.3 billion tons of coal, nearly half of which could be recovered. *Id.*

14. *Id.*

15. *Id.* at 8.

16. Warm Springs Project Preliminary Draft Environmental Impact Statement (PDEIS) 4-12 (1995). This PDEIS was the last complete version of the Smoky Hollow EIS produced before Clinton's 1996 decree; it is a comprehensive, 561-page document reflecting several previous drafts.

17. E-mail from Linda Lance (CEQ) to Tom Jensen (CEQ) (Mar. 19, 1996).

18. E-mail from Linda Lance to Kathleen McGinty (CEQ) (Mar. 21, 1996).

19. E-mail from Tom Jensen to Linda Lance, T.J. Glauthier (Office of Management and Budget), and Kathleen McGinty (Mar. 27, 1996).

20. E-mail from Kathleen McGinty to T.J. Glauthier and Linda Lance (Mar. 25, 1996).

21. Memorandum from Dave Alberswerth to A. Strasvogel (Apr. 14, 1996).

22. *Behind Closed Doors: The Abuse of Trust and Discretion of the Grand Staircase-Escalante National Monument*, H.R. Rep. 105-D, 105th Cong., 1st Sess. 7 (1997).

23. Memorandum from Kathleen McGinty to President Clinton (Aug. 14, 1996).

24. *Remarks Announcing the Establishment of the Grand Staircase-Escalante National Monument*, 32 Weekly Comp. Pres. Doc. 1785 (Sept. 23, 1996).

25. Sarah Foster, *The Utah Coal Lockup: A Trillion Dollar Lippo Payoff?* Land Rights Letter, Oct./Nov. 1996, vol. VI, no. 11, at 4-5.

26. Karen Gullo, *Clinton's National Monument Designation Blocked Clean Coal Mining Plan*, Associated Press, Jan. 7, 1997.

27. *Id.*

28. Paul Craig Roberts, *The Utah Coal Deal*, The Washington Times, Jan. 12, 1997, at 34. *A Monument to Lippo*, The Washington Times, Dec. 27, 1996, at A18.

29. *Clinton's 'Mother of All Land Grabs'*, U.S. News and World Report, Jan. 20, 1997, at 42.

30. *Dinner Raised $488,000-and Questions*, USA Today, Feb. 7, 1997, at 4A.

31. http://en.wikipedia.org/wiki/National_Monument. The purpose of these monument decrees, suggested U.S. Senator Ben Nighthorse Campbell, was to enhance Clinton's place in history: "One way for him to get past the Monica legacy is to create the public land legacy by locking up public property." Dave Boyer and Audrey Hudson, *Bush urges conservation by grants, not command*, The Washington Times, June 2, 2000.

32. Casper (Wyoming) Star Tribune, Nov. 1, 1996, at 1.

33. 16 U.S.C. § 431.

34. *Wyoming v. Franke*, 58 F. Supp. 890 (D.Wyo. 1945).

35. *Id.* at 892.

36. *Id.* at 894.

37. *Id.* at 895.

38. *Id.*

39. *Id.*

40. *Cameron v. United States*, 252 U.S. 450 (1920); *Cappaert v. United States*, 426 U.S. 128 (1976).

41. U.S. Const. art. IV, § 3, cl. 2. "Congress shall have Power to dispose of and make all needful Rules and Regulations respecting the Territory or other Property belonging to the United States."

42. David H. Getches, *Managing the Public Lands: The Authority of the Executive to Withdraw Lands* 22 Natural Resources Journal. The Supreme Court found such acquiescence in *United States v. Midwest Oil Company*, 236 U.S. 459 (1915).

43. "Effective on and after the date of this Act, the implied authority of the President to make withdrawals and reservations resulting from acquiescence of the Congress (*U.S. v. Midwest Oil Co.*, 236 U.S. 459) and the following statutes and parts of statutes are repealed." Pub. L. No. 94-579, §704(a), 90 Stat. 2744, 2792 (1976).

44. *Utah Ass'n of Counties/Mountain States Legal Foundation v. Clinton*, No. 97cv00479, slip op. (D.Utah Aug. 12, 1999).

45. *Clinton v. Utah Ass'n of Counties*, No. 00-601 (10th Cir. July 7, 2000).

46. "We have seen millions of acres of land declared off-limits and designated national monuments—just like that, with no real public involvement and no regard for the people affected by those decrees." Dave Boyer and Audrey Hudson, *Bush urges conservation by grants, not command*, The Washington Times, June 2, 2000.

47. http://seattlepi.nwsource.com/national/bush261.shtml

48. http://www.wnd.com/news/article.asp?ARTICLE_ID=17615

49. *Mountain States Legal Foundation v. Bush*, No. 00cv2072, Transcript of Motions Hearing, at 46-63 (D.D.C. Nov. 15, 2001).

50. *Id.* at 54-55.

51. *Tulare County v. Bush*, 185 F.Supp.2d 18 (D.D.C. Sept. 28, 2001).

52. *Mountain States Legal Foundation v. Bush*, 306 F.3d 1132 (D.C. Cir. 2002), and *Tulare County v. Bush*, 306 F.3d 1138 (D.C. Cir. 2002).

53. *Mountain States Legal Foundation*, 306 F.3d at 1136.

54. *Id.*

55. *Tulare County*, 306 F.3d at 1144.

56. Modern notice pleading requires only that the other party be put on notice as to the nature of the lawsuit. *Conley v. Gibson*, 355 U.S. 41 (1957).

57. *Mountain States Legal Foundation*, 306 F. 3d at 1132.

58. *Mountain States Legal Foundation*, 540 U.S. 812 (2003); *Tulare County*, 540 U.S. 813 (2003).

59. *Utah Ass'n of Counties v. Bush/Mountain States Legal Foundation v. Bush*, 316 F.Supp.2nd 1172 (D.Utah 2004).

60. *United States v. George S. Bush & Co.*, 310 U.S. 371 (1940).

61. *Bowen v. Michigan Academy of Family Physicians*, 476 U.S. 667, 681 (1986).

62. *Harmon v. Brucker*, 355 U.S. 579, 581-82 (1958).

63. *Bowen*, 476 U.S. at 667.

64. *Chamber of Commerce of U.S. v. Reich*, 74 F.3d 1322, 1330-1331 (D.C. Cir. 1996).

65. *Utah Ass'n of Counties*, 316 F.Supp.2d at 1183.

66. R. Lee, *supra*, at 68-71.

67. 16 U.S.C. § 1133.

68. 16 U.S.C. § 1531, *et seq.*

69. 43 U.S.C. § 1711.

70. 61 *Fed. Reg.* 50,223-50,226 (Sept. 18, 1996).

71. *Id.* at 50,224-50,225.

72. *Id.* at 50,224.

73. *Id.* at 50,225.

74. In *Wyoming v. United States Dept. of Agriculture*, ___ F.3d ____, 2005 WL 1607932 (10th Cir. 2005), the Tenth Circuit dismissed, as moot, a decision from Wyoming federal district court holding that Clinton's "roadless" decree closing 60 million acres of national forest violated the Wilderness Act. In the case below, *Wyoming v. United States Dept. of Agriculture*, 277 F. Supp.2d 1197, 1236-37 (D.Wyo. 2003), the Wyoming federal district court had held that the U.S. Forest Service had usurped Congress's power regarding access to, and management of, public land by a *de facto* designation of wilderness in violation of the Wilderness Act of 1964. "In [their] rush to give President Clinton lasting notoriety in the annals of environmentalism," federal officials sought to establish *de facto* wilderness in violation of the Wilderness Act. *Id.* at 1232. Their action "negates the system of wilderness designation established by Congress" and must be set aside. *Id.* at 1236.

Chapter 5: Fighting for Local Communities

1. On May 3, 2004, President Bush and Mrs. Laura Bush presented Bruce Vincent and his Provider Pals™ with one of the first four *Preserving America* President Awards in a White House ceremony. http://www.achp.gov/news-prezaward04.html

2. Jim Petersen, *The West is Burning: The 1910 Fire*, Evergreen Magazine, Winter Edition 1994-1995. http://www.idahoforests.org/fires.htm

3. *Save the Yaak Committee v. Block*, 840 F.2d 714 (9th Cir. 1988).

4. 42 U.S.C. § 4321, *et seq.*

5. 42 U.S.C. § 4332(c).

6. *Kleppe v. Sierra Club*, 427 U.S. 390, 410 n21 (1976).

7. 42 U.S.C. § 4331(b)(5).

8. 42 U.S.C. § 4331(a).

9. Bruce Vincent says that, when the wildfires start, loggers are the only ones running "the wrong way, that is, toward the fire." It puts one in mind of the heroes of New York City on September 11, 2001.

10. 42 U.S.C. § 4331(c).

11. The author has been in standing-room-only audiences frequently when Bruce Vincent delivers his "stump speech," which is always followed by a standing ovation and in which he delivers remarks such as these.

12. *Mountain States Legal Foundation v. Madigan*, No. 92cv0097 (D.D.C. filed Jan. 10, 1992). Joining Mountain States Legal Foundation as plaintiffs in the case were Lincoln County, Montana; Boundary County, Idaho; Libby, Troy, and Eureka, Montana; Bonners Ferry and Moyie Springs, Idaho; and Owens & Hurst Lumber Company. In May 2005, Owens & Hurst Lumber Company went out of business citing the "anemic Forest Service timber sale program"; 200 people lost their jobs. http://www.dailyinterlake.com/articles/2005/01/28/news/news01.txt

13. *Mountain States Legal Foundation v. Glickman*, 922 F.Supp. 628 (D.C.C. 1995).

14. *Id.* at 632. Risk of a catastrophic fire is "mere speculation," but the speculative injury to a federally protected species calls for years of additional study.

15. *Mountain States Legal Foundation v. Glickman*, 92 F.3d 1228, 1235 (D.C. Cir. 1996).

16. *Id.* at 1236.

17. *Id.*

18. *Id.* at 1338.

19. *Id.*

20. Neil A. Lewis, *A Once Doomed Nomination Wins Senate Panel Approval*, New York Times, Jan. 31, 2003, at A26.

21. The Bush administration's incredibly slow start was the result of three circumstances: first, Vice President Gore's decision to contest the election, which delayed the Bush transition; second, Senator Jefford's decision to "come out of the closet" as an Independent after a lifetime as a Republican; and, third, the attack on the United States on September 11, 2001.

22. *Lands Council v. Powell*, 395 F.3d 1019 (9th Cir. 2004).

23. Bruce Vincent and others praise the Bush administration's healthy forests efforts, the passage of which through Congress was aided by the horrifying photographs of much of the West ablaze, the result of endless delays caused by lawsuits by environmental groups. President Bush announced his Healthy Forests Initiative on August 22, 2002. http://www.whitehouse.gov/news/releases/2002/08/20020822-3.html. The Healthy Forests Restoration Act of 2003, Pub. L. No. 108-148, 117 Stat. 1887, was signed into law on December 3, 2003. 16 U.S.C. § 6501, *et seq.* Because of the cultural shift within the Forest Service during the Clinton administration, the impact of Bush administration changes have yet to be felt in Lincoln County.

24. Letter from Julia Altemus, Montana Logging Association, to Paul D. Clement, Acting Solicitor General of the United States (Sept. 22, 2004).

25. http://www.missoulian.com/articles/2005/03/31/news/mtregional/news07.txt

26. Sanders County is the poorest county in Montana and has the highest unemployment rate. The Rock Creek project would generate $237 million in payroll, buy $303 million in materials and supplies, and contribute more than $30 million in property and production taxes, $23 million in state income taxes, and $85 million in federal income taxes. Laura Skaer, Executive Director, Northwest Mining Association, Testimony, Committee on Resources, U.S. House of Representatives (Apr. 23, 2005).

27. *Rock Creek Alliance v. U.S. Fish and Wildlife Service*, No. 01cv152-DWM, 2005 WL 928604 (D.Mont. Mar. 25, 2005). "This is a huge roadblock," enthused one mine opponent. "This decision is more than a delay. This decision is the nail in the coffin." http://www.spokesmanreview.com/breaking/story.asp?submit-Date=2005330201518

28. Skaer, *supra.*

29. Bruce Vincent often begins his speeches thusly:

    Have any of you ever been to Libby, Montana? On purpose? Did you buy a major appliance while you were there? You know tourism is our future. Times are so tough, I'm sure we could find someone to weld a freezer to your bumper if you wanted to take one home.

30. *Communities for a Great Northwest v. Bush*, No. 00cv1394-GK (D.D.C. filed June 12, 2000). The Montana Coalition of Forest Counties joined the lawsuit after the terrible fires of 2000 for fear that Clinton's roadless policy would hamper fire fighting and healthy forest efforts.

31. Federal district courts in Idaho and Wyoming ruled that the Clinton plan was illegal. The ruling by Judge Brimmer in Wyoming was particularly hard hitting labeling Clinton's actions a "thinly veiled attempt to designate wilderness areas in violation of the clear and unambiguous process established by the Wilderness Act." *Wyoming v. U.S. Dep't of Agriculture*, 277 F.Supp.2d 1197, 1239 (D.Wyo. 2003). The Idaho ruling, which enjoined Clinton's plan, *Kootenai Tribe of Idaho v. Veneman*, 2001 WL 1141275 (D.Idaho May 10, 2001), was reversed by the Ninth Circuit. *Kootenai Tribe*, 313 F.3d 1094 (9th Cir. 2002). The Wyoming ruling was dismissed as moot given the new Bush administration plan. *Wyoming v. U.S. Dep't of Agriculture*, 414 F.3d 1207 (10th Cir. 2005).

32. *Campbell County solidly remains Wyoming's wealthiest*, Casper Star Tribune, July 11, 2005. "Campbell County's assessed valuation—the value of all its property for tax purposes—grew more than 12 percent to a record $3.66 billion this year. Thanks to coal, gas and oil wealth, Campbell County has been Wyoming's wealthiest since 1971, when its assessed valuation was $154 million . . . Wyoming's second-wealthiest county is Sublette County, which because of gas drilling is increasing in value fastest. Sublette County's assessed valuation this year was $2.9 billion."

33. http://www.wsgs.uwyo.edu/Coal/CBM_Info.aspx

34. *Wyoming Outdoor Council*, 156 IBLA 347, 357-59 (Apr. 26, 2002).

35. *Pennaco Energy, Inc. v. U.S. Dep't of the Interior*, 266 F.Supp.2d 1323, 1329 (D.Wyo. 2003).

36. *Id.*

37. *Id.* at 1330.

38. *Id.*

39. *Pennaco Energy, Inc.*, 377 F.3d 1147, 1156 (10th Cir. 2004).

40. *Id.* at 1157-1159.

41. *Id.* at 1156 fn 5.

42. After holding five public scoping meetings and six public hearings, the BLM issued the DEIS on February 15, 2002. During the 60-day comment period that followed, six public hearings were held throughout Montana and more than 25,000 comments, oral and written, were received. The BLM issued the FEIS on January 17, 2003, and, after a 30-day review and protest period, it issued a Record of Decision in April 2003 approving the FEIS.

43. If ever, given the situation that gave birth to these NEPA documents, such documents would be "bullet proof," it would be here. Nonetheless, the Montana federal district court ruled that the NEPA study prepared for Montana failed to comply with NEPA. *Northern Plains Resource Council v. United States Bureau of Land Management*, No. 03cv69-BLG, slip. op. (D.Mont. Feb. 25, 2005).

44. *Wyoming Outdoor Council v. Pierson*, No. IBLA 2004-76 (Feb. 19, 2004).

45. William Perry Pendley, *War on the West: Government Tyranny on America's Great Frontier* 32 (Regnery 1995).

46. 43 C.F.R. § 1502.22 (May 27, 1986). Naturally, this new regulation was the result of a court ruling that made new law. *Alaska v. Andrus*, 580 F.2d 465, 473 (D.C. Cir. 1978). *See also* Robert S. Lynch, Esq., Testimony, Committee on Resources, U.S. House of Representatives (June 18, 2005).

47. On March 24, 2004, Michael J. Kowalski, Chairman and CEO of Tiffany & Company, for example, took out a full-page advertisement in the *Washington Post* opposing the Lincoln County Rock Creek project and United States mining law, prompting praise from environmental groups. http://www.earthworksaction.org/pubs/TiffWaPoAd.pdf. http://actionnetwork.org/mpc/alert-description.tcl?alert_id=2373798. Meanwhile, environmental groups were silent about Tiffany's open pit diamond mine in Canada. http://www.mineweb.net/sections/sustainable_mining/389589.htm

48. Lynch, *supra*.

49. *Id.*

50. In 2004, the Supreme Court reversed the Tenth Circuit in an environmental, though not a NEPA, case out of Utah. *Norton v. Southern Utah Wilderness Alliance*, 542 U.S. 55 (2004). The decision the Court overturned, certainly worthy of reversal, was so extreme as to hardly have been capable of being followed. *Southern Utah Wilderness Alliance v. Norton*, No. 02cv01118, 2004 WL 2827894 (D.Utah Nov. 30, 2004). In 1998, the Court limited the ability of environmental groups to sue on overall forest plans; groups must

await completion of documents implementing the plan. This decision also imposed limits on the edge of the NEPA problem, not at its core. *Ohio Forestry Association, Inc. v. Sierra Club*, 523 U.S. 726 (1998). Sometimes the Court does not hear important cases because the federal government does not ask. In 1988, there was a huge split between the Ninth and Tenth Circuits over what was a "hard look" for oil and gas leasing. Energy advocates wanted the Court to resolve the split; the Bush administration declined. As a result, federal agencies adhered to the stricter of the two tests adding cost and delay. *Conner v. Burford*, 848 F.2d 1441 (9th Cir. 1988), *cert. denied* 489 U.S. 1012 (1989).

51. *Montana Wilderness Association v. Fry*, 310 F.Supp.2d 1127 (D.Mont. 2004).

52. Bureau of Land Management, Las Cruces Field Office, *Resource Management Plan Amendment for Federal Fluid Minerals Leasing and Development in Sierra and Otero Counties* (January 2005).

53. *New Mexico v. Bureau of Land Management*, No. 05cv0460 (D.N.M. filed Apr. 22, 2005).

54. http://www.prfamerica.org/OverviewZoningPropRts.html. The late Representative Morris K. Udall (D-AZ) was asked why he had become a foe of federal land use planning after some period of time supporting the concept. "I didn't see the light," the famously witty representative of southern Arizona deadpanned, "I felt the heat."

55. http://www.prfamerica.org/7thAnnualConferenceGreatSuccess.html

Chapter 6: Fighting "Your Land Is Our Land" State Bureaucrats

1. http://www.arlo.net/lyrics/this-land.shtml. Guthrie, "[a] lifelong socialist and trade unionist," moved to New York City in 1939 or 1940, where he was "embraced by its leftist and folk music community." "In 1940, Guthrie wrote his most famous song, 'This Land is Your Land,' which "protested the institution of private ownership of land . . . ." http://en.wikipedia.org/wiki/Woody_Guthrie

2. The SKS Rifle (Samozaryadnaya Karabina Simonova), developed by S.G. Simonov in the late 1930s as a self-loading rifle for the Soviet military, is currently manufactured in several countries including the Soviet Union, China, and Yugoslavia. It fires 7.62 mm x 39 mm ammunition.

3. Meg Jones, Gail Boxrud and Rick Barrett, *5 killed, 3 hurt in hunting rampage: Man arrested in assault rifle attack after tree-stand argument*, Milwaukee Journal Sentinel Online, Nov. 21, 2004, at http://www.jsonline.com/news/state/nov04277439.asp. "[I]t's considered poor etiquette to use another's deer stand without asking permission . . ." *Man charged with murder in Wis. slayings*, Associated Press, Nov. 30, 2004, at http://espn.go.com/outdoors/hunting/news/2004/1130/1935318.html

4. Charged was Chai Soua Vang, 36, of St. Paul, Minnesota. Joshua Freed, *Not guilty: Plea of deer-hunter killer*, Associated Press, Jan. 3, 2005, at http://espn.go.com/outdoors/hunting/news/2005/0103/1958078.html. The dead include: Bob Crotteau, 42; Joey Crotteau, 20; Jessica Willers, 27; Denny Drew, 55; Mark Roidt, 28; Al Laski, 43, all of Rice Lake, Wisconsin. http://www.rice-lake-hunters-memorial.com/

5. S.D. Codified Laws §§ 41-9-1.1, 41-9-1.3. Upon statehood, private property in South Dakota was made subject to section line easements, which, when improved, provide public access. *Reis v. Miller*, 550 N.W.2d 78, 80-81 (S.D. 1996). "The use by the public of the section line rights-of-way for recreation, which includes hunting, dates back to the 1880s and has not been successfully challenged in this state to our knowledge." *Id.* at 83; *see* S.D. Codified Laws § 41-9-1.3. A section line right-of-way is 66 feet wide, 33 feet on each side of the section line. S.D. Codified Laws § 31-18-2.

6. "[N]o person may fish, hunt or trap upon any private land not his own or in his possession without permission from the owner or lessee of such land." S.D. Codified Laws § 41-9-1; *Reis*, 550 N.W.2d at 80. South Dakota law provides that ownership of property includes the right to "use it to the exclusion of others." S.D. Codified Laws § 43-2-1.

7. S.D. Codified Laws §§ 41-9-1, 41-9-8.

8. *State v. Rumpca*, 652 N.W.2d 795, 798 (S.D. 2002) ("[A] trespass may be committed on, beneath, or above the surface of the earth with the exceptions of flight by aircraft"; "shooting at a pheasant flying over private property constitutes hunting and is prohibited under [S.D. Codified Laws] 41-9-1 unless the hunter owns or possesses the land or has the permission of the owner or lessee.").

9. S.D. Codified Laws § 41-9-1.1(2). Federal refuges and Indian tribal trust land are excepted from such invasion. South Dakota Hunting Handbook (2003), at 26, R80.

10. *See* South Dakota Hunting Handbook (2003), at 16-22, R84-90.

11. S. Dak. Const. art. VI, § 13, U.S. Const. amend. V, XIV. "If subdivision (2) of this section is declared by an advisory opinion or adjudication of the South Dakota Supreme Court to be a taking of private property requiring compensation, subdivision (2) is void." Con. Comm. Engrossed No. HB 1163, 2003 Leg. Assem., 78th Sess. (S.D. Mar. 10, 2003).

12. *Nollan v. California Coastal Comm'n*, 483 U.S. 825, 831-832 (1987) (quoting *Loretto v. Teleprompter Manhattan CATV Corp.*, 458 U.S. 419, 432-435 (1982)). "A permanent physical occupation authorized by state law is a taking without regard to whether the State, or instead a party authorized by the State, is the occupant." *Loretto*, 458 U.S. at 432 n.9.

13. *Loretto*, 458 U.S. at 433.

14. *Nollan*, 483 U.S. at 831 (internal quotations omitted).

15. *Id.* at 832.

16. *Loretto*, 458 U.S. at 433.

17. *Lucas v. South Carolina Coastal Council*, 505 U.S. 1003, 1015 (1992).

18. *United States v. Causby*, 328 U.S. 256, 264-265 (1946) ("invasions of [airspace] are in the same category as invasions of the surface").

19. *Portsmouth Harbor Land & Hotel Co. v. United States*, 260 U.S. 327, 329 (1922).

20. *Burlington Truck Lines, Inc. v. United States*, 371 U.S. 156, 168-169 (1962). "The courts may not accept appellate counsel's *post hoc* rationalizations for agency action; [] an agency's discretionary order be upheld, if at all, on the same basis articulated in the order by the agency itself."

21. The South Dakota Hunting Handbook (2003), "a synopsis of South Dakota Codified Laws and Game, Fish and Park rules regarding hunting" (at 5, R101), provides, that "[t]o be *lawfully* taken from a public road right-of-way, the hunter must be within the right-of-way boundaries when shooting, and the game must originate from or be flying over the road right-of-way." *Id.* at 33, R73.

22. S.D. Codified Laws § 41-1-8 makes it unlawful for anyone to "intentionally interfere with persons lawfully engaged in hunting." *See Reis v. Miller*, *supra*, and *State v. Tracy*, 539 N.W.2d 327 (S.D. 1995) (landowner appeals from hunter interference convictions).

23. *Benson v. South Dakota*, Civil 03-121, slip op. (6th Judicial Circuit Nov. 30, 2004).

24. *Id.* at 26.

25. *Id.*

26. *Id.*

27. http://travel.state.mt.us/fire.htm. Photographs of the various fires throughout the West are available at http://www.nifc.gov/gallery/

28. http://archives.cnn.com/2000/US/08/16/wildfires.02/

29. J.P. Plutt, *More rivers closing as weather takes its toll on state's fisheries*, and *Outdoor use limited as restrictions and closures take effect*, Dillon Tribune, Aug. 16, 2000, at A-11.

30. Mont. Code Ann. §§ 23-2-301, *et seq.*

31. *Montana Coalition for Stream Access v. Curran*, 682 P.2d 163 (Mont. 1984); *Montana Coalition for Stream Access v. Hildreth*, 684 P.2d 1088 (Mont. 1984).

32. "All surface, underground, flood and atmospheric waters within the boundaries of the state are the property of the state for the use of its people and subject to appropriation for beneficial uses as provided by law." Montana Const. art. IX, § 3(3).

33. *Day v. Armstrong*, 362 P.2d 137, 145-46 (Wyo. 1961).

34. Mont. Code Ann. §§ 23-2-301, *et seq.*

35. *Galt v. State Dept. of Fish, Wildlife & Parks*, 731 P.2d 912 (Mont. 1987).

36. The landowners included Harvey and Doris Madison of Absarokee, Montana; Charles and Elena d'Autremont of Alder, Montana; and Harrison Saunders of Ennis, Montana.

37. *Madison v. Graham*, 126 F. Supp.2d 1320 (D.Mont. 2001).

38. *Madison*, 316 F.3d 867 (9th Cir. 2002).

39. The Supreme Court has long recognized that claims may arise under either or both the Takings Clause and the Due Process Clause because those constitutional provisions address two different types of governmental conduct. A claim under the Takings Clause assumes the validity of the regulation but seeks just compensation for the property taken, whereas a substantive due process claim challenges the validity of the regulation itself. *See United States v. Great Falls Mfg. Co.*, 112 U.S. 645, 656 (1884) (if an owner demands just compensation, he has accepted the validity of the taking); *City of Monterey v. Del Monte Dunes at Monterey, Ltd.*, 526 U.S. 687, 747 n. 7, 748 (Souter, J., concurring in part and dissenting in part) (a substantive due process claim asserts a "lack of authority. But this is not so in the usual case where damages are sought;" "inverse condemnation enforces payment for the owner's value in property *lawfully* taken" (emphasis added)).

40. *Madison*, 538 U.S. 1058 (2003).

41. *Del-Rio Drilling Programs, Inc. v. United States*, 146 F.3d 1358 (Fed. Cir. 1998); *Villas of Lake Jackson, Ltd. v. Leon County*, 906 F. Supp. 1509 (N.D. Fla. 1995), *aff'd*, 121 F.3d 610 (11th Cir. 1997).

42. *City of Coeur d'Alene v. Simpson*, Memorandum Decision (1st Judicial District, Oct. 24, 2002).

43. *Simpson*, ___P.3d ___, 2005 WL 286936 (Idaho Feb. 8, 2005).

44. *Simpson*, No. 29299 (Idaho Apr. 12, 2005).

45. *Kelo v. City of New London, Connecticut*, ____ U.S. ____, 125 S.Ct. 2655 (2005).

46. *County of Wayne v. Hathcock*, 684 N.W.2nd 765 (Mich. 2004).

47. http://www.landusecoalition.org/stories.htm

48. *Id.*, "Real People. Real Stories."

49. Colo. Rev. Stat. § 30-28-139.

50. *Williamson County Regional Planning Commission v. Hamilton Bank of Johnson City*, 473 U.S. 172 (1985).

51. *San Remo Hotel, L.P. v. City and County of San Francisco*, ___ U.S. ___, 125 S.Ct. 2491 (2005).

52. *San Remo Hotel*, 364 F.3d 1088, 1095 (9th Cir. 2004).

53. The Constitution grants to federal courts the authority to hear cases "arising under" the Constitution. U.S. Const. art. III, § 2. The Supreme Court maintained, in *San Remo Hotel*, that its ruling was required by a federal statute, the Full Faith and Credit Act, 28 U.S.C. § 1738. It may also be required by the Rooker-Feldman doctrine, which provides that lower federal courts have no subject matter jurisdiction to review state court decisions unless Congress has authorized such review. *Rooker v. Fidelity Trust Co.*, 263 U.S. 413 (1923); *District of Columbia Court of Appeals v. Feldman*, 460 U.S. 462 (1983).

54. Michael M. Berger, *Supreme Bait & Switch: The Ripeness Ruse in Regulatory Takings*, 3 Wash. U.J.L. & Pol'y 99 (2000).

55. *San Remo Hotel*, ___ U.S. at ___, 125 S.Ct. at 2509-10 (Rehnquist, C.J., concurring) ("[F]urther reflection and experience lead me to think that the justifications for [*Williamson County's*] state-litigation requirement are suspect, while its impact on takings plaintiffs is dramatic.... In an appropriate case, I believe the Court should reconsider whether plaintiffs asserting a Fifth Amendment takings claim based on the final decision of a state or local government entity must first seek compensation in state courts.").

56. Substantive due process is "[t]he doctrine that governmental deprivations of life, liberty or property are subject to limitations regardless of the adequacy of the procedures employed...." *Pearson v. City of Grand Blanc*, 961 F.2d 1211, 1216 (6th Cir. 1992) (quoting *Comment, Developments in the Law—The Constitution and the Family*, 93 Harv. L. Rev. 1156, 1166 (1980)).

57. *Weinberger v. Salfi*, 422 U.S. 749, 768-770 (1975); *Village of Willowbrook v. Olech*, 528 U.S. 562, 562 (2000) (*per curiam*).

58. *See, e.g., Adarand Constructors, Inc. v. Peña*, 515 U.S. 200 (1995).

59. One of most important sticks in the bundle of rights that make up property is the right to devote that property to "essential uses." *See Curtin v. Benson*, 222 U.S. 78, 86 (1911). The consummate "essential" use of real property is the right to establish a home thereon. *See Lucas*, 505 U.S. at 1031.

60. The Fifth Amendment prohibits government from "forcing some people alone to bear public burdens, which in all fairness and justice, should be borne by the public as a whole." *Armstrong v. United States*, 364 U.S. 40, 44 (1960).

Chapter 7: Fighting the Closure of "Sacred" Public and Private Lands

1. Native American Rights Fund, *Court rules for Indian religious freedom*, 23 NARF Legal Review, No. 1, Winter/Spring 1998; *available at* www.narf.org/pubs/nlr/nlr23-1.htm

2. *Cholla Ready Mix, Inc. v. Civish*, 382 F.3d 969, 977 (9th Cir. 2004).

3. The Sheridan Inn was built in 1892. From 1894 to 1901, Colonel William F. "Buffalo Bill" Cody was a part owner of the hotel, which is today a National Historic Landmark. www.sheridaninn.com

4. www.wyomingsawmills.com

5. www.fs.fed.us/r2/bighorn/index.shtml. U.S. Department of the Interior, Bureau of Land Management, *Public Land Statistics 1992* 5 (1993).

6. Multiple Use Sustained Yield Act of 1960, 16 U.S.C. § 528.

7. The Organic Act of June 4, 1897, 16 U.S.C. § 475, provides: "No national forest shall be established, except to improve and protect the forest within the boundaries, or for the purpose of securing favorable conditions of water flows, and to furnish a continuous supply of timber for the use and necessities of citizens of the United States...."

8. Although environmental groups vehemently deny the obvious, failure to manage forests to preserve forest health results in dreadful forest fires, such as the 2002 Rodeo-Chediski fire, the worst in Arizona history; more than 467,000 acres (an area two-thirds the size of Rhode Island) went up in flames. http://en.wikipedia.org/wiki/Rodeo-Chediski_fire. The White Mountain Apache Tribe, for example, prevented even greater devastation of its forest by its aggressive forest thinning and fuel reduction program. http://64.233.167.104/search?q=cache:sPdj3CpJUf0J:www4.nau.edu/itep/about/assets/docs/_NV_Summer2002FINAL.pdf 1 rodeo 1 chediski 1 forest 1 fire 1 navajo 1 lands 1 saved&hl=en. Not surprisingly, an environmental group sued to prevent the Forest Service from engaging in post-fire timber sales to prevent future fires in the Rodeo-Chediski area. Ultimately, and perhaps for one of few times, that attempt to delay harvesting failed. *Forest Conservation Council v. U.S. Forest Service*, No. 03-16511, 2004 WL 2180022 (9th Cir. Sept. 15, 2004), *en banc denied* (Nov. 15, 2004).

9. http://www.fs.fed.us/r2/bighorn/recreation/heritage/nativeamericans. http://wyoshpo.state.wy.us/medwheel.htm. The Medicine Wheel is a "roughly circular alignment of rocks and associated cairns enclosing 28 radial rows of rock extending out from a central cairn" some 75 feet in diameter at an elevation of 9,642 feet. *Id.*

10. http://www.sacredland.org/historical_sites_pages/medicine_wheel.html

11. *Id.*

12. Memorandum of Agreement Among the Bighorn National Forest, Advisory Council on Historic Preservation, Wyoming State Historic Preservation Officer, Medicine Wheel Coalition For Sacred Sites Of North America, Big Horn County Commissioners, and Federal Aviation Administration Regarding the Long-Term Management of the Medicine Wheel National Historic Landmark and Historic Properties on Medicine Mountain, I-1 (June 21, 1993).

13. U.S. Forest Service, Draft Medicine Wheel/Medicine Mountain Historic Preservation Plan (April 1996).

14. U.S. Forest Service, Final Medicine Wheel/Medicine Mountain Historic Preservation Plan, Sec. III-5 (September 1996).

15. *Id.* at I-2. The National Forest Management Act of 1976 (NFMA), 16 U.S.C. § 1600, *et seq.*, requires each unit of the national forest system (forests and grasslands) to adopt plans pursuant to which the unit will be managed. General plans are followed by specific plans authorizing the previously approved management activity. Each plan must be adopted in accordance with the extensive paperwork and public comment mandates of the National Environmental Policy Act of 1969 (NEPA), 42 U.S.C. § 4321, *et seq.* These plans, often referred to as "environmental reviews," include Environmental Assessments (EAs) and Environmental Impact Statements (EISs).

16. U.S. Forest Service, Addendum to the Environmental Assessment for the Management and Historic Preservation Plan for the Medicine Wheel National Historic Landmark and Vicinity, Analysis of Effects of Proposed Forest Plan Amendment No. 12.

17. *Id.*

18. U.S. Forest Service, Final Medicine Wheel/Medicine Mountain Historic Preservation Plan, Sec. IX-51 (September 1996).

19. American Indian religious practitioners often assert that such demands are merely a request that the government "accommodate" their free exercise of religion. Government action respecting religion is not constitutional "accommodation," however, unless it removes a "discernible burden" on the free exercise of religion, *Lee v. Weisman*, 505 U.S. 577, 607 (1992), which was "government-created." *Corporation of Presiding Bishop of Church of Jesus Christ of Latter-Day Saints v. Amos*, 483 U.S. 327, 338 (1987). The accommodation doctrine is "not a principle without limits," *Board of Education of Kiryas Joel Village Sch. Distr. v. Grumet*, 512 U.S. 687, 706 (1984), because, "[a]t some point, accommodation may devolve into an unlawful fostering of religion." *Amos*, 483 U.S. at 334-335.

20. U.S. Forest Service, Amendment to Horse Creek Timber Sale Environmental Assessment (Aug. 8, 1997).

21. U.S. Forest Service, Bid Package for Horse Creek Timber Sale (Sept. 19, 1997); U.S. Forest Service, Forest Supervisor's Notice of Cancellation of Horse Creek Timber Sale (Oct. 1, 1997).

22. U.S. Forest Service, Forest Supervisor's Notice of Cancellation of Horse Creek Timber Sale (Oct. 1, 1997).

23. U.S. Const. amend. I.

24. *Lemon v. Kurtzman*, 403 U.S. 602, 612-13 (1971) (state-provided aid to church-related elementary and secondary schools regarding secular instruction violates Establishment Clause).

25. *Id.* at 612-13 (citing *Walz v. Tax Commission*, 397 U.S. 664, 674 (1970)).

26. *Lynch v. Donnelly*, 465 U.S. 668, 690 (1984) (O'Connor, J., concurring), adopted in *Wallace v. Jaffree*, 472 U.S. 38, 57 (1985) (state-authorized daily period of silence in all public schools for meditation or voluntary prayer violates Establishment Clause).

27. *Lee v. Weisman*, 505 U.S. 577, 587, 592 (1992) (quoting *Lynch*, 465 U.S. at 678) (public school requirement that students stand and remain silent during "nonsectarian" prayer at graduation ceremony violates Establishment Clause).

28. *Santa Fe Independent School Dist. v. Doe*, 530 U.S. 290, 309-310 (2000) (quoting *Lynch*, 465 U.S. at 688 (O'Connor, J., concurring)) (elected student giving a prayer over public address system at each varsity football game violates Establishment Clause).

29. *Badoni v. Higginson*, 638 F.2d 172, 178 (10th Cir. 1980) (quoting *Otten v. Baltimore & O. R. Co.*, 205 F.2d 58, 61 (2nd Cir. 1953) (Learned Hand, J.)).

30. *Lyng v. Northwest Indian Cemetery Protective Ass'n*, 485 U.S. 439, 452-53 (1988) (emphasis in original).

31. *Wyoming Sawmills, Inc. v. United States Forest Service*, 179 F.Supp.2d 1279 (D.Wyo. 2001). Outrageously, these types of delays are not uncommon. One case litigated by MSLF was briefed fully and ready for decision on July 5, 2001; the federal district court did not rule for more than four years. *Mount Royal Joint Venture v. Norton*, No. 99cv2728 (D.D.C. Aug. 26, 2005).

32. *Wyoming Sawmills*, 179 F.Supp.2d at 1297. Standing is required by the Constitution's "case" or "controversy" requirement, U.S. Const. art. III, § 2, which the Supreme Court interprets to require: (1) an "injury in fact," which is an invasion of a legally protected interest that is "(a) concrete and particularized, and (b) actual or imminent, not conjectural or hypothetical;" (2) a causal relationship between the injury and the agency action; and (3) a likelihood that the injury will be redressed by a favorable decision. *Lujan v. Defenders of Wildlife*, 504 U.S. 555, 560-561 (citations and footnotes omitted).

33. William Matthews, Forest Service Historian, U.S. Forest Service, Lovell, Wyoming.

34. By the time the Bush administration filed its brief in December 2002, all of its high-level and intermediary officials were in place. Moreover, the terrible 2002 fire season had energized the Bush administration into addressing, at least legislatively, the forest health issue. Furthermore, Governor Bush and Secretary Cheney had campaigned against Clinton's western policies. None of these was a sufficient basis for Bush administration lawyers to change their litigating posture in *Wyoming Sawmills*. In fact, to the writer's knowledge, on every lawsuit filed against the Clinton administration that challenged Clinton's

western, environmental, or natural resources policies, the Bush administration aggressively defended its predecessor.

35. Medicine Wheel Coalition On Sacred Sites Of North America. Friend of the court (*amici curiae*) briefs in support of the Forest Service were filed by the National Congress of American Indians, National Trust for Historic Preservation, The Becket Fund for Religious Liberty, Bureau of Catholic Indian Missions, General Conference of Seventh-day Adventists, Clifton Kirkpatrick, Stated Clerk of the General Assembly of the Presbyterian Church (U.S.A.), Union of Orthodox Jewish Congregations of America, Baptist Joint Committee on Public Affairs, and Council on American Islamic Relations.

36. *Wyoming Sawmills Inc.*, 383 F.3d 1241, 1247 (10th Cir. 2004). This is ludicrous. *See, e.g.*, *Two Guys From Harrison-Allentown, Inc. v. McGinley*, 366 U.S. 582(1961) (corporation has standing to challenge whether law respected establishment of religion).

37. *Foremaster v. City of St. George*, 882 F.2d 1485 (10th Cir. 1989).

38. *See County of Allegheny v. ACLU*, 492 U.S. 573 (1989) (local residents had standing to challenge the presence of a creche on city and county property). In fact, in only one circuit must one who seeks to challenge an alleged Establishment Clause violation modify his behavior in response to that offending religious symbol. *ACLU v. City of St. Charles*, 794 F.2d 265, 269 (7th Cir. 1986). The Supreme Court knows of this split and may yet resolve it. *See City of Edmond v. Robinson*, 517 U.S. 1201 (1996) (Chief Justice Rehnquist, with Justices Scalia and Thomas, dissenting from denial of *certiorari*).

39. *Wyoming Sawmills, Inc. v. United States Forest Service*, ___ U.S. ___, 126 S.Ct. 330 (2005).

40. "A petition for a *writ* of *certiorari* is rarely granted when the asserted error consists of erroneous factual findings or the misapplication of a properly stated rule of law." Sup. Ct. R. 10.

41. Exec. Order No. 13,007, Indian Sacred Sites, 61 *Fed. Reg.* 26,771 (May 26, 1996).

42. Devils Tower, a vertical monolith that rises 1,267 feet above the Belle Fourche River in Crook County, near Hulett, Wyoming, is the nation's first national monument and was created by President Theodore Roosevelt on September 24, 1906. www.nps.gov/deto/index.htm

43. The Tenth Circuit ruled: as to the commercial climber, that he had failed to show an economic injury; as to climbers who objected to the NPS's policy but climbed anyway, that they had not suffered an injury; and, as to climbers who refused to climb for fear that if they did climb the NPS would close Devils Tower to all climbing year-round, that their fears were "remote and speculative." *Bear Lodge Multiple Use Ass'n v. Babbitt*, 175 F.3d 814, 821-22 (10th Cir. 1999). Petitions for rehearing *en banc* and for *writ* of *certiorari* were both denied. *Bear Lodge*, reh'g denied (Aug. 18, 1999), *cert. denied*, 529 U.S. 1037 (2000).

44. The Lewis and Clark National Forest covers portions of 13 counties in central and north-central Montana. www.fs.fed.us/r1/lewisclark. Its Rocky Mountain Division overlies the Overthrust Belt, a vast geological feature estimated to be the largest natural gas deposit in the continental United States.

45. *Rocky Mountain Oil and Gas Association and Independent Petroleum Association of America v. U.S. Forest Service*, 2001 WL 470022 (9th Cir. May 3, 2001). A petition for *writ* of *certiorari* was denied. *Independent Petroleum Association of American Association v. U. S. Forest Service*, 534 U.S. 1018 (2001). Despite the Bush administration's public commitment to finding new energy sources, its lawyers opposed Supreme Court review of a decision closing one million acres of land thought to contain an abundant amount of natural gas.

46. Rainbow Bridge National Monument, the world's largest natural bridge, was designated by President Taft on May 30, 1910, and today is managed by the National Park Service. www.nps.gov/rabr/home

47. *Natural Arch and Bridge Society v. Alston*, 98 Fed Appx. 711 (10th Cir. Mar. 23, 2004). A petition for rehearing *en banc* was denied, No. 02-4099 (10th Cir. June 15, 2004), as was a petition for *writ* of *certiorari* on behalf of the one visitor who the district court held had standing. *DeWaal v. Alston*, ___ U.S. ___, 125 S.Ct. 1294 (2005).

48. *Lyng*, 485 U.S. at 453.

49. *Cholla Ready Mix, Inc.*, No. 02cv1185, slip op. at 4 (D.Ariz. Jan. 21, 2003).

50. *Cholla Ready Mix, Inc.*, 382 F.3d at 975.

51. *Id.* at 977.

52. *Buono v. Norton*, 371 F.3d 543, 548-550 (9th Cir. 2004).

53. *Cholla Ready Mix, Inc.*, No. 03-15423 (9th Cir. Oct. 14, 2004). *Cholla Ready Mix, Inc., v. Mendez*, ___U.S.___, 125 S.Ct. 1828 (2005).

54. Cave Rock is a basalt plug rising 300 feet above the shores of Lake Tahoe on federal land along U.S. Highway 50. The U.S. Forest Service manages Cave Rock as part of the Lake Tahoe Management Unit. www.fs.fed.us/r5/ltbmu/. The Access Fund, a climbing group, filed the lawsuit in December 2003.

55. *The Access Fund v. Veneman*, No. 03cv00687, Transcript 54-55 (D.Nev. Jan. 28, 2005) (quoting *Cholla v. Civish*, 382 F.3d 969, 976 (9th Cir. 2004).

56. U.S. Department of Agriculture, Forest Service, Cave Rock Management Direction, Final Environmental Impact Statement 3-72 (2002).

57. *Id.* at 2-1.

58. *Id.* at 2-6.

59. *Id.*

60. *See, e.g., Lyng v. Northwest Indian Cemetery Protective Ass'n*, 485 U.S. 439, 448–450 (1988).

61. Final Environmental Impact Statement, *supra*, 3-20.

62. *Id.* That the conversation of climbers at Cave Rock is not the "dominant noise source in the area" is a bit of an understatement; the four lanes of Highway 50, which transect Cave Rock, generate a continuous roar of speeding trucks, automobiles, and motorcycles.

63. *Id.* at 3-72.

64. *Id.* at 3-24.

65. *Id.* at 3-4, 3-5.

66. *Id.* at 2-7. A similar sign on federal land in California regarding a Latin cross erected to honor those killed in World War I yielded this ruling: "[D]espite the sign—indeed, perhaps because of it—'observers might [still have] reasonably perceive[d] the city's display of such a religious symbol on public property as government endorsement of the Christian faith.'" *Buono*, 371 F.3d at 549 (quoting *Separation of Church and State Comm. v. City of Eugene*, 93 F.3d 617, 626 (9th Cir. 1996).

67. *Buono, supra.*

68. "'Do not come any closer,' God said. 'Take off your sandals, for the place where you are standing is holy ground.'" Exodus 3:5 NIV.

69. *McCreary County, Kentucky v. ACLU of Kentucky*, ___ U.S. ___, 125 S. Ct. 2722, 2748 (2005) (Scalia, J., dissenting); *Van Orden v. Perry*, ___ U.S. ___, 125 S. Ct. 2854 (2005) (Rehnquist, C.J., plurality); *Wallace v. Jaffree*, 472 U.S. 38, 100–103 (1985) (Rehnquist, J., dissenting).

70. Michael Novak, *On Two Wings: Humble Faith and Common Sense at the American Founding* (Encounter Books 2002). "In one key respect, the way the story of the United States has been told for the past one hundred years is wrong. It has cut off one of the two wings by which the American Eagle flies, her compact with the God of the Jews—the God of Israel championed by the nation's first Protestants.... Believe that there is such a God or not—the founding generation did, and relied upon this belief. Their faith is an 'indispensable' part of their story." *Id.* at 5.

71. *McCreary County, Kentucky v. American Civil Liberties Union of Kentucky*, ___U.S.___, 125 S.Ct. 2722, 2726 (2005).

72. *Id.* at 2724.

73. *Id.* at 2725 (quoting *Stone v. Graham*, 449 U.S. 39, 41 (1980)).

74. *Id.* at 2737.

75. *Van Orden v. Perry*, ___U.S.___, 125 S.Ct. 2854, 2871 (2005).

76. *Id.* at 2869.

77. *Id.* at 2869, 2870.

78. *Id.* at 2871.

Chapter 8: Fighting the Federal Government When It Wears Two Hats

1. http://www.brainyquote.com/quotes/authors/g/george_washington.html

2. http://www.brainyquote.com/quotes/authors/r/ronald_reagan.html

3. As of March 9, 1990, the BLM's "case abstract" for Mr. Mann's lease, NM 40957, erroneously listed Crowne as the owner of the lease.

4. Lease determination letter from Bureau of Land Management, District Manager, Las Cruces District Office, to Stanley K. Mann (Nov. 12, 1993).

5. In fact, the BLM had not taken the action that it asserted it would take, within 30 days, if Stanley Mann did not respond to the "lease determination" notice.

6. *Stanley K. Mann*, IBLA 95-705 (Nov. 3, 1995).

7. *Stanley K. Mann* (On Reconsideration), IBLA 95-705 (Mar. 15, 1996).

8. *Mann v. United States*, 53 Fed. Cl. 562 (Fed. Cl. 2002).

9. *Mann*, 334 F.3d 1048, 1051-1052 (Fed. Cir. 2003).

10. *Id.* at 1052.

11. 31 U.S.C. § 1304.

12. *Cannon v. United States of America*, 338 F.3d 1183, 1185 (10th Cir. 2003).

13. *Id.*

14. *Id.* at 1184-1185.

15. *Id.* at 1186.

16. *Id.*

17. *Id.* at 1187.

18. *Id.*

19. *Id.* at 1188. The federal government did list the Cannon property as a Formerly Used Defense Site (FUDS) for future cleanup by the U.S. Department of Defense. The Army Corps of Engineers testified that the Cannon property is scheduled for cleanup in 2008-2010, that is, if Congress appropriates the funds. Congress spends only $2 million annually on the 2,700 FUDS properties, whose total cleanup cost is $19 billion.

20. *Cannon*, 338 F.3d at 1194.

21. *Id.* at 1188.

22. One has to wonder at this advice and what it says about the federal government and the type of society America is to become. The Tenth Circuit told the Cannons that they should not have waited for the federal government, which was in the midst of an investigation, to finalize its work before suing. Whether all the facts are known or not, the Tenth Circuit implies, sue anyway.

23. *Cannon*, 338 F.3d at 1194. In July 2005, the Cannon family filed a claim against the United States under the Resource Conservation and Recovery Act (RCRA), 42 U.S.C. § 6901, *et seq.*, to force the U.S. government to do exactly what it compels others to do, on pain of civil and criminal prosecution: clean up its mess. Subsequently, they filed a lawsuit. *Cannon v. Rumsfeld*, No. 05cv00922 (D.Utah filed Nov. 4, 2005).

24. http://www.rdsdrive-in.com/about.htm

25. *Garcia v. Spun Steak Co.*, 998 F.2d 1480, 1489 (9th Cir. 1993).

26. http://deseretnews.com/dn/view/0,1249,450022058,00.html

27. In *Garcia*, 998 F.2d at 1489, the Ninth Circuit refused to "defer to an administrative construction of a statute where there are 'compelling indications that it is wrong,'" holding instead that "Nothing in the plain language of [Title VII] supports EEOC's English-only rule . . . ."

28. *Jewish World Review*, Nov. 27, 2000/22 Kislev, 5763.

29. Roger Clegg, *Help Wanted: The administration has some civil-rights issues*, National Review Online, Dec. 2, 2002.

30. *EEOC v. Kidman*, No. 02cv01911 (D.Ariz. Sept. 14, 2004).

Chapter 9: Fighting the Federal Government's Bad Neighbor Policies

1. Bartlett's Familiar Quotations 244-11 (16th ed. Little, Brown and Company 1992). George Herbert, 1593-1633, was an English poet and orator. http://en.wikipedia.org/wiki/George_Herbert

2. Bartlett's Familiar Quotations, *supra*, at 506-11. Walter Bagehot, 1826-1877, was an English social scientist. http://www.infoplease.com/ce6/people/A0805734.html

3. As ESPN has broadcast, Watersmeet is "Home of the Watersmeet Nimrods." A nimrod is "a mighty hunter before the Lord." http://www.watersmeet.k12.mi.us/nimrod.html

4. http://www.watersmeet.org/index.shtml

5. *Id.*

6. http://www.fs.fed.us/r9/ottawa/index.shtml

7. http://www.fs.fed.us/r9/ottawa/images/maps/sylvania_04.pdf

8. http://www.lakegogebic.com/about.htm. Kathy Stupak-Thrall recalls that her grandparents "lived year round on Crooked Lake until age and health issues dictated otherwise."

9. http://www.watersmeet.org/index.shtml

10. "Funds appropriated under this Act shall not be used for the acquisition of forest lands . . . without approval of the local government concerned." Pub. L. No. 89-53 (Mar. 1, 1911), Administrative Provisions, Forest Service, 36 Stat. 961. http://www.lib.duke.edu/forest/Research/usfscoll/policy/Agency_Organization/NF_System/weeks_law/

11. The Gogebic County Board of Supervisors voted to allow the Forest Service to acquire the property but conditioned its approval upon "the fact that the Forest Service . . . would practice multiple use management of the area."

12. 16 U.S.C. § 1131(a); *see* Wilderness Act of 1964, 16 U.S.C. § 1131, *et seq.*

13. *See Wyoming Outdoor Coordinating Council v. Butz*, 484 F.2d 1244 (10th Cir. 1973).

14. Final Environmental Impact Statement: Roadless Area Review and Evaluation ("RARE II FEIS"). *See State of California v. Block*, 690 F.2d 753, 758 (9th Cir. 1982).

15. RARE II FEIS at 73. The Forest Service recognized that "non-federal lands included within boundaries of an area classified as wilderness are not themselves classified." In 1986, the Forest Service finalized its management plan for the Ottawa noting that "the management prescriptions defined in the Forest Plan apply to National Forest System lands only. They do not apply to any lands in state, county, private or other ownership." Forest Plan Map of Alternative 7, *in* U.S. Forest Service, Final Environmental Impact Statement, Land and Resources Management Plan, and Record of Decision for the Ottawa National Forest.

16. Michigan Wilderness Act, Pub. L. No. 100-184 (Dec. 8, 1987), 101 Stat. 1274.

17. *Id.* 101 Stat. at 1275. "Subject to valid existing rights, each wilderness area designated by the Act shall be administered by the Secretary of Agriculture in accordance with the provisions of the Wilderness Act of 1964."

18. Under Michigan law, riparian owners share in common the right to use the entire surface of Crooked Lake for boating, swimming, and fishing, and other activities so long as they do not interfere with the reasonable use of other riparians. *Hall v. Wantz*, 57 N.W.2d 462, 464 (Mich. 1953); *Burt v. Munger*, 23 N.W.2d 117, 119 (Mich. 1946). Although the term "riparian," meaning one who owns land on the banks of a river, is often used regarding Kathy Stupak-Thrall and her neighbors, the precise term is "littoral," which means "belonging to the shore, as of seas and great lakes." *Black's Law Dictionary* 1327 (6th ed. 1991).

19. Her neighbors, who were with her during the entire litigation, were Michael A. Gajewski, Major (Retired/Disability), United States Army, and his wife Bodil Gajewski. Sadly, as this litigation drew to an end, Major Gajewski died.

20. *Stupak-Thrall v. United States*, 843 F. Supp. 327, 330 (W.D. Mich. 1994).

21. *Id.* at 331, 333.

22. *Stupak-Thrall*, 70 F.3d 881, 889-891 (6th Cir. 1995).

23. *Stupak-Thrall*, 81 F.3d 651 (6th Cir. 1996).

24. *Stupak-Thrall*, 89 F.3d 1269 (6th Cir. 1996) (*en banc*).

25. *Stupak-Thrall*, 843 F.Supp. at 332 (citing *Kleppe v. New Mexico*, 426 U.S. 529 (1976)).

26. *Kleppe*, 426 U.S. at 547. Article IV, § 3, cl. 2, of the United States Constitution provides, "The Congress shall have Power to dispose of and make all needful Rules and Regulations respecting the Territory or other Property belonging to the United States. . . ."

27. *Stupak-Thrall*, 519 U.S. 1090 (1997).

28. *Id.* at 1063-64.

29. Section 4 of the Michigan Wilderness Act provides:

As soon a practicable after [this law] takes effect, the Secretary of Agriculture shall file maps and legal descriptions of each wilderness area designated by this title with the Committee on Energy Land Natural Resources, United States Senate, and the Committee on Interior and Insular Affairs, House of Representatives, and each such map and legal description shall have the same force and effect as if included in this Act: *Provided, however,* That correction of clerical and typographical errors in such legal descriptions and maps may be made. Each such map and legal description shall be on file and available for public inspection in the office of the chief of the Forest Service, Department of the Agriculture.

101. Stat. 1274, 1275-76.

30. Willis Burt, a surveyor of impeccable reputation, performed the survey of the area around Crooked Lake and, in accordance with established surveying principles, meandered the section line around Crooked Lake, setting the requisite "meander corners" and resuming his survey of the section line on the opposite side of Crooked Lake. Because the original GLO surveys meandered Crooked Lake, no section lines cross Crooked Lake. In 1966, the Forest Service retraced the original GLO surveys; in 1982, the Forest Service remarked the meandered corners on Crooked Lake.

31. *Stupak-Thrall*, No. 98cv113, slip. op. at 8, 20 (D.Mich. Apr. 2, 1999).

32. *Kleppe*, 426 U.S. at 546.

33. *U.S. v. Armstrong*, 186 F.3d 1055, 1061 (8th Cir. 1999) (citing *Kleppe*, 426 U.S. at 546).

34. "[E]very man must use his own property so as not to injure that of his neighbor." *People v. Hulbert*, 131 Mich. 156, 91 N.W. 211, 215 (1902); *see also Camfield v. United States*, 167 U.S. 518, 525 (1897), where the United States sought to prevent what was "clearly a nuisance." There is no private property right under common law to create a nuisance.

35. American Heritage Rivers Initiative: Proposal With Request for Comments, 62 *Fed. Reg.* 27253 (May 19, 1997). Private citizens were not the only ones who wanted more details. On April 25, 1997, one low-level federal bureaucrat from New Mexico declared: "The initiative would be a lot stronger if, at a national level, federal agencies and others point to SPECIFIC programs and resources that will be dedicated to supporting proposals."

36. *Id.* The term "economically sustainable" is an immediate warning sign to westerners. Environmental groups maintain that almost no economic activity that takes place in the West—ranching, mining, energy development, or forestry—is "economically sustainable."

37. *Id.* at 27254.

38. *Id.*

39. 16 U.S.C. § 1271, *et seq. See also* William Perry Pendley, *War on the West: Government Tyranny on America's Great Frontier* 123-124 (Regnery 1995).

40. *Village of Belle Terre v. Boras*, 416 U.S. 1, 13 (1974) ("[Z]oning is a complex and important function of the State. It may indeed be the most essential function performed by local government....").

41. Federal lands are under the exclusive control of Congress. U.S. Const. art. IV, § 3, cl. 2.

42. Exec. Order No. 13,061, 62 *Fed. Reg.* 48445 (Sept. 17, 1997).

43. David Almasi, *River-Borne Trojan Horse*, The Washington Times, July 25, 1997, at A18. *See also* Adriel Bettelheim, *River Proposal Doesn't Flow in the West*, The Denver Post, Sept. 8, 1997.

44. More than 100 federal programs were addressing the ostensible goals of the AHRI. Alexander F. Annett, *Navigating the American Heritage Rivers: Wasting Resources on Bureaucracy* Backgrounder No. 1231 (The Heritage Foundation Nov. 4, 1998).

45. *Id.* Clinton designated the Willamette River in Oregon, which borders both the First and Fifth Congressional Districts, held by Democrats who each won in 1996 with but 52 percent of the vote. Clinton also designated the Upper Mississippi River in Iowa, Illinois, Minnesota, and Wisconsin. In the 1998 congressional elections, seven seats in those States would be in play. Democrats would seek to hold Illinois' 17th Congressional District (52 percent), Wisconsin's 3rd (52 percent), and Iowa's 3rd (49 percent) and would try to defeat Republicans in Minnesota's 1st (53 percent), Iowa's 1st (53 percent) and 2nd (53 percent),

- and Illinois' 20th (50 percent). In all of these districts, the green of environmental group politics and the green of millions of federal dollars could make a potent political combination.

46. *Id.*

47. Two of the ten "most endangered" rivers were removed from eligibility for AHRI designation by local congressional representatives; not one of the eight "most endangered" rivers that remained was designated by President Clinton. *Id. See* http://www.amrivers.org

48. Alex Annett, *Good Politics, Bad Policy: Clinton's American Heritage Rivers Initiative F.Y.I.* No. 171 at 3 (The Heritage Foundation Feb. 2, 1998).

49. *Chenoweth v. Clinton,* No. 97cv2954 (D.D.C. filed Dec. 10, 1997). In June 1997, Representative Chenoweth and 46 co-sponsors introduced H.R. 1842 to terminate AHRI funding by any federal agency; the bill passed the House Resources Committee by a voice in November 1997 but went no further. Annett, *supra.*

50. 16 U.S.C. §§ 1271-1273; 28 U.S.C. § 1254(1); 31 U.S.C. § 1301; 42 U.S.C. § 4331(b); 43 U.S.C. §§ 1701(a)(4), 1714(a).

51. The Clinton administration also argued that Congress either had failed to enact legislation that would bar the AHRI or had acquiesced in Clinton's adoption of the AHRI. The argument turns the Constitution on its head!

52. *Chenoweth v. Clinton,* 997 F.Supp. 36, 37 (D.D.C. 1998).

53. *Id.* at 41.

54. For example, the District of Columbia Circuit had ruled that Senator Ted Kennedy (D-MA) had standing to sue President Nixon for his use of a pocket veto. *Kennedy v. Sampson,* 511 F.2d 430 (D.C. Cir. 1974). The District of Columbia Circuit "has repeatedly recognized Members' standing to challenge measures that affect their constitutionally prescribed lawmaking powers." *Byrd v. Raines,* 956 F.Supp. 25, 30 (D.D.C. 1997).

55. *Chenoweth v. Clinton,* 181 F.3d 112, 115 (D.C. Cir. 1999). *Raines v. Byrd,* 521 U.S. 811, 824 (1997) ("In the vote on the [Line Item Veto] Act, [the *Raines* plaintiffs'] votes were given full effect. They simply lost that vote.").

56. *Chenoweth,* 181 F.3d at 116.

57. *Coleman v. Miller,* 307 U.S. 433 (1939).

58. The District of Columbia court claimed that Representative Chenoweth and her colleagues had the ability to vote, which made them like Senator Byrd and his fellow litigants. *Chenoweth,* 181 F.3d at 116 ("Congress could terminate the AHRI were a sufficient number in each House so inclined."). However, Representative Chenoweth's vote would have been to "repeal" an illegal act by Clinton, for which, assuming a presidential veto, she would have needed a two-thirds majority vote, not the simple majority with which Senator Byrd could have carried the day in passing an act of Congress. "[A] *majority* of Senators and Congressm[e]n can [still] pass or reject [ ] bills . . ." *Raines,* 521 U.S. at 823. Plus, since when must Congress "repeal" illegal presidential "acts."

59. *Chenoweth,* 529 U.S. 1012 (2000).

60. The Supreme Court's ruling in *Raines* was applied by the Tenth Circuit to deny standing to Congressman Bob Schaffer (R-4th CO) who sought to challenge federal legislation that provided an annual pay raise to Senators and Representatives in violation of the Twenty-Seventh Amendment to the Constitution. During oral argument, the Tenth Circuit recognized that to deny Congressman Schaffer the right to sue to enforce that amendment meant that no one had standing to enforce it. *Schaffer v. Clinton,* 54 F.Supp.2d 1014 (D.Colo. 1999), 240 F.3d 878 (10th Cir. 2001), *cert. denied, Schaffer v. O'Neill,* 534 U.S. 992 (2001).

61. 59 *Fed. Reg.* at 60266, 60280.

62. Oddly, the Fish and Wildlife Service did not propose to return the Rocky Mountain wolf (*Canis lupus irremotus*) to the area but instead to place the Canadian gray wolf there.

63. An eastern reporter once asked me, "Do you have coyotes in the northern Rockies?" I said, "Yes." "What's the difference between a coyote and a wolf?" "About 100 pounds and the Endangered Species Act," I responded. "If you want wolves, why don't you put them in Rock Creek Park in Washington, D.C.?" I added. "People live there," she said.

64. http://www.cnn.com/EARTH/9712/13/wolf.ruling/. In the early 1900s, because of predation by wolves on livestock, the federal government authorized the killing of wolves throughout the region. By 1930, the federal government had eliminated nearly all the wolves in this region.

65. http://www.wildlife.alaska.gov/regulations/pdfs/regulation_process.pdf. It is estimated that there are between 52,000 and 60,000 wolves in Canada.

66. http://www.azstarnet.com/clips/980126wolves.html

67. *Wyoming Farm Bureau Federation v. Babbitt*, No. 94cv286 (D.Wyo. filed Nov. 25, 1994).

68. http://www.cnn.com/EARTH/9801/27/mexico.wolf/cage.jpg

69. *National Audubon Society v. Babbitt*, No. 95cv1015 (D.Wyo. filed Feb. 24, 1995).

70. http://www.nps.gov/yell/nature/animals/wolf/wolfrest.html

71. *Wyoming Farm Bureau Federation*, 987 F.Supp. 1349 (D.Wyo. 1997).

72. U.S. Fish and Wildlife Service, 2005, Rocky Mountain wolf recovery 2004 annual report, *available from* U.S. Fish and Wildlife Service, Ecological Services, 100 N. Park, Suite 320, Helena, Montana.

73. http://www.cnn.com/EARTH/9712/13/wolf.ruling/

74. http://www.sublette.com/examiner/v4n42/v4n42s3.htm

75. http://www.fbi.gov/congress/congress05/lewis051805.htm

76. U.S. Fish and Wildlife Service, *supra*, fn 70.

77. *Wyoming Farm Bureau Federation*, 199 F.3d 1224 (10th Cir. 2000).

78. U.S. Fish and Wildlife Service, *supra*, fn 70.

79. http://www.supremecourtus.gov/about/biographiescurrent.pdf

80. http://www.billingsgazette.com/index.php?id=1&display=rednews/2005/01/06/build/wyoming/15-wolves.inc

81. http://www.ens-newswire.com/ens/apr2004/2004-04-26-10.asp

82. *Defenders of Wildlife v. Secretary, U.S. Dep't of the Interior*, No. 03cv1348 (D.Ore. Jan. 31, 2005), Nos. 05-35735, 05-35691 (9th Cir. filed July 1, 14, 2005).

83. http://fwp.state.mt.us/mtoutdoors/HTML/Articles/2002/Elkvswolves.htm

84. http://www.bozemandailychronicle.com/articles/2004/12/17/news/02latehunt.txt

85. http://www.livescience.com/animalworld/ap_050819_wolf.html. In 1995, Secretary Babbitt and Governor Romer agreed to import lynx into Colorado. In 1998, the federal and state agencies declined to prepare an environmental impact statement on the impacts of placing scores of lynx in Colorado's national forests. When ranchers and outfitters, who would bear the brunt of the plan, sued, a Colorado federal district court ruled that they had no right to sue. *Colorado Farm Bureau Federation v. U. S. Forest Service*, No. 98cv02696 (D.Colo. Jan. 15, 1999). The Tenth Circuit implicitly recognized that the ranchers and outfitters could sue but held that they had failed to allege final agency action that caused an injury. *Colorado Farm Bureau Federation v. U.S. Forest Service*, 220 F.3d 1171, 1174 (10th Cir. 2000). Although the ranchers and outfitters pointed out, in a petition for rehearing *en banc*, that, "a failure to act is final agency action," in December 2000 the Tenth Circuit denied the petition. In 1999, the lynx were released; in 2000, lynx were listed under the Endangered Species Act and access to the national forests was restricted. *Lynx force new look at forests*, The Denver Rocky Mountain News, July 8, 2000. Access to private property in the Pike and San Isabel National Forests also has been denied because of lynx habitat.

Chapter 10: Fighting the Criminalization of Everything

1. Gene Healy, ed., *Go Directly to Jail: The Criminalization of Almost Everything* cover inside flap (Cato Institute 2004).

2. http://www.wildwilderness.org/wi/unser.htm

3. Purportedly, Bobby Unser violated 16 U.S.C. § 551 and 36 C.F.R. § 261.16(a), which provide, respectively:

The Secretary of Agriculture shall make provisions for the protection against destruction by fire and depredations upon the public forests and national forests . . . and he may make such rules and regulations . . . to regulate their occupancy and use and to preserve the forests thereon from destruction; and any violation of the provisions of this section, sections 473 to 478 and 479 to 482 of this title or such rules and regulations shall be punished by a fine of not more than $500 or imprisonment for not more than six months, or both.

The following are prohibited in a National Forest Wilderness (a) Possessing or using a motor vehicle, motorboat or motorized equipment except as authorized by Federal Law or regulation . . . .

4. *United States v. Unser*, No. 97-CR-110-B (D.Colo. June 17, 1997).

5. *Unser*, 165 F.3d 755 (10th Cir. 1999).

6. *Staples v. United States*, 511 U.S. 600, 606 (1994).

7. *United States v. Freed*, 401 U.S. 601, 609 (1971) ("[O]ne would hardly be surprised to learn that possession of hand grenades is not an innocent act."). *See Morissette v. United States*, 342 U.S. 246 (1952), which followed, *inter alia*, *United States v. Balint*, 258 U.S. 250 (1922).

8. *Staples*, 511 U.S. at 620.

9. *Liparota v. United States*, 471 U.S. 419, 433 (1985).

10. *Id*. at 426.

11. Government bears the burden of proof beyond a reasonable doubt of each element of a criminal offense. *In re Winship*, 397 U.S. 358, 372 (1970) ("[T]he requirement of proof beyond a reasonable doubt in a criminal case is bottomed on a fundamental value determination of our society that it is far worse to convict an innocent man than to let a guilty man go free.") (Harlan, J., concurring).

12. Citing the "pragmatic element" that defendants in cases such as this may have superior access to the facts necessary to prove or disprove a defense, the Tenth Circuit held that shifting the burden of proof of the necessity defense to Mr. Unser did not violate his Fifth Amendment Due Process rights. *Unser*, 165 F.3d at 764-65.

13. *United States v. Semenza*, 835 F.2d 223 (9th Cir. 1987); *United States v. Launder*, 743 F.2d 686 (9th Cir. 1984); *United States v. Wilson*, 133 F.3d 251 (4th Cir. 1997); *Holdridge v. United States*, 282 F.2d 302, 310 (8th Cir. 1960).

14. Of course, this assumes that *United States v. Unser* made the "discuss list," "a list of cases deemed important enough for discussion and a vote. As many as three-quarters of the petitions for *certiorari* are denied a place on the list and thus rejected without further consideration." *The Supreme Court at Work*, Congressional Quarterly, 1990, at 68.

15. *Unser*, 528 U.S. 809 (1999).

16. "Laguna" in Spanish means "small lake." A "sinkhole" is formed by the erosion of an underlying salt structure and its subsequent collapse. A "playa," on the other hand, is formed by wind erosion or by the wallowing of buffalo.

17. Final Rule for Regulatory Programs of the Corps of Engineers, 51 *Fed. Reg*. 41206, 41217.

18. Letter from James L. Collins, Esq., EPA Associate Regional Counsel, to Larry Squires (Aug. 13, 1987).

19. Letter from Myron Knudsen, Water Management Division Manager, EPA, Dallas, Texas, to Larry Squires (Mar. 26, 1991).

20. Highly mineralized springs flowing into Laguna Gatuna contain salt concentrations much higher than that of the brine disposed there: 300 parts per million as compared to 80 parts per million.

21. Letter from Kenton Kirkpatrick, Acting Director of Water Management Division, EPA, Dallas, Texas, to Larry Squires (Oct. 10, 1991).

22. 33 U.S.C. § 1311, *et seq*.

23. *Laguna Gatuna, Inc. v. Browner*, 58 F.3d 564, 564-65 (10th Cir. 1995).

24. *Abbott Laboratories v. Gardner*, 387 U.S. 136, 140 (1967).

25. *Laguna Gatuna, Inc. v. Browner*, 516 U.S. 1071 (1996).

26. U.S. Const. amend. V.

27. *Solid Waste Agency of Northern Cook County v. United States Army Corps of Engineers*, 531 U.S. 159 (2001).

28. *Laguna Gatuna, Inc. v. United States*, 50 Fed. Cl. 336, 343 (2001).

29. *Laguna Gatuna, Inc. v. United States*, No. 96cv157 (Fed. Cl. Oct. 31, 2002). On March 19, 2003, his attorneys were awarded $225,000.00 under a federal fee-shifting statute that requires payment of attorneys' fees in cases like the one brought by Larry Squires. Uniform Relocation Assistance and Real Property Acquisition Policies Act (URA) 42 U.S.C. § 4654(c).

Chapter 11: Fighting for the Equal Protection Guarantee

1. *Plessy v. Ferguson*, 163 U.S. 537, 559 (1896) (Harlan, J., dissenting).

2. *Adarand Constructors, Inc. v. Peña*, 515 U.S. 200, 239 (1995) (Scalia, J., concurring).

3. *See also* William Perry Pendley, *War on the West: Government Tyranny on America's Great Frontier* (Regnery 1995), Appendix C—What No One Knows About the West, 225-229; Public Land Law Review Commission, *One-Third of the Nation's Land: A Report to the President and to the Congress* (1970); and U.S. Department of the Interior, Bureau of Land Management, *Public Land Statistics—1992* 5.

4. General Services Administration, *Federally Owned Land by Agency, Bureau and State, as of September 30, 1992* 14-15 (table 24).

5. *Adarand Constructors, Inc.*, 515 U.S. 200.

6. On March 6, 1961, President Kennedy signed Executive Order 10925 requiring the following of those entering into contracts with the federal government: "The contractor will take affirmative action to ensure that applicants are employed, and that employees are treated during employment, without regard to their race, creed, color, or national origin." In 1977, as Congress considered the Public Works Employment Act (PWEA), a $4 billion economic stimulus program, Congressman Parren Mitchell (D-MD) offered an amendment to set aside a portion of the program for minority-owned business enterprises. 123 Cong. Rec. 5327 (1977). A challenge to the constitutionality of the race-based set-aside was filed immediately. After Congressman Mitchell's amendment was upheld as constitutional in *Fullilove v. Klutznick*, 448 U.S. 448 (1980), Congress, in 1982, required minority business set-asides for all federally financed highway construction projects. Surface Transportation Assistance Act of 1982 (STAA), 96 Stat. 2097 (1982).

7. *Fullilove*, 448 U.S. at 489.

8. *Richmond v. J.A. Croson Co.*, 488 U.S. 469 (1989). "[N]or shall any State . . . deny to any person within its jurisdiction the equal protection of the laws." U.S. Const. amend. XIV, § 1. The Fifth Amendment provides, "[n]o person shall . . . be deprived of life, liberty, or property, without due process of law," which the Supreme Court has read to include an equal protection guarantee or "the equal protection component of the Due Process Clause." *Bolling v. Sharpe*, 347 U.S. 497 (1954).

9. *Metro Broadcasting, Inc. v. FCC*, 497 U.S. 547 (1990).

10. In 1987, Congress replaced STAA when it adopted the Surface Transportation and Uniform Relocation Assistance Act (STURAA) (101 Stat. 132), which was replaced in 1991 with the Intermodal Surface Transportation Efficiency Act of 1991 (ISTEA) (105 Stat. 1914), which was replaced in 1998 with the Transportation Equity Act for 21st Century (TEA-21) (112 Stat. 107), which was replaced with the Safe, Accountable, Flexible, and Efficient Transportation Equity Act of 2005 (SAFETEA), signed by President Bush on August 10, 2005. All contain the race-based contracting set-aside challenged in *Adarand*.

11. 49 C.F.R. Part 23.

12. *Affirmative Action Has Outlived Its Value*, The Denver Post (Feb. 1, 1995).

13. *Colorado Case Could Sound Death Knell for Affirmative Action*, Conservative Chronicle (Jan. 20, 1995).

14. Ann Devroy, *Clinton Orders Affirmative Action Review; At Stake: Principles and Political Base*, The Washington Post (Feb. 24, 1995).

15. It was consistent with and based upon the decision that gave MSLF its first victory before the U.S. Supreme Court, *Wygant v. Jackson Board of Education*, 476 U.S. 267 (1986).

16. *Adarand*, 515 U.S. at 206.

17. *Id.* at 210, 212.

18. *Id.* at 213.

19. *Id.* at 223-24.

20. *Id*. Internal citations omitted.

21. *Id*. at 224. For emphasis, Justice O'Connor repeats Justice Powell's "defense of this conclusion:" "When [political judgments] touch upon an individual's race or ethnic background, he is entitled to a judicial determination that the burden he is asked to bear on that basis is precisely tailored to serve a compelling governmental interest." *University of California Regents v. Bakke*, 438 U.S., 265, 299 (1978) (opinion of Powell, J.) (footnote omitted).

22. *Adarand*, 515 U.S. at 225.

23. *Id*. at 226.

24. *Id*., quoting *Croson, supra*, 488 U.S. at 493 (plurality opinion of O'Connor, J.).

25. *Adarand*, 515 U.S. at 226-27.

26. *Id*.

27. *Id*. at 227.

28. *Id*. The Court also effectively reversed *Fullilove*, "Of course, it follows that to the extent (if any) that *Fullilove* held federal racial classifications to be subject to a less rigorous standard, it is no longer controlling." *Adarand*, 515 U.S. at 235.

29. *Id*. at 227-31. On this issue, Justice O'Connor was joined only by Justices Scalia, Thomas, and Kennedy. Chief Justice Rehnquist did not join in this part.

30. *Id*. at 234.

31. *Id*. at 232.

32. *Id*. at 235.

33. *Id*.

34. *Id*. at 237.

35. *Id*. at 230.

36. *Id*. at 230.

37. *Id*. at 237. The Court also saw a need to address unresolved questions "concerning the details of the complex regulatory regimes implicated by the use of subcontractor compensation clauses," including whether a particularized inquiry into the economic disadvantage of a participant is required; whether race-based presumptions apply both to social and economic disadvantage; whether the definition of socially disadvantaged differs between the various Small Business Act programs; and whether any use of a subcontractor compensation clause can survive strict scrutiny. *Id*. at 238.

38. *Id*. at 239-41. Justice Scalia wrote that the government can never have a "compelling interest" for discrimination on the basis of race to "make up" for past wrongs. While wronged individuals "should be made whole," under the Constitution, "there can be no such thing as either a creditor or debtor race." *Id*. at 239. "In the eyes of government, we are just one race here. It is American." *Id*. Yet Scalia believes the challenged program will fail even under Justice O'Connor's view of strict scrutiny. "It is unlikely, if not impossible, that the challenged program would survive . . . I am content to leave that to be decided on remand." *Id. See* Kevin A. Ring, ed., *Scalia Dissents: Writings of the Supreme Court's Wittiest, Most Outspoken Justice* 96-97 (Regnery 2004).

    Justice Thomas agreed with the majority's conclusion that "strict scrutiny applies to all government classifications based on race." Thomas wrote separately to disagree with the premise underlying the dissents of Justices Steven and Ginsburg: "Government cannot make us equal; it can only recognize, respect, and protect us as equal before the law." "[T]he paternalism that appears to lie at the heart of this program is at war with the principle of inherent equality that underlies and infuses our Constitution. . . [T]he equal protection principle reflects our Nation's understanding that such classifications ultimately have a destructive impact on the individual and our society. . . [Since] [t]hese programs stamp minorities with a badge of inferiority and may cause them to develop dependencies or to adopt an attitude that they are 'entitled' to preferences." *Id*. at 240.

39. Justice Stevens filed a dissenting opinion in which Justice Ginsburg joined. *Id*. at 242. Justice Souter filed a dissenting opinion in which Justices Ginsburg and Breyer joined. *Id*. at 264. Justice Ginsburg filed a dissenting opinion in which Justice Breyer joined. *Id*. at 271.

40. Said Peter Jennings of ABC World News Tonight, "We begin tonight with one of the hottest political and social debates in the country today: affirmative action and racial discrimination. The Supreme Court has handed down two enormously important civil rights decisions today . . . [In *Adarand*] the power of the federal government to encourage the hiring of minorities will be quite severely limited." Reported Dan Rather of CBS Evening News, "The United States Supreme Court delivered a significant roll back of civil rights law enforcement today on two fronts: in the work place and in the class room. The Court set new restrictions on federal affirmative action programs designed to fight job discrimination." Intoned Tom Brokaw of NBC Nightly News, "The fuse that has been burning toward an explosive political confrontation on affirmative action in this country is burning even faster tonight. The United States Supreme Court, in a ruling on federal programs designed to help minorities, set new, tougher standards. Those standards make it much more difficult for affirmative action."

41. Linda Greenhouse (June 13, 1995).

42. June 13, 1995.

43. Frank J. Murray (June 13, 1995). George F. Will wrote later, "The nation's fundamental law would be improved by incorporating the Scalia-Thomas doctrine that such programs, being starkly incompatible with the equal protection guarantee, cannot be 'improved' to the point of constitutional respectability." Conservative Chronicle (June 28, 1995).

44. Abigail Thernstrom, *Don't mend it, defend it— Pres Clinton's stance on affirmative action*, National Review (Sept. 2, 1996).

45. *Id.* The statement is by Duval Patrick, Assistant Attorney General for Civil Rights.

46. Clinton administration lawyers were also busy creating documents to demonstrate to the federal courts that Congress had a "compelling governmental interest" for adopting the program and that the program was "narrowly tailored." In addition to being the work of lawyers, self-serving, and not probative of discrimination, the documents had never been considered by Congress. Congress, which had not debated the constitutionality of the use of racial preferences since 1977, finally debated the subject in 1997 and 1998 when it reauthorized the use of the racial preferences first adopted in 1982. The amendment to abandon a program labeled as unconstitutional in 1995 was defeated handily in a bipartisan effort. Many asserted that it was not Congress's role to ensure the highway program was constitutional; that was a job left to the federal courts.

47. *Adarand Constructors, Inc. v. Slater*, 965 F.Supp. 1556, 1581 (D.Colo. 1997).

48. *Adarand*, 169 Fed.3d 1292, 1297 (10th Cir. 1999).

49. *Adarand*, 528 U.S. 216, 224 (2000) (*per curiam*).

50. *Adarand*, 228 F.3d 1147, 1188 (10th Cir. 2000).

51. *Adarand Constructors, Inc. v. Mineta*, 534 U.S. 103 (2001). http://www.abanet.org/publiced/preview/scprimer.pdf, at 7

52. Nor would there be a ruling on the constitutionality of Colorado's implementation, on non-federal lands, of the federal highway program, which requires states to utilize racial preferences. Days following his 1997 victory at the Colorado federal district court, Randy Pech sued the State of Colorado. After a long, convoluted, and tortured trip through the federal courts accompanied by some clever slight of hand by federal and state employees, the case was dismissed as a result of the Tenth Circuit's 2000 ruling.

53. In a small victory of sorts, the United States admitted that its position from August 10, 1990, when Adarand filed its complaint, until September 25, 2000, when the Tenth Circuit ruled, was "not substantially justified," and it agreed to and did pay Adarand's attorneys $310,000.

54. In *Fullilove,* Chief Justice Burger set forth racially "discriminatory barriers" that prevented minority businesses from participating in government contracting: "deficiencies in working capital, inability to meet bonding requirements, disabilities caused by an inadequate 'track record,' lack of awareness of bidding opportunities, unfamiliarity with bidding procedures, pre-selection before the formal bidding process." *Fullilove*, 448 U.S. at 467. Nine years later, Justice O'Connor, writing for the Court, held that these "barriers" were race-neutral, were not caused by purposeful discrimination in the contracting industry, and were the result of societal discrimination, which could be addressed only by race-neutral means. *Croson*, 458 U.S. at 507-510. Justice Marshall, dissenting, asserted that the *Fullilove* "barriers" were the result of racial discrimination. *Id.* at 531-533. Six years later, the dissent in *Adarand* continued to maintain that the *Fullilove* "barriers" were the result of racial discrimination and could be remediated through the use of racial preferences. *Adarand*, 515 U.S. at 261 (Stevens, J., dissenting). The Tenth Circuit, in upholding the constitutionality of the federal government's use of racial preferences in its highway construction contracting program, ignored the holdings in *Croson* and *Adarand* and relied instead on *Fullilove* and the dissents in *Croson* and *Adarand* for its ruling that the *Fullilove* "barriers" justify the use of racial preferences. Held the Tenth Circuit: "Nothing in *Adarand* [1995] undermines the conclusion of the lead *Fullilove* opinion that 'Congress had abundant evidence from which it could conclude that minority businesses have been denied effective participation in public contracting opportunities. . . .'" *Adarand*, 228 F.3d at 1176 (citation to *Fullilove* omitted).

55. An earlier challenge to Denver's policy of awarding contracts based on race won a quick victory when the Denver Public Schools settled a lawsuit challenging its decision to award a school construction contract on the basis of race. *Bassett and Associates, Inc. v. School District No. 1, City and County of Denver*, No. 97cv1405-DBS (D.Colo. Aug. 27, 1997).

56. *Concrete Works of Colorado, Inc. v. City and County of Denver*, 36 F.2d 1513, 1530-31 (10th Cir. 1994).

57. *Concrete Works*, 86 F.Supp.2d 1042, 1079 (D.Colo. 2000).

58. *Concrete Works*, 321 F.3d 950 (10th Cir. 2003).

59. *Concrete Works*, 540 U.S. 1027 (2003).

60. *Id.*

61. *Id.*

62. *Id.*

63. *Id.*

64. *Id.*

65. *Sherbrook Turf, Inc. v. Minnesota Department of Transportation*, 345 F.3d 964 (8th Cir. 2003).

66. *Sherbrook*, 124 S.Ct. 2158 (2004).

67. Exactly why did the Supreme Court decline to hear *Concrete Works*. Certainly, given the Court's opinion in its 1995 *Adarand* ruling, Justices Kennedy and Thomas were as opposed to racial preferences as Justice Scalia and the Chief Justice; the four of them were sufficient to grant *certiorari*. The question would have been, however, was there a fifth vote to reverse the Tenth Circuit. In light of Justice O'Connor's embrace of racial preferences by colleges and universities a few months earlier in *Grutter v. Bollinger*, 539 U.S. 306 (2003), it is suspected that the strength of her opposition to racial preferences had dissipated. After all, in 1990, in *Metro Broadcasting*, she wrote that racial diversity was not a compelling government interest whereas, in 2003, in *Grutter*, she wrote that it was. What might have happened had the Bush administration urged the Court, in 2001, to issue a final ruling in *Adarand Constructors, Inc. v. Mineta* instead of engaging in a duplicitous paper shuffle to persuade the Court that the case had "outlived itself"? The author believes that, in 2002, the Court would have made final what it determined preliminarily in its 1995 *Adarand* ruling. With the Court's precedent thus so firmly established, the outcome in *Grutter* would have been much different.

68. *How Rehnquist Changed America*, Time (June 30, 2003).

69. *Id.*, quoting Professor A.E. Dick Howard, University of Virginia School of Law.

70. Meanwhile, Jeffrey Roehm of Enterprise Flasher, Inc., continues his challenge to the federal program in Delaware federal district court. *Enterprise Flasher, Inc. v. Mineta*, No. 03cv198 (D.Del. filed Feb. 14, 2003).

71. *NAACP v. City of Niagara Falls*, 65 F.3d 1002, 1016 (2d Cir. 1995).

Chapter 12: Fighting Demands for Racial Gerrymandering of Election Districts

1. Seth Lipsky, *Editorial*, Wall St. J., June 20, 2001; *available at* http://www.opinionjournal.com/columnists/ slipsky/?id=95000667. "My concerns were augmented in mid-April when *The Jewish Forward* (edited by Seth Lipsky, who came to the paper from the *Wall Street Journal*) published a critical article about me.... [T]he article reminded me that I could easily become a lightning rod for controversy." Lani Guinier, *Lift Every Voice: Turning a Civil Rights Setback into a New Vision of Social Justice* 31 (Simon & Schuster 1998). *Lift Every Voice* is "an enormously self-indulgent vanity piece, with insufficient consideration of, and a marked lack of honesty about, the controversial theories that ultimately sank her nomination. The book spreads more noise than light on the issues. . . . The essential fact is that Ms Guinier does not believe that the United States Constitution, with it's system of representative democracy, adequately defends the rights of minorities. Therefore, she proposes adoption of schemes like cumulative voting, geared towards allowing the losing minority to win actual representation regardless of their election loss." http://www.brothersjudd.com/index.cfm/fuseaction/reviews.detail/book_id/175/Lift%20Every%20V.htm

2. http://www.chinookmontana.com/about.html

3. Lee was not Clinton's first radical nominee to head the Civil Rights Division; that was Lani Guinier, whose nomination was withdrawn after Clinton read of his friend's views, allegedly for the first time. "Had I read [her writings] before I nominated her, I would not have done so." http://www.security-policy.org/papers/1993/93-D45.html

4. A short time later the author received an envelope from Montana. Inside was a photocopy of a tiny article about the threat made at the meeting. MSLF called the commissioners and offered its free legal services.

5. Ratified in 1870, the Fifteenth Amendment provides: "The rights of citizens of the United States to vote shall not be denied or abridged by the United States or by any State on account of race, color, or previous condition of servitude. Congress shall have the power to enforce this article by appropriate legislation." U.S. Const. amend. XV, § 1-2.

6. 16 Stat. 140 (amended 16 Stat. 433 (1871)) (federal penalties for interfering with ability of African Americans to vote in federal elections).

7. 71 Stat. 634 (Attorney General authorized to initiate legal action on behalf of African Americans denied the right to register or vote).

8. 74 Stat. 86 (federal courts authorized to identify "patterns and practices" of racially discriminatory activity preventing African Americans from voting and to order the registration of such persons).

9. 78 Stat. 241 (prohibited use of tests or standards as a prerequisite to registering or voting if those tests or standards had not been administered previously to those registered to vote).

10. Pub. L. No. 89-110, 79 Stat. 437 ("VRA") (*inter alia*, targeted "methods and tactics used to disqualify blacks from registering and voting in Federal and state elections . . . ." S. Rep. No. 97-417, Report of the Subcommittee on the Constitution, *reprinted in* 1982 U.S.C.C.A.N. 177, 290).

11. *South Carolina v. Katzenbach*, 383 U.S. 301 (1966). *See, inter alia, City of Rome v. United States*, 446 U.S. 156 (1980).

12. *City of Mobile Alabama v. Bolden*, 446 U.S. 55, 65 (1980).

13. *Whitcomb v. Chavis*, 403 U.S. 124 (1971).

14. *City of Mobile*, 446 U.S. at 69-71.

15. "S. 1992 amends Section 2 of the Voting Rights Act of 1965 to prohibit any voting practice, or procedure [that] results in discrimination . . . to make clear that proof of discriminatory intent by the legislative body is not required to establish a violation of Section 2." S. Rep. No. 97-417, Report of the Subcommittee on the Constitution, reprinted in 1982 U.S.C.C.A.N. 177, 179.

16. *Id.* at 281.

17. *Id.* at 214.

18. 42 U.S.C. § 1973 (emphasis added). Prior to the 1982 amendments, Section 2 read as follows:

Sec. 2. No voting qualification or prerequisite to voting, or standard, practice, or procedure shall be imposed or applied by any State or political subdivision to deny or abridge the right of any citizen of the United States to vote on account of race or color.

19. This is according to the 1990 Census. Montana was also the poorest state.

20. In the partisan primaries held in Blaine County, candidates with a plurality win the nomination. Thus, bloc voting by American Indians in the Democratic primary would have meant that, in the two elections in which an American Indian ran, their candidates of choice would have been elected, if American Indian voters had turned out to vote at the rate of non-Indian voters.

21. *Muntaqim v. Coombe*, 366 F.3d 102, 119 (2d Cir. 2004), *cert. denied*, __ U.S. __, 125 S.Ct. 480 (2004), *rehearing en banc granted sue sponte*, 396 F.3d 95 (2d Cir. 2004). Those Supreme Court cases included:

Florida Prepaid Postsecondary Education Expense Board v. College Savings Bank, 527 U.S. 627 (1999); *Kimel v. Florida Board of Regents*, 528 U.S. 62 (2000); *U.S. v. Morrison*, 529 U.S. 598 (2000); *Board of Trustees of the University of Alabama v. Garrett*, 531 U.S. 356 (2001); *Nevada Department of Human Resources v. Hibbs*, 538 U.S. 721 (2003); and *Tennessee v. Lane*, 541 U.S. 509, 124 S. Ct. 1978 (2004).

22. *City of Boerne v. Flores*, 521 U.S. 507, 518 (1997).

23. *See, e.g., City of Rome v. U.S.*, 446 U.S. 156, 179 (1980).

24. *Boerne*, 521 U.S. at 530.

25. *Garrett*, 531 U.S. at 368.

26. *Florida Prepaid*, 527 U.S. at 64 (citing *Boerne*, 521 U.S. at 526); *accord Morrison*, 529 U.S. at 626-627; *Garrett*, 531 U.S. at 368).

27. That motion was denied as untimely; fifteen months had passed since the Justice Department filed its lawsuit. The ACLU's appeal was denied. The ACLU then filed a separate case and moved to consolidate; that motion was denied. When Blaine County appealed to the Ninth Circuit, the ACLU sought to intervene; that motion was denied and its brief was stricken. When Blaine County appealed to the Supreme Court, the ACLU filed a brief, which was stricken. Why so relentless? The ACLU may collect attorneys' fees if it prevails in a Voting Rights Act case.

28. *United States v. Blaine County, Mont.*, No. 99cv122, Transcript of Proceedings (D.Mont. Oct. 9-11, 15-18, 2001, docket entries 88-94).

29. These are referred to as exogenous elections; elections regarding the office being disputed under the Voting Rights Act are endogenous. Two of these elections were for the Montana House of Representatives in racially gerrymandered districts in which American Indians comprised a substantial majority of the voting-age population. However, a low turnout by those American Indians voters doomed the American Indians candidates.

30. A handful of these laws restricted the right to vote, on proposals to increase property taxes and to float bonds secured by real property, to property owners; however, these laws did not apply exclusively to American Indians but to all county residents who did not own property. The Supreme Court eventually declared all such laws unconstitutional, *Kramer v. Union Free School District* No. 15, 395 U.S. 621 (1969), after which Montana's laws were either null and void or were repealed.

31. In adopting the Fourteenth and Fifteenth Amendments, the States agreed to federal regulation for their transgressions of the Civil War Amendments; however, they never waived their sovereignty to allow the United States to remedy its own allegedly racially discriminatory policies by taking action against state electoral systems.

32. Mr. Hay testified that he is an enrolled member of the Turtle Mountain Band of the Chippewa Nation, which Reservation is in Belcourt, North Dakota. He carries a tribal identification card showing that he was enrolled shortly after his birth. Mr. Hay's grandfather on his mother's side was a full-blood Chippewa. His mother was a half-blood Chippewa and Mr. Hay is a quarter-blood Chippewa. His wife is Assiniboine and Chippewa. These family members resided, for some time, at Fort Belknap Reservation, where Mr. Hay's wife's father was an Assiniboine elder.

33. Blaine County also objected to the so-called scientific testimony that the United States elicited from its witnesses. One expert, for example, sought to demonstrate how Blaine County's American Indians voted. Instead of using the best test for who is an American Indian, that is, "self-identification" by the voter himself, the expert used political activists—most likely the same people who had demanded that the Civil Rights Division file its lawsuit—to identify American Indian voters. One of them used the following tests to identify the 1,834 American Indians in Blaine County: (1) because she did not obtain the Fort Belknap Tribal membership list, she worked from her memory of who was a member; (2) her "intense personal knowledge of someone's family" of the sort that is "emphasized at cultural gatherings"; (3) whether a purported American Indian had "act[ed] on [his] Indianness and [his] identity." (Tr. 1344-45, 1350). These and other deficiencies in the expert testimony offered by the United States violate Federal Rule of Evidence 702 because they are unreliable under *Daubert v. Merrell Dow Pharmaceuticals, Inc.*, 509 U.S. 579 (1993), and *Kumho Tire Co. Ltd. v. Carmichael*, 526 U.S. 137 (1999).

34. www.naco.org

35. The Defendant, the State of Montana, did not contest the issues of discrimination at trial, presumably for political reasons.

36. *United States v. Blaine County*, No. 99cv122-GF-PMP (D.Mont. Mar. 2, 2002).

37. Civil Docket, No. 99cv122-GF-PMP (D.Mont. June 17, 2002) (ruling from Bench).

38. http://www.alamosachamber.com. http://www.alamosa.org/

39. *United States v. Alamosa County, Colorado*, 306 F.Supp.2d 1016, 1018 (D.Colo. 2003).

40. *Id.*

41. *Id.* at 1019.

42. *Id.* at 1018.

43. *Id.* at 1019.

44. *Id.* at 1040.

45. *Id.*

46. *Id.* at 1039.

47. *Id.* at 1037.

48. *Id.* at 1025-26. "[I]n each instance, the appeal was made by the Hispanic rather than the Anglo candidate...." *Id.*

49. *Id.* at 1033, fn 42.

50. The victory did not come cheap. Although Alamosa County did not pay for the free legal services it received from MSLF, it did reimburse MSLF for the out-of-pocket expenses incurred on its behalf: $278,000!

51. Declared the Supreme Court:

The mere fact that one interest group or another... has found itself outvoted and without legislative seats of its own provides no basis for invoking constitutional remedies, where, as here, there is no indication that this segment of the population is being denied access to the political system.

Whitcomb v. Chavis, 403 U.S. at 149, 154-155 (1971) (emphasis added). Moreover,

There are communities in which minority citizens are able to form coalitions with voters from other racial groups... Those candidate may not represent perfection to every minority voter, but minority voters are not immune from the obligation to pull, haul, and trade to find common political ground.

Johnson v. DeGrandy, 512 U.S. 997, 1020 (1994).

52. Without proof of "private discrimination," "claims of vote dilution [are no more than] 'a euphemism for political defeat at the polls.'" *League of United Latin American Citizens, Council No. 4434 v. Clements*, 999 F.2d 831, 850-851 (5th Cir. 1993) (en banc). "When racial antagonism is not the cause of an electoral defeat ... the defeat does not prove a lack of electoral opportunity but a lack of whatever else it takes to be successful in politics." *Uno v. City of Holyoke*, 72 F.3d 973, 981 (1st Cir. 1995).

53. *N.A.A.C.P. v. City of Columbus, S.C.*, 850 F.Supp. 404, 418 (D.S.C. 1994), *aff'd with modifications not relevant here*, 33 F.2d 52 (4th Cir. 1994) ("[T]here is nothing to be thwarted" without "distinctive political interests.").

54. *See, e.g., Farrakhan v. Washington*, 359 F.3d 1116, 1124 (9th Cir. 2004) (Kozinski, J., dissenting from denial of rehearing en banc) ("Despite a 1984 case summarily affirming a district court decision upholding its constitutionality ... Section 2's constitutionality remains an open question.").

55. The Ninth Circuit panel's ruling conflicts with Supreme Court rulings in *Boerne, supra,* through *Lane, supra,* and with the rulings of two other circuits. *Miller v. King*, 384 F.3d 1248, 1269 (11th Cir. 2004), and *Muntaqim v. Coombe*, 366 F.3d 102, 119 (2d Cir. 2004), *cert. denied*, __ U.S. __, 125 S.Ct. 480 (2004).

56. Section 2's constitutionality remains an open question: *Johnson v. De Grandy*, 512 U.S. 997, 1028-1029 (1994) (Kennedy, J., concurring in part and in judgment); *Chisom v. Roemer*, 501 U.S. 380, 418 (1991) (Kennedy, J., dissenting). *See also Bush v. Vera*, 517 U.S. 952, 991 (1996) (O'Connor, J., concurring)("In the 14 years since enactment of § 2(b) ... [we have] never directly addressed its constitutionality."); see *also, generally, Holder v. Hall*, 512 U.S. 874, 891-945 (1994) (Thomas, J. concurring, joined by Scalia, J.).

57. Although Blaine County did not pay for the free legal services it received from MSLF, it did reimburse MSLF for the out-of-pocket expenses incurred on its behalf: over $74,000!

58. The ACLU recently sued Fremont County, Wyoming, making the same claims against that rural county as made by the U.S. Department of Justice against Blaine County, Montana, and Alamosa County, Colorado. *Large v. Fremont County*, No. 05cv270 (D.Wyo. filed Oct. 11, 2005).

59. The fight over the Voting Rights Act will return to Congress in 2006; some of its most controversial provisions are up for reauthorization in 2007. One legal scholar asserts that fundamental changes are necessary: "the act should be changed back to its pre-1982 language, to require a showing of actual racial discrimination—that people are being treated differently because of race"; "the law should be amended to make clear that there is no requirement that districts be drawn with the racial bottom line in mind—and, indeed, that such racial gerrymandering is in fact illegal"; "the act should be amended to make clear that it guarantees nothing for one racial group that it does not guarantee for all racial groups." Roger Clegg, *Revise Before Reauthorizing*, National Review Online, Aug. 4, 2005. http://www.nationalreview.com/clegg/clegg200508040826.asp

Chapter 13: Fighting "Takings" Committed "Without Just Compensation"

1. *Pennsylvania Coal Co. v. Mahon*, 260 U.S. 393, 415-416 (1922).

2. *Armstrong v. U.S.*, 364 U.S. 40, 49 (1960).

3. *Glosemeyer v. United States*, 45 Fed. Cl. 771, 775 (2000).

4. The MKT's application with the Interstate Commerce Commission was to abandon 200 miles of right-of-way between Machens and Sedalia, Missouri. *Glosemeyer v. Missouri-Kansas-Texas Railroad Company*, 685 F.Supp. 1108 (D.Mo. 1988).

5. The Glosemeyers' right was a "present but non-possessory fee interest. They do not hold a 'reversionary interest' in the strict common law sense of the word in that the interests are present as opposed to future." *Glosemeyer*, 45 Fed. Cl. at 776.

6. Pub. L. No. 98-11 (Mar. 28, 1983), 97 Stat. 42, 16 U.S.C. § 1247(d).

7. http://en.wikipedia.org/wiki/Hindenburg_disaster

8. *Glosemeyer*, 685 F.Supp. at 1119-1120.

9. *Glosemeyer v. Missouri-Kansas-Texas Railroad*, 879 F.2d 316 (8th Cir. 1989).

10. *Preseault v. ICC*, 494 U.S. 1, 9 (1990).

11. *Preseault v. United States*, 100 F.3d 1525, 1529 (Fed. Cir. 1996).

12. *Preseault v. ICC*, 853 F.2d 145, 150 (2nd Cir. 1999).

13. *Preseault*, 494 U.S. at 19. Deference to Congress, a co-equal branch of the federal government, may be one thing; however, deference to a ragtag bunch of city councilmen, as the Court did in *Kelo v. New London*, ___ U.S. ___, 125 S.Ct. 2655 (2005), *reh'g denied* ___ U.S. ___, 126 S.Ct. 24 (2005), is quite something else again.

14. *Preseault*, 494 U.S. at 20-25.

15. *Glosemeyer v. Missouri-Kansas-Texas Railroad*, 494 U.S. 1003 (1990).

16. *Preseault v. United States*, 27 Fed.Cl. 69 (1992).

17. *Preseault*, 66 F.3d 1167 (Fed. Cir. 1995).

18. *Id.* 1190 (Fed. Cir. 1995).

19. *Preseault*, 100 F.3d 1525 (Fed. Cir. 1996) (*en banc*).

20. *Id.* at 1540, 1538.

21. *Id.* at 1552.

22. *Id.* at 1551.

23. *Id.* at 1552.

24. *Id.* In May 2002, the Federal Court of Claims awarded the Preseaults just compensation for the taking of their property in the amount of $234,000, plus interest from the date of the taking, February 5, 1986, which interest totaled $356,526.19. The Preseaults' attorneys, both for-profit and nonprofit public interest law firms (PILFs), were awarded $894,855.60. *Preseault v. United States*, 52 Fed. Cl. 667, 684 (2002). The Preseaults were represented by New England Legal Foundation of Boston, Massachusetts.

25. *Glosemeyer*, 45 Fed.Cl. at 776.

26. *Id.* at 778.

27. *Id.* at 779.

28. *Id.* at 781.

29. *Id.*

30. *Id.*

31. *Id.*, quoting *Loretto v. Teleprompter Manhattan CATV Corp.*, 458 U.S. 419, 435 (1982).

32. *Glosemeyer*, 45 Fed.Cl. at 782, quoting *Pennsylvania Coal Co. v. Mahon*, 260 U.S. 393, 416 (1922).

33. *Hussey v. United States*, No. 95cv00360 (D.Idaho Dec. 20, 1996).

34. See Chapter 1.

35. *Loretto*, 458 U.S. at 433, quoting *Kaiser Aetna v. United States*, 444 U.S. 164, 176 (1979). Justice Scalia, writing for the Court in the famous *Nollan* case, quoted *Loretto* by noting, "We have repeatedly held . . ." *Nollan v. California Coast Commission*, 483 U.S. 825, 831 (1987).

36. *Benson and Messmer v. South Dakota*, Civil 03-121, slip op. (6th Judicial Circuit Nov. 30, 2004). See Chapter 6.

37. *Madison v. Graham*, 316 F.3d 867 (9th Cir. 2002), *cert. denied*, 538 U.S. 1058 (2003). See Chapter 6.

38. *City of Coeur d'Alene v. Simpson*, ___P.2d ___, 2005 WL 286936 (Idaho 2005).

39. Nollan, supra.

40. Migratory Bird Treaty Act, 16 U.S.C. §§ 703-711, 40 Stat. 755 (July 3, 1918). Bald and Golden Eagle Protection Act, 16 U.S.C. §§ 668, 668a-668d, 54 Stat. 250 (June 8, 1940).

41. *Andrus v. Allard*, 444 U.S. 51, 65-66 (1979).

42. *Hodel v. Irving*, 481 U.S. 704, 716 (1987). The Court reached the same conclusion ten years later in *Babbitt v. Youpee*, 519 U.S. 234 (1997).

43. *Hodel*, 481 U.S. at 719 (Scalia, J., concurring).

44. *U.S. v. Kornwolf*, 276 F.3d 1014 (8th Cir. 2002).

45. *Kornwolf v. U.S.*, 537 U.S. 813 (2002).

46. What is the cause of such "Orwellian snooping," author Steven Vincent asked regarding a similar statute, the Native American Graves Protection and Repatriation Act. "The answer involves the weighted history of Indian relations, a vaguely written federal law, and the zealous agencies that seek to enforce it, as well as aspects of Native American culture that strike some non-Indians as confusing and often contradictory." *Grave Injustice: Federal laws about burial remains put politics before science*, Reason, June 2004. http://www.reason.com/0407/fe.sv.grave.shtml. An art critic and freelance writer, Mr. Vincent's life was changed on September 11, 2001, when, from atop his East Village apartment building, he saw the second plane hit the World Trade Center. Confronted with the evil of Islamic terrorism, he believed he had to do something. He went to Iraq to write and report. After completing In the *Red Zone: A Journey into the Soul of Iraq* (Spence 2004), he returned to Iraq. On August 2, 2005, he was abducted and murdered. He was the first American reporter to be attacked and killed during the Iraq war. *New York Times*, August 3, 2005, A8. A hero of 9/11 as surely as the firefighters on that day or the men and women in uniform on the days following, my friend Steven Vincent was laid to rest on August 15, 2005.

47. Some 47,000 acres were purchased pursuant to the Weeks Act of 1911, 16 U.S.C. § 480, *et seq.*

48. *United States v. Welch*, 217 U.S. 333, 339 (1910).

49. *Curtin v. Benson*, 222 U.S. 78 (1911). "The right of the property owner to pasture his cattle upon his land and the right of access to it are the very essence of his proprietorship." *Id.* at 88.

50. *Nollan*, 483 U.S. at 831.

51. 30 U.S.C. § 1272(2).

52. *Stearns Co., Ltd. v. United States*, 53 Fed. Cl. 446, 447, 450-451 (2002).

53. *Stearns*, 396 F.3d 1354, 1357-1358 (Fed. Cir. 2005).

54. http://www.opinionjournal.com/extra/?id=110007209

55. *Stearns*, ___ U.S. ___, 126 S.Ct. 385 (2005).

56. U.S. Const. amend. V.

57. *Id.*

58. *Berman v. Parker*, 348 U.S. 26 (1954).

59. *Hawaiian Housing Authority v. Midkiff*, 467 U.S. 229, 243-44 (1984).

60. *99 Cents Only Stores v. Lancaster Redevelopment Agency*, 2001 WL 811056 (C.D. Cal. 2001).

61. *Poletown Neighborhood Council v. Detroit*, 410 Mich. 616, 304 N.W.2d 455 (1981).

62. *County of Wayne v. Hathcock*, 684 N.W.2nd 765 (Mich. 2004).

63. *Kelo v. New London*, ___ U.S. ___, 125 S.Ct. 2655 (2005), reh'g denied ___ U.S. ___, 126 S.Ct. 24 (2005). Justice Stevens delivered the opinion of the Court, in which Justices Kennedy, Souter, Ginsburg, and Breyer joined. Justice Kennedy filed a concurring opinion. Justice O'Connor filed a dissenting opinion, in which Chief Justice Rehnquist and Justices Scalia and Thomas. Justice Thomas filed a dissenting opinion.

64. *Id.* at 2663-4.

65. *Id.* at 2671, 2677 (O'Connor, J., dissenting).

66. *Id.* at 2676.

67. *Id.* at 2678, 2679 (Thomas, J., dissenting).

68. *Lochness Properties, Inc. v. City of Sheridan*, No. 05cv5997 (Colo. Dist. Ct. filed Dec. 8, 2005).

Chapter 14: Fighting for Access to Private Property

1. Edwin Meese III, Editorial, Wall St. J., Sept. 5, 2005; available at: http://www.opinionjournal.com/extra/?id=110007209

2. The lands that comprise the O'Haco Cabins Ranch were conveyed on April 26, 1920, to Seltzer Tillman when President Woodrow Wilson signed Patent No. 746772. This grant was made pursuant to the Act of May 20, 1862, entitled, "To Secure Homesteads to Actual Settlers on the Public Domain" (12 Stat. 392-93) (repealed 1976). When it was made, the O'Haco Cabins Ranch was surrounded by lands owned by either the United States or third parties.

3. The Quiet Title Act of 1972, 28 U.S.C. § 2409a, is the exclusive means by which citizens may challenge an adverse claim by the United States to property that the citizen believes he owns. Once the citizen is on notice that the United States believes its property interest is "adverse" to that of the citizen, the citizen has 12 years in which to file his Quiet Title Act lawsuit or his claim is forever barred.

4. *Fitzgerald v. United States*, 932 F. Supp. 1195 (D.Ariz. 1996).

5. Federal Land Policy and Management Act Private Road Easement FDR 11-56B.

6. "Where a landowner conveys to another an inner portion of land and retains the land surrounding the portion conveyed, the common law presumes the grantee has a right to pass over the retained property if such passage is necessary to reach the granted property." *United States v. Jenks*, 129 F.3d 1348, 1353 (10th Cir. 1997). "These rights-of-way are referred to as 'easements by necessity,' " *Leo Sheep Co. v. U. S.*, 440 U.S. 668, 679 (1979), and are "founded in a public policy favoring utilization of land," *Id.*, (citing *Powell on Real Property* § 34.07 (rev. ed. 1997)). Without such an easement, the granted lands would be worthless. *Montana Wilderness Ass'n v. United States Forest Service*, 496 F.Supp. 880, 888 (D.Mont. 1980), *aff'd on other grounds*, 665 F.2d 951 (9th Cir. 1981).

7. *Superior Oil Co. v. United States*, 353 F.2d 34, 36-37 (9th Cir. 1965).

8. *Hunter v. United States*, 388 F.2d 148, 153-154 (9th Cir. 1967) (noting the "well-settled rule that the grant of a right in real property includes all incidentals possessed by the [grantor] and without which the property granted cannot be fully enjoyed.").

9. *Fitzgerald v. United States*, No. CIV 02-0069-PCT-DKD, slip op. at 11 (D.Ariz. Mar. 30, 2004).

10. See *United States v. Dunn*, 478 F.2d 443 (9th Cir. 1973); *United States v. Jenks*, 129 F.3d 1348 (10th Cir. 1997); *Mantle Ranches Inc. v. U.S. Park Serv.*, 945 F. Supp. 1449 (D.Colo. 1996) (plaintiff landowners have historic access and an easement by necessity); *Mackie v. United States*, 194 F. Supp. 306 (D.Minn. 1961) (an easement by necessity applies against the United States, but not established by facts of the case); *Byd-*

lon v. United States, 175 F. Supp. 891 (Ct. Cl. 1959) (an easement by necessity applies against the United States); *United States v. C.M. Balliet*, 133 F.Supp.2d 1120, 1127 (W.D. Ark. 2001) ("an easement by necessity or by implication may arise when the United States issues a patent for public lands"); *Burdess v. United States*, 553 F. Supp. 646 (E.D. Ark. 1982) (an easement by necessity applies against the United States).

11. *Dolan v. City of Tigard*, 512 U.S. 374 (1994). By the time the Supreme Court ruled in Dolan, Mr. Dolan had died.

12. Glacier National Park was created on May 11, 1910. 36 Stat. 354, 16 U.S.C. § 161.

13. *Id.*

14. National Park Service, Land Protection Plan 7, 28, 35 (August 1985).

15. Quiet Title Act, 28 U.S.C. § 2409a: Administrative Procedure Act, 5 U.S.C. § 551, et seq.

16. *McFarland v. United States*, No. 00cv0020-DWM (D.Mont. July 9, 2003).

17. *McFarland v. Norton*, 425 F.3d 725 (9th Cir. 2005).

18. Act granting the Right of Way to Ditch and Canal Owners over the Public Lands, and for other purposes, 14 Stat. 251-53 (codified at 43 U.S.C. § 661); Irrigation or General Right of Way Act of March 3, 1891, 26 Stat. 1101-02 (codified as amended at 43 U.S.C §§ 946-49).

19. *Roth v. United States*, 326 F.Supp.2d 1163 (D.Mont. 2003).

20. *Jamestown & N.R. Co. v. Jones*, 177 U.S. 125 (1099), *Barlow v. Northern Pac. Ry. Co.*, 240 U.S. 484 (1916).

21. *Roth*, 326 F. Supp.2d at1173.

22. *Id.* at 1175.

23. *Id.* at 1176.

24. See *Dunbar v. United States*, No. CV 02-191-M-LBE (D.Mont. filed on Nov. 15, 2002); *Big Creek Lakes Reservoir Ass'n v. United States*, No. CV 04-39-M-DWM (D.Mont. filed Mar. 10, 2004); *Carlton Creek Irrigation Co. v. United States*, No. CV 04-152-M-DWM (D.Mont. filed Aug. 5, 2004).

25. In October 1937, George L. and Myrtle Gibson transferred their interest in the South Fork Dam and Reservoir to Maybelle Callender.

26. The ranchers believe, although it could not be proven, that a Forest Service employee blew up the headgate.

27. *Big Creek Lakes Reservoir Ass'n v. United States*, No. CV 04-39-DWM (D.Mont. filed Mar. 10 2004).

28. *In the Matter of the Adjudication of the Existing Rights to the Use of All the Water, Both Surface and Underground, Within the Westside Subbasin of the Bitterroot River Drainage Area, Including all Tributaries of Tributaries of the Westside Subbasin of the Bitterroot River in Ravalli County, Montana*, Case 76HF-168, 76H-W-120062-00 (Mont. Water Court July 21, 2005).

29. *Id.*

30. Of course, the answer is yes. Miners in Colorado's Park County were told by U.S. Forest Service employees and a federal lawyer that they should not submit a plan of operation to conduct operations on their claims; it would be rejected, the miners were told. Illegally denied access to their claims, they sued. The Colorado federal district court ruled against them on the merits. *Park Lake Resources, LLC v. U.S. Dep't of Agriculture*, 979 F.Supp. 1310 (D.Colo. 1997). The Tenth Circuit upheld that ruling but on different grounds: the miners had not suffered an injury and had no standing because Forest Service lawyers insisted during oral arguments that the miners should have filed a plan of operations anyway. *Park Lake*, 197 F.3d 448 (10th Cir. 1999). This reveals yet another problem in dealing with the federal governments, its agencies, bureaucrats and lawyers: no one ever truly speaks for the United States!

Chapter 15: Fighting Illegal Immigration and Other Abuses

1. Heather MacDonald, *Mexico's Undiplomatic Diplomats*, City Journal (Manhattan Institute), Autumn 2005; *available at* http://www.city-journal.org/html/15_4_mexico.html

2. David R. Henderson, *What part of "no law" doesn't Congress get?* Hoover Institution Weekly Essays, Mar. 11, 2002; *available at* http://www-hoover.stanford.edu/pubaffairs/we/2002/henderson_0302.html

3. Randy Pullen's view is that the word "benefit" includes all the public benefits listed under the 1996 Welfare Reform Act, 8 U.S.C. §1621; that is, any grant, contract, loan, or professional or commercial license, as well as any retirement, welfare, health, disability, public housing, post-secondary education, food assistance, unemployment, or other similar benefit funded by a state or local government. Excluded are benefits providing emergency medical care, short-term in-kind disaster relief, public health assistance for immunization and treatment of communicable diseases, community soup kitchens and shelter services, and services "necessary for the protection of life or safety."

4. http://www.yesonprop200.com/news/news.html

5. On September 1, 2004, *The Arizona Republic* reported that the opposition groups would spend between one and two million dollars to kill Proposition 200. One opposition advertisement featured an Anglo-appearing accident victim, his arm pinned beneath a boulder, who is told by the paramedic that he cannot be rescued until he shows his citizenship papers.

6. The "Findings and declaration" of Proposition 200 could not have been more reasonable:

   This state finds that illegal immigration is causing economic hardship to this state and that illegal immigration is encouraged by public agencies within this state that provide public benefits without verifying immigration status. This state further finds that illegal immigrants have been given a safe haven in this state with the aid of identification cards that are issued without verifying immigration status, and that this conduct contradicts federal immigration policy, undermines the security of our borders and demeans the value of citizenship. Therefore, the people of this state declare that the public interest of this state requires all public agencies within the state to cooperate with federal immigration authorities to discourage illegal immigration.

   16. A.R.S. § 152.

7. That is not all. Also opposed were the mayors of Phoenix, Tucson, and Flagstaff, Arizona Chamber of Commerce, AFL-CIO, most state and municipal government employee unions, Arizona Catholic Conference, League of Women Voters, Phoenix Convention and Visitors Bureau, Western Growers Association, and every daily newspaper in the state.

8. On September 10, 2004, *The Arizona Republic* announced that 66 percent of those polled favored passage of Proposition 200. The poll, of registered 600 voters, was taken September 3-5, 2004. Republicans favored passage by 8-1, whereas Democrats supported it by 3-1. The results of this poll were similar to those of earlier polls.

9. *Friendly House v. Napolitano*, No. 04cv649 (D.Ariz. Dec. 22, 2004).

10. 42 U.S.C. § 1973, *et seq.* The letter read, in part, "[t]he Attorney General does not interpose any objection to" Proposition 200's requirement that voters provide evidence of their citizenship to register and to receive a ballot.

11. Chris Hawley, *Mexico threatens to take Prop. 200 rights to tribunal*, The Arizona Republic, January 28, 2005, at A22. Apparently, that is not the half of it. See Heather MacDonald, supra.

12. http://www.internationaljusticeproject.org/nationalsJMedellin.cfm

13. *Medellin v. Dretke*, 371 F.3d 270 (5th Cir. 2004).

14. On February 28, 2005, the Bush Administration filed a friend of the court brief noting that President Bush had asked Texas to conduct new hearings for Medellin and the 50 other Mexican nationals included in the ICJ ruling, which, "the president has determined is an appropriate means to fulfill this nation's [Vienna Convention] treaty obligations." A week later, Secretary of State Rice advised the U.N. Secretary-General, the United States "hereby withdraws" from the Vienna Convention. That same day the Supreme Court authorized the Solicitor General to participate in the March 28th oral arguments. It is likely that the Bush administration embraced the ICJ ruling in *Medellin v. Dretke* to prevent the Court—after its shocking juvenile death penalty ruling that saved two of Medellin's co-defendants from execution—from ruling that foreign nationals facing criminal prosecution have more rights than do U.S. citizens. *Roper v. Simmons*, ___ U.S. ___, 125 S.Ct. 1183 (2005). Meanwhile, Secretary Rice emasculated the ICJ for all future criminal proceedings by withdrawing from the Vienna Convention.

15. http://www.supremecourtus.gov/docket/04-5928.htm

16. Chris Hawley, Mexico report: Ariz. "xenophobia" hotbed, The Arizona Republic, April 2, 2005.

17. Personal Responsibility and Work Opportunity Reconciliation Act of 1996 (PRWORA or PRA) (also known as Welfare Reform Act), Pub. L. 104-193 (Aug. 22, 1996), 110 Stat. 2105, 8 U.S.C. § 601, et seq., 42 U.S.C. § 1601, et seq.

18. 8 U.S.C. §§ 1611 , 1621.

19. 8 U.S.C. § 1601(g).

20. 8 U.S.C. §§ 1644, 1373.

21. 8 U.S.C. § 1625.

22. DeCanas v. Bica, 424 U.S. 351, 358 (1976).

23. *Friendly House v, Napolitano*, 419 F.3d 930 (9th Cir. 2005), No. 04cv649, on remand dismissed with prejudice (D.Ariz. Sept. 19, 2005).

24. Ariz. Att'y Gen. Op. I04-010 (Nov. 12, 2004).

25. Yes on Proposition 200 v. Napolitano, No. CV2004-09299 (Ariz. Sup. Ct. 2004).

26. Press Release, Jan Brewer, Ariz. Sec. of State, Atty. Gen. & legislative leaders agree on voter ID at polls, new procedures requires all voters to provide identification at the polls (July 1, 2005).

27. Congressman Tom Tancredo, High noon for Denver sanctuary policy, Rocky Mountain News, May 17, 2005 available at http://michellemalkin.com/archives/002423.htm

28. http://www.commoncause.org/site/pp.asp?c=dkLNK1MQIwG&b=186966.

29. The Montana Chamber of Commerce was the first to file a lawsuit on the gag law in February 1997.

30. *Montana Chamber of Commerce v. Argenbright*, 28 F.Supp.2d 593, 599 (D.Mont. 1998), aff'd 226 F.3d 1049 (9th Cir. 2000).

31. *Id.*, 28 F.Supp.2d at 601.

32. *Montana Chamber of Commerce v. Argenbright*, No. 98cv037, Transcript of Proceedings, at 243-244 (D.Mont. Oct. 22, 2004).

33. An expert, Jerome Anderson, testified, "Using a week or ten days of television and radio time immediately before the election is not effective." Instead, "[a] consistent television and radio campaign that is continued for at least four weeks is critical to the success of an election educational effort." Moreover, such a last minute blitz was not even possible because "TV time must be pre-purchased as early as 90 days before use in order to obtain effective spot placement." "It's too late to mount an effective campaign at this point in time," eleven days before an election. See also, Argenbright, 28 F.Supp.2d, at 597.

34. According to the State of Montana, 169,991 voted for the initiative and 155,034 voted against it, a margin of 14,957 votes. http://www.state.mt.us/sos/assets/elections/98gen/98gen.htm. A change of only 7,479 of the 325,025 votes cast, or 2.2 percent, would have changed the result. The associations and group believe that, had they been able to participate, they would have changed the outcome and the anti-mining initiative would have been defeated.

35. *Montana Chamber of Commerce v. Argenbright*, No. 98cv037 (D.Mont. Nov.13, 2004). Subsequently, the anti-mining initiative had the effect sought by its proponents. After the expenditure of $70 million, a Montana mining project near Lincoln, Montana, which would have recovered 9 million ounces of gold and 20 million ounces of silver, was killed. The Montana Supreme Court ruled that no just compensation was owed. *Seven Up Pete Venture v. State of Montana*, 114 P.3d 1009 (Mont. 2005), petition for cert. filed Nov. 4, 2005.

36. *Montana Chamber of Commerce v. Argenbright*, 226 F.3d 1049, 1058 (9th Cir. 2000).

37. *Red Lion Broadcasting Co. v. F.C.C.*, 395 U.S. 367, 390 (1969).

38. *Communities for a Great Northwest v. Vaughey*, 534 U.S. 817 (2001).

39. Bipartisan Campaign Reform Act of 2002, Pub.L. 107-155 (Mar. 27, 2002), 116 Stat. 81.

40. *McConnell v. Federal Election Commission*, 540 U.S. 93 (2003).

41. *Forum for Academic & Institutional Rights v. Rumsfeld*, 292 F.Supp.2d 269 (D.N.J. 2003), 390 F.3d 219 (3rd Cir. 2004).

42. *Id.*, 390 F.3d at 246.

43. *Id.* at 251.

44. *Id., cert. granted*, ___ U.S. ___, 125 S.Ct. 1977 (May 2, 2005).

45. U.S. Const. art. I, § 8.

Epilogue

1. Sonny Bono. http://en.wikipedia.org/wiki/Sonny_Bono. The epitaph on the headstone of the late Con-gressman Sonny Bono (R-44th CA) reads, "And The Beat Goes On."

2. Yogi Berra. http://rinkworks.com/said/yogiberra.shtml

3. Frank Sinatra. http://www.cool-lyrics-place.com/As_Time_Goes_By_Lyrics.html

4. Pennsylvania Coal Co. v. Mahon, 260 U.S. 393, 415 (1922). "[T]he natural tendency of human nature is to extend the qualification more and more until at last private property disappears. But that cannot be accomplished in this way under the Constitution of the United States....We are in danger of forgetting that a strong public desire to improve the public condition is not enough to warrant achieving the desire by a shorter cut than the constitutional way of paying for the change." *Id*. at 415-416.

5. *First English Evangelical Lutheran Church of Glendale v. Los Angeles County, Cal.*, 482 U.S. 304 (1987); *Nollan v. California Coastal Commission*, 483 U.S. 825 (1987).

6. *Tahoe-Sierra Preservation Council, Inc. v. Tahoe Regional Planning Agency*, 535 U.S. 302 (2002); *San Remo Hotel, L.P. v. City and County of San Francisco*, ___ U.S. ___, 125 S.Ct. 2491 (2005); *Kelo v. New London*, ___ U.S. ___, 125 S.Ct. 2655 (2005).

7. *Plessy v. Ferguson*, 163 U.S. 537 (1896).

8. *Brown v. Board of Education*, 347 U.S. 483 (1954).

9. *Fullilove v. Klutznick*, 448 U.S. 448 (1980).

10. *Adarand Constructors, Inc. v. Peña*, 515 U.S. 200 (1995).

11. *Plessy*, 163 U.S. at 559 (Harlan, J., dissenting) ("But in view of the constitution, in the eye of the law, there is in this country no superior, dominant, ruling class of citizens. There is no caste here. Our constitution is color-blind, and neither knows nor tolerates classes among citizens. In respect of civil rights, all citizens are equal before the law. The humblest is the peer of the most powerful.")

12. *Concrete Works of Colorado, Inc. v. City and County of Denver*, 540 U.S. 1027 (2003) (Scalia, J., dissenting).

13. *A.L.A. Schechter Poultry Corp. v. United States*, 295 U.S. 495 (1935). For much of that time, the Court's Commerce Clause cases involved preventing states from unduly burdening interstate commerce.

14. *NLRB v. Jones & Laughlin Steel Corp.*, 301 U.S. 1 (1937); *Wickard v. Filburn*, 317 U.S. 111 (1942).

15. *U.S. v. Lopez*, 514 U.S. 549 (1995). Although the Rehnquist Supreme Court declared several federal acts unconstitutional, it did not do so on Commerce Clause grounds but because those acts exceeded the powers granted by Section 5 of the Fourteenth Amendment. *Florida Prepaid Postsecondary Education Expense Board v. College Savings Bank*, 527 U.S. 627 (1999); *Kimel v. Florida Board of Regents*, 528 U.S. 62 (2000); *U.S. v. Morrison*, 529 U.S. 598 (2000); *Board of Trustees of the University of Alabama v. Garrett*, 531 U.S. 356 (2001); *Nevada Department of Human Resources v. Hibbs*, 538 U.S. 721 (2003); *Tennessee v. Lane*, __ U.S. __, 124 S. Ct. 1978 (2004).

16. *Gonzales v. Raich*, ___ U.S. ___, 125 S.Ct. 2195 (2005).

17. http://www.warmuseum.net/revolutionarywarhall/PATRICK-HENRY.NET/

18. *The Federalist*, No. 15. http://www.quoteworld.org/docs/fed15.php

19. http://www.gmu.edu/departments/economics/wew/quotes/govt.html

20. http://www.brainyquote.com/quotes/quotes/t/thomasjeff136269.html

21. http://www.brainyquote.com/quotes/quotes/j/johnadams169381.html

22. http://www.ccrkba.org/JacksonFarewellAddress.html

23. http://www.presidentreagan.info/speeches/thatcher.cfm

24. U.S. Const. preamble.

25. http://www.presidentreagan.info/speeches/in2.cfm

26. http://www.townhall.com/columnists/billmurchison/bm20040203.shtml

INDEX

Get a FREE chapter
of Regnery's latest bestseller!

Visit us at
www.Regnery.com

- Hot New Releases

- Upcoming Titles

- Listings of Author Signings
  and Media Events

- Complete Regnery Catalog

- Always a Free Chapter
  of a Brand-New Book!